XML

In Record Time™

Natanya Pitts

San Francisco • Paris • Düsseldorf • Soest

Associate Publisher: Amy Romanoff
Contracts and Licensing Manager: Kristine O'Callaghan
Acquisitions Editor: Krista Reid-McLaughlin
Developmental Editor: Kim Crowder
Editor: Diane Lowery
Technical Editor: B. K. DeLong
Book Designers: Franz Baumhackl, Patrick Dintino, Catalin Dulfu
Graphic Illustrator: Tony Jonick
Electronic Publishing Specialist: Nila Nichols
Production Coordinators: Shannon Murphy, Jeremy Crawford
Indexer: Nancy Guenther
Cover Designer: Design Site
Cover Illustrator/Photographer: Adri Berger/Tony Stone Images

Library of Congress Card Number: 98-88755
ISBN: 0-7821-2340-6

Manufactured in the United States of America

10 9 8 7 6 5 4 3 2 1

To DJ. For everything that has been, is, and ever will be. Without you, I wouldn't be me.

Acknowledgments

This book would not have seen the light of day (or the printing press) without the hard work and support of many people. First and foremost, thanks to my parents Charles and Swanya for always believing in me. Special thanks to my dear friends DJ and Jim who are always there rooting for me, even when I don't necessarily deserve it. Thanks to the team at LANWrights, Inc.—Ed Tittel, Mary Burmeister, and Dawn Rader—whose professional and personal support helped me through the little things and many of the big ones.

A very special thanks to the wonderful editorial staff at Sybex for their hard work and commitment to a quality book: Krista Reid-McLaughlin, Diane Lowery, and Kim Crowder. Sybex's production staff also deserve a thank you for their work: Nila Nichols, Shannon Murphy, Jeremy Crawford, and Tony Jonick. Also, thanks to B. K. DeLong, the best tech editor any author could ever ask for. Each and every one of you helped make this the best book project I've ever had the privilege to work on.

And finally a loving thank you to Robby, who only appeared on the scene at the very end of this project but has, it seems, been here for much longer than either of us could have ever known.

Contents at a Glance

Table of Contents

Introduction

XML is the future of the Web. In a year or two, we will all wonder how we ever got along without it. Media and technical gurus are talking up XML for all it is worth, touting it as a revolution in the way we communicate and disseminate information across the Web and within intranets. They are not exaggerating.

As with every other new Web technology that appears on the horizon, XML raises many issues in the minds of veteran and newbie developers alike:

- Is XML a passing fad or is it here to stay?
- Is XML really all that (with a slice of cheese as well)?
- What can XML do for me?
- What are the realities of implementing XML?
- What new skills, hardware, and software will I have to acquire to work with XML?
- What XML tools are already available and which ones are being developed?
- What about HTML?

Very often it is difficult to get past the hype of any new technology and into the nitty-gritty of its realities. XML is no different.

XML is not your mama's HTML. This new and powerful markup language can help you do things with your data that you never before thought possible. However, by itself XML can't do much of anything. To develop a complete XML solution, you'll need much more than just a few tags you create yourself and a Web browser.

This book is designed to demystify and dissect XML so you can see straight into the core of its reality. When you're done with the last page of the book, you'll know and understand exactly what XML is, how it is going to affect the future of the Web, what you'll have to do to implement an XML solution, and even what it takes to create your own markup language using XML.

Who This Book Is For

This book is for anyone who wants to use Web technologies to disseminate information across the Internet or an intranet. Veteran HTML developers and newcomers to the field alike will find the information contained within these pages of value. If you've been working with HTML for some time now, you will find that XML isn't just another way to format a document for display with a Web browser. Instead, XML is a powerful tool for describing content to be processed by a wide variety of applications. To use XML correctly and effectively, you'll need to learn some new habits and maybe even break a few old ones. This book is designed to bring you up to speed quickly without forcing you to trudge through information you already know.

What's in This Book?

If you are a new Web developer with little or no HTML experience, then you are in for a real treat. Before diving headfirst into the future of the Web, the first few skills in the book teach you about the here and now of the Web—HTML and Web page development. Then, after you're comfortable with the basics of Web page design and development, the book's remaining skills introduce you to the basic concepts of XML and help you prepare for the future as well as work effectively in the present.

In the first part of the book, you'll meet XML and learn the basics of both markup languages—HTML and XML—at work on the Web today. The key skills that you pick up in Part I will provide you with the foundation you need to begin working in depth with the core building blocks of HTML, as covered in Part II. In the third part of the book, you'll use the skills you acquired in Parts I and II to begin thinking about deploying your XML documents in the real world. Then, in Part IV, you'll have a chance to see what others are already doing with XML. Finally, in Part V, you will learn how to deal with the realities of deploying XML in the real world. Together, all of these parts of the book will prepare you to begin working with XML as part of a total information dissemination solution.

This book was created as a first look at HTML and is designed to provide the reader with a strong working knowledge of the principles and practices of XML. In addition to explaining the nuts and bolts of XML, the book also takes a hard and practical look at what it really takes to implement XML. Code samples throughout the book let you see how XML DTDs and documents are formed and provide you with working examples to use as you learn the ins and outs of XML. When you are done with this you will be prepared to consider XML as a practical solution to a wide variety of information dissemination needs.

This book also includes additional information in the following forms:

NOTE

Notes look like this and they'll be used to indicate points of special concern. For example, the XML specification is constantly under development. Look for notes that highlight specific parts of the specification that may change radically in the coming months. You'll also find pointers to relevant and useful Web sites within notes.

TIP

Tips look like this; they are written to save you some time, and they may point out additional information that can be of help. In either case, they were created to provide you with something extra.

Warnings look like this and are included to prepare you for common pitfalls you might encounter.

The Web Component

As an added bonus, we've also put together a Web site for the book that includes a hyperlinked list of all the URLs listed in the book, a special XML software page, and regularly updated information about the Extensible Stylesheet Language (XSL). Take advantage of this useful online resource at `www.sybex.com`.

The world of XML is constantly changing direction, much like a roller coaster, but even though it is often unpredictable, the ride is definitely fun and interesting. Hop on board and join me for a trip to the future of the Web.

PART I

Introducing XML

SKILL 1
Learning about XML

- Answering key questions about XML
- Understanding XML's role as a Web technology
- Realizing the realities of working with XML

Extensible Markup Language (XML) bridges the gap between the complex world of SGML (Standard Generalized Markup Language) and the sometimes limited Web world of HTML (Hypertext Markup Language). This chapter answers some common XML questions and, in doing so, investigates what XML really is, the role it is going to play as a Web technology, and how this book will help bring you up to speed with XML.

Answers to Some Common XML Questions

Welcome to the new and exciting world of XML. As the newest addition to the Web technology pantheon, XML has caused quite a stir. While the excitement surrounding XML has been quick to grow and is full of promises, it seems that the answer to "What is XML?" is quite often conspicuously absent. If you're reading this book, then you probably know that XML will allow you to create your own tags and that it's going to be the next big Web "thang." Both of those statements are accurate, but there's much more to XML than just the ability to create your own tags. XML will pave the way for Web-based, customized document description and dissemination solutions. No longer will Web developers have to force all of their content into the HTML mold. Once XML takes off, it will change the way we design and deploy Web documents.

Although all of this is well and good, many questions about XML have elusive or difficult-to-find answers, and without those answers, you won't know whether XML is the right technology for you. I've found that while even the best computer books explain many things very well and provide tutorials, sample code, and other things that a user might need to get started with the technology, they don't really address fundamental questions the user might have. The wide variety of FAQs—lists of frequently asked questions and their answers—available for most Internet- and Web-related subjects indicates that basic questions about a technology do need to be answered before one can jump into the learning of how to use it. The same is true for XML.

XML FAQs Online

XML FAQs are just beginning to appear on the Internet, and most are focused on one particular implementation or another of XML. Two good XML FAQs are:

- The W3C's XML Working Group's XML FAQ maintained by Peter Flynn at `http://www.ucc.ie/xml/`
- The Microsoft XML FAQ maintained by Microsoft at `http://www.microsoft.com/xml/xmlfaq.htm`

Peter Flynn's XML FAQ is a bit on the technical side, but it is updated regularly and is a wonderful quick reference when you're wondering about some aspect of XML. This FAQ is maintained by Flynn on behalf of the World Wide Web Consortium's (W3C) XML Working Group—the powers that be in the XML world—and is the closest thing to an official FAQ as there will ever be. The Microsoft XML FAQ is less extensive than Flynn's, but it is easy to read and contains a lot of useful information. Granted, this FAQ is written from the Microsoft point of view and does contain some purely Microsoft-oriented material, but it is a solid resource that Microsoft updates on a regular basis.

By way of introduction to XML, and this book, I've put together my own XML FAQ that answers the most common and important XML questions. My FAQ is not exhaustive by any means, but it does highlight key XML issues, dispel any myths about XML from the beginning, and provide you with a strong foundation with which to begin learning about and working with XML. In addition, because FAQs are designed to highlight the most important aspects of any subject, many of the other skills in the book—beginning with Skill 6, "Understanding the Basics of XML DTDs and Documents"—include a FAQ at the end that summarizes the important topics and ideas covered in each chapter. That said, on with the Q&A.

The World Wide Web Consortium: The Ultimate Authority

The Internet and World Wide Web are built on worldwide accepted standards. These standards make it possible for different kinds of computers, running different operating systems and software, to talk to each other. The W3C was created to ensure the standards governing the Internet and Web do not favor one vendor or operating system over another. In addition, the W3C oversees the maintenance of existing standards to ensure they are kept up-to-date to meet the growing needs of the Internet and Web. The W3C is also responsible for organizing the teams of industry specialists who develop new standards.

The official standards for HTML, graphics, style sheets, Web servers, and a wide variety of other Web technologies have all been developed and are maintained by the W3C. The W3C can recommend only new standards and hope that individual companies create products that adhere to those standards. Generally, if a company wants its product to sell well and have a large user base, the company will design the product by the W3C's recommended standard. All of the major Internet and Web software and hardware developers are members of the W3C and involve themselves directly in the development of the standards their products should adhere to.

The W3C maintains a Web site at `http://www.w3.org/` that includes full documentation for all the standards they are responsible for as well as information about those standards and initiatives still under development. If you're working with Internet or Web technologies and haven't visited the W3C's Web site, you should take some time to do so now. The resources available at the site are second to none.

What Is XML?

The W3C XML Activity page, located at `http://www.w3.org/XML/Activity.html` provides this answer to the question:

> XML—the eXtensible Markup Language—is a simple and very flexible language based on SGML. Although originally envisaged to

> meet the challenges involved in large-scale publishing, XML is set to play an increasingly important role in the markup of a wide variety of data on the Web. Not only will XML help people find the information they want but the wealth of XML metadata on the Web—information about information—will help many Web-based applications.
>
> XML will make it easier for information consumers and producers to find each other; many tasks involving search or information exchange can be automated with XML, providing a common framework for representing information—everyone should benefit.

In nongeek speak, this means that XML is a language for creating markup languages—or a meta–markup language—specifically geared toward one type of content. A markup language uses tags embedded directly into the text to describe the various pieces and parts of the text. In the following example, the <PARA> and <ITALICS> tags describe a paragraph and an italicized word:

```
<PARA>"XML - the eXtensible Markup Language - is a simple and very
flexible language based on SGML. Although originally envisaged to meet
the challenges involved in large-scale publishing, XML is set to play
an increasingly important role in the markup of a wide variety of data
on the Web. Not only will XML help people find the information they
want, but the wealth of XML metadata on the Web - information <ITALICS>
about</ITALICS> information - will help many Web-based
applications.</PARA>
```

A markup language does not worry about how the content it describes is formatted but is, instead, concerned with accurately describing its content. HTML is a markup language, and the concept of a markup language is key to understanding and implementing XML. In this book, you'll learn a great deal about markup languages, starting with Skill 2, "Making Sense of Markup," and when you finish Part II, you'll be able to use XML to write your own markup language.

In short, XML is a markup language that can run on any platform, operating system, or environment and is designed to provide developers with a mechanism to better describe their content. It was originally designed for publishing projects but has been developed to make the exchange of data on the Web easier and more efficient. XML does this by allowing developers to write their own *document-type definitions* (DTDs) that describe sets of tags and attributes that can be used to describe specific kinds of content. DTDs are markup language rule books that define what markup elements can be used to describe a document. If you want to create your own tags, you'll have to first define them in a DTD. Skill 2 introduces DTDs; Skill 6, "Understanding the Basics of XML DTDs and Documents," discusses

DTDs in depth. The individual markup languages that XML defines are called *XML vocabularies*, or applications, and XML defines these through DTDs.

XML is being developed under the auspices of the W3C's XML Working Group to ensure that its mechanisms are standard and don't promote one vendor over another. While each XML vocabulary will have a specific purpose and type of content it is designed to describe, all must adhere strictly to the rules of XML, making all the vocabularies XML subsets. Two examples of XML vocabularies are the Genealogical Markup Language (GedML) and the Chemical Markup Language (CML). Both are XML vocabularies and have been developed according to the XML specification, but each has a very different purpose. GedML is designed to describe ancestral data, whereas CML was created specifically to describe chemical formulas and molecules. Both are defined by DTDs that specify the elements that can be used to describe genealogical and chemical information, respectively. Skill 6 includes an in-depth discussion of how the DTDs and documents of a particular XML vocabulary work together. In general, XML provides a standardized set of rules for describing DTDs and their documents for exchange over the Internet and Web. You can use XML to write the DTD that defines your own vocabulary and documents to go along with it or to create documents according to a DTD for a vocabulary that someone else has already written.

XML is sufficiently robust and extensive that it can be used to describe not only content but also *metadata*. Metadata is information that describes other information. An example of metadata we've all worked with is a card catalog in a library. Each card, or electronic entry in a computerized catalog, is an information resource that provides information about another information resource, usually a book, magazine, or bit of film. A consistent method for describing metadata, such as with XML, will eventually lead to more organized cataloging of Web resources, making it easier for denizens of the Web to conduct efficient searches of the millions of existing Web pages.

In a nutshell, XML provides both a more extensive means for describing document content and a mechanism for describing metadata, using a method that will work on all computers, regardless of platform or operating system. XML takes Web data to the next level, using vocabularies defined by DTDs tailored to specific kinds of content.

Why Was XML Developed?

XML was developed because document designers and content specialists realized that HTML was simply too narrow in scope to handle the many tasks it had been given. Not all content can be described as paragraphs, lists, tables, and forms.

Because HTML was the only available mechanism for describing Web content, all Web content was squeezed into paragraph, list, table, and form molds. If you've ever tried to put a square peg into a round hole, you'll know why this paradigm simply wasn't working.

The members of the W3C's various working groups realized that HTML simply couldn't be expanded to accommodate every type of data because it would become too cumbersome. They could have opted to develop a series of markup languages, each with its own specific purpose, but they realized there was no way they could anticipate everyone's markup needs. Returning to the world of SGML wasn't an option either, because SGML was an overkill solution.

XML was developed to provide a structured environment for developers to create DTDs for content that doesn't fit into the HTML mold. By defining a *meta-language* for creating Web-based markup languages, rather than a whole new group of markup languages, the W3C provided a mechanism for creating customizable solutions for the Web that works within the existing Web infrastructure.

If you're new to the Web and this discussion of HTML and SGML leaves you a bit confounded, never fear. Skill 2 introduces you to the basics of markup, the foundation for working with both XML and HTML. Skills 3 and 4, "Forming a Foundation with HTML" and "Using HTML Tags to Describe Documents," provide a crash course in HTML and will help you create your first HTML-based Web pages in preparation for the greater task of using XML to define content for dissemination over the Web.

What Is XML's Relationship to HTML?

In many ways, XML is a distant cousin of HTML and may in the future actually be its parent. Both XML and HTML are descendants of SGML, but while XML is a meta–markup language, HTML is a specialized markup language. SGML is the granddaddy of all markup languages and the basis for both XML and HTML. In Skill 2, you will read about how and why each of the three markup languages were developed and the different roles they play in information description and dissemination. Eventually HTML will probably become an XML vocabulary, used to describe simple documents and to make Web sites backward-compatible with older Web browsers.

HTML paved the way for XML by giving developers a taste of what is possible when you combine a nonproprietary markup language and data exchanged over the Internet. The extensive use of HTML to describe documents of all kinds rooted out the many needs and issues for which developers would have to find solutions. HTML was created to meet a specific need at the European Laboratory for Particle Physics in Switzerland (CERN) and soon became the solution for a wider variety of needs. XML is being built expressly to serve the needs revealed by widespread use of HTML.

If you know something about HTML, you know something about XML. For the time being, the Web is still built with HTML, so you'll need to know HTML to implement your XML solutions. Many of the new tools being built to parse and display data described with XML vocabularies are programmed in Java for easy implementation in the Web environment. To include a Java applet in a Web page, you have to use HTML—and that probably won't change any time soon. At least for the foreseeable future, HTML and XML are going to coexist in the Web world, and HTML will be a necessary part of implementing XML solutions on the Web.

Can I Use XML to Design Web Pages?

Unfortunately, this question can't be answered with a simple "Yes" or "No." Both Internet Explorer 4 and 5, as well as Netscape Navigator 5, have some support for XML—as described in the answer to the next question—but it is limited in scope and application. You can't simply create an XML document, stick it on your Web site, and expect your average Web browser to know what to do with it. At present, there's no easy way to include XML in a Web page. Determined developers have to program their Web pages with a scripting language, such as ECMAScript (formerly known as JavaScript), to convert an XML document into HTML for viewing in a Web browser—not a very practical solution. Skills 20 through 24 discuss current, real-world, Web-based implementations of XML, most of which require special software to implement and view. For now, the most practical reason for learning XML is that many emerging Web technologies include XML as part of their solution, and future Web pages will almost certainly be built using XML.

Do Internet Explorer and Netscape Navigator Support XML?

The developers at both Microsoft and Netscape realize the importance of including XML support in their browser offerings; however, the status of XML as a developing technology currently has limited that support. Internet Explorer 4 for Windows 95/98/NT currently ships with a nonvalidating XML parser written in C++. You can also download a validating Java-based parser as an add-in.

NOTE A *parser* is a software component that reads an XML document and creates output that an application, such as a Web browser, can generate a display from. The section "How Do I Process and Display XML Documents?" later in the skill includes more detailed information about parsers, as does Skill 14, "Processing XML Documents."

Either parser can hand off the results of a parsed document to an XML viewer written in Java or ActiveX. In addition, Internet Explorer includes support for an XML Object Model (XOM). The XOM provides Web scripts created in JavaScript or Visual Basic access to all the elements in an XML document, as parsed by either the IE C++ or Java parser.

Internet Explorer also supports the Channel Definition Format (CDF) and the Open Software Description (OSD) vocabularies. CDF is the mechanism that makes Internet Explorer's channels possible and is the first full implementation of an XML vocabulary at work on the Web. For more information on CDF, see Skill 20, "Automating Web Sites with WIDL." OSD is designed to describe software packages as part of a system that allows for hands-off software installation over a network. For more information on OSD, see Skill 22, "Installing Software with OSD."

Netscape's release of the Mozilla source code—also known as Navigator 5—includes a version of the *expat* parser written by James Clark and includes support for the Resource Description Frameworks (RDF) vocabulary. RDF is intended to describe Web resources in a standard and consistent way, and it may soon change the way we all search for information on the Web. For more information on how RDF is implemented in Navigator 5, see Skill 18, "Browsing XML with the Latest Web Clients."

As XML becomes less a developing technology and more an implemented technology, you can expect to see full support for XML in Web browsers. Still, because XML developers will be able to create their own DTDs and documents, we can't expect every browser to know how those documents should be displayed. Most likely, the browsers will support a handful of the key XML vocabularies and leave the creation of browsers for other vocabularies to the vocabulary developers themselves. Skill 17, "Turning Existing HTML Documents into Valid XML Documents," focuses on the issue of Web browser support for XML and the realities of creating XML documents for browsing by Web clients.

Can I Really Create and Use My Own XML Tags?

Yes, you can. Although the answer is simple, creating and implementing your own tags isn't as simple. Remember that tags are used to describe a document's content and a DTD specifies which tags can be used in a document. To create your own tags, you'll have to create your own DTD as we discussed earlier in this skill. To make things even more fun, you have to play by the rules of XML for your DTDs and documents to function correctly. Skill 7, "Creating Well-Formed and Valid Documents," addresses this important issue in detail. The mechanisms that make up a DTD aren't that complicated to define and describe, but designing an efficient, effective, and extensible DTD is a whole other story, as described in Skill 6.

Don't think I'm trying to scare you away from XML or from creating your own markup; rather, I'm pointing out that XML isn't the walk in the park that HTML is. When you're finished with this book, I'm confident you'll be able to create your own DTDs and documents to go with them; you'll also have a whole new knowledge base to drawn upon. After a strong introduction to DTDs in Skill 6, the skills in Part II of the book will walk you through the creation of not one but two DTDs, and then they will show you how to create documents to go along with those DTDs. The key to creating your own markup isn't in understanding how to define elements and attributes but in the quiet art of DTD design. Although Skill 6 includes a discussion of good DTD design elements, becoming a DTD design pro takes a bit of practice and the willingness to learn from others and from your own mistakes. The two example DTDs that we build in Part II will provide you with a solid introduction to good DTD design.

Finally, although you can create your own markup, it's important to know when to design your own DTD and when to use someone else's. Many XML vocabularies are already under development to meet an assortment of Web content needs, including describing mathematical and chemical content, identifying Web metadata, facilitating financial transactions over the Web, and more. Companies or groups of companies are building the majority of these vocabularies to meet their own needs. Inevitably, specialized tools and browsers will be developed for these vocabularies, making their implementation much easier. New vocabularies are being developed every day, as well; if a current one doesn't meet your needs, it's quite possible that one will be released in the not-so-distant future that will. Skill 19, "Creating Documents for XML Applications," includes a close look at the different varieties of XML vocabularies, and Skills 20 through 24 examine in detail five of the current vocabularies under development.

The whole motivation behind XML is to provide developers with a standard environment in which to develop specialized markup. However, for the standard environment to be extensible enough to meet a wide variety of needs it has to be a bit sophisticated, so working within the environment requires some study. But you bought this book, so you already know that.

How Do I Process and Display XML Documents?

XML documents are processed by applications called *parsers*. The parser reads the document and generates output based on the document's content and the markup used to describe that content. In some instances, the document must be compared to and abide by the rules specified in its DTD. When properly constructed, these documents are called *valid*. Parsers that have the ability to compare a document to its DTD and determine whether the document is valid are called *validating parsers*. Even if a document does not have to be validated, it must still conform to the general rules of document creation established in the XML specification. Documents that obey all the general rules are considered well formed. All parsers check to make sure an XML document is well formed, but only validating parsers also check to see if a document is valid. While all documents must be well formed, not all must be valid. Skill 7, "Creating Well-Formed and Valid XML Documents," explains this distinction.

Specialized browsers are currently being developed that know how to interpret the output from a parser and render a display of the XML document using that output. XML is a new technology, so parsers and browsers are just beginning to appear. A parser can process any XML document and a validating parser can discern the validity of any XML document, but most browsers currently under development are designed to display documents written for one DTD or another. For example, the JUMBO browser was developed specifically to display documents described with the Chemical Markup Language (CML), an XML vocabulary. CML is used to describe chemical and molecular compounds, and JUMBO is designed to display those compounds based on the results of parsed CML documents. Although JUMBO can understand and might attempt to display the contents of other parsed non-CML documents, the end results might not be as effective as with CML documents.

Skill 14, "Processing XML Documents," examines the issues surrounding the processing of XML documents and includes information about some of the current parsers and browsers available for processing XML documents. The discussions of the different XML vocabularies in Skills 20 through 25 also include a look at how the documents written for those particular vocabularies can be processed.

Because XML is an Internet and Web technology and the developers of the various vocabularies realize that specialized browsers will be needed to properly view their documents, the majority of the parsers and browsers are being written as Java applets. Because all the major browsers support Java, specialized XML browsers written in Java can be embedded easily in Web pages, and the display of XML documents can be quickly integrated into the current Web infrastructure. There are many issues associated with parsing and browsing XML documents. Skill 14 examines them in-depth with an eye toward the realities of making XML part of an overall information dissemination and management solution.

Is XML Just a Passing Fad?

This question can be asked of almost every Web technology and probably of the Web itself. In my opinion, based on reading the opinions of the powers that be, XML is here to stay. XML provides an elegant and extensible solution to many needs that have arisen since HTML became the language of the Web. XML requires that document developers understand some new concepts and learn a few new skills. Web browsers will have to handle documents differently and support a wider variety of markup vocabularies. However, developers will be able to choose from a collection of languages rather than having to mangle a single language, and browser developers won't have to create proprietary solutions to a wide variety of user needs. Indeed, if XML works as it was intended, it will bring a long-awaited standardization to the Web that will propel the dissemination of information into a new era, probably just as we celebrate the new millennium.

Getting Ready to Work with XML

As the answers to this skill's XML FAQ have shown, XML is not just another version of HTML. There are many issues a budding XML developer must address, including how to read a DTD and write documents for it, how to process an XML document, and what kind of XML support is included in the different Web browsers. The status of XML as a developing technology means resources and information about it are scarce, and it is difficult to put your finger on how you can use XML as part of a workable, real-world solution.

The remaining skills in this book are designed to introduce you to the fundamentals you'll need to understand and work with and to teach you how to create XML DTDs and documents. The last few skills of the book show you how to decide whether XML is the right solution for your information needs and how to choose the XML vocabulary that best fits your content. A look at how XML is already being used in the real world helps make XML more of a reality than a nice theory, and a survey of some of the XML software currently available will help you find the right tool for developing your own DTDs and documents. By the end of this book, you'll be armed with the knowledge and tools you need to fully understand and work with XML.

Are You up to Speed?

Now you can...

- ☑ **Explain what XML is and why it was developed**
- ☑ **Describe how XML is related to HTML**
- ☑ **Discuss how XML can be currently used in Web pages**
- ☑ **Clarify how XML is supported in current Web browsers**
- ☑ **Be confident that XML is not a fleeting fancy**

SKILL 2

Making Sense of Markup

- Exploring the history of markup
- Understanding how markup works
- Separating structure from display
- Leaving bad HTML habits behind

Web page developers have been using markup languages for years now, but the concept of what a markup language really is remains elusive. It's impossible to create Web pages without the Hypertext Markup Language (HTML), but in reality, most Web developers don't even know the difference between a markup language and a formatting language. In fact, a Web page is built every minute that violates at least three or four rules of markup.

This casual shrugging off of the basic principles of markup is due in large part to the accepting nature of Web browsers, the rapid development of HTML as a formatting language, and the emergence of WYSIWYG (What You See Is What You Get) editors that rival page-layout applications in sophistication and design prowess. Add to this the relative simplicity of HTML and the lack of focus on the markup aspect of HTML, and you have a population of skilled Web developers who have only begun to learn how to harness the true powers of a markup language.

TIP The issues of Web standards are so important and complex that a whole organization was created to combat these same problems that have contributed to the regular HTML user's lack of markup knowledge. Read more about the Web Standards Project (WaSP) at `http://www.webstandards.org`.

By its very design, XML (Extensible Markup Language), unlike HTML, takes full advantage of every strength associated with markup languages. If you're coming into the XML world from the HTML world, you must understand what a markup language is, recognize the benefits of separating structure from formatting, be willing to play by the rules of markup, and break bad HTML habits before you even learn the basics of XML. If, however, you're a denizen of the SGML (Standard Generalized Markup Language) world, then you are probably a long-time student of markup, an advocate of its uses in document development and dissemination, and well aware of the consequences of breaking the rules. If you're new to the Web and HTML, then you'll have the distinct advantage of learning about XML, and markup languages in general, without any baggage brought along by HTML veterans.

This chapter discusses what markup is, the role it plays in describing documents, the advantages of separating structure from formatting, and why adhering to markup rules can be a benefit instead of a nuisance. Those of you new to markup theory (yes, I mean HTML veterans, too—just because you know HTML doesn't mean you know markup) will find that, after reading this chapter, you will have a whole new perspective on your favorite Web page development language and a revised notion of what a document really is, as well as the foundation you'll need to begin learning about XML. Markup veterans will find a discussion of those concepts that you've always known to be true, with a new idea or two thrown in for good measure. Either way, XML relies on the fundamental understanding of markup languages, and this chapter is designed to provide you with just that.

A Brief History of Markup

Before I jump right into what markup is, let's take a trip down memory lane to see how we got to where we are. As Cicero said, "Not to know what happened before you were born is always to be a child." Although markup may have come into being long after you were born, the same principle applies.

SGML: The Granddaddy of All Markup

The Standard Generalized Markup Language (SGML) was created in the 1960s by the folks at IBM who were looking to solve some problems associated with porting documents from one platform and operating-system configuration to another. Their first effort was called General Markup Language (GML) and was a proprietary language for use at IBM. The originators of GML—Charles Goldfarb, Ed Mosher, and Ray Lorie—realized a few years later that they had devised a solution for the creation of easily portable documents that would work anywhere, not just at IBM. GML eventually fell under the auspices of the International Organization for Standardization (ISO) and became an official standard (ISO 8879) in the 1980s.

Not long afterward, SGML was adopted by the Department of Defense as its official technical-specification format. Contractors were, and still are, required to submit all documentation in SGML format to facilitate ease of sharing and to guarantee compatibility. SGML is at work in many other large organizations as the language of choice for document description and output. Although SGML is a powerful and robust language, it is both complex and extensive, as well as expensive, to implement and maintain. SGML isn't practical for describing simple documents, and DTD creation isn't for the faint of heart.

HTML: SGML for the Masses

In the late 1980s, a gentleman named Tim Berners-Lee joined the European Laboratory for Particle Physics (CERN) ostensibly to study physics. However, once he got there, he found a problem that needed solving. Physicists regularly came to CERN for short periods of time—three to five years—to study and generate research. Each physicist used a different method for storing and outputting data, making it very difficult for new researchers to take advantage of the work of previous colleagues or for current members of the center to collaborate and share data. Tim went to work on a system that would be platform-independent and easy to use. The result was HTML.

Built on the concept of hypertext—a method for linking documents together and traversing the links by clicking chunks of text—and markup, HTML is a platform- and device-independent markup language. HTML uses markup to describe documents and hypertext links (described by markup) to link and traverse documents. The basic building blocks of SGML—markup, attributes, entities, and others—are at the core of HTML. However, HTML authors don't have to write their own DTDs but, instead, work with a set, or sets, of tags proscribed by the HTML DTD.

Berners-Lee's hypertext functioned entirely in a text-based world and was designed to work only at CERN. The idea that HTML might one day lead to a World Wide Web of distributed documents accessible via the Internet wasn't part of the original plan. However, because HTML is text-based and nonproprietary, it was a perfect way to share information over the Internet. The Internet predates HTML, and it works because it is based on a collection of protocols that define how information is transmitted from one computer to another, regardless of type or platform. E-mail, file transfer, news, and other Internet services were already governed by protocols long before HTML was an idea in Tim's mind. Once the Hypertext Transfer Protocol (HTTP) was defined to govern the exchange of HTML documents, the Web was on its way.

In the early 1990s, HTML documents, and all other Internet Services, were still processed by text-only applications. However, in 1992, Mark Andreesen, a grad student at the University of Illinois at Urbana-Champaign (UIUC), created Mosaic, the first graphical interface for HTML documents. Andreesen later left UIUC to form Netscape. With the advent of a simple graphical interface to the Web and other Internet services, HTML became a major player in the information-dissemination world. However, as I've mentioned previously, HTML was never intended to describe complex documents or carry the weight of the Web as it does now. There's nothing wrong with HTML per se; it's just being stretched beyond its capabilities.

XML Bridges the Gap

In the last one or two years, the W3C has come to realize that HTML wasn't engineered to accomplish what it's being asked to accomplish. The working groups at the W3C saw a need for an extensible markup system that would allow document developers to create markup suited for their content. The immediate answer to the problem was the already established SGML. However, SGML was not a practical solution.

Their answer was XML. XML truly bridges the gap between SGML and HTML, allowing developers to write their own DTDs and develop documents for DTDs other than HTML. However, XML is not the simple markup language that HTML has proven to be. Although there will be a plethora of XML tools and plenty of DTDs to work with, XML requires a complete understanding of not only what a markup language is but the specifics of each individual DTD for which developers design documents. XML requires a shift in the way developers look at their documents, and the transition to XML from HTML will be a bumpy one.

There has been speculation that HTML will simply cease to exist in the wake of XML. Although the jury is still out on that particular subject, I'm more inclined to believe, based on my own reading and experiences, that HTML will become—as it was originally intended—another DTD in the pantheon of growing XML vocabularies. Although XML is more difficult to learn than HTML, it is more extensible and robust than HTML. XML is the best hope the Web has for accurately and precisely describing, transmitting, and outputting information on a level equal to the information itself.

What Is a Markup Language?

Before we get into what a markup language is, let's discuss what it isn't. Contrary to what HTML may lead you to believe, a markup language is not a formatting language. Formatting languages focus on describing the final display of a document without trying to describe the document's content. An example of a formatting language is RTF (Rich Text Format). RTF was created specifically to describe the final format of a document using codes embedded in a document. These codes are readable by a wide variety of applications, from word processors to page-layout programs, but they are generally invisible to the document developer. RTF's mission in life is to allow the formatting of a document to be transferred intact from one application to another. In contrast, formatting information is not built into a markup language at all. (See the section "The Benefits of Separating Structure from Display" later in this chapter to learn more about this topic.)

In addition, a markup language isn't a programming language. A programming language creates a set of instructions that are interpreted or compiled into a program or application. Java is an example of a programming language. Java applets are miniature applications that can run only inside another application, such as a Web browser, that understands Java. To remember the difference, keep in mind that programming languages generate programs or applications, but markup languages generate documents. In fact, markup is interpreted by a program.

Finally, markup is not limited to HTML. HTML is an individual instance of a markup language, but it certainly isn't the only markup language. In the grand scheme of things, HTML is just a drop in the markup bucket.

Markup Describes Documents

Now that you know what markup isn't, it's time to dive headfirst into what it really is. Simply put, markup is used to describe the pieces and parts of a document. By way of example, take a look at this text snippet:

```
De Bello Gallico
Gallia est omnis divisa in partes tres
```

Unless you speak Latin or know something about Julius Caesar's recounting of the Gaelic War, then the snippet is Greek (or Latin in this case) to you. Add the following markup to the text and you'll find you know more about the text than you did before:

```
<BOOK>
     <TITLE>De Bello Gallico</TITLE>
<CHAPTER NUMBER=1>
     <PARAGRAPH>
     <FIRST>Gallia est omnis divisa in partes tres</FIRST>
     </PARAGRAPH>
</CHAPTER>
</BOOK>
```

If you're entirely new to markup of any kind, then the addition of text between less-than (<) and greater-than (>) symbols may have served only to confuse you more. For those of you familiar with markup, you'll find that you know much more about the text snippet than you did before, even though you may still not know what it says.

Markup Notation

Markup is added to a document in the form of tags. Tags assign a markup label to parts of a document and are created using a specific type of notation. Most tags come in pairs and comprise start and end tags. A few tags are singletons; that is, they have only a START tag but no END tag. In general, pairs of tags are designed to describe content, such as a paragraph or heading level, whereas singleton tags are used to insert something into a document, such as an image or a line break. All tags begin with a less-than symbol (<), followed by a string of text that identifies the tag—such as TITLE or CHAPTER—and end with a greater-than (>) symbol. END tags—the second tag in a tag pair—include a slash (/) after the less-than symbol but before the text string. A sample tag pair is:

```
<TITLE>...</TITLE>
```

The ellipsis (...) between the START and END tag is a convention that indicates there will probably be text and possibly other markup between the START and END tags of the tag pair.

Notice that the text strings within the start and end pair are the same. If the text strings don't match, the tag pair is not legal. Examples of illegal tag pairs are:

```
<TITLE>...</TITL>
<TITLE>...</CHAPTER>
```

The tag pairs used to describe the content in the previous text snippet assign a specific, appropriate label to the text they surround.

- The <BOOK>...</BOOK> tags that have been added before and after the snippet indicate (intuitively) that the following information is from or about a book.
- The <TITLE>...</TITLE> tags around the phrase *De Bello Gallico* are a pretty good indication that the phrase serves as the book's title.

- The <CHAPTER>...</CHAPTER> tags with an attribute of NUMBER=1 let us know that the information contained within them is relevant in some way to Chapter 1 of the book entitled *De Bello Gallico*.
- The <PARAGRAPH>...</PARAGRAPH> within the <CHAPTER>...</CHAPTER> tags delimit a paragraph in the chapter.
- The final set of tags, <FIRST>...</FIRST>, indicate that the text within them is a first of some sort, most probably the first line of the paragraph.

Based on the markup, you now know that *De Bello Gallico* is the title of a book and that the first line of the first paragraph of Chapter 1 is "Gallia est omnis divisa in partes tres." For the curious, the book's title translates as *"The Gallic War"* and the first line as "All of Gaul is divided into three parts." And they said my degree in Latin would never pay off.

It seems I'm not the only one who enjoys using classical literature to test my XML. XML markup has already been applied by Jon Bosak to religious texts and some Shakespearean literature. Download a zip file of religion texts and the works of Shakespeare at `http://sunsite.unc.edu/pub/sun-info/xml/eg/religion.1.10.xml.zip` and `http://sunsite.unc.edu/pub/sun-info/xml/eg/shakespeare.1.10.xml.zip` respectively.

As the previous example shows, markup is used to define the pieces and parts of a document and to describe the role they play in a document. By nesting markup tags within markup tags, you can provide more precise descriptions of the parts of a document. Text within <TITLE>...</TITLE> tags is just a title, but when the <TITLE>...</TITLE> tags are nested within <BOOK>...</BOOK> or <CHAPTER>...</CHAPTER> tags, the role of the title becomes more apparent.

You'll notice that the markup simply describes the text but doesn't say much about how it should be formatted. That's because it's not the job of the markup, or the document designer really, to specify how the described text should be rendered. That's left up to the rendering agent, be it a printer, computer screen, Braille reader, or other output device. The key function of markup is to add labels to bits of text, and based on the label, the output device can decide how best to format the content. This is called separating structure from display, and its advantages are discussed in more detail later in this skill.

NOTE

The issue of Web accessibility is an important one, and XML will go a long way in making Web-based content easily available to everyone, regardless of how they surf the Web. To read more about the W3C's Web Accessibility Initiative (WAI), visit `http://www.w3.org/WAI/`.

The most important thing to remember about markup is that it is designed specifically to describe the contents of a document. As a document developer, you should go out of your way to describe your documents as accurately as possible without regard for the final display. HTML designers have been twisting and mangling markup for a few years now in order to achieve a certain look and feel for their Web pages, regardless of the rules they had to break in the process. Web browsers are very forgiving, so they've been getting away with it. The result is Web pages that look good on some versions of some browsers and horrible on others. Hence, the source of the now famous (and exasperating) browser incompatibility problems. If all of the Web-page designers in the world had to play by the rules of the current HTML standards, the Web would be a better place. But I digress. This digression (or soapbox oration) continues later in the chapter and is more relevant than you may think to the successful creation of XML documents.

Markup Works on Any Computer

You've probably noticed that markup exists side-by-side with the content that it describes. This is contrary to the ways of modern word processor and page-layout programs. In these WYSIWYG Graphical User Interface (GUI) environments, we are accustomed to pressing buttons or choosing styles from drop-down menus and seeing the final product displayed on our screen immediately. Tedious things, such as the commands and instructions responsible for that final product, are hidden from us.

However, all of these relevant and necessary commands and instructions are written in languages only the application can understand and that is often platform-specific. Although converters and translators make life a bit easier, it's often difficult, if not impossible, to view a document when you don't have a copy of the application that created it handy or aren't working on the same platform the document developer did. Markup solves cross-platform and application-specific issues because it and the content it describes are simply text. Any computer that reads plain text— and that's any computer at all—can read marked documents.

Because markup language is limited to ASCII text, you may be wondering how markup can be useful in a variety of contexts. ASCII text is limited to the characters you see on your keyboard: the alphabet in lowercase and uppercase, the digits zero through nine, and some assorted punctuation marks. Non-English characters, accented characters, and other special characters, such as the copyright symbol and the yen sign, are not part of this most basic character set. But, after all, there's more to documents and languages than just ASCII text. Never fear, markup of any kind has a complete mechanism for representing non-ASCII characters. This mechanism uses a series of ASCII characters to represent non-ASCII characters. For example, the entity `é` in HTML represents a lowercase *e* with an acute accent (*é*). I'll discuss how XML deals with non-ASCII and special characters in much the same way as HTML in Skill 11, "Employing Entities in DTDs and Documents."

You've probably got one of those applications on your computer right now—your Web browser. As with all other applications, Web browsers differ a bit from platform to platform. However, because they read, interpret, and display ASCII documents described by markup, they can process documents regardless of the platform on which they are written and stored. Instead of attempting to make a variety of platform-independent applications, markup focuses on creating platform-independent documents that can be read by any application that understands markup.

Markup Is Governed by a DTD

If you're HTML savvy, you've worked with at least one DTD, and probably more, each time you've created a Web page. The various HTML specifications released by the W3C as well as additional elements and attributes added by the major browser vendors—Microsoft and Netscape—are all actually DTDs that spell out in detail what tags you can use with your text to create Web pages. You know that to describe text as boldface, you enclose it in the `<B>...</B>` tags. You also know that there's no such thing as `<BOLD>...</BOLD>` tags, so you can't use them to label text as boldface. These rules, and the hundreds of others like them, are part of the DTD for HTML 4.0.

Each time a new version of HTML is released, it is in the form of a DTD. That means that documents written by the HTML 4.0 DTD may have elements in them, such as frames, that aren't supported by earlier DTDs, such as the HTML 2.0

DTD. The browser vendors maintain their own versions of the various HTML DTDs that include elements that only work with their browser and not their competitors'. These browser-specific elements are collectively known as proprietary markup, which means that they are not part of the official HTML specification. Rarely do Web developers even think twice about which DTD they are designing by or that they are designing by a DTD at all. Because browsers support the most current official version of HTML as well as their own version of HTML, but not their competitors' versions, most developers don't even know whose version (aka DTD) to follow.

Many of you may be wondering why you haven't ever heard of DTDs and their relationship with HTML, or other markup for that matter, even though you've been working with HTML for a while now. HTML was designed to be simple and intuitive, and that design goal was achieved, with bells on. There was no need to read long, technical documentation to create your first Web page. All you needed to know were a few tags, and you were on your way. Most Web design books and HTML primers don't mention markup at all except as part of the expansion of HTML into the Hypertext Markup Language. So-called how-to articles, tip sheets, and design guides focus on final display in a browser but not proper form. In many ways, the concept of a DTD has been deliberately kept out of most major HTML discussions because it was thought it would only cloud them and make something so simple too difficult.

To make matters worse, DTDs aren't the easiest things in the world to read, and they weren't exactly made accessible to document developers. Early designers learned from trial and error, guided wholly by the final results displayed in their Web browsers. No one bothered to explain what a markup language was or how it was different from formatting. Later books and articles focused on how to bend the rules of markup to achieve a desired effect with a Web page, but these books never mentioned that we were actually bending the rules. The creators of WYSIWYG Web page editors all insist that you don't even need to know HTML, much less markup theory, to create dazzling Web pages. It's almost as if markup were doomed to be just the M in HTML.

Luckily, the advent of XML has brought markup and DTDs back into the spotlight. A solid understanding of markup theory and DTD design are prerequisites for working with XML. You can't design your own markup—the key design goal of XML—without them, and you can't take advantage of the DTDs designed by others either. And maybe, just maybe, you'll see your Web pages in a whole new light.

TIP

I bet you didn't know that for a Web site to be fully HTML 4.0 compliant, it should have a DTD declared at the very beginning, using a `<!DOCTYPE>` declaration like this one: `<!DOCTYPE HTML PUBLIC "-//W3C//DTD HTML 3.2 Final//EN">`. I will cover this in more detail in Skill 3, "Forming a Foundation with HTML."

The Benefits of Separating Structure from Display

In at least two places in the previous section, I hinted that separating structure from display is a very good thing. I'm done hinting and will now proceed to bang you over the head with the idea.

A Simple Scenario

Moving away from markup for a moment, imagine a common scenario that occurs in small and large offices on an all-too-regular basis. A document is created in a word processor by research staff that will eventually be poured into a page-layout program by production staff for final printing. The word processor version of the document is edited and updated many times, deemed acceptable, and forwarded to the production staff. The production staff pours the contents of the document into a page-layout application and returns the newly formatted document to the research staff for comment. In addition to making changes to the look and feel of the document, the research staff tweaks the content a bit more along the way. Now the version of the document in page-layout form is no longer identical to the version in word-processing form and is, in fact, more up-to-date. The document works its way through the production process and is ultimately printed and distributed.

A few months later, the research staff decides to update the printed document, but when they return to the last version of the word-processing file they forwarded to production, they discover, to their chagrin, that it's not the same as the printed copy. Someone then remembers all the changes made to content during production. To get the most recent version of the document, they must ask production to pour it out of the page-layout software and into the word-processing software. Needless to say, this isn't the most efficient or accurate way to handle documents. But for most people, it's the only available option.

Now, imagine that the original document from research was written in plain text and described with markup. Research revises and corrects the document in their markup editor of choice until it's deemed acceptable and forwarded to production. The page-layout application production uses is markup-aware and creates a final print version of the document based on the markup used by research. Any tweaks to the look and feel of the document are not made to the document itself, but to how the page-layout application interprets the markup. Tweaks to the content are made to the document itself, not a version of the document used by production. If the document lives on a common file server, then both production and research have access to the same document. Multiple version, platform, and application issues are eliminated, and the document's content is retained even if its final display is changed.

Let's follow the scenario one step further. Mike, a member of the research group, wants to make a presentation about the document, using slides of the document's salient points as a visual aid. Although he may hand out printed copies at the presentation, he definitely doesn't want to display the entire document on his slides. Using the conventional, nonmarkup method, Mike would first have to get the latest version of the document from production converted into word-processing format. Then, using the word processor's table-of-contents generator, Mike could generate a list of the document's headings, import them into a presentation application document, and then proceed to add look-and-feel elements to make the presentation pretty. If you've ever had to do something like this, you know it's not as quick and easy as it may seem.

If, however, the document were described by markup, Mike would only have to open the document in a markup-aware presentation application and instruct it to cull and display only the heading sections and perhaps other parts of the document based on their markup. Try to get a word processor's table-of-contents generator to do that. To change look-and-feel elements of the presentation, Mike can tweak the application's interpretation of markup and not the document itself. Later, when the document is updated, the presentation could be updated by simply loading the new version of the document into the presentation application.

In short, the nonmarkup solution leads to multiple versions and forms of the same document, whereas the markup solution generates multiple displays and outputs for multiple purposes from a single document. The nonmarkup solution inexorably links structure with content. Content must be re-created or reformatted each time it is needed for a new purpose. The markup solution separates display from structure, allowing a single document to be displayed in several different ways without creating several versions. A change to the document leads to an automatic change in each display, without any assistance from the document's developer.

One Document, Many Output Options

The scenario in the previous section described two possible output options for a single document:

- Print
- Presentation slides

Although these are two common forms of document output or display, a few more can be added to the list:

- Web browser display by
    - Graphical Web browsers
    - Nongraphical Web browsers
- Audio interpretation by text-to-speech readers
- Multiple print versions
    - Abstracts
    - Large print
    - Brochures
    - Student materials
    - Tip sheets
- Braille output

Any given document might need to be output to one, several, or all of these different formats. And to make things even more interesting, you might need multiple versions with a different look and feel for each option.

Until the Web made its mark as a major information source, most document developers were concerned only with the dissemination of information in print and presentation form. Entire departments are devoted to production of printed documents, and smart presentation software has been developed to import large documents and export key-topic presentations. Although this is all well and good, the ultimate weakness in this system is that a new version of the same document is created each time the document is reformatted to meet a new output need. If you have five different print versions of a single document, you'll have to change five files when you update or edit the document.

Markup and markup-aware applications overcome this weakness by separating structure from display and output. The document's content is contained in a single file described carefully with markup. Markup-aware applications process and interpret the markup and generate one or many different outputs with formats appropriate to the purpose of the output. Even though several different outputs are created, each is based on the same document—instead of creating new documents each time. It's a subtle difference, but an important one.

Markup-aware applications create output from a markup document based on the way the document is described with markup. For example, print output for a document may render paragraphs in 12-point Arial with a first line indentation of half an inch, line spacing of 24 points, and left and right margins of one inch. The same paragraph output into HTML may have the tags `<P><FONT FACE="Arial">...</FONT></P>` included before and after it. Yet a third output for a large print version of the document might render paragraphs in 36-point Times with a first line indentation of an inch, line spacing of 72 points, and left and right margins of one inch. Each final output has a different look and feel, but each is based on the same markup description of paragraphs.

To bring this theoretical discussion to life, here's what a single paragraph from Skill 1, "Learning about HTML, the Web, and the Internet," of the book *HTML 4.0: No Experience Required* would look like when described by a markup language that uses the tag <PGRAPH>...</PGRAPH> to label paragraphs:

```
<PGRAPH> The Internet began in the mid-1960s as a project of the United
States Department of Defense's Advanced Research Project Agency.
Scientists and researchers developed the Internet as a way to communicate
and share information between various research institutions. To do this,
they created new protocols, or agreements to establish how computers
should talk to each other when they exchange information. The modern
Internet is based on these protocols.</PGRAPH>
```

If this single paragraph were to be displayed in each of the three outputs (as a regular print document, as a Web page, and as a large-print document) the content would remain the same, but the final look and feel would be dictated by the output itself. Figure 2.1 shows the paragraph as it might appear in a printed document, Figure 2.2 is a sample of the paragraph's display in a Web browser, and Figure 2.3 shows the paragraph in large print.

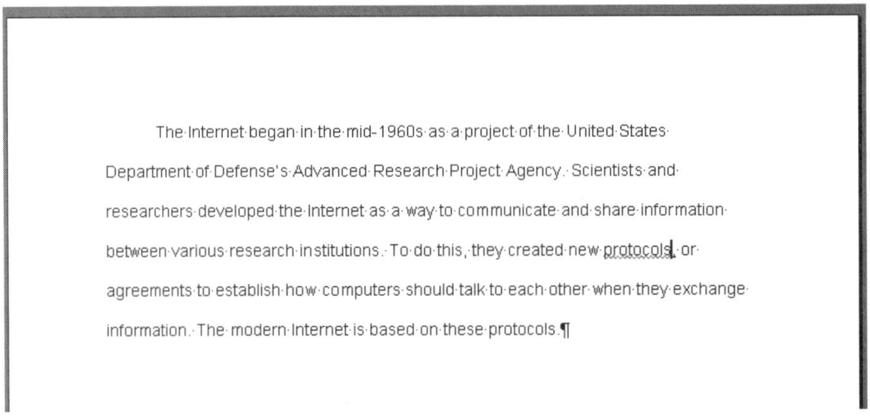

The·Internet·began·in·the·mid-1960s·as·a·project·of·the·United·States·
Department·of·Defense's·Advanced·Research·Project·Agency.·Scientists·and·
researchers·developed·the·Internet·as·a·way·to·communicate·and·share·information·
between·various·research·institutions.·To·do·this,·they·created·new·protocols,·or·
agreements·to·establish·how·computers·should·talk·to·each·other·when·they·exchange·
information.·The·modern·Internet·is·based·on·these·protocols.¶

FIGURE 2.1: The sample paragraph as it might be rendered by a standard printer

D:\NatStuff\zzz.html - Microsoft Internet Explorer
File Edit View Go Favorites Help
Back Forward Stop Refresh Home Search Favorites History Channels Fullscreen Mail Print
The Internet began in the mid-1960s as a project of the United States Department of Defense's Advanced Research Project Agnecy. Scientists and researchers developed the Internet as a way to communicate and share information between various research institutions. To do this, they created new protocols, or agreements to establish how computers should talk to each other when they exchange information. The modern Internet is based on these protocols.
My Computer

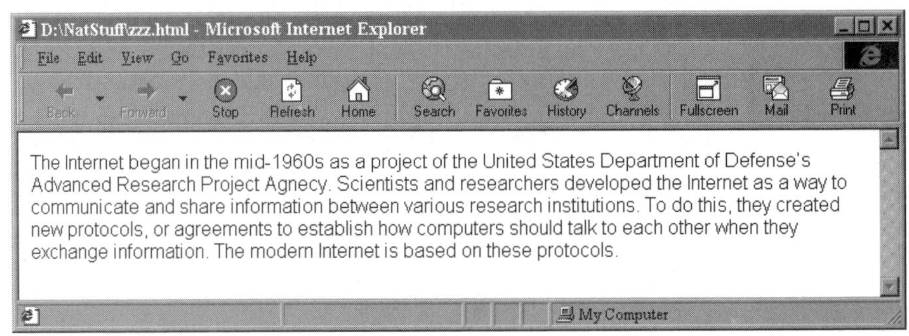

FIGURE 2.2: The sample paragraph as it might be rendered by a Web browser

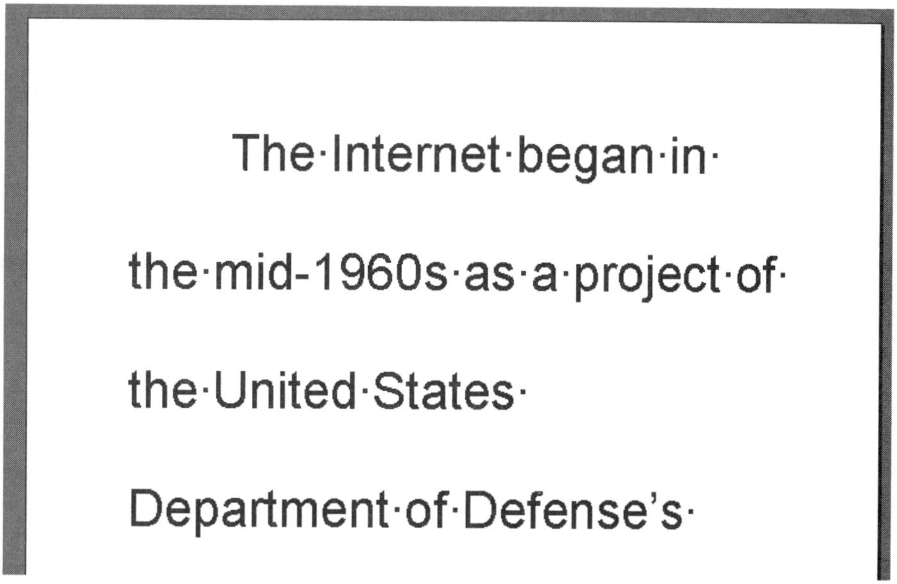

The·Internet·began·in·
the·mid-1960s·as·a·project·of·
the·United·States·
Department·of·Defense's·

FIGURE 2.3: The sample paragraph as it might be rendered in large-print format

Each device interprets the <PGRAPH>...</PGRAPH> tag in a different but appropriate way. Keep in mind that for this example to work, all three devices used to generate the different displays of the single document would have to be able to read and process markup. The document dissemination world isn't there yet, but XML is certainly a step in the right direction.

HTML Was Intended to Separate Structure from Display

If you've ever been frustrated with the way your Web pages are displayed differently by various versions of Web browsers, then you have been caught in the trap of treating HTML as a formatting language instead of the markup language that it really is. Believe it or not, HTML was intended—as with all other markup languages—to separate document structure from display. The original idea behind HTML was to provide document developers with a platform- and device-independent way to describe and exchange information. The idea was that HTML would be used to describe the different parts of a document, and then Web browsers would display Web pages based on that description. Developers weren't supposed to take the final display of the document into much account because every browser is different from every other; instead, they were supposed to concentrate on an accurate description of their documents. To that end, a separate Web style mechanism called Cascading Style Sheets (CSS) was developed to provide a way for developers to create correctly structured HTML and still control its layout. The idea was that markup should define the content, and CSS style sheets should control the final display. Skill 14, "Adding Style with CSS," will cover CSS in more detail.

A quick tour of the Web shows that all the supposed tos and should haves never quite came to fruition. Frustrated by HTML's apparent lack of formatting tags—not a surprise because structure was supposed to be separate from display in theory—developers began using markup to manipulate the final display of a document without regard to the correct description of the document. A perfect example of this all-to-common phenomena is the use of the `<BLOCKQUOTE>...</BLOCKQUOTE>` tag to create margins for Web pages.

The `<BLOCKQUOTE>...</BLOCKQUOTE>` tag is meant to describe long quotations or excerpts. To set text labeled as *blockquote* off from the text around it, most graphical Web browsers add a line break and a space both before and after the quoted text and indent both sides of the text between half and one inch. Remember, the description is provided by the markup language and the final formatting by the Web browser. Developers quickly noticed that labeling text as a blockquote caused it to be displayed with indents on both sides by all the major browsers. Because HTML itself doesn't provide a mechanism for defining indentations on a page (that's a display issue better left to the Web browser), Web page developers began to define entire documents as blockquotes just to achieve a final visual effect and with complete disregard for the actual meaning of the tag.

Shortcuts and tricks like this violate the very nature of a markup language because structure is no longer separated from display. Instead, an incorrect structure is imposed on a document with a final display in mind. Although the repercussions of such abuses of HTML have not been widespread—Web browsers don't up and die because of them—they have ingrained a large number of bad habits in Web page developers that will have to be broken before they can become successful XML developers. See the final section of the skill for a further discussion of breaking bad habits.

Different Markup Languages for Different Documents

Part of separating structure from display is choosing the correct markup language, or DTD, to describe the structure of a document. One of the reasons HTML developers have felt they need to mangle their markup is because HTML is intentionally limited in scope. HTML was originally intended as a simple document description language. Its tags focus on paragraphs, headings, some simple text-formatting instructions, feedback forms, and table development. Tables and frames, two recent additions (HTML 3.2 for tables and HTML 4.0 for frames) to the HTML specification are evidence of the growing needs of Web developers to describe more than just paragraphs. Tables, one of the most popular groups of HTML tags, are not used much by XML developers because the Web is full of tabular information. This markup is so popular because tables, with the right massaging, provide developers with a level of control over final display that no other markup can. Frames divide a browser page up into multiple display areas and allow developers to prescribe how many pages should be displayed at one time and in what arrangement. Notice the frequent use of the word display in this paragraph? That's just more evidence of HTML's status as a pseudo–formatting language and not as the markup language it was intended to be.

If HTML were better equipped to describe advanced and complex documents correctly, then the need for massaged markup would go away. However, if HTML continued to grow to meet every developer's specific needs, the specification and its implementation by browsers would soon grow to be unwieldy. Just as important as using markup correctly is choosing the right markup language to describe your documents. Until the advent of XML, HTML was the only markup language available for use on the Web. The idea behind XML is for developers to be able to create their own specialized DTDs that address information-specific needs. A brief look at Table 2.1, which lists some of the XML DTDs currently under development, shows that there will be many content-specific DTDs to choose from, and the undue manipulation of markup will no longer be necessary.

TABLE 2.1: XML DTDs in Development

DTD	Description
Channel Definition Format (CDF)	Sets up server-push channels for routine delivery of Web-based information to users
Chemical Markup Language (CML)	Describes chemistry formulas and data
Genealogical Data in XML (GedML)	Provides a description format for genealogical data
Mathematical Markup Language (MathML)	Describes mathematical data
Open Software Description (OSD)	Describes software packages to set up remote installation of software and components of an intranet or the Internet
Synchronized Multimedia Integration Language (SMIL)	Describes collections of multimedia resources, such as audio and video files, that are played together in a single presentation
Resource Description Framework (RDF)	Describes resources of all types for easy cataloging, searching, and referencing
Web Interface Definition Language (WIDL)	Defines Application Programming Interfaces (APIs) for Web services and information

These DTDs are just a small sampling of those being developed with XML. As you can see, they are intended to work with specific kinds of data, from chemical formulas, to genealogical information, to application programming interfaces. By choosing—or developing your own if one doesn't suit your needs—the correct DTD or markup language to describe your documents, you remove the need to mangle the markup.

Describing Complex Documents Using Markup

One of the greatest advantages provided by separating structure from display is that highly complex documents—technical specifications and scientific findings, for example—can be described accurately without worrying about having a display mechanism immediately available to handle the display. Documents can be prepared for addition to an archive or compilation of other documents, with the only concern being accurate description, not accurate formatting. If every manufacturer involved in building an airplane used the AML (Airplane Markup Language)—a figment of my imagination—to describe their technical schematics, they could collaborate and exchange data without worrying about the computer platforms or operating systems the other manufacturers were using. As long as they all had an application that understood markup, and more specifically, was geared toward processing and displaying AML, they could all work together to build a working airplane.

Data on the Web is becoming more and more complex as financial transactions, advanced databases, and multimedia are all added into the fray. HTML is not suited to the description of these types of information, so complex scripts and programs are currently used in conjunction with HTML pages to link this data to Web pages. With the addition of XML awareness to Web browsers, many of the convoluted and complex workarounds created by Web designers will become a thing of the past.

The Importance of Playing by the Rules

I've said it before, and I'll say it again: Web browsers are very forgiving. You can break all kinds of HTML rules, and your Web pages will still be displayed. Some browsers are more forgiving than others, hence the disparity in display of mangled markup. You break one rule to solve a problem in one browser only to cause a half-dozen other problems in a different browser. In the end, HTML pages have become a collection of the least offensive markup workarounds.

Although Web browsers are forgiving, parsers and other applications that process XML are not. If you forget even a single closing tag, misspell an attribute, or leave out a quotation mark, your document is invalid and won't be processed. The previous discussion of the benefits of separating structure from display focused heavily on the importance of the accurate description of a document with markup. The correct use of markup is key to the success of markup because the final output of marked-up documents is entirely dependent upon the accuracy of the markup used to describe a document's content.

Unforgiving applications may seem like a burden, but they are really a blessing in disguise. If correct output is dependent on correct markup, an application that hangs on incorrect markup alerts you to bugs so you can fix them sooner rather than later. Granted, most XML applications can't force you to use a `PARAGRAPH` tag instead of a `HEADING` tag to identify paragraphs, but they can ensure that you follow all the rules set by the DTD or, barring that, the general rules of creating correct markup.

In the markup world there are two kinds of documents:

- Well formed
- Valid

A well-formed document follows all the general rules of markup but doesn't necessarily adhere to a specific DTD. A valid document does both. It uses all the correct conventions of markup and follows all of the rules set down by a DTD. Some applications that process XML require that a document is both valid and well formed, whereas others only care if the document is well formed. At a most basic level, a marked-up document should always be well formed, or it simply can't be processed by a markup-aware application.

Skill 6, "Creating Well-Formed and Valid XML Documents," is devoted to a discussion of valid and well-formed documents. For now, it's important to remember that, barring Web browsers, all other markup-aware applications require that documents be either valid or well formed. Although HTML teaches developers that breaking the rules leads to (seemingly) positive results, other markup will quickly show that breaking the rules only leads to broken documents.

Breaking Bad Habits

Speaking from my own experiences, it's the seasoned Web page developer who will have the hardest time making the transition from HTML to XML, only because we all have assorted bad habits that we'll have to unlearn. I've already discussed a couple of them in earlier sections of the chapter, but I'd like to list all of them here. If you are a seasoned Web developer, you'll need to readjust your thinking and treat HTML as a markup language instead of a formatting language. Separate your structure from your display—in other words, don't twist your markup to create a specific effect—and you'll find that your pages display more consistently from browser to browser. If you're new to HTML and other markup languages, don't lose sight of the benefits of separating structure from markup. Don't be sucked into the idea that you should do anything necessary to achieve a certain look in a certain browser. Instead, stay true to the spirit of the markup language and create accurately described documents for precise output and display in any medium.

Bad HTML habits to break (or never form) include:

1. Thinking of HTML as a formatting language. Get used to describing the parts of your documents rather than describing how you would like them formatted by the various Web browsers. Also, avoid mangling the markup to achieve a desired affect. Don't call a duck a goose simply because you want it to look like a goose. Remember that XML provides you with an avenue for creating your own tags or finding a DTD that better suits your needs.
2. Designing for one browser or another. The idea behind a markup language is that the document can be output by any application that is markup-aware. If you concentrate on accurate markup instead of browser display, your documents will look good in any environment, including text-only, text-to-speech, and print.
3. Using markup to specify formatting. Do your best to separate structure from display. Many of the HTML formatting tags like `<FONT>...</FONT>` and `<CENTER>...</CENTER>` have been deprecated (made obsolete) by Cascading Style Sheets in HTML 4.0. Skill 14, "Processing XML Documents," includes a comprehensive discussion of using CSS with markup.
4. Leaving out important structural elements. Many Web browsers don't care whether you forget to define a document as HTML by using the `<HTML>...</HTML>` tag or separate the document into head and body sections using the `<HEAD>...</HEAD>` and `<BODY>...</BODY>` tags. Many also forgive the exclusion of quotation marks and other important syntax conventions. XML processors will not be so forgiving. Learn to pay attention to detail now, and save yourself hours of document correction later.

All of these habits relate in one way or the other to viewing HTML as a formatting language or creating sloppy code because the browser lets you get away with it. In the end, markup languages are formal beasts that expect you to do things in a certain way. If you can shift your thinking from format issues to description issues and can get used to being meticulous, you'll be well on your way to creating quality markup documents of any kind.

Are You up to Speed?

Now you can...

☑ Explain how XML fits into the bigger markup picture

☑ Understand the benefits of separating structure from display

☑ Describe in general how a markup language works

☑ Recognize the limitations of HTML that have lead to the development of XML

☑ Keep in mind that it's vital when working with markup to play strictly by the rules

☑ Avoid common mistakes picked up in the current Web page development environment

SKILL 3

Forming a Foundation with HTML

- Understanding the basics of the Web
- Linking documents with URLs
- Working with the building blocks of HTML
- Being mindful of key HTML issues

Before moving full force into XML, it's important to understand the fundamentals of HTML. HTML and XML will likely coexist for some time in the Web development arena, and in fact, they depend on each other in many ways. HTML is the backbone of every Web page posted on the World Wide Web today. You simply cannot create a Web page without using HTML. In this chapter, we will look at some of the basics of Web page creation, including how HTML tags and their attributes work and the role hyperlinks play in most Web documents. The all-important issues of content and browser incompatibilities are also addressed.

The Web: A Series of Linked Documents

The World Wide Web comprises millions of documents all written in the common language of HTML and linked together using hyperlinks. What makes the Web really work is the hypertext in HTML. You'll recall from Skill 2 that Tim Berners-Lee is the creator of HTML and the "father of the Web." In March 1989, when Berners-Lee first proposed what became the World Wide Web, he described his idea as a "linked information system." Berners-Lee described the working version of this information system at CERN as a "multiply-connected Web whose interconnections evolve with time." This is an accurate and succinct description of what the Web has become.

As envisioned by Berners-Lee, a linked information system allows information to be gathered in a manner that lets the system grow and evolve as the data it contains grows and evolves. For that to occur on an extended level like the Web, the storage mechanism cannot retain the information as traditional fixed hierarchical systems tend to. Instead, Berners-Lee envisioned a "web" of notes with "links" or references. This differed from the traditional model of "trees" with branches and leaves that traverse up and down fixed paths. In a "web" environment, a link could be made from the very tip of one branch to the tip of another, whereas in a tree, you'd need to travel back up to the trunk before you could move down the next branch. The linking methodology provided flexibility that wasn't possible with hierarchical systems. Berners-Lee had experimented with hypertext systems as early as 1980, when he wrote a program for keeping track of information relating to a software. In extending the idea of hypertext and links, Berners-Lee realized that it provided a solution to linking constantly changing data.

The system of hypertext and linking that Berners-Lee created at CERN was eventually expanded into the World Wide Web. The Web itself is spread out over millions of computers all around the world. These computers run a wide variety of operating systems on a number of different platforms. However, because hypertext and hyperlinks are described with a markup language (HTML) and are saved as text files, any computer with a Web browser can easily read the Web pages stored on another computer. In short, a hyperlink is a link between two HTML documents stored on any computer connected to the Internet anywhere in the world. Every hyperlink in the world is created using this syntax:

```
<A HREF="URL"></A>
```

The tag is officially called the ANCHOR tag, hence the letter *A* after the less-than sign, and the HREF attribute points to the URL or location of the other resource the link is linking to. This link points to the home page of W3C:

```
<A HREF="http://www.w3.org">World Wide Web Consortium</A>
```

Don't worry if you're not 100 percent clear on how tags, URLs, and attributes work just yet. They'll all be explained in their own good time. In addition, Skill 4, "Using HTML Tags to Describe Documents," includes a complete rundown on the syntax for creating and embedding hyperlinks in an HTML document.

Finding Your Way with Uniform Resource Locators

The idea of being able to link from one document to any other document available on the Web is quite exciting. But the prospect of trying to actually get to that other document can be somewhat daunting. Where is it? How do you get there? How do you identify it?

Think about a more common problem. Joe, an acquaintance from work, invites you over to his house for a barbecue after work on Friday evening. How do you find Joe's house? Even the most knowledgeable long-time resident of your city isn't likely to know where Joe's house is if it is identified only as "Joe's house." (Unless you happen to live in a town with only one Joe, of course.) You need an address to effectively find your way to the party.

The same applies to Web pages; they all must have addresses in order for visitors to find them and for other Web pages to provide instructions (directions) for where to reach them. An address on the Web is known as a *Uniform Resource Locator*, or URL. These locator addresses are uniform in that they provide a common addressing syntax for any Internet-connected computer around the world.

If you've ever had any correspondence with foreign companies or individuals, you'll know how confusing addressing conventions can be in different countries. On the Web, URLs take the same basic form no matter where in the world a computer is located.

Deconstructing Addresses

The root of all URLs is the *domain name*. Many businesses today have domain names that are the same as or similar to their business name. For example, the publisher of this book, Sybex, has the domain name `sybex.com`. Technically, the `com` portion of that name is what's known as the *top-level domain*, or TLD. For domains administered within the U.S., there are six major top-level domains:

- `Com` currently serves as a sort of catch-all for domain names that don't fit into any of the other categories. When created, it meant "commercial."
- `Org` is used for organizations. Generally, it is used for nonprofit entities.
- `Edu` is used for educational institutions.
- `Net` is used for network companies, most often by ISPs.
- `Mil` is used for all networks related to the military.
- `Gov` is used for all government organizations and institutions.

NOTE The top-level domain naming system is in the process of being expanded to provide for the increasing number of individuals and organizations that want their own Web addresses. What the new top-level domains are going to be and when they will begin to be assigned is still very much up in the air.

In our example domain name, `sybex.com`, the `sybex` portion is what's known as the second-level domain. When people are discussing domain names, the full `sybex.com` is the entity in question.

To link to specific documents on a Web site, you need more information than just the site's domain name. Many Web sites make use of a third-level domain, a name written to the left of the second- and top-level domain; for example, `www.sybex.com`. The `www` in this instance is the third-level domain. The vast majority of Web servers connected to the Internet today use `www` as a third-level domain for their Web sites. The tradition began with many system administrators naming their computers, for purposes of domain names, according to the function that they served. A machine that functioned as a Web server, as opposed to an FTP server or mail server, was typically named www. It should be noted that a Web server can be named anything the administrator wants to name it; the www third-level domain is not required. In fact, some administrators choose not to use third-level domains at all. The Netscape Web site is an example of this; it can be accessed at `http://netscape.com`. (So as not to confuse users though, Netscape also makes use of the www third-level domain by way of the `http://www.netscape.com` URL. Both syntaxes will connect a user to the same machine.)

Another critical piece of a URL is the protocol, a part often overlooked by many users and quite a few marketing and advertising types when they add URLs to brochures or television spots. The protocol is the portion of the URL before the double slash (//). For Web sites, the protocol is `http`, or Hypertext Transfer Protocol. A full and well-formed URL contains the protocol and at least a second- and top-level domain.

Now, before your eyes glaze over completely, we're finished with the real technical talk about URLs. We've already seen that just knowing the primary address for a Web site isn't necessarily enough information to provide an accurate link to a specific document. What you now need is the path to the document in question. You should be familiar with directory paths from working with your computer. On Windows 95/98 and NT machines, many programs are installed within the Program Files directory on your hard drive. If you have a program called "Wizard," the files for that program might reside in `c:\program files\wizard`. On a Web site, the same concept applies.

Let's say we need to link to a particular technical support FAQ document about the fictional Tech Guru, Inc.'s Wizard software. Their primary Web site URL is `http://www.techguru.com`. All of their support documents are located in a directory known as Support, and FAQs have their own subdirectory called FAQ. The document in question is titled `wizard-faq.html`.

Like a path on your hard drive, all paths on a Web site travel down from the root-level or primary address (`http://www.techguru.com`). Traveling through the Support directory, into the FAQ directory, and to the individual file, the URL would be constructed as `http://www.techguru.com/support/faq/wizard-faq.html`.

URL Shorthand: Relative Addressing

When working in your own Web site, you can save time and space by using a form of shorthand for URLs. This shorthand is officially called *relative addressing*. As with your computer, a Web server will assume that you are working on files within the current directory unless you explicitly state otherwise. This gets really handy when you're working with images or other objects that are also included in your document.

To write a URL for a document or object in the same directory as your current document, you need to use only the file name. Keeping with our Tech Guru example, if one FAQ on the site needed to link to the `wizard-faq.html` file, the Webmaster could simply use `<A HREF="wizard-faq.html">` when creating that link.

From Links to Building Blocks

Hypertext and hyperlinks are what make the Web what it is. Without links, Web pages would be stand-alone files on a computer system somewhere that could be shared only by users on a local-area network who save them to disk and pass them around the office. Although links make the connection of documents possible, they are only one piece in the larger Web puzzle. Before you can use a hyperlink to link two documents together, you must have documents to link. The following sections examine the building blocks of HTML documents: tags, attributes, and content. Even though HTML is a standard markup language, there is more than one version of HTML, and Web browsers don't always interpret HTML in the same way. Therefore, there are some important HTML issues you'll need to keep in mind as you get ready to create your own HTML documents.

The Basics of Web Page Creation

To create and publish a Web page, all you need is a simple text editor and an account with an ISP (Internet Service Provider) that provides Web hosting (or, of course, your own server, but we'll assume that you don't have the significant resources that such an undertaking requires). There are dozens, if not hundreds, of software tools available to assist you in creating your Web pages. These programs range from enhanced text editors that are free or are available at very little cost to full enterprise-oriented RAD (Rapid Application Development) packages retailing for thousands of dollars. The most widely available editors come with your computer's operating system: Notepad in Windows, SimpleText on the Mac, or vi on UNIX-based systems. Open a new file and you're ready to begin.

A New Paradigm for Document Creation: The Edit-Review Cycle

When new Web developers begin work on HTML documents, one of the toughest things to get used to is that the document looks different in the editor than it looks when it's uploaded to the Web server. The rising popularity of tools that purport to be WYSIWYG (What-You-See-Is-What-You-Get) don't help the problem.

In the arena of desktop publishing, which is one of the computing activities most similar to Web site production, authors are familiar and comfortable with tools that create documents as they will be seen, right in the document development tool. The word processor that this text was written in operates in that manner. The margins, spacing, font styling, text placement, and so on, will look similar on paper to how it looks on the screen. The key is that the output of these programs is intended to be paper. Once something is printed, unless scissors are taken to it or coffee is spilled on it, it remains the same size and color. You don't have to concern yourself with what font someone might select for their paper or how many colors their paper is capable of displaying. You know what paper you are printing the material on and can make those decisions during the production process.

On the Web, however, you have no control over the type of system on which your documents will be viewed. It could be someone with a palm-top computer that has a 3-inch by 6-inch monochrome backlit screen or a graphics professional sitting in front of a giant 21-inch monitor set to 16 million colors.

In order to create effective documents in this wildly variable environment, many authors have developed the habit of using an edit-review cycle during their document creation efforts. The concept is pretty simple:

1. The author begins work on the document and stops at a point where the look or layout needs to be checked.
2. The document is saved and then opened in as many browsers and on as many platforms as the author has access to. This enables the author to see how the markup ideas have been interpreted by these various devices.
3. If an inconsistency is found, the document can then be edited and reviewed again until the author is satisfied with the display that users are most likely to encounter.

The number of browsers or platforms on which you choose to review your documents will certainly vary. Not everyone that uses a PC will have access to a

Mac or a Unix box, nor will you necessarily have a wide array of browsers to work with—but that's okay. The important part is that you check your work by viewing it in the environment that your users will be seeing it, which is a Web browser.

Tags: The Building Blocks of HTML

HTML relies on markup for relaying structural instructions. Markup consists of elements, or *tags*. Each tag provides formatting information that the browser uses to interpret and display the content of the HTML document. We'll discuss the most current version of HTML 4.0 in detail in Skill 4,"Using HTML Tags to Describe Documents"; for now, let's review the function of tags in HTML.

As we saw in Skill 2, markup notation consists of a key word enclosed in angle brackets, such as `<TITLE>`, and, if required, a closing tag that leads off with a slash, as in `</TITLE>`. HTML provides tags that denote the beginning of a document, details about the document's origins, language, and content, and of course, the content itself. Within the body of the document, where the content is written, additional tags provide a means of organizing the information being presented in blocks (such as paragraphs), in tables, or in forms that retrieve information from a document's readers.

By way of example, the following tags describe an unordered list:

```
<UL>
     <LI>List item 1</LI>
     <LI>List item 2</LI>
     <LI>List item 3</LI>
</UL>
```

The unordered-list tag (`<UL>`) identifies the list as a bulleted list, and the list-item tag (`<LI>`) marks each individual item in the list. In HTML, and every other markup language for that matter, every tag is used to describe a particular kind of content. In the following example, the definition-list tag (`<DL>`) identifies the list as a list of definition terms, whereas the definition-term tag (`<DT>`) marks the terms, and the definition-description tag (`<DD>`) identifies the description of each term:

```
<DL>
     <DT>XML</DT>
          <DD>Extensible Markup Language</DD>
     <DT>HTML</DT>
          <DD>Hypertext Markup Language</DT>
</DL>
```

Figures 3.1 and 3.2 show what the definition-list and unordered-list markup look like when viewed in a Web browser.

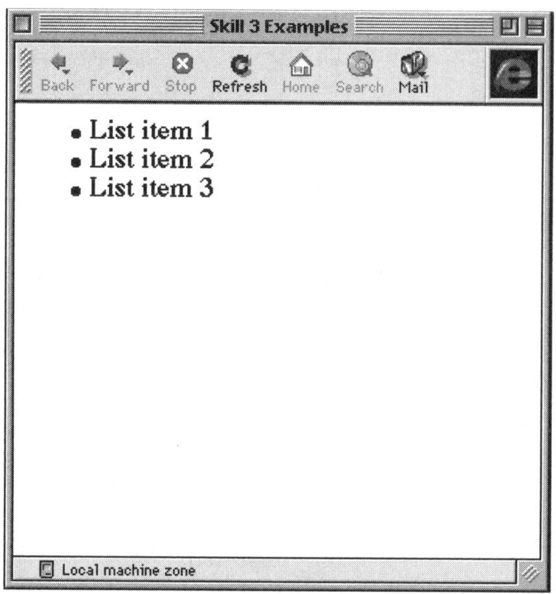

FIGURE 3.1: Unordered-list markup as displayed in a Web browser

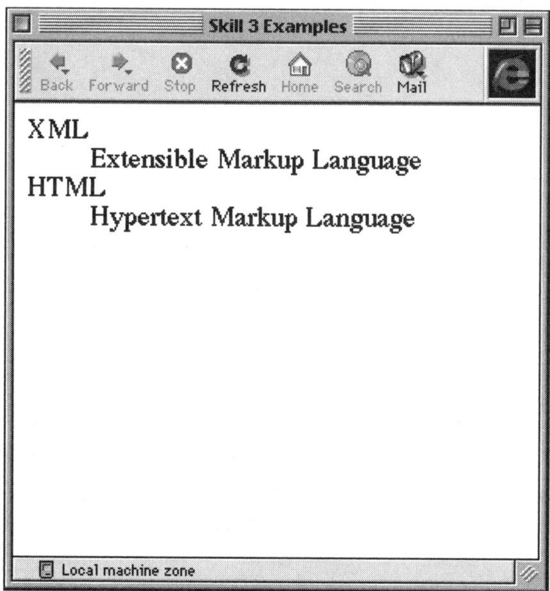

FIGURE 3.2: Definition-list markup as displayed in a Web browser

The way content is finally displayed in a Web browser is entirely dependent upon the tags used to describe it. If I change the list identifier in the unordered-list example from <UL> to <OL> (an ordered-list identifier), the new code looks like this:

```
<OL>
     <LI>List item 1</LI>
     <LI>List item 2</LI>
     <LI>List item 3</LI>
</OL>
```

The list is now labeled as an ordered list instead of an unordered list, so the display is different, as shown in Figure 3.3.

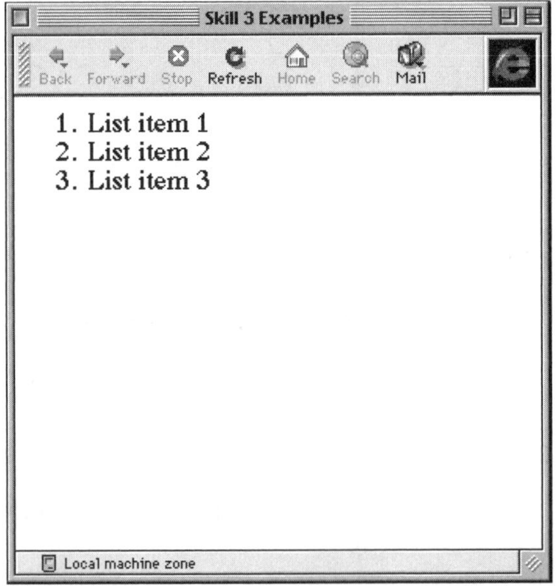

FIGURE 3.3: Ordered list markup as displayed in a Web browser

In HTML, tags are the first step in describing your content, so a large part of learning HTML is learning what tags you have at your disposal and what kind of content they are used to describe. Skill 4 investigates all of the HTML tags and the content they describe in depth.

Getting Specific with Attributes

Attributes are a markup mechanism that allow additional details to be added to a tag that describes a block of content. Generally, attributes either provide details to the browser about how to format the tag's content, or they supply extended flexibility to allow one tag to be used to describe a wide variety of content. The attributes you can use with each individual HTML tag are predefined in the HTML DTD, and you can't mix and match attributes from one element to another. Part of learning HTML is learning which attributes work with which tags and what they're for. For instance, the tag that allows authors to insert images into their documents, the IMAGE tag, has one required attribute, the SRC attribute. While the <IMG> tag describes an image in general, the SRC attribute points to the location of the image file to be embedded within the HTML file, as seen here:

```
<IMG SRC="myphoto.gif">
```

Attributes will always be written as part of a name/value pair; that is, the attribute's name is written first, with the = symbol providing the link to the value assigned to that attribute, and the value is enclosed in quotation marks. In our image example, the attribute name is SRC (source), and the value is the file name myphoto.gif.

Not all possible attributes are required in every instance of an HTML tag. The IMAGE tag has many more attributes than are commonly used. However, only the SRC attribute is required; the additional attributes serve only to enhance or refine the instructions relayed to the browser by that tag. For instance, the TABLE tag has an optional attribute of BORDER. This attribute takes a numerical value, and the number assigned as a value to the attribute specifies how many pixels wide the border around the element should be. This code specifies an image with a border of 0:

```
<IMG SRC="banner.gif" BORDER=0>
```

This code specifies an image with a border of 20:

```
<IMG SRC="banner.gif" BORDER=20>
```

Figures 3.4 and 3.5 show how the change in the value of the BORDER attribute changes the final display of the code in a Web browser.

FIGURE 3.4: An image with a border of 0 pixels

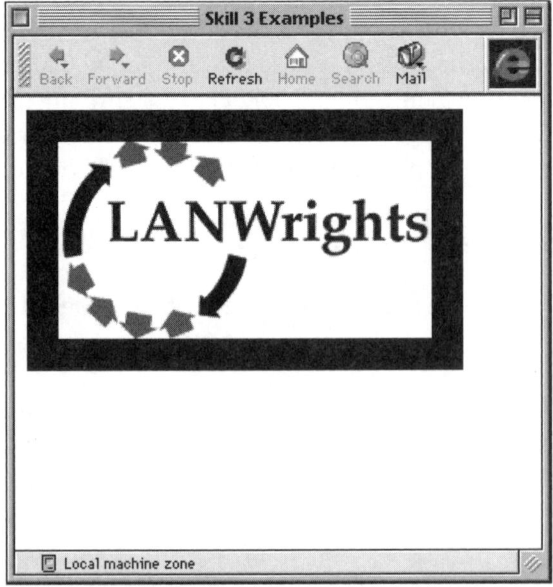

FIGURE 3.5: An image with a border of 20 pixels

Often, if an attribute is not present in a tag, its default value is assumed. If the BORDER attribute is not defined in the IMAGE tag, the browser uses the default value of "1" when rendering the image content.

A few attributes have only one possible value, so by their mere presence, the value is constant and need not be written. An example of this is found in the FORM tag for a checkbox, as seen here:

```
<INPUT TYPE="checkbox" NAME="box1" VALUE="foo" CHECKED>
```


In this sample, three attributes, TYPE, NAME, and VALUE, appear as you'd expect them to, in name/value pair format. CHECKED, on the other hand, stands alone. By its presence in the INPUT tag, it instructs the browser to display this checkbox with a checkmark already placed in it.

This differs from a default value for an attribute in an important way: A default value may be changed through overriding it by declaring the attribute in the tag and setting a value other than the default value. For an attribute without a value, if it is present, the value is on or activated. If it is not present, the value is turned off or remains unexpressed.

It's obvious that attributes are just as important as tags in creating HTML tags. In fact, you'll almost never find a tag that doesn't have at least one attribute. Skill 4 includes a complete discussion of all of the attributes you have at your disposal and how they affect the final rendering of their tags.

Content Is King

No matter how well organized your document may be, how creatively it has been designed, or how precisely you followed the HTML specifications while creating it, you've wasted all that effort if your document doesn't have content. As someone once said about southern California, "There's no *there* there." You don't want to have someone say that about your Web site!

The Web site for Claremont Graduate University in Claremont, California, is a good example of a site that provides quality information, as seen in Figure 3.6.

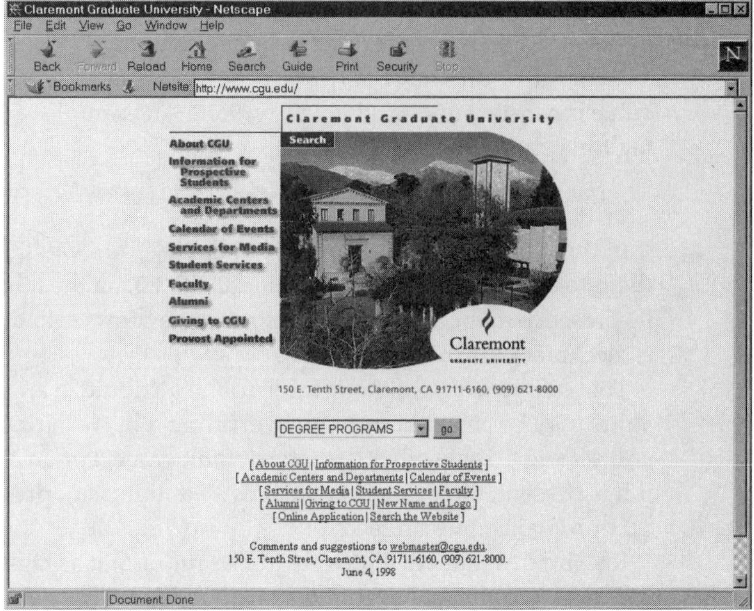

FIGURE 3.6: Claremont Graduate University's Web site provides detailed information to students, faculty, and other interested parties.

The CGU site's major sections include:

- About CGU
- Information for Prospective Students
- Academic Centers and Departments
- Calendar of Events
- Services for Media
- Student Services
- Faculty
- Alumni
- Giving to CGU
- News announcements

In addition to providing information, the site interacts with potential students by providing an application form right online! (See Figure 3.7.)

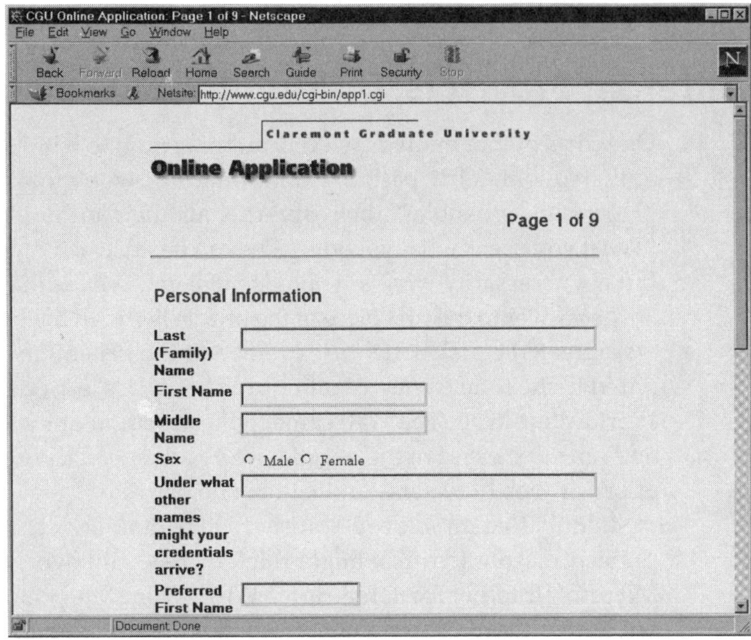

FIGURE 3.7: Interactivity can greatly increase the usefulness of your site for your intended audience.

As with any good Web site, the sections and layout of the site are driven entirely by the content the site is presenting. Every Web site will be different because everyone's content is different. Before you begin to code your first batch of HTML, make sure you carefully evaluate the content you'll be describing and always keep your content in mind as you create your pages. In the end, if you describe your content as accurately as possible with the markup available, you'll find that you'll have a clean, content-driven site that quickly and easily leads visitors to the information they are looking for.

Important HTML Issues

Before diving into creating your own HTML documents, it's important to understand a few key issues about HTML, browsers, and the way they interact.

Different Browsers, Different Platforms

One concept that many new Web authors struggle with is how HTML documents, authored with fairly basic HTML formatting, won't look the same to every user. "How is this possible?" they ask. After all, their authoring tool tells them that "What you see is what you get!" The catch is that what you see is what *you* get but not necessarily what anyone else will get. Why is that?

The answer to the first piece of the puzzle lies with the browsers. Not all browsers were created equal. Software development in general moves at light speed compared to the time frames of other product cycles, especially as it pertains to the World Wide Web. The Web came to the attention of the general public in 1994, and now at the end of the decade, we've advanced through more than five generations of Web browsers—more than one per year!

Multiply that rapid development by the number of browsers that have been publicly distributed. You might think there's only two: Netscape Navigator and Microsoft Internet Explorer, right? Wrong! One site popular with Web developers, aptly named BrowserWatch, has been keeping track of how many unique browsers have visited. As of mid-June, 1998, over 356 different browsers had visited the site! Many of those 356 different browsers are actually different versions of the same browser (often called a *user agent*). Twelve browsers have collected a "market share" of more than 25 percent of that site's visitors. When you consider how many versions of each of those dozen browsers may be out there, we're talking about quite an astounding number of browsers! In fact, according to another browser-oriented Web site, BrowserCaps, there are 54 unique user agents running around the Web today.

NOTE

The statistics collected by BrowserWatch (`http://browserwatch.internet.com/`) are heavily tilted toward those who have an interest in browsers. This means that some fairly obscure browsers are noted in their stats and that the numbers also reflect various beta versions of browsers and browsers on a wide number of platforms.

The number of browsers being used today might just sound like an interesting statistic to you at this point. But consider this: not every browser displays HTML in the same way, and this is *by design*. Before deciding that the W3C members have suffered a collective lapse of sanity, remember what we discussed in Skill 1, "Learning about XML," about the origins of HTML: HTML was designed to describe the *structure* of a document, not its presentation.

For instance, a structural description could say that related text is grouped together into distinct units known as paragraphs. Based on that statement, what should a paragraph look like? You can't tell, other than knowing that it's a block of text. The description doesn't say that the text within the block should use a serif font, be justified, and have one-inch margins on all sides; it simply says it is text that is distinctly grouped together to form a unit.

The examples given in Figures 3.8 and 3.9 show the same Web page, the LANWrights, Inc. home page, as displayed by Internet Explorer and Netscape Navigator. The content is the same, but the margins, fonts, and font sizes are different.

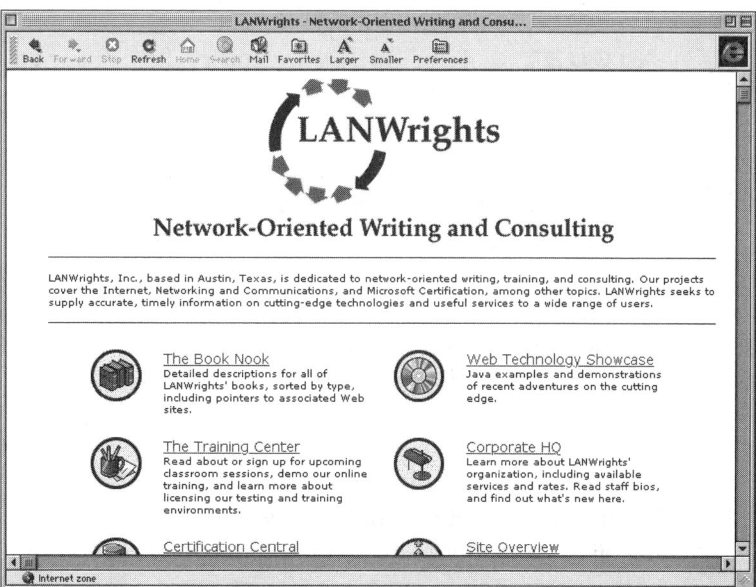

FIGURE 3.8: The LANWrights, Inc. home page as seen with Internet Explorer

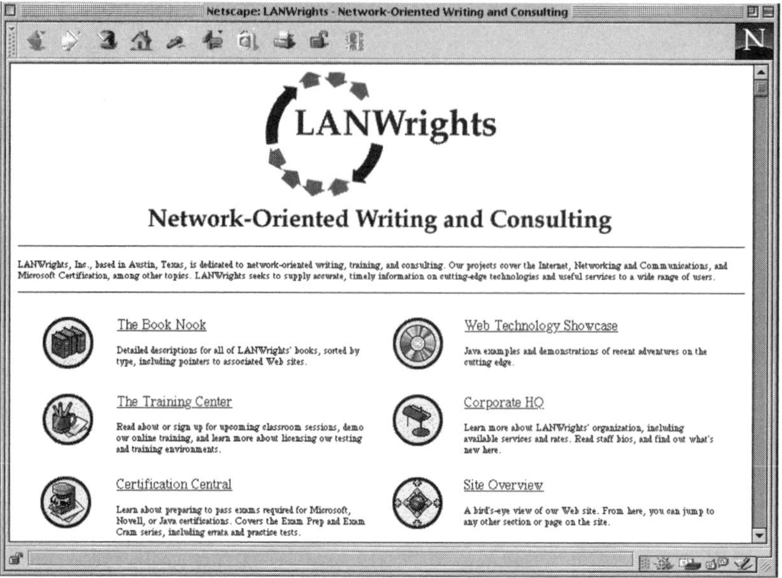

FIGURE 3.9: The LANWrights, Inc. home page as seen with Netscape Navigator

That's the quandary software developers face when creating browsers. Traditions started by the first browsers can support specific methods of display for various HTML elements, but the HTML specifications rarely dictate exactly how an element should look. As we'll discuss in Skill 4, "Using HTML Tags to Describe Documents," convention may dictate that *emphasis* is indicated by italicized text, but the programmers writing a new browser are free to use giant purple wingdings for emphasis if they choose. (Their customers might complain, but that's another topic.)

The second major piece of the puzzle is the fact that each major computer platform inherently handles various basic functions differently. PC users often take for granted the options they have with a right-click of the mouse. Mac users, on the other hand, normally don't have a right mouse button. The basic look and feel of the browser often must be different in order to accommodate these differences in basic functionality.

TIP

If you're interested in the amount of time it takes to program cross-browser and cross-platform compatible Web sites, check out the Web Standards Project at `http://www.webstandards.com`.

From Building Blocks to Building

So now that you know what building materials you have to work with, I'm sure you're ready to get started constructing your own HTML pages. Even when you're up to your neck in HTML tags and attributes, don't lose sight of some of the very important concepts and issues this skill covers. Remember that content is always king, and that tags and attributes are used to describe content, not format it. Don't get too frustrated when your pages don't look exactly the same from version to version, that's just the difference in the way the browsers interpret your markup. Let go of your desire to format content and concentrate on describing it, and you'll have a much more enjoyable Web page development experience.

Skill 4 looks at all of the HTML 4.0 tags, grouped by type, and shows you the attributes you can use with each tag. You can copy the helpful code samples into the text editor of your choice and practice writing your own HTML with just a little help from me. HTML is quite a bit of fun, you'll see. By the time you're done with Skill 4, you'll be creating Web pages like a pro.

Are You up to Speed?

Now you can...

- ☑ **Describe how hyperlinks connect the millions of documents on the Web**
- ☑ **Explain how HTML tags and attributes describe content**
- ☑ **Discuss the importance of content in Web page development**
- ☑ **Address some of the key HTML and browser issues that affect Web page development**

SKILL 4

Using HTML Tags to Describe Documents

- Using HTML to describe a document
- Understanding structure versus presentation
- Reviewing the major HTML element groups

In order to use XML successfully in your Web development efforts, you should have a solid understanding of the most recent HTML specification, HTML 4.0. This skill examines most of the HTML 4.0 tags in detail. I've divided the tags by type so they'll be easier to digest.

HTML as a Document Description Tool

HTML's origins are in providing a framework or structure for a document. Rather than establishing how a document should look, HTML describes how it should be built. To use a more visual metaphor, HTML tells you how to secure six square wooden panels together to create a cube. It doesn't, however, specify whether that wood should be oak, pine, or mahogany, or whether it should be unfinished, varnished, stained, or painted.

Over the years, user demand has encouraged the addition of presentational elements into the HTML specifications. As this continued, it became clear that the original idea of HTML providing structure rather than decoration was the most practical approach. So the determination of a document's look and feel was removed from HTML and placed in the domain of style sheets. CSS2—Cascading Style Sheets level 2—can handle almost any stylistic issue a designer can dream up. The addition of XML to the markup world for describing the structure of documents completes the arsenal for document description.

A Rundown of the HTML 4.0 Specification: HTML Tags by Category

The HTML 4.0 specification is a large and complex document. Even at the simplest level, there are three versions of which authors need to be aware: HTML 4.0 Strict, Transitional, and Frameset.

NOTE

The complete specification, which contains elements that apply to one or all of these versions, is available online at the W3C's Web site at `http://www.w3.org/TR/REC-html40`. Any known errors in the specification are being tracked and can be viewed at `http://www.w3.org/MarkUp/html40-updates/REC-html40-19980424-errata.html`.

In order to simplify your review of HTML and to provide a meaningful reference segment for you to refer to throughout your adventures in XML later in this text, I've formed 10 groups of elements that are similar in usage or that work together to produce a specific function, such as tables and forms.

Setting Up the Document Structure

All HTML documents are composed of four parts:

- A line declaring which version of HTML is being used to create the document.
- An HTML element that describes the document as an HTML document.
- A declarative header section, which is enclosed in the <HEAD> element
- The main body of the document, which contains the actual document content. The body can be contained within either the <BODY> or <FRAMESET> elements.

Which Version of HTML?

To be valid, an HTML document must declare which version of HTML was used to compose it. This statement is the *document-type declaration* for the document. It names the *document-type definition* (DTD) that's being used for the document. The DTD is a concise definition of the HTML version being used. It could be likened to an HTML "periodic table of the elements"—it describes all the necessary information about HTML in a brief, compact manner.

Each of the three versions of HTML 4.0 has its own DTD, as shown here:

- **HTML 4.0 Strict** includes all elements that have not been deprecated or are not used in framesets. This means that no presentational elements are found here. To use this DTD, include the following document-type declaration at the beginning of your document:

  ```
  <!DOCTYPE HTML PUBLIC "-//W3C//DTD HTML 4.0/EN"
  "http://www.w3.org/TR/REC-html40/strict.dtd">
  ```

- **HTML 4.0 Transitional** includes everything in the Strict DTD but adds deprecated elements and attributes that deal with presentation. It does not, however, include frameset elements. To use this DTD, include this document-type declaration:

  ```
  <!DOCTYPE HTML PUBLIC "-//W3C//DTD HTML 4.0 Transitional//EN"
  "http://www.w3.org/TR/REC-html40/loose.dtd">
  ```

- **HTML 4.0 Frameset** includes everything in transitional DTD and adds in the elements necessary for framesets. This DTD includes elements used to create Web pages with frames not a part of the transitional HTML 4.0 specification. Frames are a particular kind of HTML markup that let you divide your page into sections and display several documents at one time, each in its own frame. The section on frame elements later in the chapter discusses this markup in detail. To use this version, include the following document-type declaration:

```
<!DOCTYPE HTML PUBLIC "-//W3C//DTD HTML 4.0 Frameset//EN"
"http://www.w3.org/TR/REC-html40/frameset.dtd">
```

Admittedly, these document-type declarations look pretty intimidating, but when you break them down, they're fairly easy to read. They look as they do because they're a carryover from SGML. A well-formed SGML document must have a document-type declaration in order to tell the SGML parser (processor) how to process it. Web browsers don't generally rely on parsers to display HTML documents, so the document-type declaration isn't required in that context. However, it is still required for a document to be considered valid, and more importantly, including the document-type declaration that assists you in validating the entire document against the specification you have chosen.

Let's break down the declaration for HTML 4.0 Transition:

```
<!DOCTYPE HTML PUBLIC "-//W3C//DTD HTML 4.0 Transitional//EN"
"http://www.w3.org/TR/REC-html40/loose.dtd">
```

The document-type declaration is opened with a left-angle bracket and a bang (exclamation mark). `DOCTYPE` (document type) and `HTML` are fairly self-explanatory. `PUBLIC` identifies the DTD as being generally available. The next string, enclosed in quotation marks, is known as the public identifier for this particular DTD. The first segment, `//W3C`, indicates that the W3C was the author of this DTD. The second segment, `DTD HTML 4.0 Transitional//`, is the common name for the DTD. `//EN` indicates that we're using the U.S. English version. The URL provided in the next section is where the public copy of this DTD is available on the Web.

The HTML Element

All of the contents of an HTML document, with the exception of the document-type declaration, must be included within the element `<HTML>...</HTML>`. So, the first markup tag you use in any HTML document should be `<HTML>` and the last should be `</HTML>`. This snippet of code shows the beginnings of an HTML document written by the HTML 4.0 Transitional specification and with its HTML element already in place:

```
<!DOCTYPE HTML PUBLIC "-//W3C//DTD HTML 4.0 Transitional//EN"
"http://www.w3.org/TR/REC-html40/loose.dtd">

<HTML>

</HTML>
```

The remainder of the document's markup and content will go between the open HTML (<HTML>) and close HTML (</HTML>) tags. It's a good idea to get into the habit of always beginning every HTML document you create with a document-type declaration and an HTML element.

Just as all HTML documents should begin with an HTML element, so should they be saved with the suffix `.html` or `.htm`. These two suffixes let both the computer serving the HTML document (the Web server) and the Web browser know that a file is an HTML file and should be treated as such.

The Document Head

After the HTML tag comes the document-header data. This section is also a container and uses the <HEAD> element. This section will hold descriptive information about the document, such as its title and *metadata*. Metadata is data that describes data (just as XML is a meta–markup language that describes other markup) and includes information, such as keywords or short descriptions for use with search engines, the document's author, version control information, and any other data that is generally not considered actual document content. Most user agents do not display the contents of the <HEAD> element.

Within the HEAD element, every document *must* have a <TITLE> element. This should be a short descriptive phrase or sentence that uniquely identifies the document. The title used by the W3C for the HTML 4.0 specification was just that: "HTML 4.0 Specification." Choose your titles carefully, as many search engines display them as links to your documents. You'll want visitors to be able to differentiate between individual documents on your site rather than have all of the documents use the same "Foo, Inc." title. Title is a container, so a closing </TITLE> tag is required.

TIP

The text included within the <TITLE>...</TITLE> tags appears in the browser window's title bar after the Web page is loaded into the browser. Unlike all of the other text within your HTML page, you can't add any formatting tags to the text within the TITLE tags.

META elements are highly versatile. Any descriptive information that needs to be included can be placed into a META tag. Each META element consists of a property and that property's content. For example, Foo, Inc. requires that all HTML documents have an author's name included in them. A META tag for authorship would appear as

```
<META name="author" content="Jane Campbell">
```

NOTE

Quotation marks play an important role in both HTML and XML. In general, you should always include all attribute values within quotation marks. Although some Web browsers will forgive you if you don't, they are a required part of XML syntax, so it's best to get into the habit of using them with every attribute value in any type of markup.

An additional attribute is available for META elements that indicates the language in which the content is provided. For example, if Napoleon Bonaparte had access to the Web, his documents could be identified as

```
<META name="author" lang="fr" content="Napoleon Bonaparte">
```

Identifying the original language of the content helps speech synthesizers apply appropriate pronunciation to the content. Unless you specify otherwise, the original language of the content is considered to be English.

NOTE

A reference list of language codes to be used for this purpose can be found in RFC1766 "Tags for the Identification of Languages," by H. Alvestrand, at http://ds.internic.net/rfc/rfc1766.txt.

Additional uses for metadata are continually being developed. Proposals are underway for PICS (Platform for Internet Content Selection) labels, profiles, and other more global descriptive methods.

So, an HTML document with a document-type declaration, an HTML element, and a header section with a title looks like this:

```
<!DOCTYPE HTML PUBLIC "-//W3C//DTD HTML 4.0 Transitional//EN"
"http://www.w3.org/TR/REC-html40/loose.dtd">
```

```
<HTML>

    <HEAD>
        <TITLE>My first HTML document</TITLE>
    </HEAD>

</HTML>
```

TIP

Notice the interesting use of white space in the previous code sample? Web browsers ignore hard returns and groups of spaces in a document. You could, in theory, include all of your HTML document on one line and the Web browser would process it in the exact same manner it would when the document is spread out over several lines. This means you can use white space to make your documents easier to manage and read.

Figure 4.1 shows what this document looks like when displayed in an HTML browser.

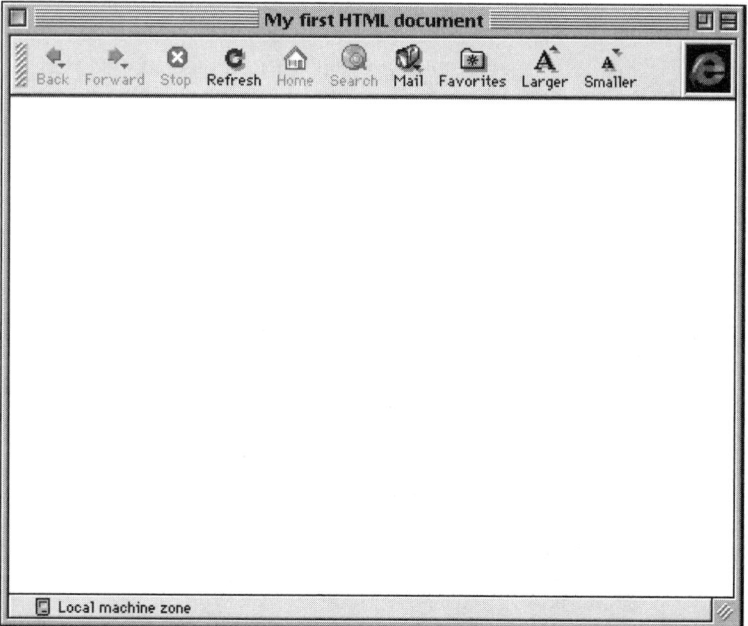

FIGURE 4.1: A short HTML document with only header information, as displayed by a Web browser

Notice the window is empty; however, the title described in the HTML header is in the window's title bar. The content that will be displayed in the window itself is contained within the document-body elements, not coincidentally the topic of the next section.

The Document Body

As the name implies, the document body contains the content for the document. This is what you'd think of as the "meat" of the document or the actual text of a book rather than the front matter, such as the title page, dedications, and other pages you'll find at the beginning of most books. The contents need to be enclosed in the <BODY> element, which is a container that is opened immediately after the closing <HEAD> element, and the contents remain open until just before the larger closing <HTML> element, as shown in this code snippet:

```
<!DOCTYPE HTML PUBLIC "-//W3C//DTD HTML 4.0 Transitional//EN"
"http://www.w3.org/TR/REC-html40/loose.dtd">

<HTML>

     <HEAD>
          <TITLE>My first HTML document</TITLE>
     </HEAD>

     <BODY>

     </BODY>

</HTML>
```

In past versions of HTML, several descriptive attributes were seen in the <BODY> element, including background coloring or image selection, colors for primary text, and colors for links in each of their various states (visited, unvisited, active, etc). These attributes have been deprecated in favor of style sheets, although they are allowed in HTML 4.0 Transitional and Frameset. Table 4.1 includes a list of the attributes you can use with the <BODY> element and a brief description of each.

TABLE 4.1: The <BODY>...</BODY> Attributes

Attribute	Description
ALINK="(#RRGGBB | colorname)"	Specifies the color of a link when it is active (i.e., after a user has clicked on it but before the resource it points to is displayed)

TABLE 4.1 CONTINUED: The <BODY>...</BODY> Attributes

Attribute	Description
BACKGROUND="URL"	Specifies a graphic to be used as a tiled background for the document
BGCOLOR="(#RRGGBB | colorname)"	Specifies a background color for the document
LINK="(#RRGGBB | colorname)"	Specifies the color for links in the document
TEXT="(#RRGGBB | colorname)"	Specifies the color for text in the document
VLINK="(#RRGGBB | colorname)"	Specifies the color for visited links in the document

Notice that all of the attributes that involve color can take one of two kinds of values: #RRGGBB or colorname. Color on the Web is specified in one of two ways. The first is a hexadecimal color-notation system that uses a combination of numbers and letters to specify a color. This system is based on the Red-Green-Blue (RGB) system for identifying color. Colors can also be specified as one of 16 recognized color names, including:

Aqua	Lime	Silver
Black	Maroon	Teal
Blue	Navy	White
Fuchsia	Olive	Yellow
Gray	Purple	
Green	Red	

For example, when specifying a white background for a document, you can use either of these two methods:

```
<BODY BGCOLOR="white">
<BODY BGCOOR="#RRGGBB">
```

If you're going to use hexadecimal notation, you'll want to make sure you include a pound sign (#) before the 6-digit notation code.

TIP Hexadecimal codes are computed using a specific formula. The easiest way to see which code generates a specific color is to visit an online color resource, such as the one at `http://www.mcp.com/que/developer_expert/htmlqr/reference.html#color`.

To add BODY attributes to the growing HTML sample page, use this code:

```
<!DOCTYPE HTML PUBLIC "-//W3C//DTD HTML 4.0 Transitional//EN"
"http://www.w3.org/TR/REC-html40/loose.dtd">

<HTML>

     <HEAD>
          <TITLE>My first HTML document</TITLE>
     </HEAD>

     <BODY BGCOLOR="teal" TEXT="white" LINK="navy" VLINK="maroon">

     </BODY>

</HTML>
```

Structuring Document Content with Headings

Almost any document can be broken down into distinct blocks of text or other information provided by illustrations and photographs. The most basic of HTML documents will describe this structure for you. For example, you may have two paragraphs, an image, a quotation, and then a final paragraph. Your document can be described as having five distinct blocks. To help organize your information, you might choose to provide several headings that divide up these blocks. You use the heading elements to do this in HTML.

Headings come in six levels, <H1> through <H6>. An H1 head denotes the most important information; H6 is the least important. Headings can be thought of as levels in an outline, where Roman numerals I and II would be H1-level headings and section IA would be an H2-level heading, etc. Headings are containers that should envelop a descriptive title for the sections to follow.

This code sample shows how headings might be used in a Web-based résumé to divide the document into logical sections:

```
<!DOCTYPE HTML PUBLIC "-//W3C//DTD HTML 4.0 Transitional//EN"
"http://www.w3.org/TR/REC-html40/loose.dtd">

<HTML>

     <HEAD>
          <TITLE>Resume</TITLE>
     </HEAD>

     <BODY BGCOLOR="white" TEXT="black">
```

```
        <H1>Employment History</H1>
        <H1>Education</H1>
            <H2>Undergraduate</H2>
            <H2>Graduate</H2>
        <H1>Skills</H1>
            <H2>Managerial</H2>
            <H2>Computer Related</H2>
                <H3>Hardware/Software</H3>
                <H3>Internet/Web</H3>
        <H1>References</H1>
        </BODY>
    </HTML>
```

Figure 4.2 shows this HTML code as viewed by a Web browser.

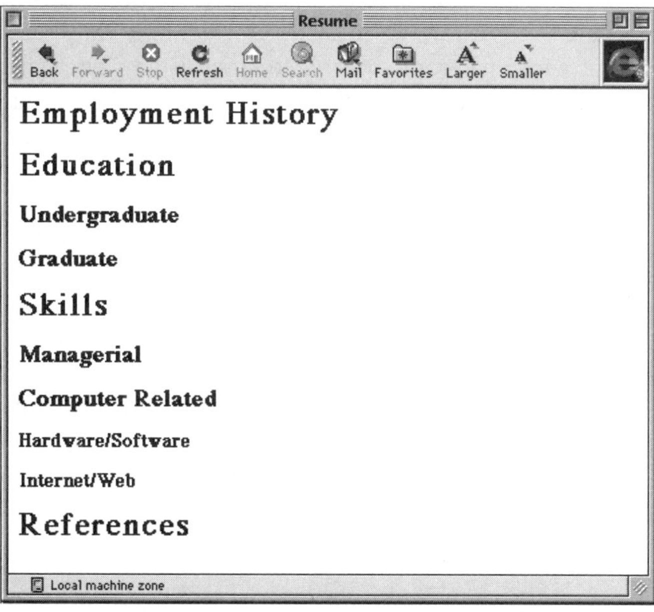

FIGURE 4.2: Heading markup as viewed by a Web browser

Text Formatting

The idea of text formatting may seem at first to go against my previous statements that HTML should only provide structure for the document. When you look more closely at the idea, you'll see I am still discussing structure as opposed to presentation.

The most basic text formatting is the grouping of sentences into paragraphs. The PARAGRAPH element is a container, as shown in this bit of code:

```
<P>The idea of text formatting may at first seem to go against our pre-
vious statements that HTML should only provide structure for the docu-
ment. When we look more closely at the idea, you'll see we are still
discussing structure as opposed to presentation.</P>
```

A paragraph is considered to be a block of text and usually describes a group of information that goes together. You may want to specify that specific sections of a paragraph be formatted in a specific way, usually to convey an emphasis of some kind or another or to identify text as technical text. The next few sections describe the tags you should use to add these descriptions to your HTML documents.

Providing Emphasis

In almost any block of text, there will be a portion that, if spoken, would be given a different vocal inflection that emphasizes the words being spoken. HTML can provide this with the EMPHASIS <EM> element. Emphasis acts as a container and instructs the browser to visually distinguish the emphasized text from the rest of the text block. Traditionally, this is done using *italicized* text. In this bit of code the words "really don't" are emphasized using the EM element:

```
<P>"I <EM>really don't</EM> want to go to school today,"
the little girl said.</P>
```

Strong Emphasis

As with almost everything in life, there are degrees of emphasis. Something might be *important;* then again, it could be **extremely important!** Strong emphasis can be conferred to text blocks using the <STRONG> element. Strong emphasis is also a container. It is traditionally rendered as boldfaced type but without italics. The previous code sample, with the STRONG element replacing the EMPHASIS element, looks like this:

```
<P>"I <STRONG>really don't</STRONG> want to go to school today,"
the little girl said.</P>
```

Figure 4.3 shows how a Web browser renders this markup using both EMPHASIS and STRONG EMPHASIS tags.

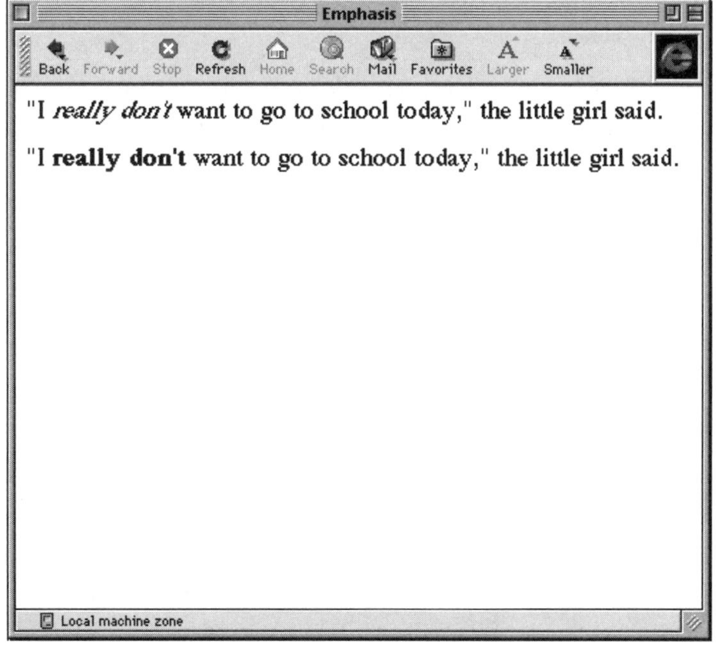

FIGURE 4.3: Emphasis and strong emphasis markup are rendered differently by Web browsers.

NOTE There are two deprecated HTML tags that are usually displayed in Web browsers in the same way as the <STRONG> and <EM> tags: <B> (for bold) and <I> (for italics). These two tags are strictly for formatting and should be avoided. (The <STRONG> and <EM> tags are structural.) In fact, if you validate a Web page that uses these tags against the HTML 4.0 Strict DTD, you'll get an error message listing the tags as invalid.

Structure for Technical Documents

There are eight additional elements that can provide structure to text fragments within a document. These each have highly specialized uses and, as with the

EMPHASIS elements, presentation depends on the design of the user agent. Table 4.2 provides a summary of these elements, which I'll discuss in more detail presently.

TABLE 4.2: Text-Formatting Elements

Element	Usage
ACRONYM	Indicates the enclosed text is an acronym, e.g., the word *radar.*
ABBR	Denotes an abbreviated form of the word or phrase, such as WWW for World Wide Web.
CITE	Shows that the text provided is a citation from or reference to another work.
CODE	Displays a segment of computer code.
DFN	Highlights the defining instance of the word or phrase; e.g., this book uses the convention of italicizing the defining instances of new terms.
KBD	Displays text that should be entered by the user; helpful for tutorials or other instructional material.
SAMP	Shows the display sample output from programs or scripts.
VAR	Highlights a variable or other program argument.

It is important to remember that not all user agents support each of these PHRASE elements, and how they treat the elements when they do support them is not necessarily consistent with other user agents. The important factor is that they do set apart the text in question, allowing the reader to differentiate the general body of a document from the designated examples.

Lists

Lists in HTML come in three basic categories: *unordered lists, ordered lists,* and *definition lists*. The first two, unordered and ordered, have just two elements: the LIST element—<UL> or <OL>, respectively—and the LIST ITEM <LI> element.

The LIST elements are containers, so a closing tag is required. Each individual item to be included is assigned its own <LI> tag.

Unordered Lists

An unordered list is one that is not inherently dependent on the order in which the items appear, although they are rendered in the order in which they are written in your source file. The idea is to set apart a collection of items or ideas. Most visually-oriented browsers display unordered lists as bulleted lists.

To create an unordered list, first use the <UL> element to identify the list as unordered, and then add LIST ITEM elements (<LI>) for each item in the list:

```
<P>Vehicles I have owned</P>
<UL>
     <LI>1993 Saturn SL1</LI>
     <LI>1996 Ford Contour</LI>
     <LI>1999 Ford Ranger</LI>
</UL>
```

Figure 4.4 shows this markup as rendered by a Web browser.

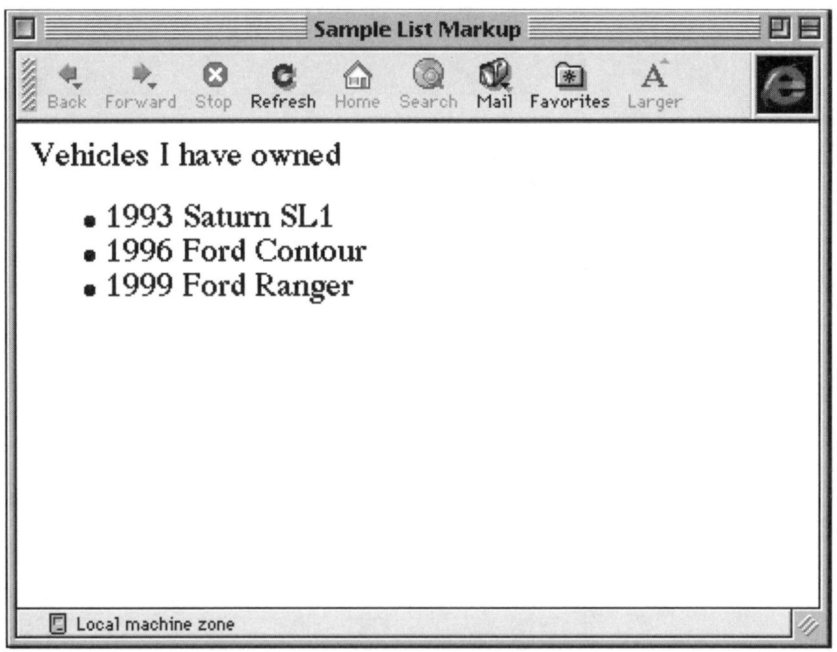

FIGURE 4.4: Markup rendered by a Web browser

Ordered Lists

An ordered list is one that is dependent on the order in which the items are presented. For example, the steps for following a recipe are likely to be presented as an ordered list, as are the instructions for assembling a child's bicycle. The ordering method and starting point—using numbers, letters, roman numerals, etc., and deciding whether to start with 1 or 100—is determined by using the TYPE= attribute.

To create an ordered list, first identify the list as an ordered list by using the <OL> tag, and then add <LI> tags for each item in the list:

```
<P>Things to do today</P>
<OL>
     <LI>Check email</LI>
     <LI>Write a chapter</LI>
     <LI>Teach class<LI>
</OL>
```

Figure 4.5 shows what this markup looks like as viewed by a Web browser.

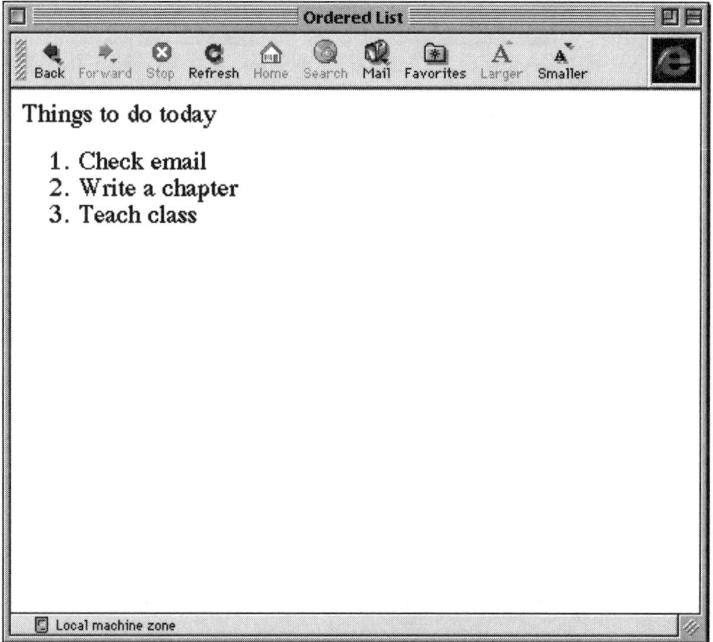

FIGURE 4.5: Ordered list markup as displayed by a Web browser

Definition Lists

Definition lists differ from the ordered and unordered lists in that each item consists of two parts: the definition term, <DT>, and the definition description,<DD>. The list opens with the definition-list tag, <DL>. Each definition *must* have both a term and a description, such as in the short list of computer-related acronyms in Figure 4.6:

```
<DL>
<DT>RAM
     <DD>Random Access Memory</DD>
</DT>
<DT>BIOS
     <DD>Basic Input Output System</DD>
</DT>
</DL>
```


It is not necessary to use definition lists for only dictionary applications as seen here; they can be used for any purpose that needs to set off text that relates to a shorter term or idea. For example, in the script for a play or movie the character name can be set off as the definition term and the corresponding dialog and actions written in the definition description.

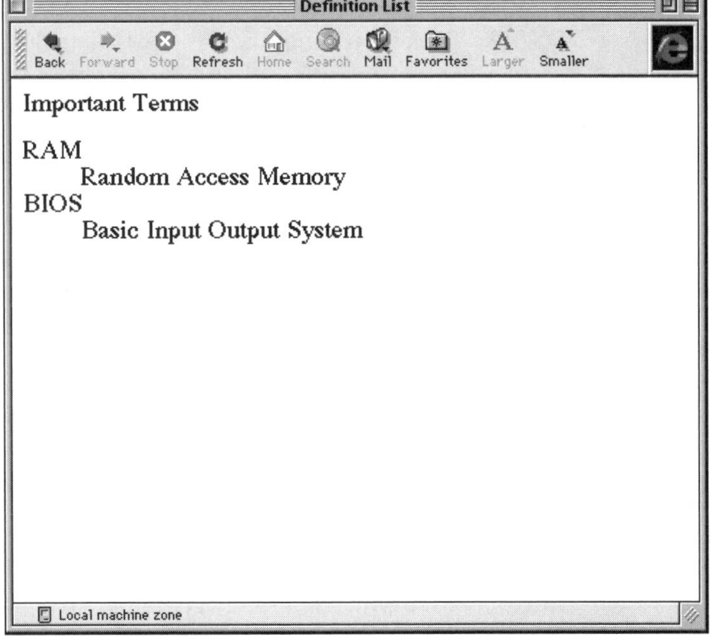

FIGURE 4.6: A definition list as displayed in a Web browser

Tables

Of all the elements in HTML, tables probably have undergone the most changes in version 4.0. Many attributes were added, while others were deleted. Significant improvements were made in terms of accessibility options as well as a logical way of connecting the content of cells to rows and columns.

We begin with the <TABLE> element itself. An important point to keep in mind is that not all user agents, even the most current ones (at this writing, the version 4.0 generation browsers), can support all of the new attributes and features of the TABLE element. This should improve with the next release of the major browsers.

The TABLE element accepts seven primary attributes. The attributes are

SUMMARY This value holds a text summary that describes the content and structure of the table. It is primarily used by alternative browsers, such as speech readers or Braille devices.

WIDTH This is a value for how wide the table should be rendered within the available screen real estate. It is measured as a percentage of available space (e.g., "100%" takes up 100 percent of the available space within the current browser dimensions; it does not mean "full screen").

BORDER This determines the width of the table border, measured in pixels. A value of 0 (zero) here removes the border.

FRAME A frame is also available to surround the table. The default value for this attribute is "void," which means the frame is not present. Alternative values are available to allow individual sides or a combination of the frame sides to be displayed. (It is important to note that the frame is not synonymous with the border. It is a separate visual element.)

RULES Rules are visual dividers between rows, columns, or groups of either within the table. This allows, for example, for a vertical divider between columns but no horizontal rules between cells in that column. The default value is "none," which means that no rules will be rendered. Rules are distinct visual elements apart from any borders defined.

CELLSPACING Space provided between table cells, measured in pixels. The default value is set to 0 (zero).

CELLPADDING Space between the cell wall and the cell content. This measurement is also in pixels, with a default of 0 (zero).

An important innovation in HTML 4.0 is the concept of grouping cells within tables. Both rows (the cells on the same horizontal level across the table) and columns (the cells in the same vertical space within the table) can be grouped together.

On the horizontal rows, three new elements are provided: TABLE HEAD <THEAD>, TABLE FOOT <TFOOT>, and TABLE BODY <TBODY>. Each group element must contain at least one row, which is still defined by the TABLE ROW <TR> element. The TABLE HEAD and TABLE FOOT elements are intended to contain descriptive information about the table columns to be displayed within the table body. Actual content data should be presented only in the table body. The following code sample provides an example of the expected HTML construction when using these elements.

```
<TABLE>
<THEAD>
<TR>table head contents</TR>
</THEAD>
<TFOOT>
     <TR>table foot contents</TR>
</TFOOT>
<TBODY>
     <TR>first row of table contents</TR>
     <TR>second row of table contents, etc</TR>
</TBODY>
</TABLE>
```

You'll notice that the table foot is declared before the table body. This is so that browsers can render the foot before beginning to fill in the data for the table body. Also note that this example just shows the beginning structures of an HTML table. It is far from complete, and if you tried to view this markup in a Web browser, you'd see nothing. Just wait, there's more.

When using head or foot and body groups within your table, each group *must* have the same number of columns in order for the table to be rendered properly.

Columns, on the other hand, have a single element that controls their grouping, the <COLGROUP> element. <COLGROUP> has two important attributes: SPAN and WIDTH.

SPAN This attribute defines the number of columns to be contained within the column group. The value must be an integer greater than 0 (zero), and the default is 1 (one).

`WIDTH` This attribute defines a default width for *each column* within the column group (rather than the width of the entire group). Values may be expressed in pixels, percentages, and relative values that are typically seen in the layout of frames. A special value of 0* (zero asterisk) may also be used; it defines the width of each column as the minimum width required to hold the column's contents and no more. (This also means that the browser must receive the entire content before it can make this determination and begin displaying the data).

The SPAN attribute can greatly reduce the amount of work required to format a large table of similarly sized cells. For example, a table designed to hold spreadsheet-type information may have 10 columns that all should be 50 pixels wide. The author then needs to declare this size only once, using the tag set

```
<COLGROUP SPAN="20" WIDTH="50">
...content...
</COLGROUP>
```

rather than

```
<COLGROUP>
     <COL WIDTH="50">
     <COL WIDTH="50">
     ... eight more times
</COLGROUP>
```

If one or a few columns in a large group need special formatting, an exception can be declared using style sheets. The irregular column is assigned an ID attribute that allows the style sheet to format that individual column apart from the others.

Column group definitions are declared within the <TABLE> element but before any HEAD or FOOT elements and before the ROW elements, as seen here:

```
<TABLE>
<COLGROUP SPAN="5" WIDTH="50">
<COLGROUP SPAN="2" WIDTH="100">
<THEAD>
     ...head content...
</THEAD>
<TFOOT>
     ...foot content...
</TFOOT>
<TBODY>
     ...body content...
</TBODY>
</TABLE>
```

It is important to remember that the <COLGROUP> tag provides *structure* for the columns; that is, it defines how may columns are in the group and provides the width measurements for those columns. It does not provide any other formatting support; that is the function provided by the <COL> element.

<COL> can also contain SPAN and WIDTH attributes that act in the same manner as when they are found in the <COLGROUP> element. SPAN is an integer greater than zero that defines the number of columns on which the element will operate. WIDTH defines the width for each of the columns in the element's SPAN. If a differing WIDTH were set in a <COLGROUP> element that impacts the <COL> element, the WIDTH defined for the <COL> tag will override the previous declaration.

TIP

<COL> elements do not have to be placed within a column group; they can stand both inside and outside a group element. Although attributes can be inherited or overridden between the two elements, they are not dependent upon each other for accurate display of your table. Use each only when they can simplify the table organization.

Table Cells

Two elements are available for defining table cells within rows: the TABLE HEADER CELL <TH> and the TABLE DATA CELL <TD>. Five primary attributes are available for these elements, as described below:

HEADERS Used for table data cells, this attribute defines which other header cells describe the contents of the current cell. The value is written as a space-delimited list of cell names. (The ID attribute then becomes required in those cells in order for them to be properly identified.)

SCOPE Used for table header cells, this attribute provides the connection between the header cell and its corresponding data cells. Four values are available:

- ROW provides header details for the remaining cells in the current row.
- COL provides header data for the remaining cells in the current column.
- ROWGROUP provides details for the remaining cells in the current row group.
- COLGROUP provides details for the remaining cells in the current column group.

`ABBR` An abbreviated form of the cell's content is presented with this attribute and may either be presented by the browser in place of the cells or read before the cell's contents by speech readers or other adaptive browsers.

`ROWSPAN` This attribute gives the number of rows spanned by the current cell, defaulting to 1 (one). The 0 (zero) value, while not particularly intuitive, indicates that the cell spans not only the current row but all remaining rows in the table.

`COLSPAN` This attribute follows the rowspan values. The default is 1 (one) and 0 (zero) indicates a span from the current cell to the end of the table.

When you put all of these `TABLE` elements together, you can create a pretty impressive display in a Web page. Figure 4.7 shows a table in a Web page inspired by Dr. Seuss.

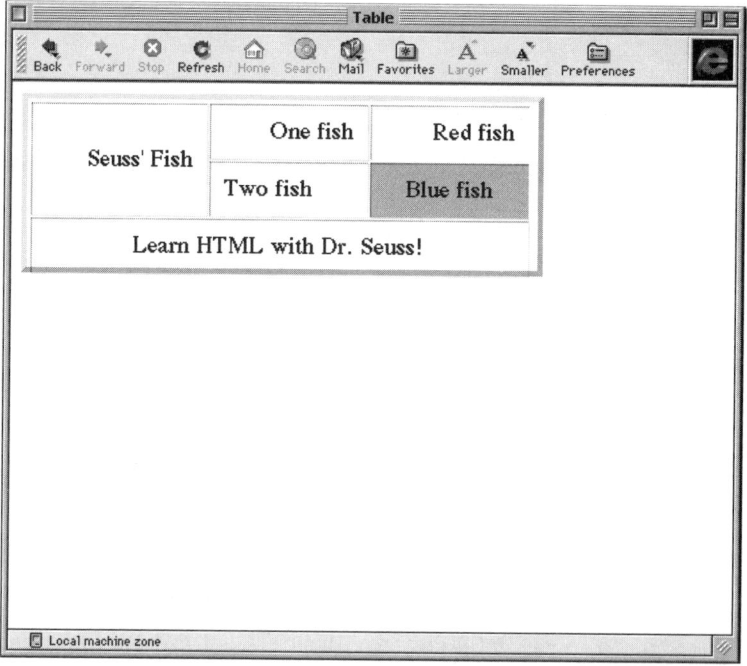

FIGURE 4.7: The Dr. Seuss fish table as shown in a Web browser

The code behind the fish table looks like this:

```
<TABLE WIDTH="75%" BORDER="5" CELLPADDING="10">
   <TR ALIGN="RIGHT">
      <TD ROWSPAN="2">Seuss' Fish</TD>
      <TD>One fish</TD>
      <TD BGCOLOR="red">Red fish</TD>
   </TR>

   <TR>
      <TD>Two fish</TD>
      <TD BGCOLOR="blue" ALIGN="CENTER">Blue fish</TD>
   </TR>

   <TR>
      <TD COLSPAN="3" ALIGN="CENTER">Learn HTML with Dr. Seuss!</TD>
   </TR>
   </TABLE>
```


Creating Links

Links are what the "hypertext" in Hypertext Markup Language is all about. Web pages are unique in that they don't lead viewers down a linear path of information that's always displayed in the same predictable order. The beauty of the Web is that you can move from one document about jazz music on a server in San Francisco and be transported directly to another document about musicians based in New Orleans and, from there, to other spots around the world.

The basic text link is provided with the ANCHOR <A> element. The <A> element actually has two pieces: the anchor, or beginning of the link, and the destination, or the resource, on the Web that's being linked to. A typical text link would appear within a paragraph:

```
<P>Additional details about our new widgets can be found on the
<A HREF="details.html">widgets details page</A>.
```

Figure 4.8 shows how a Web browser renders this code.

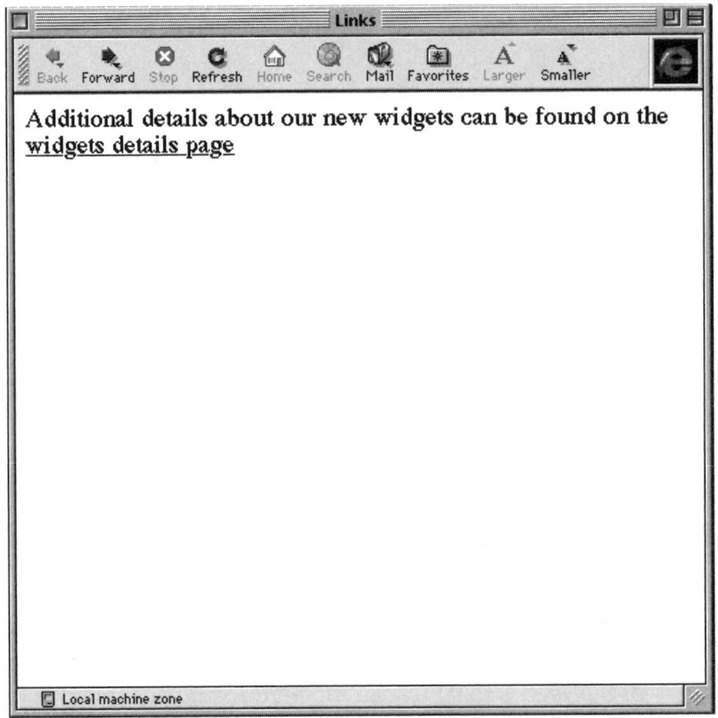

FIGURE 4.8: A hyperlink as seen with a Web browser

The HREF attribute indicates either the hyperlinked resource file or the file that you're linking out to. The value will always be a URL. In this example, we've used a relative URL. If a file is on your site in the same directory as the current document, you can use a sort of URL shorthand and write out only the file name you want to link to. However, if the document resides on another server or in another directory on your site, additional details will be needed. For instance, if the `details.html` file were located at the manufacturer's site elsewhere on the Web, rather than the retailer's site where this first document resided, the HREF value might look like `HREF="http://www.wemakethem.com/widgets/details.html"`.

Adding Internal Anchors

Links don't necessarily have to reach out to other documents on your site or elsewhere on the Web. In large documents, it's often convenient to provide links to sections farther down the page. For example, a directory of 50 faculty members at the local high school might be on a single page. A set of links can be provided at the top to make finding individual listings easier by transporting the reader to specific sections, such as jumping down to names beginning with *F* without having to scroll through the entire alphabet.

To do this, you need to introduce the NAME attribute into your ANCHOR tags. To set the anchor that can be linked to, create an empty ANCHOR tag—that is, one that does not contain an HREF attribute. Using our directory metaphor, an anchor would be created at the beginning of the *M* section and would appear as:


```
<A NAME="M">
```

Back at the top of the document, you can link to this anchor using special notation seen here:

```
<A HREF="#M">
```

The hash mark (#) indicates that the link is to an empty anchor on the current page. To jump directly to specific information, you can combine a link to a new page with a link to an empty anchor on that new page. Keeping with our directory example, a Web page designer who wants users to be able to link to the *M* section from another page on the school's site can write

```
<A HREF="directory.html#M">
```

to take their visitors directly to that section.

Specifying Presentation

There are now two methods for authors to apply presentation instructions in HTML documents. When using HTML 4.0 Strict, authors are required to employ style sheets for all stylistic elements. If the author prefers, he or she may use HTML 4.0 Transitional, in which decorative specifications may still be made, and the document will remain valid.

Style sheets were developed as a means of keeping HTML "pure" in its original structural intent. Cascading Style Sheets level 1 was the first implementation;

Cascading Style Sheets level 2 has just recently been published as a W3C specification. Style sheets will be covered in detail in Skill 15, "Adding Style with CSS."

NOTE See `http://www.w3.org/Style/` for the Cascading Style Sheets level 2 W3C specification.

There are several presentational elements that can be easily employed using HTML 4.0 Transitional. One of the most popular ways of changing a document's appearance is the use of font styling. We touched on some of these—the emphasis and strong emphasis elements—briefly in the earlier section on text formatting.

Table 4.3 provides a list of font style elements that are available and their usage.

TABLE 4.3: Font Style Elements

Element	Usage
B	Renders the text in bold-face type
BIG	Displays the enclosed text in a larger font size
I	Renders as italicized text
STRIKE	Displays text with a horizontal line through the midpoint, used to display text that has been struck from the document (often seen in legal settings)
SMALL	Renders the text in a smaller font size
TT	Displays the text in teletype format (a monospaced font)
U	Displays the text with an underline

This next chunk of code shows each of these elements as applied to a bit of text, and Figure 4.9 shows the results when the code is viewed with a Web browser.

```
<B>This is boldface type</B>
<BIG>This is big type</BIG>
<I>This is italicized type</I>
<STRIKE>This is struck type</STRIKE>
<SMALL>This is small type</SMALL>
<TT>This is teletype type</TT>
<U>This is underlined type</U>
```

FIGURE 4.9: Presentation markup as rendered by a Web browser

Modifying Font Styles

FONT STYLE elements change the style of the original font. FONT MODIFIER elements actually change the base font being used. The change can be to an entirely new font face (from Arial to Times New Roman, for example), or changes can be made to a font's standard color or size.

Table 4.4 relates the possible values for these attributes to the <FONT> element.

TABLE 4.4: FONT ELEMENT Attributes

Attribute	Usage
COLOR	Sets the color for the text enclosed within the <FONT> element
FACE	Shows a comma-delimited list of font names that should be attempted for display, in order of preference
SIZE	Determines the size of the font display, using integer values between 1 and 7

The font face is the actual name of the font to be employed. Familiar font faces are Arial, Helvetica, Times, Verdana, Courier, etc. It's important to note that the font you choose must be present on the viewer's system before your document can be displayed in that font. In order to have your document look its best, you should provide a second, third, or even fourth choice in the list of font names, in the order that you prefer. For example, if you want your document to be displayed in the Arial font face, you can set your face value to "Arial, Helvetica, sans serif." Arial is primarily a PC-based font, while Helvetica is a very similar font on the Macintosh platform. Sans serif isn't a particular font face; it tells the browser "If you can't find Arial or Helvetica, choose the default sans serif font that is installed on this system."

To specify that a section of text should be three steps larger than the document's regular font size, teal in color, and in Comic Sans font face, you would use this markup:

```
<FONT SIZE=+"3" COLOR="teal" FACE="Comic Sans">The text to be
changed</FONT>
```

TIP

The majority of presentation control tags, from <B> to <FONT>, are deprecated and not a part of the HTML 4.0 Strict DTD. To control the way your documents look, use the HTML style mechanism Cascading Style Sheets (CSS), which is discussed in depth in Skill 15, "Adding Style with CSS."

Setting Up Frames

Frames can be one of the most abused concepts in Web development. The most typical—and most appropriate—usage is to provide a static navigation panel along the left side or top of the browser display or to retain a static banner that will always "frame" the content found elsewhere on the site. Web authors need to be careful when the temptation arises to use frames because you can rather than because the design of the site requires it. Frames present more accessibility hurdles than almost any other HTML-based design option, not only for those using adaptive technologies but also for those using older browsers. So use frames with care, and explore whether acceptable alternative formatting methods are available before choosing to implement them. That said, let's review the structure of frames.

Frames begin with the <FRAMESET> container, which describes the layout of content within the browser window. This is accomplished using the following attributes:

> ROWS defines the size and number of horizontal frame divisions. The value is a comma-delimited list of values, defined in pixels, percentages, or relative lengths. Should no value be assigned, the default is "100%" (one row).
>
> COLS defines the size and number of vertical frames, also described in a comma-delimited list of values. The default here is "100%" (one column), as well.

For example, if you want to break up the browser window into four equal quadrants that fill the available browser window space, you'll need two rows and two columns. The frame-set declaration would look like this:

```
<FRAMESET rows="50%, 50%" cols="50%, 50%">
      ...content...
</FRAMESET>
```

Within the frame set, the content for each frame must be directed to the proper place. This information is defined in the <FRAME> element, as follows:

```
<FRAME src="doc1.html" name="box1">
```

The SRC attribute determines which HTML file is loaded into that frame. The NAME attribute identifies which framed area the content is placed in. The browser fills frames from left to right and from top to bottom.

TIP

In our example of four equally-sized quadrants for a display, we'll simply number our frames, calling them box1 through box4. In other instances, such as when a navigation frame is used beside a main content window, you might choose "nav" and "main" for your frame names. Choose something that will be meaningful to you.

The full frame-set container now looks like this:

```
<FRAMESET rows="50%, 50%" cols="50%, 50%">
      <FRAME src="doc1.html" name="box1">
      <FRAME src="doc2.html" name="box2">
      <FRAME src="doc3.html" name="box3">
      <FRAME src="doc4.html" name="box4">
</FRAMESET>
```

Frame names have a few conventions you'll need to remember. The name *must* begin with an alphabetical character, in either case (that is, any letter from *a* to *z*, in upper- or lowercase). Each of these names is case-sensitive to the lowercase. In order to load new content into individual frames, a method of targeting a specific frame is needed. This is accomplished using the TARGET attribute in elements that create links (e.g., A, AREA for image maps, etc). The syntax is as follows:

```
<A HREF="NewFrameContent.html" TARGET="FrameName">
```

Additional attributes are available for the <FRAME> element. These include

NORESIZE This attribute stands alone, without a value. When present, it indicates that the browser should not allow the user to change the size of the frame by dragging on one of the frame borders.

SCROLLING As with the main browser window, when a frame's content length or width exceeds the available viewing space, scrollbars will appear on the right side of the frame (for vertical scrolling) or at the bottom (for horizontal scrolling). Scrolling behavior can be set with this attribute, using one of three values:

AUTO This attribute is the default value. The browser will insert scrollbars when it encounters a document that cannot be viewed fully within the available frame space.

YES The browser will supply scrollbars, whether or not the content exceeds the available frame space.

NO No scrollbars will be displayed, regardless of whether or not they are needed. Take care to test any frames that use this attribute, as display on a monitor with a resolution smaller than yours may be considerably different from how you see it.

FRAMEBORDER Frames, by default, are displayed with a visible divider. The default for this attribute is 1 (one), representing "on" or "true." A value of 0 (zero) turns the border off. Be aware that if an adjoining frame has the borders turned on, a border will still appear next to a frame that has set this attribute value to 0.

MARGINWIDTH The margin—the space between the frame border and the content—can be set with this attribute. Values are provided in pixel and must be a whole number of 1 (one) or greater. The default presentation varies from browser to browser.

MARGINHEIGHT The vertical margin is set with this attribute. Values also are specified in whole numbers of pixels, and default presentation is browser-dependent.

Providing Alternate Content

Because there are a considerable number of instances when a browser may not support frames, it becomes important to provide an alternate means for users to access the frame content. The container element <NOFRAMES> takes care of this for you. A common practice when creating <NOFRAMES> content is to provide a short statement and link to a version of the site that does not rely on frames, as seen here:

```
<FRAMESET rows="50%, 50%">
     <FRAME src="frame1.html">
     <FRAME src="frame2.html">
     <NOFRAMES>
     <P>We do maintain a <a href="no-frames.html">non-framed ver-
sion</a> of this site.
     </NOFRAMES>
</FRAMESET>
```

A set of training materials I designed uses this frame markup:

```
<HTML>
   <HEAD>

      <TITLE>Intro to the WWW and HTML - Module 1</TITLE>

   </HEAD>


   <FRAMESET ROWS="*,50" BORDER="0" FRAMEBORDER="0" FRAMESPACING="0" >

      <FRAMESET COLS="130,*" FRAMEBORDER="0" FRAMESPACING="0" >

         <FRAME NAME="nav" SRC="nav-m1.htm" FRAMEBORDER="0" MARGINWIDTH="5"
            NORESIZE SCROLLING="NO" MARGINHEIGHT="25">

         <FRAME NAME="body" SRC="body.htm" FRAMEBORDER="0" MARGINWIDTH="15"
            NORESIZE SCROLLING="auto">
      </FRAMESET>

      <FRAME SRC="message.htm" NAME="message" MARGINHEIGHT=1" NORESIZE>
   </FRAMESET>

<NOFRAMES>
   <BODY BGCOLOR="#FFFFFF" TEXT="#000000">
```

```
    <P>A frames-compatible browser is required to access this site.
      Please see the student handbook at http://www.lanw.com/training/
      wwwintro/student/manual.htm for more information about obtaining
      a browser that supports this training.</P>
</NOFRAMES>

</BODY>

</HTML>
```

The final results of this frameset are shown in Figure 4.10.

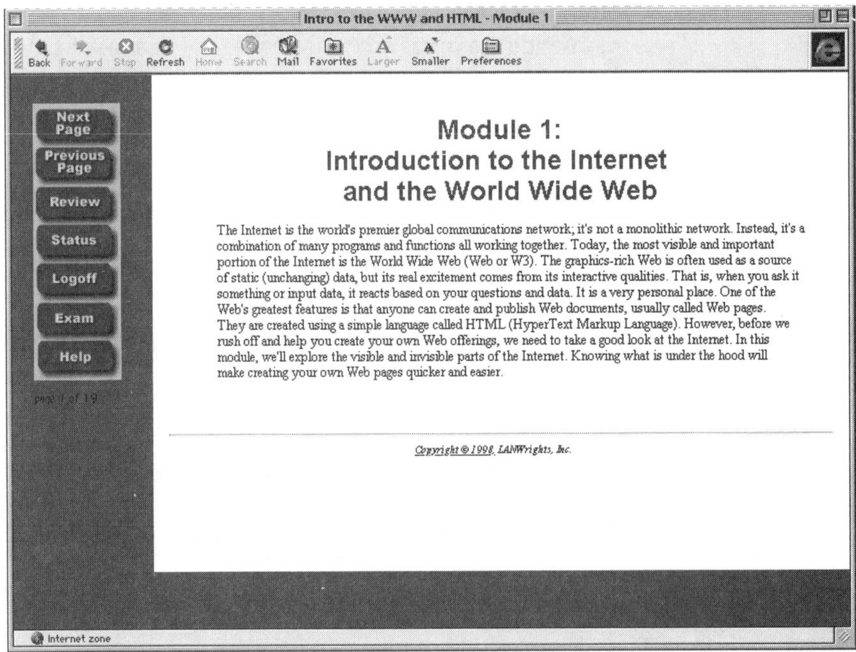

FIGURE 4.10: A frameset as displayed by a Web browser

Try to avoid creating frame-only Web sites. They are often inaccessible to a wide variety of users and can be difficult to navigate. When you do use frames be sure to include a navigation system that works outside of the frameset and that is easy to find and use.

Generating Forms

The ability of site owners and site visitors to effectively communicate with each other has become an important part of the World Wide Web experience. A site might want to solicit feedback about its products or services or provide product registration online, shopping systems, or user-to-user discussion areas. All of these objectives can be accomplished through the use of forms.

Forms have two major sections: the form container itself and the content, comprising a set of Input controls and any necessary accompanying text or images.

The form container has two attributes: `METHOD` and `ACTION`.

> `METHOD` describes how the data collected by the form should be sent to the form processor. For most modern purposes, this value will be "post."
>
> `ACTION` defines the form processor to be used. Two options are generally available: an e-mail processor and a CGI script (or other script-based method, such as Active Server Pages).

The container appears as follows:

```
<FORM method="post" action="http://www.mycompany.com/cgi-bin/form.cgi">
```

The URL defined as the `ACTION` value points to a CGI script that will receive and act upon the data sent by the browser when the user hits the "submit" button. Should you wish to send the form data directly to e-mail (with no preprocessing or formatting), you can do so by substituting a `mailto:` link for the URL:

```
<FORM method="post" action="mailto:you@yourcompany.com">
```

This choice should really be used only for the simplest of forms because the data arrives in raw URL-encoded format straight from the browser, and even then, not all browsers can support this functionality because it requires an integrated (or recognized) e-mail client.

Form Input controls are the elements on a Web page that a visitor to your site uses to interact with the form. Examples of Form Input controls are

- Text boxes
- Radio buttons
- Checkboxes
- Drop-down menus

The bulk of HTML form markup is designed to help you create a variety of Input controls that you can use to solicit information from users.

Form Input Controls

There are ten commonly supported Form Input controls, which are summarized in Table 4.5.

TABLE 4.5: Form Input Controls

Input Control	Result
Text	This control creates a text input box. It can only be a single line wide or tall.
Password	This control creates a specialized text input box. The characters typed are visually obscured to maintain security.
Checkbox	This control creates a box that holds a checkmark or *x* when selected and acts as a toggle between an "on" and "off" state.
Radio	This is a control similar to the checkbox but used in groups. Only one option per group may be selected at any one time.
Hidden	This control allows the author to preload the name and value of controls that don't need to be changed on a user-by-user basis.
Submit	This control creates a standard button used to instruct the browser to apply the action defined in the <FORM> element.
Image	This control provides an image to be used in place of the standard submit button.
Reset	This control creates a button similar to the submit button, which will return all form elements to their original state.
Select	This control provides a list of options from which the user can choose. It can be displayed as a drop-down menu or a list box.
Textarea	This control creates a text input area that can contain more than one line.

Each of these control elements takes similar syntax:

```
<INPUT TYPE="ControlType" NAME="MyControl">
```

The TYPE attribute defines which type of control is being created. Each control must have a NAME attribute, so the data collected can be identified as corresponding with that particular control. You can name a control anything you want, but most designers choose a name that is indicative of the data the control will be collecting. For example, a text box that collects the user's surname can have the name value "LastName." Some controls accept additional attributes, as we'll explore further.

Text Boxes

The text box is one of the most common controls you'll see on the Web, simply because it's so versatile. Any information that can be expressed as a word, number, phrase, etc., can be placed into a text box. As mentioned in Table 3.4, a text box can be displayed visually as a single line only. This means that while the browser cannot render a box wider than the available browser screen width, a text box *can* accept more data than that. Should the visible space be filled, the browser will continue to accept input, and most browsers will simply scroll the text to the left.

Three additional attributes are commonly used for text boxes.

`SIZE` When applied to textboxes, `SIZE` indicates how many character spaces wide the box will be (up to the available width of the browser window). This does not limit the number of characters the box can accept.

`MAXLENGTH` This attribute limits the acceptable size of the user input. You may choose to set this to the same value as your `SIZE` attribute or to set it to some length longer than that.

`VALUE` The `VALUE` attribute acts differently depending on the kind of Input control you are using. When used with text boxes, the value of `VALUE` is displayed in the text box for the user when the page is loaded. Some designers like to have text preentered into text boxes, either as a suggested response or as an additional indicator of what the user should enter. A text box designed to accept the user's name might have a value set to "Enter your name here."

Password Control

A Password control is a special instance of a text box and can accept the same attributes and input. What's different is that when the user types in the space provided, the characters are obscured from view and replaced with a constant character (often the * character). This maintains the security of a password by protecting it from prying eyes.

Checkboxes

Forms can allow the Web author to collect detailed information from visitors. In order to extract meaningful results, questions are often stated with a predefined set of answers to choose from, such as the "Check all that apply" options that you often see on paper-based forms. The Checkbox control provides this functionality on Web pages.

A basic checkbox uses two attributes: TYPE and NAME. In order to label them visually, you can place text immediately to the right of the control, as follows:

```
<INPUT TYPE="checkbox" NAME="label"> label
```

A checkbox acts as a toggle switch: it is either selected (on) or it has been left blank (off). If the sample checkbox here were to be used on a real form and were selected, the NAME=VALUE pair submitted would be `label=on`.

When using a large group of checkboxes, it can be helpful to use the VALUE attribute to provide more obvious results. In order to do this, use the same value with the NAME attribute for each control rather than assigning each checkbox a unique name. Then, add a unique value for the VALUE attribute. For example, the user is asked to choose what kind of sandwich fixings they'd like: mayo, mustard, lettuce, tomato, or pickles. The HTML would appear as:

```
<INPUT TYPE="checkbox" NAME="fixings" VALUE="mayo"> mayo
<INPUT TYPE="checkbox" NAME="fixings" VALUE="mustard"> mustard
<INPUT TYPE="checkbox" NAME="fixings" VALUE="lettuce"> lettuce
<INPUT TYPE="checkbox" NAME="fixings" VALUE="tomato"> tomato
<INPUT TYPE="checkbox" NAME="fixings" VALUE="pickles"> pickles
```

If the user then chooses mayo and lettuce, the name value pairs sent would be `fixings=mayo` and `fixings=lettuce`, rather than five pairs of `mayo=on`, `mustard=`, `lettuce=on`, `tomato=`, and `pickles=`. This occurs because when a VALUE attribute is present, the checkbox returns a `name=value` pair only when the control is in the "on" state. Figure 4.11 shows a Web browser's interpretation of the checkbox markup.

FIGURE 4.11: A Web browser's rendering of checkbox markup

Radio Buttons

What about situations in which you want a user to be able to select only a single option? There isn't an attribute that disables the selection of more than one checkbox. There is, however, a control type just for this situation: the radio button. Visually, the radio button is most often rendered as an empty circle. When marked, the circle contains a black dot.

The VALUE attribute is required rather than optional for the Radio control type. Additionally, the NAME attribute *must* be the same for each item in the radio-button group; that's how the browser knows to treat them as a group where only one choice may be selected.

For example, you want to ask the user to select their favorite color from among red, blue, and green. A radio-button set would appear as

```
<INPUT TYPE="radio" NAME="color" VALUE="red"> red
<INPUT TYPE="radio" NAME="color" VALUE="blue"> blue
<INPUT TYPE="radio" NAME="color" VALUE="green"> green
```

The value that's reported with the name=value pair for this control group will be assumed based on which option is selected. If the user chooses blue, the browser reports color=blue.

Skill 4

Suggesting a Selection

You can guide your visitors into selecting certain choices by displaying the form with your preferred responses already selected. In text boxes, suggestions are inserted using the VALUE attribute. Checkboxes and radio buttons use the VALUE attribute for another purpose. For these situations, the CHECKED attribute does the job.

CHECKED stands on its own; it takes no value. When present, it tells the browser to mark the item as selected. On some sites, you may have run across a situation in which a checkbox or radio button is provided, asking you whether you wish to receive product updates or other company news via e-mail. The form will often have this option preselected, requiring the user to then opt out of the messages rather than opt in.

Select Lists

The Select control provides another way for users to choose from more than one option. These take one of two forms:

Dropdown menu A list of choices are revealed by "dropping down" when the user clicks on the arrow provided.

List box A list that is presented in a bordered box with at least the first few choices in view. A scrollbar can be provided to view the rest of the list if it is especially long.

List construction begins with the SELECT element, which acts as a container for the list. Each individual item in the list is then entered using the OPTION tags, as follows:

```
<SELECT NAME="music">
     <OPTION VALUE="classical"> classical
     <OPTION VALUE="jazz"> jazz
     <OPTION VALUE="rock"> rock
     <OPTION VALUE="blues"> blues
</SELECT>
```

This example will result in a drop-down menu, as shown below.

To turn the drop-down menu into a list box, you need to add the SIZE attribute to the SELECT tag. SIZE determines how many rows will be displayed at a given time. The default is 1, resulting in a drop-down menu as seen in the previous graphic (if an attribute isn't declared at all, the default value is assumed). A size of 2 or greater will create the list-box display. The list box below has been set to a SIZE value of 4.

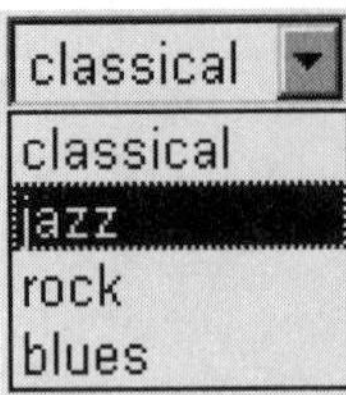

The SIZE value doesn't have to be equal to the number of option tags in your list. A small list is more convenient for the user. However, the choice remains yours. A scrollbar appears if the SIZE value is less than the total number of options, as seen below.

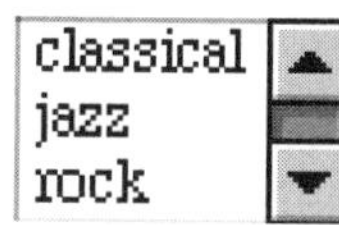

Drop-down menus and list boxes can be set to accept more than one selection using the MULTIPLE attribute. Like the CHECKED attribute, its value is assumed by its presence. The user can choose a second (or third or more) option by holding down the Control key (the Command key for Mac users) before clicking the additional choices. Each of the selected options is then highlighted, as shown below.

Larger Text Areas

There are times when significant blocks of text need to be collected from the user. Online problem reports, feedback forms, suggestion boxes, and other applications that require extended commentary are good candidates for the Textarea control.

The syntax used is a bit unusual. It's a container tag and has attributes for ROWS and COLS (columns).

```
<TEXTAREA NAME="comments" ROWS="5" COLS="80"></TEXTAREA>
```

The control has a name, like all other Input controls. The ROWS and COLS attributes define its size in two dimensions. ROWS indicates how many lines high the space should be, and COLS defines how many columns of characters wide it should be. Our width of 80 indicates the text area can hold 80 characters across, five lines deep. As with a text box, the input is not restricted to what can fit in the Textarea container.

Supplying Hidden Information

In almost any information exchange between users and site owners, there is some information that you'll need to collect every time but which doesn't change based on user selection. For example, a Canadian company may offer information in both English and French. The CGI script that processes their forms always returns data in English, regardless of the original format. The site owner can track how many responses originated from the English or French version by including a hidden control on each version of the form, as follows:

```
<INPUT TYPE="hidden" NAME="language" VALUE="english">
```

This control is invisible to the user (unless they happen to look at your page source) but returns the `name=value` pair `language=english` when the form is submitted. For the French version, simply change the value to French and you can easily track which users came from which form version.

The Submit Button

A method for sending a form needs to be provided so after the user completes all the form fields, the form can get back to you. The Submit control type and its resulting button are objects that almost any Web surfer will recognize. Its function is intuitive: it's a button that users are used to "pushing," and the label typically says "Submit," giving users an instruction for its use. The control is written as follows:

```
<INPUT TYPE="submit" VALUE="Submit">
```

The control can function with no more than the TYPE attribute. Most browsers will insert the label "Submit" by default if the author has not set it. Not all browsers do this, however (Netscape Navigator 4 defaults to "Submit query"), so it's considered good practice to always define the value for this control.

Using an Image to Replace Submit

Some authors have been dissatisfied with the rather stark, industrial look that comes with the default Submit buttons. In order to counter this, the Image control type allows authors a choice of replacing that ordinary gray button with a custom image.

```
<INPUT TYPE="image" SRC="mybutton.gif" HEIGHT="20" WIDTH="50" ALT=
"submit button">
```

This control includes attributes you're familiar with from image handling—namely the height and width in pixels of the image—and a text description of the image in the ALT attribute.

Changing Your Mind

There may be times when a user wants to clear a form and start over. A second Button control is provided for this task and is usually universally labeled as the Reset button. When activated, this control resets all form fields to their original values, whether unchecked (empty), checked, or with preselected text in place. The syntax is the same as that for the Submit button:

```
<INPUT TYPE="reset" VALUE="reset">
```

Additional Control Types

The HTML 4.0 specification provides for several additional controls that could prove to be very handy. Unfortunately, as of this writing the major browsers don't yet support them. In part, this is due to HTML 4.0 maturing after the release of the 4.0 generation browsers. We expect that more control types will be supported in future versions. These controls are described in Table 3.5.

TABLE 4.6: Additional Input Controls

Control	Function
BUTTON	This control provides a button similar to the Submit button, with no default behavior. Actions are specified through scripting.
FILE	This control allows the user to select and then manipulate a file on their local computer (intended for file uploads or similar transactions).
OBJECT	The control submits generic objects along with other FORM elements. It is similar to the hidden Input control.

Scripts

Functionality that isn't available in HTML or in XML can be added to documents using various scripting languages, such as JavaScript, VBScript, and others. In order to include these features, HTML needs an element that can enclose the script to isolate it from the rest of the document for proper processing. The <SCRIPT> element takes care of this for us.

NOTE SCRIPT elements can appear in either the HEAD or BODY elements (or both) of a document, depending on the purpose of the script.

The attributes used are familiar by now and include

- SRC links to a script stored in an external file. The value here would be the URL for that file.
- TYPE specifies the language being used and overrides any default scripting language set by the user agent. The language is named in content-type format, for example "text/javascript" for JavaScript. The author must set this attribute value; there is no default in the HTML specification.
- DEFER is similar to CHECKED in FORM elements; it is a Boolean attribute that is "turned on" by its mere presence. When included, it tells the user agent that the script is not going to dynamically generate document content, so the browser can continue to render the HTML without having to reserve space for the script output and without having to first stop and process the script.

Scripts are most often implemented to handle intrinsic events, such as the user moving the mouse pointer over an object or clicking the mouse. Authors should be aware that the W3C is conducting work on what's known as the Document Object Model, which can impact how intrinsic events are dealt with within HTML, which impacts the use of the SCRIPT element. As of this writing, it is not possible to determine the direction this research will lead the W3C to take on the subject.

Learning More about HTML

And there you have your crash course into HTML. Although I've tried to cover all the basics of HTML, I've only really scratched the surface. There are whole books devoted to HTML (as a trip to your local bookstore will quickly show), and the Web itself is full of content-rich sites devoted entirely to the creation of HTML. To learn more about HTML online, point your Web browser at any one of these great resources:

- The Web Design Group
  `http://www.htmlhelp.com`
- Webmonkey
  `http://www.webmonkey.com`
- Builder.com
  `http://www.builder.com/`

- The HTML Writers Guild Web Site
  `http://www.hwg.org`
- The Bare Bones Guide to HTML
  `http://www.werbach.com/barebones/`

To peruse the current HTML print offerings visit Amazon.com at `http://www.amazon.com/` and search for "HTML" or "Web Design."

From HTML to XML

If you didn't know HTML before, you're certainly on your way to being up to speed now. Beginning with Skill 5, "Investigating XML," we leave the topic of HTML behind and attack the topic of XML with full force. However, because HTML is still the prominent markup language of the Web—and promises to be for a while—we'll often use it for reference or comparison with XML. Skill 5 answers your most basic XML questions and introduces you to XML's basic constructs. Come along, it's time to immerse ourselves in the wonderful world of XML.

Are You up to Speed?

Now you can...

- ☑ **Describe your document in terms of blocks and elements**
- ☑ **Create an HTML page that includes tables, frames, and forms**
- ☑ **Specify how text in your HTML document should be presented**

SKILL 5

Investigating XML

- Looking at the building blocks of XML
- Examining a real-world DTD
- Understanding the roles of elements, attributes, and entities
- Working with the XML specification
- Preparing to create XML DTDs and documents

Now that you understand the general mechanisms of a markup language and have taken a look at the markup language used by thousands of Web developers every day, you're ready to learn more about the principal subject of the book—XML. This skill introduces XML's main components and discusses the important role the XML specification plays in the overall scheme of XML. When you've finished this skill, you'll have a solid understanding of the basic terms and concepts used in XML and will be ready to move on to the nitty-gritty of creating XML documents.

Introducing XML's Main Components

Regardless of the goal of a DTD (document-type definition) and the methods the DTD uses to achieve that goal, all XML DTDs and documents employ certain structures and components. The following sections are intended as a general introduction to the constructs used in XML DTDs and documents. The idea is to become familiar with the terminology and get a general idea of what each construct is used for and how they all work together. Don't panic if it doesn't all make sense immediately. The material in Skills 8 through 12 is designed to explore these constructs in detail. This skill is just an introduction to some ideas and components you'll use every time you work with any aspect of XML.

By way of example, each of the following sections will take a brief look at the Open Software Description (OSD) vocabulary. This XML vocabulary was designed to describe a software package for installation on a client computer across a network. OSD enables a single software package to be described once and to be installed on as many client computers hooked up to that network as necessary. OSD is a Web-based technology, so the network a software package can be installed on could include the Internet as well as a company intranet.

DTDs

A DTD describes the components and guidelines included in any XML vocabulary. Remember that an XML vocabulary is an XML markup language created according to the rules of the XML specification. The DTD defines the elements that make up the vocabulary, attributes those elements can take, any entities (such as graphics or non-ASCII characters) that may be included in documents written for the DTD, and the rules for how all these components may interact with each other. The DTD is the rule book for any document written for the XML vocabulary. Valid documents must strictly adhere to the structures and rules as defined by the DTD, and no XML document, even well-formed documents, is actually without a DTD, even if it is a small one.

The current standard for HTML (HTML 4.0) is written in the form of a DTD because HTML is a markup language, and markup languages are described by DTDs. Even though you may never have seen the DTD, it's there. Because DTDs are the central element in any XML vocabulary, the majority of XML constructs are used in the creation of DTDs. By way of example, the Open Software Description (OSD) specification looks like this:

```
<!ELEMENT ABSTRACT (#PCDATA)>

<!ELEMENT CODEBASE EMPTY>
<!ATTLIST CODEBASE FILENAME CDATA #IMPLIED>
<!ATTLIST CODEBASE HREF CDATA #REQUIRED>
<!ATTLIST CODEBASE SIZE CDATA #IMPLIED>

<!ELEMENT DEPENDENCY (CODEBASE|SOFTPKG)* >
<!ATTLIST DEPENDENCY ACTION (Assert|Install) "Assert">

<!ELEMENT DISKSIZE EMPTY>
<!ATTLIST DISKSIZE VALUE CDATA #REQUIRED>

<!ELEMENT IMPLEMENTATION (CODEBASE | DEPENDENCY | DISKSIZE | IMPLTYPE |
LANGUAGE | OS | PROCESSOR | VM)*>

<!ELEMENT IMPLTYPE EMPTY>
<!ATTLIST IMPLTYPE VALUE CDATA #REQUIRED>

<!ELEMENT LANGUAGE EMPTY>
<!ATTLIST LANGUAGE VALUE CDATA #REQUIRED>

<!ELEMENT LICENSE EMPTY>
<!ATTLIST LICENSE HREF CDATA #REQUIRED>

<!ELEMENT MEMSIZE EMPTY>
<!ATTLIST MEMSIZE VALUE CDATA #REQUIRED>

<!ELEMENT OS (OSVERSION)*>
<!ATTLIST OS VALUE CDATA #REQUIRED>

<!ELEMENT OSVERSION EMPTY>
<!ATTLIST OSVERSION VALUE CDATA #REQUIRED>

<!ELEMENT PROCESSOR EMPTY>
<!ATTLIST PROCESSOR VALUE CDATA #REQUIRED>
```

```
<!ELEMENT SOFTPKG (ABSTRACT | IMPLEMENTATION | DEPENDENCY | LICENSE |
TITLE)*>

<!ATTLIST SOFTPKG NAME CDATA #REQUIRED>
<!ATTLIST SOFTPKG VERSION CDATA #IMPLIED>

<!ELEMENT TITLE (#PCDATA) >

<!ELEMENT VM EMPTY>
<!ATTLIST VM VALUE CDATA #REQUIRED>
```

NOTE Don't worry, the OSD DTD isn't supposed to make sense just yet. By the time you've finished this book, you'll be reading and writing DTDs just like this one. If you're curious about OSD, you'll learn all you ever wanted to know and more about it in Skill 22, "Installing Software with OSD."

Elements

XML documents are divided into containers called *elements*. In HTML <P>…<P>, <BR>, <TABLE>…</TABLE>, and other tags are all elements that represent logical structures within an HTML document. Elements are the key structures in an XML document, and DTDs specify which elements may be used in documents written for that DTD. Every bit of content within an XML document must be described using an element from the document's DTD. Other XML constructs, such as attributes and content declarations, provide additional information about elements and how they may be used together. To get truly technical about terminology, elements are defined in DTDs, and tags are used to represent those elements in documents.

The elements used in the OSD specification include

ABSTRACT	CODEBASE	DEPENDENCY
DISKSIZE	IMPLEMENTATION	IMPLTYPE
LANGUAGE	LICENSE	OS
OSVERSION	PROCESSOR	SOFTPKG
TITLE	VM	

These elements are used to describe the software package that is going to be installed on a client machine across a network. They include descriptors for the different versions of a package, the different operating systems a package may be installed on, the specific kind of processor a computer must have to run the software package, and a descriptive title for the software-package installation.

Attributes

Attributes are element modifiers. They provide additional and more specific information about an element and its content. In the world of HTML, attributes are used most often to provide the browser with a suggestion for formatting the final display of the element's content by a Web browser. For example, the `BODY` element includes the following attributes for specifying formatting guidelines for the visible content of an HTML file:

`BGCOLOR` Specifies a background color for the page

`BACKGROUND` Identifies an image to be included as a tiled background for the document

`TEXT` Specifies the color for rendering the document's text

`LINK` Defines a color for rendering the document's links

`ALINK` Defines a color for rendering the document's active links

`VLINK` Defines a color for rendering the document's visited links

While the majority of HTML attributes are formatting-oriented, the same doesn't necessarily have to be true for XML attributes. For example, the OSD element `SOFTPKG` includes the following attributes:

- `NAME`
- `VERSION`

Remember that OSD is used to describe software packages to be installed across a network. The `SOFTPKG` element uses the `NAME` and `VERSION` attributes to provide title and version information for the software package described by the OSD document. The attributes are used to provide further information about the package itself and are attached to the general element called `SOFTPKG`.

Because the true goal of XML is to separate markup from display, you will rarely see formatting attributes in XML DTDs. Style sheets (discussed briefly in this skill and in depth in Skills 15 and 16, "Adding Style with CSS" and "Converting XML to HTML with XSL") are responsible for assigning formatting information to an XML document.

Entities

In general, an entity is a unit of data. Entities can comprise binary data and take the form of graphics and sound files or even Java applets. Entities can just as easily comprise textual data and represent chunks of text to be included in an XML file. HTML developers will be familiar with a specific type of entity, the character entities used to represent non-ASCII or reserved characters in HTML documents. The entity < represents the less-than sign (<) while the À entity represents a capital letter *A* with an accent grave (*À*).

Regardless of the type, every entity included in an XML document must be predefined in the document's DTD; even well-formed documents have a DTD because they invariably have entities. You're probably wondering how a general DTD can anticipate all the entities—especially nontext entities such as graphics and audio files—any document developer might need. They don't have to because every XML document has both an external DTD and an internal DTD. The external DTD holds all of the general declarations—such as elements and attributes—that will apply to all the documents referencing the DTD. The internal DTD holds declarations that are specific to the document, such as entity declarations for graphics that will only be used within the individual document. Skill 6, "Understanding the Basics of XML DTDs and Documents," will make it all clear.

Entities are one of the most powerful features of XML. The inclusion of non-ASCII characters and graphics files are just the tip of the entity iceberg. With entities, you can combine several XML files into one and even create groups of frequently used elements and attributes for quick reference while building DTDs. Skill 12, "Employing Entities in DTDs and Documents," explores the creation and power of entities in depth.

Content Models

A common feature of any HTML file is nested markup. Nested markup means that one element is contained within the other element. An example from HTML might look like this:

```
<P>This is a paragraph. <B>This is bold text within in the
paragraph</B></P>
```

The PARAGRAPH tag (<P>...</P>) contains the BOLD tag (<B>...</B>), so the BOLD tag is said to be nested within the PARAGRAPH tag.

For an unordered list to function correctly, you have to label it as an unordered list by first using the <UL> tag and then marking list items inside the list with <LI> tags. The markup looks like this:

```
<UL>
     <LI>List item 1
     <LI>List item 2
     <LI>List item 3
</UL>
```

In fact, the HTML DTD states that you can't use <LI> tags without first beginning an unordered (<UL>) or ordered (<OL>) list. The DTD also says that you have to include list items as the first level of markup underneath ordered or unordered-list tags. If you follow <UL> or <OL> with any other tag besides <LI>, you've violated the rules of the DTD.

Rules that describe how tags must be nested within each other are called *content models*. They prescribe which tags must be nested within which other tags and in what order, and they often also prescribe how many instances of each nested tag are allowed. The content models for any given XML vocabulary are defined as part of the vocabulary's DTD, specifically as part of the various element declarations in the DTD. If a tag doesn't have any content listed for it, then no other tags can be nested within it. Careful manipulation of content models can help DTD developers ensure that documents contain required information.

For example, in the OSD specification, no elements explicitly require that other elements be contained within them. Several element definitions do allow other elements to be nested within them as necessary. The SOFTPKG element can contain zero or more instances of the ABSTRACT, IMPLEMENTATION, DEPENDENCY, LICENSE, and TITLE tags. However, the OS tag may contain the only OSVERSION tag, and several of the other tags can't contain any other tags at all.

Because XML vocabularies are meant to accurately describe content, it only makes sense that the nesting of tags be closely controlled to prevent inaccurate descriptions. HTML actually has similar rules of content, but they are for the most part ignored by developers and browsers alike. XML parsers won't tolerate such oversight. Skill 11, "Defining Content Models for Elements," discusses the art of creating content models and shows how they can be used to direct document designers in the right direction.

Links

Hyperlinks are one of the basic building blocks of the Web; without hyperlinks the Web wouldn't really be the Web. The hyperlinks with which Web page designers are so familiar are severely limited in scope. They link only one way and are difficult to maintain and catalog. Most hyperlinks are static creatures that allow users to move from one static page to the other.

XML revolutionizes linking by including mechanisms for multidirectional hyperlinks, links between documents that don't have to be stored in either of the documents that make up the link (out-of-line linking), and other advanced linking concepts. For example, Figure 5.1 shows how, with XLink's out-of-line linking capabilities, a linking document can contain descriptions of links among other documents without actually linking to any of those documents. Linking in XML is so extensive that it is being developed as a specification called XLink, which is independent of XML. Any element in an XML document can become one of many types of hyperlinks. Skill 13, "Linking Up with XLink," looks at XLink in detail.

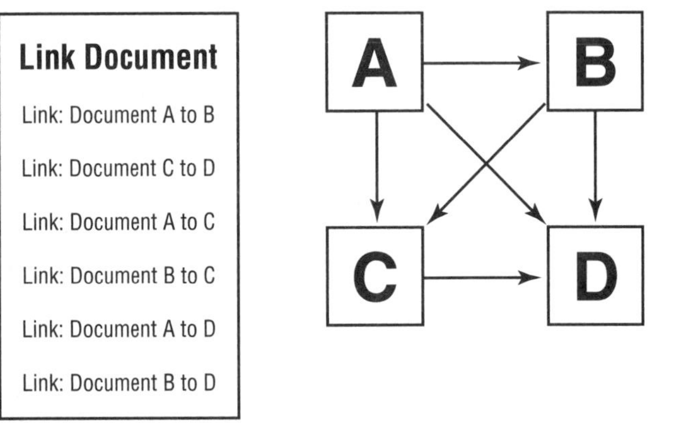

FIGURE 5.1: The principle behind XLink's out-of-line links

Styles

As I've alluded to more than once, XML strives to fully separate markup from display. Attributes designed to describe formatting will not be part of XML DTDs and documents. Instead, XML is going to rely on an advanced style-sheet mechanism, currently called the Extensible Style Language (XSL), to provide browsers with formatting and display information. XML also supports Cascading Style Sheets (CSS), the HTML style-sheet mechanism.

XSL is derived from the Document Style Semantics and Specification Language (DSSSL), the style-sheet mechanism used with SGML. XSL goes beyond the simple task of assigning styles to markup to the more complex chore of transforming documents from one DTD to another. XSL will probably be the primary tool that developers use to convert XML documents into HTML documents during the time of transition from HTML- to XML-based Web pages.

Like XLink, XSL is being developed as a separate specification from XML. The primary weakness in this method of specification development is the XLink and XSL specifications are almost a year behind XML in development. While XML is already a specification, XLink and XSL won't be recommendations until some time in 1999. Developers will have to watch the evolution of the XLink and XSL specifications closely, adapting their documents as the working drafts change and keeping their exercises in linking and style sheets purely experimental. Welcome to the bleeding edge of technology. It's comforting to know that the style sheets and links you create during the development of the specifications should work even after the final specification has been released. It's still a good idea to update your documents to meet the official standard whenever possible.

Documents

After what probably seems like an eternity, we're down to the nitty-gritty of XML, the documents themselves. As you've probably surmised by now, XML documents comprise text-based content described by the markup prescribed by a DTD. Documents contain an internal DTD for declaring entities and performing other housekeeping duties, the content to be described by the markup, and of course, the markup itself. Most documents also contain a collection of both binary and text entities. An example of an OSD document is

```
<CHANNEL HREF="http://www.acme.com/intropage.htm">
    <SELF="http://www.acme.com/software.cdf" />
    <TITLE>A Software Distribution Channel</TITLE>

    <SOFTPKG
            HREF="http://www.acme.com/aboutsoftware.htm"
            NAME="{D27CDB6E-AE6D-11CF-96B8-444553540000}"
            VERSION="1,0,0,0">

        <IMPLEMENTATION>
            <OS VALUE="WinNT"><OSVERSION VALUE="4,0,0,0"/></OS>
            <OS VALUE="Win95"/>
            <PROCESSOR VALUE="x86" />
            <CODEBASE HREF="http://www.acme.com/test.cab" />
        </IMPLEMENTATION>
    </SOFTPKG>
</CHANNEL>
```

Unlike HTML documents that follow a pretty predictable pattern, the only things two XML documents may have in common are the less-than and greater-than signs used to delineate markup (assuming, of course, they aren't using the same DTD or XML implementation). Documents are generally designed according to a DTD and must always be well formed, if not valid. Ultimately, XML and its unlimited vocabularies are all about describing content in documents. Although not everyone who works with XML will create DTDs, they will all create documents.

The two most important things to remember about any XML document are

- They must always follow the basic rules of markup. In other words, make sure all of your documents are well formed. An XML parser can't completely process a document until it is 100 percent correct.
- Documents use markup to describe content, not formatting. When you're creating your XML documents, regardless of the DTD, push any thought of how the document will be rendered by a browser into the farthest corner of your mind, and leave it there. Keeping markup and display firmly separated leads to happy, well-designed documents.

Virtually every skill in the book refers to XML documents in one way or another, but Skill 6, "Understanding the Basics of XML DTDs and Documents," Skill 7, "Forming Well-Formed and Valid Documents," and Skill 19, "Creating Documents for XML Applications," focus on the document-centric topics of DTDs and documents, valid and well-formed documents, and creating documents for individual XML vocabularies.

A Look at the Role of the XML Specification

If XML is the metalanguage of XML vocabularies, the XML specification is the metalanguage for XML. XML plays by the rules as defined by the W3C in the XML specification, an official recommendation of the W3C. Although there are many HTML specifications at work in the Web world, there is only one XML specification, and the W3C is working hard to keep it that way.

TIP XML is currently at version 1.0 and is defined by the recommendation available on the Web at `http://www.w3.org/TR/1998/REC-xml-19980210`.

The recommendation document includes an overview of XML as well as a detailed description of its constructs and structures. The recommendation is informative, if you read geek-speak; if not, you might want to wait until after you're more familiar with XML and its terminology before reading your way through it. If you try it any earlier, you're apt to run away screaming.

The official specification as listed at the W3C will always be your best source for accurate and timely information about XML. Although you will work with many other XML resources, the recommendation is the official horse's mouth.

TIP Visit the W3C's XML site at `http://www.w3.org/XML/` regularly to keep up with the latest XML developments.

When a new specification is released, probably in mid-1999 or so, you'll want to read through it to learn about all of the latest changes and newest additions. Get used to reading the spec, because as long as you're working with XML, you'll be working with it.

TIP By way of introduction to the XML 1.0 specification, Tim Bray has created an annotated version of the specification maintained by XML.com at `http://www.xml.com/xml/pub/axml/axmlintro.html`. If you're anxious to read the specification right now, start there.

Continuing the Investigation

Even though this skill is entitled "Investigating XML," your investigation of this wondrous language is actually just beginning. In the next skill, we take our first close look at DTDs and the role they play in documents. You'll learn about how DTDs and documents are inextricably tied together. For those of you interested in creating your own DTDs, there are sections on planning DTDs and characteristics of good DTD design. Even if you're not planning on diving into DTD design any time soon, the skill includes important information on XML document design and ends with the important points about DTDs and documents summed up in two FAQs.

Are You up to Speed?

Now you can...

- ☑ Identify an XML DTD
- ☑ Describe the main components of XML
- ☑ Understand basic XML terminology
- ☑ Discuss the importance of the XML specification

SKILL 6

Understanding the Basics of XML DTDs and Documents

- The basic structures of a DTD
- The basic structures of a document
- How DTDs and documents work together
- The roles of the internal and external DTD subsets

Now that I've answered some basic XML questions and given you a preview of the components you'll be using throughout your XML journey, it's time to examine the key XML structures: *document-type definitions* (DTDs) and documents. DTDs and documents are really what XML is all about. You know a little about both already, but an understanding of how each works alone and how they work together is crucial to your success with XML. In this skill, I'll look at the roles DTDs and documents play in an overall XML solution as well as examine their basic structures. You'll learn about the difference between the internal and external subsets of DTDs and what you should include in which subset. The skill ends with an XML DTD and document FAQ. DTDs and documents will be part of all your XML efforts, so it's best if you're well acquainted with them from the very start.

How DTDs and Documents Work Together

DTDs define the markup you use to describe the contents of a document, and the majority of XML documents are designed with a particular DTD in mind. XML allows developers to create their own customized DTDs to accurately describe a specific set or kind of information. In reality, the DTD is part of the document itself, even when the DTD is stored in another file. So DTDs and documents aren't two separate entities but are a single unit separated into two distinct sections. An XML document is divided this way because the two sections contain two different types of information, and each has its own distinct role to play. Even though I (and many others) often refer to the DTD as separate from the document, the two really do work together in perfect harmony. The following sections examine the different and equally important roles played by DTDs and documents.

By way of example, in the rest of the skill I'll describe a fictitious DTD called `library.dtd` and the document that goes with it (`books.xml`), which is used to catalog all the books in my personal library. Along the way, you'll probably think of a lot of things you'd add to the DTD or ways that you would make it different, but remember that this is just an example—and consequently not fully developed—to get us through the skill. If you want to play around, be my guest and add to it. You'll learn lots along the way, I promise.

The Role of the DTD

As I have already mentioned, the DTD establishes the rules by which its associated documents must play. The DTD includes specifics about the markup that can be used within a document. The specifics take the form of

- Element declarations
- Attribute list declarations
- Content models
- Entity declarations

The "Basic DTD Structures" section describes each of these specifics in detail and introduces you to the syntax used to create them.

My `library.dtd` lists all the elements I have available to describe my books and attributes to go with them. `library.dtd` also has specifics about which tags I can nest within which other tags, and it also declares which text and binary entities I can use in my descriptions.

My DTD's most important role is as a guide to help me describe my growing collection of books. The DTD helps me keep my descriptions standard and consistent, making it easier for me to sort through my books. Rules are not always a bad thing, as you'll soon see. As I describe the different structures found in DTDs, I'll show you how they're employed in `library.dtd`. By the end of the skill you will have seen an entire DTD built.

The Role of the Document

Documents use the markup and guidelines specified in the DTD to describe content. Content is described in a document using these basic document structures:

- Prolog
- Document element
- Elements
- Attributes
- Content
- Comments
- Processing instructions

Notice that the names of these structures resemble the names of many of the structures in a DTD. That should come as no surprise because the DTD uses declarations to define the structures that can be used in documents to describe content. I will discuss each of these basic document structures in detail shortly.

My `books.xml` document written according to the `library.dtd`, holds the actual information about the books in my library, described with the markup designated in the DTD. The document's most important role is to hold the content and its markup descriptions in a format that can be read by any XML processor. A document should be well organized and accurate. It should use markup consistently and correctly to describe its contents. Creating a document that fulfills all these "shoulds" is up to the developer, of course, but I'm working under the assumption that all developers want to create good XML documents. As I develop `library.dtd` right before your eyes, I'll design a small document to go along with it.

The DTD and Document FAQ

What is the difference between a DTD and a document?

A DTD defines the elements, attributes, content models, and entities that make up an XML vocabulary and can be used to develop a document for that vocabulary. The document uses the structures defined in the DTD to describe content for processing by an XML processor. DTDs and documents are not necessarily separate entities but work together to describe information in an accurate and useable way.

What are the basic structures of DTD?

A DTD includes element declarations to define the elements that make up a vocabulary and attribute-list declarations that specify attributes to be used with the elements. Content models describe which kind of content—regular text-based data or other elements—can be contained within an element, and entity declarations describe those text and binary entities that can be included within documents built for the DTD.

continued ➧

What are the basic structures of a document?

Every XML document begins with an XML declaration that labels the document as an XML document and a declaration that identifies the DTD for which the document was developed. The document uses elements in the form of tags to describe content and uses attributes to provide more specific information about the tags. Documents may also include references to text or binary entities and processing instructions (PIs) that provide specific information to the document processor about how to deal with the document.

What is the difference between an external DTD subset and an internal DTD subset?

A DTD may have its elements stored in a subset external to a document as well as in an internal subset included within the document itself. The two subsets form the whole DTD for the document. Generally, the external subset contains the majority of element and attribute-list declarations as well as entity declarations any document developed for the DTD might need. The internal subset contains entity declarations specific to the document. It also contains any additional element and attribute declarations that affect only the individual document. The internal subset will not affect other documents that may also reference the external subset of the DTD.

Basic DTD Structures

All of the structures in a DTD are designed to describe in exquisite detail the markup that can be used by its documents. Every aspect of the markup should be specified in the DTD. The attributes that can be used by elements, what kinds of values the attributes themselves take, which attributes are required, and what the default values are for each attribute are as important as the elements themselves. As I describe the DTD structures in the next few sections, I'll concentrate on the roles they each play rather than on the how-to's of creating them. Don't worry if the illustrative code samples are a bit confusing; they are there to give you an idea of the different types of syntax used in developing DTDs and documents. Each major structure has its own skill in Part II, in which I'll get into the real guts of each structure.

Element Declarations

As the name implies, an element declaration specifies a single markup element. Every tag you use in a document is defined by an element declaration in a DTD. The `library.dtd` contains these elements:

`BOOK` identifies a book record

`TITLE` describes the book's title

`AUTHOR` identifies the book's author

`PUBLISHER` identifies the book's publisher

`COVER` describes the book as hardback or paperback

`CATEGORY` identifies the book's type; i.e., general fiction, fantasy, sci-fi, etc.

`ISBN` identifies the book's ISBN number

`RATING` rates the book on a scale of one to five

`COMMENTS` provides a section for comments about the book

The element declarations for these elements, in proper DTD syntax, look like this:

```
<!ELEMENT book>
<!ELEMENT title>
<!ELEMENT author>
<!ELEMENT publisher>
<!ELEMENT cover EMPTY>
<!ELEMENT category EMPTY>
<!ELEMENT isbn>
<!ELEMENT rating EMPTY>
<!ELEMENT comments>
```

You'll notice that the declarations for the `COVER`, `CATEGORY`, and `RATING` elements have the word `EMPTY` added to their declaration. This means that they are empty, or singleton, tags (like `IMAGE` or `LINE-BREAK` tags in HTML) and won't contain any text. After you see the attributes for these tags, you'll understand why.

Many elements have attributes that provide additional or more specific information about the content that they describe. We'll visit attributes next, but we will revisit elements before we're done.

Attribute-List Declarations

Just as element declarations declare elements, attribute-list declarations declare sets of attributes. Each attribute-list declaration is created to define a set of attributes for a specific element; and the attributes in the list can be used only for that element. Of the elements in my `library.dtd`, these three can take the attributes listed after them:

COVER: TYPE. The values for TYPE are hardback and paperback.

CATEGORY: CLASS. The values for CLASS are fiction, fantasy, scifi, mystery, horror, nonfiction, historical, and biography.

RATING: NUMBER. The values for NUMBER are 1, 2, 3, 4, and 5.

You'll note that the DTD doesn't extend to my technical library, and nonfiction is limited to a generic nonfiction category and to the historical and biography types. I'm sure you could add many more types to this list in the fiction category alone, and the addition of technical books to the fray would make the list grow even longer. But since I'm just creating an example, these few will do.

Not every element has attributes because not every element needs them. You'll notice that in this particular DTD I assigned attributes only to the three elements that were empty. Because the tags built by empty element descriptions can't contain text or other elements, I had to find a way to include more specific information within the tag itself. The attributes with specific values provide me with a way to do so.

The attribute-list declarations in `library.dtd` look like this:

```
<!ATTLIST COVER
TYPE (HARDBACK | PAPERBACK) "PAPERBACK" #REQUIRED>

<!ATTLIST CATEGORY
CLASS (FICTION | FANTASY | SCIFI | MYSTERY | HORROR | NONFICTION |
HISTORICAL | BIOGRAPHY) "FICTION" #REQUIRED>

<!ATTLIST RATING
NUMBER (1 | 2 | 3 | 4 | 5) "3" #REQUIRED>
```

Each of these attribute-list declarations includes the name of the element the list is for immediately after !ATTLIST. The attribute is then defined, and the possible values it can take is included in parenthesis [( )] and divided by vertical lines (|). The default value for the attribute follows the list of options and is enclosed in quotation marks. Finally, the #REQUIRED label indicates the attribute is required each time the element is used in a document. Attributes may take many forms and values other than those I've used here, and they'll all be covered in Skill 10, "Assigning Attributes to Elements."

Now that I've set up the DTD's basic elements and attributes, I need to put some finishing touches on the document, starting with specifying which tags must or can be nested inside which other tags.

Content Models

A content model is part of an element declaration and describes what kind of content can be nested within the element. There are three different types of content in the XML world:

- Data content, which contains regular text-based characters. Data content is the most basic kind of content you'll find within any given element. Plain data content is described in a content model as `(#PCDATA)`.
- Element content, which contains other markup elements. An element content model can define not only which elements can be nested within any given element but also specify which elements must appear and in what order. If an element's content model contains just element content, no regular text (data content) can be included as content within the element.
- Mixed content, which contains both data and element content. A mixed content model allows both regular text and other elements (as specified) to be used as content within an element. You can't specify element order or require that certain elements be used as content as you can with a straight element content model.

Note that a content model extends only to the first level of content within an element. If an element can take only element content, it doesn't mean that the elements it contains can't have mixed or data content. If this is all a bit confusing, don't worry; all will be made clear in Skill 11, "Defining Content Models for Elements."

The elements in `library.dtd` should nest in this way:

- `BOOK`
  - `TITLE`
  - `AUTHOR`
  - `PUBLISHER`
  - `COVER`

- TYPE
- ISBN
- RATING
- COMMENTS

Essentially, the BOOK element contains all the other elements, which in turn contain text or, in the case of EMPTY elements, nothing at all. After I add the content-model information, the new element declarations look like this:

```
<!ELEMENT book (title, author, publisher, cover, category, isbn,
➥ rating, comments?)>
<!ELEMENT title (#PCDATA)>
<!ELEMENT author (#PCDATA)>
<!ELEMENT publisher (#PCDATA)>
<!ELEMENT cover EMPTY>
<!ELEMENT cateogry EMPTY>
<!ELEMENT isbn (#PCDATA)>
<!ELEMENT rating EMPTY>
<!ELEMENT comments (#PCDATA)>
```

The content models now indicate that the TITLE, AUTHOR, PUBLISHER, COVER, CATEGORY, ISBN, and RATING elements must all be contained in that order and followed by an optional COMMENTS element, as indicated by the question mark (?) after the comment within the BOOK element. All of the other, nonempty, elements will just contain regular data.

I've set up my elements and defined their attributes and content models. Now it's time to specify any text or binary entities that I might need in my documents.

Entity Declarations

An entity declaration creates an entity, which is essentially an alias that associates a unique name with a group of data. The data associated with the name can take on one of several formats:

Internal entity maps the unique name to a text phrase included in the entity declaration itself

External text entity maps the unique name to a block of text stored outside of the document

External binary entity maps the unique name to a non-XML data object, such as a graphics file, word-processing document, or audio file stored outside of the document

A character or numeric entity used specifically to include non-ASCII characters in XML files. Character and numeric entities map a string of characters or numbers to a specific non-ASCII character such as the lowercase *e* with an acute accent (*é*).

For example, an internal entity that associates the three-letter string "XML" with the phrase "Extensible Markup Language" takes on this format:

```
<!ENTITY XML "Extensible Markup Language">
```

An external binary entity associates the string "picture1" with the `GIF` file stored in the `/graphics/picture1.gif` file:

```
<!ENTITY picture1 "graphics/picture1.gif" NDATA GIF SYSTEM>
```

As you can see, the specific syntax for declaring entities varies based on the entity's type. Skill 12, "Employing Entities in DTDs and Documents," investigates each of the different kinds of entities in detail and discusses how to reference them in XML documents.

In my simple DTD, the only entities I have to worry about are character entities. I'll use the ones specified in a predefined set of encoded characters and referenced in my document with a processing instruction rather than with an entity declaration. This means `library.dtd` doesn't have any entity declarations at all, and we're effectively done with our tour of the basic DTD structures.

The Final Product: library.dtd

Before moving on, let's take a look at what `library.dtd` looks like when it's all put together:

```
<!ELEMENT book (title, author, publisher, cover, category, isbn,
rating, comments?)>

<!ELEMENT title (#PCDATA)>

<!ELEMENT author (#PCDATA)>

<!ELEMENT publisher (#PCDATA)>

<!ELEMENT cover EMPTY>
     <!ATTLIST COVER
     TYPE (HARDBACK | PAPERBACK) "PAPERBACK" #REQUIRED>

<!ELEMENT cateogry EMPTY>
     <!ATTLIST CATEGORY
```

```
     CLASS (FICTION | FANTASY | SCIFI | MYSTERY | HORROR | NONFICTION |
     HISTORICAL | BIOGRAPHY) "FICTION" #REQUIRED>

<!ELEMENT isbn (#PCDATA)>

<!ELEMENT rating EMPTY>
     <!ATTLIST RATING
     NUMBER (1 | 2 | 3 | 4 | 5) "3" #REQUIRED>

<!ELEMENT comments (#PCDATA)>
```

Not too bad for an example created on the fly. Now that you've seen what goes into the DTD, it's time to take a look at the structures that, based on the definitions in the DTD, describe the content of a document. Now that we've built `library.dtd`, it's time to do something with it. As a wise man once said, "If you build it, they will come." Come along then.

Basic Document Structures

Skill 6

Now you know what a DTD looks like. Of course, `library.dtd` is a small and relatively simple DTD, but you've got to start somewhere. The other half of XML is the document. Documents use the structures defined in DTDs to describe content, so many document structures have names and functions similar to those in DTDs. Documents also have a couple of structures of their own not found in DTDs, but these aren't anything to get excited about. For your introduction to document structures, I'll take the same approach as I did in the previous DTD structures section. After a brief explanation of the structure, I'll show you how it's used in the `books.xml` document I use to catalog the books in my personal library. By the time I've finished, you'll have a complete XML document to complement the DTD from the DTD structures section. Once again, I remind you not to get too worried or frustrated if you don't understand all the markup specifics and semantics I used in the examples. All will be explained in good time.

The Prolog

The document prolog contains all the information relevant to the document other than content or markup. You'll find the statement that declares the document as an XML document, called the XML declaration, and the statement that links the document to its DTD, also called the DTD. (You'll see why soon.) The prolog usually includes special instructions to any application processing; the document is called, not surprisingly, processing instructions (PI).

An XML Declaration

The XML declaration has two parts and performs two important tasks. The first is to identify the document as an XML document; the second is to let the application processing the document know whether it should process only the document or the document as well as its DTD. A basic XML declaration uses this syntax:

```
<?XML VERSION="1.0" RMD= "ALL" ?>
```

The declaration begins with a question mark (?), so it's technically a processing instruction. I'll get to what exactly a processing instruction is in a minute. The `VERSION=` attribute identifies the version of XML for which the document was written. Because XML is currently at version 1.0, the majority of the documents you create for the time being will have `"1.0"` as the value for `VERSION` in their XML declarations.

RMD stands for Required Markup Declaration. The `RMD` attribute gives the document developer a way to let the application processing the document know whether it should also process the associated DTD. The value `ALL` indicates that all DTDs associated with a document should be processed along with the document. I look at RMDs in more detail in Skill 7, "Creating Well-Formed and Valid Documents," in which I'll discuss the other values the `RMD` attribute might take and which attribute you want to use when. For now, just knowing that RMDs exist is enough.

A Document-Type Declaration

Before you start to protest that I've spent half a skill describing DTDs in general only to tell you there's more than one kind of DTD, put your mind at rest. We're still talking about the same DTD here, but you've got to have a way to link the DTD to the document.

The DTD portion of an XML document has three purposes. It identifies an externally stored DTD for processing along with the document; it gives the document developer an opportunity to add his own elements, attributes, content models, or entities to the document; and it defines the top-most document element for the document.

That's right, you can add to the DTD you're designing for your document. There are all kinds of reasons why you might not want to do this and why you should be careful if you do, including the possibility that you might create an element, a set of attributes, or a content model that conflicts with the ones already included in the external DTD. Skill 19, "Creating Documents for XML Applications," discusses in depth the issues and problems associated with adding to an established DTD.

The one thing this internal subset of the DTD is good for is identifying entities that are unique to the document. Imagine if the DTD designer were held responsible for anticipating all the entities that a document developer might want to use. The designer would go crazy or the developer would have a very short list of entities from which to choose. Imagine what a boring place the Web would be if HTML supported only 50 or so graphics.

The document element is the element within which all the other elements are nested. The document element for an HTML document is `<HTML>…</HTML>`. (I cover document elements in more detail further on.) This is the internal DTD for `books.xml`:

```
<!DOCTYPE library SYSTEM "library.dtd">
```

`<!DOCTYPE` is the syntax a document-type declaration begins with, `library` is the name of the document element, and `SYSTEM` indicates that the DTD is stored elsewhere on the computer system and is called `library.dtd`.

`books.xml` doesn't employ any entities, so there isn't an internal subset of the DTD. I could, however, include the entire DTD inside of the document instead of storing the DTD in a separate file called `library.dtd`. If the DTD were included within the document, then the DTD for the document would take this form:

```
<!DOCTYPE library [
<!ELEMENT book (title, author, publisher, cover, category, isbn,
rating, comments?)>

<!ELEMENT title (#PCDATA)>

<!ELEMENT author (#PCDATA)>

<!ELEMENT publisher (#PCDATA)>

<!ELEMENT cover EMPTY>
     <!ATTLIST COVER
     TYPE (HARDBACK | PAPERBACK) "PAPERBACK" #REQUIRED>

<!ELEMENT cateogry EMPTY>
     <!ATTLIST CATEGORY
     CLASS (FICTION | FANTASY | SCIFI | MYSTERY | HORROR | NONFICTION |
```

```
    HISTORICAL | BIOGRAPHY) "FICTION" #REQUIRED>

<!ELEMENT isbn (#PCDATA)>

<!ELEMENT rating EMPTY>
    <!ATTLIST RATING
    NUMBER (1 | 2 | 3 | 4 | 5) "3" #REQUIRED>

<!ELEMENT comments (#PCDATA)>
]>
```

Notice that the system and file identifiers are gone and that the entire DTD is contained between brackets ([ ]). The initial `<!DOCTYPE` declaration still remains, as does the `library` document element. Pretty slick, huh? Now you see why a document and its DTD are never truly separate. Generally, you only want to embed the entire DTD within a document when you're only going to use that DTD for one document. By storing the general DTD as a separate file, you can reference it in as many documents as you'd like. When you embed a DTD within a document, it can be used only with that document. The section "Making Use of External and Internal DTD Subsets" later in the chapter describes these concepts in more detail.

Processing Instructions (PI)

A PI is used specifically to pass messages to the application that will be processing the XML document. As you saw earlier, the XML declaration is really a PI. Although declarations begin with a less-than sign and exclamation mark pair (`<!`) and end with a greater-than sign (>), PIs begin with a less-than sign and question mark pair (<?) and end with a question mark and greater-than sign pair (?>). You can use PIs anywhere in a document, although they're generally found in the prolog, and the attributes and values they include are determined entirely by the application processing the document. Skill 14, "Processing XML Documents," explains PIs and their role in document processing in greater detail.

In addition to the XML declaration PI, the `book.xml` document uses one other PI:

```
<?XML ENCODING="UTF-8" ?>
```

This PI specifies which character-encoding system I'll be using to describe non-ASCII characters in my document. This is an 8-bit character encoding scheme that includes most of the non-ASCII characters I might need to describe my books. Even though a PI is used to describe the encoding scheme, non-ASCII characters are still included in documents as entities. I'll visit the topic of character entities in more depth in Skill 12, "Employing Entities in DTDs and Documents."

If I use the short form of the DTD (where the `library.dtd` is stored external to the document instead of inside of it) and include the XML declaration and character encoding PIs, the prolog for `books.xml` looks like this:

```
<?XML VERSION="1.0" RMD="ALL" ?>
<!DOCTYPE library SYSTEM "library.dtd">
<?XML ENCODING="UTF-8" ?>
```

The Document Element

The document element defined by the document's internal DTD is the top-level PARENT element and includes all the document's other elements and content. The document element for `books.xml`, as prescribed by the DTD, is <LIBRARY>...</LIBRARY>. Within this tag pair, I'll add all the other basic document structures as needed to describe a book from my library.

Elements

Elements are the main markup components and are defined in the DTD by element declarations. Elements are manifested in documents as markup tags. Tags provide the most basic description of content; if you've used HTML even a little bit you're accustomed to using tags. As you'll recall from earlier discussions, most tags come in pairs, with a START tag placed at the beginning of a description and an END tag placed at the end of the description. The described content resides between the START and END tags.

A tag can also be a singleton tag and is labeled an EMPTY tag in XML lingo. An EMPTY tag can't contain other elements or regular data because it doesn't have a START tag and END tag to contain anything. Instead, EMPTY elements are used to insert entities into a document—as the IMAGE tag is used in HTML—or to provide content via attribute values rather than by describing content, as the COVER, CATEGORY, and RATING tags are used in `library.dtd`. Skill 9, "Engineering Elements for a DTD," includes complete coverage of these two different types of tags.

The following is a book described in `books.xml`, using the elements defined in `library.dtd`.

```
<BOOK>
     <TITLE>King of the Murgos</TITLE>
     <AUTHOR>Eddings, David</AUTHOR>
     <PUBLISHER>Del Ray</PUBLISHER>
     <COVER TYPE="PAPERBACK" />
     <CATEGORY CLASS="FANTASY" />
     <ISBN>0-345-41920-0</ISBN>
```

```
    <RATING NUMBER="5" />
    <COMMENTS>Book 2 of the Malloreon. Garion continues the
    search for Geran and meets Urgit, King of the Murgos
    who turns out to be Silk's half-brother. The party is
    betrayed by Toth and captured by Mallorean soldiers and
     prepares to meet Zakath.
    </COMMENTS>
</BOOK>
```

Note that the COVER, CATEGORY, and RATING elements all end with a slash (/) before their final greater-than sign (>). This is the XML syntax that indicates that the tags are empty. All the other tags are pairs and, with the exception of <BOOK>… </BOOK>, contain regular text content as specified by their content models.

Content

You probably noticed in the last bit of sample code from books.xml that all the tags and their content are nested within the <BOOK>…</BOOK> tag. That's because the content declaration for the BOOK element indicates that it must contain exactly one instance of the <TITLE>…</TITLE>, <AUTHOR>…</AUTHOR>, <PUBLISHER>… </PUBLISHER>, <COVER />, <CATEGORY />, <ISBN>…</ISBN>, and <RATING /> elements, in that order. The last element, <COMMENTS>…</COMMENTS>, is optional. The content models for the other, non-EMPTY elements allow them to contain only regular text-based data—and that's exactly what you find in between the START and END tags nested within the <BOOK>…</BOOK> tag pair.

Your documents will be molded as much by the elements you use as by the content those elements can contain. I designed the content models in library .dtd specifically to ensure that each book record would be contained entirely within the BOOK element. I also wanted to guarantee that all the other required elements—and by extension the contents those elements describe—would be part of every book record. If a record is missing a tag and its information, the document is invalid. Granted, I can't guarantee that the content described by the tags will be accurate, but markup languages are not designed to replace human actions and knowledge, only to supplement them.

Attributes

Attributes exist to provide additional information about the element. Many elements take one or more attributes that are defined in a DTD's attribute-list definition. In HTML, for the most part, attributes provide formatting suggestions to Web browsers for the final display of the content. In XML, attributes do much more than just provide formatting information. They add a level of specification to a description that would otherwise require tags nested within tags nested within tags.

By way of example, let's examine the three tags in the books.xml document that have attributes:

```
<COVER TYPE="PAPERBACK" />
<CATEGORY CLASS="FANTASY" />
<RATING NUMBER="5" />
```

The <COVER /> tag describes what kind of a cover a book has, the <CATEGORY /> tag assigns the book to a particular category of books, and the <RATING /> tag allows the document developer to rate the quality of the book. The tag provides a general description of the type of information—cover, category, or rating—but the attributes that go with each tag supply the specifics: cover type, category class, or rating number. There are several other ways that I could have used the DTD to provide the same information, but I chose attributes. If, for instance, I had chosen to use nested tags instead of attributes, I would have had to define three extra elements—TYPE, CLASS, and NUMBER—and make the COVER, CATEGORY, and RATING elements regular elements instead of EMPTY elements. The following would be the resulting code:

```
<COVER>
   <TYPE>Paperback</TYPE>
</COVER>

<CATEGORY>
   <CLASS>Fantasy</CLASS>
</CATEGORY>

<RATING>
   <NUMBER>5</NUMBER>
</RATING>
```

Using attributes is a much more efficient way to achieve the same affect. In the discussions of attributes in Skill 10, "Assigning Attributes to Elements," I'll show you why attributes are such a powerful tool in DTD and document design.

Attributes can take many different types of values, including predefined values chosen from a list and user-defined text. Some attributes may be required while others are optional. Regardless of the form they take or their requisite status, you'll find that you use attributes almost as often as you use tags. One of the keys to good DTD design is knowing how and when to use attributes, and one of the keys to good document design is taking full advantage of the attributes given to you by the DTD.

Entities

Even though the simple books.xml document doesn't use any entities, the majority of XML documents do. As you know, entities allow you to include in your document text or binary files stored on your system. DTD developers can use entities to better organize their DTDs, and as a document developer, you'll need to know how to read and understand entity declarations so you can correctly use entities in your documents. Skill 12, "Employing Entities in DTDs and Documents," has the lowdown on everything you'll need to know about entities.

Comments

There may be times when you want to include notes to yourself or others in an XML document that aren't part of the processed or displayed content. These notes can include comments on the content, markup you've used in a document, or sections of the document that you want temporarily hidden from the processor. To facilitate this notation system, XML, just like HTML, makes use of comments. In fact, XML uses the same comment syntax as HTML does. All comments begin with <!– and end with –>. Anything included between the START and END comment tags is ignored by the XML processor but is readable by anyone reading the source of the document. By way of example I'll throw these two comments into the books.xml document:

```
<!- begin book entry ->
<BOOK>
     <TITLE>King of the Murgos</TITLE>
     <AUTHOR>Eddings, David</AUTHOR>
     <PUBLISHER>Del Ray</PUBLISHER>
     <COVER TYPE="PAPERBACK" />
     <CATEGORY CLASS="FANTASY" />
     <ISBN>0-345-41920-0</ISBN>
     <RATING NUMBER="5" />
     <COMMENTS>Book 2 of the Malloreon. Garion continues the
     search for Geran and meets Urgit, King of the Murgos
     who turns out to be Silk's half-brother. The party is
     betrayed by Toth and captured by Mallorean soldiers and
      prepares to meet Zakath.
     </COMMENTS>
</BOOK>
<!- end book entry ->
```

The Final Product: books.xml

After putting everything together and adding another entry for good measure (but leaving the DTD in its own file), books.xml takes this final form:

```
<?XML VERSION="1.0" RMD="ALL" ?>
<?XML ENCODING="UTF-8" ?>
<!DOCTYPE library SYSTEM "library.dtd">

<LIBRARY>

<!- begin book entry ->
<BOOK>
     <TITLE>King of the Murgos</TITLE>
     <AUTHOR>Eddings, David</AUTHOR>
     <PUBLISHER>Del Ray</PUBLISHER>
     <COVER TYPE="PAPERBACK" />
     <CATEGORY CLASS="FANTASY" />
     <ISBN>0-345-41920-0</ISBN>
     <RATING NUMBER="5" />
     <COMMENTS>Book 2 of the Malloreon. Garion continues the
     search for Geran and meets Urgit, King of the Murgos
     who turns out to be Silk's half-brother. The party is
     betrayed by Toth and captured by Mallorean soldiers and
     prepares to meet Zakath.
     </COMMENTS>
</BOOK>
<!- end book entry ->

<!- begin book entiry ->
<BOOK>
     <TITLE>Demon Lord of Karanda</TITLE>
     <AUTHOR>Eddings, David</AUTHOR>
     <PUBLISHER>Del Ray</PUBLISHER>
     <COVER TYPE="PAPERBACK" />
     <CATEGORY CLASS="FANTASY" />
     <ISBN>0-345-36331-0</ISBN>
     <RATING NUMBER="5" />
     <COMMENTS>Book 3 of the Mallorean. Garion and Zakath
     meet for the first time and a friendship almost begins
     to emerge. Zakath is determined to hold Garion and his
     friends so Silk, Velvet, and Sadi instigate open war
     the halls of Zakath's castle. Durnik kills a demon and
     becomes Aldur's newest desciple.
     </COMMENTS>
</BOOK>
<!- end book entry ->

</LIBRARY>
```

There you have it, a complete document to go with the complete DTD. See, it's not so hard. Before I leave the explicit discussion of DTDs and documents—and they will keep popping up throughout our discussion of XML—I'd like to address the particulars of the external and internal subsets of a DTD. You'll hear about them often enough, both from me and other XML resources, so let's spend a bit of time with them now.

Making Use of External and Internal DTD Subsets

As I briefly discussed in my explanation of document structures, you can define DTD elements within the document just as you can within the DTD itself. I've also said that DTDs and documents are not really separate entities at all but are part of the same whole. You can link an external DTD to a document from within the document's own DTD, or you can include the entirety of a DTD in the document itself.

The first question this raises is why the DTD and document should be separate at all? Storing a DTD in an external file and referencing it in documents is more efficient and easy to maintain. Imagine that you have a thousand copies of a DTD stored inside a thousand different documents. If you want to make a change to even one line of the DTD, you'll have to make that change a thousand times. This isn't a practical approach to DTD management, even with powerful search-and-replace software that can batch process a large number of documents at one time. If you store the DTD in a single document by itself and make a thousand links to it, you'll only have to make one change to affect a thousand documents.

DTDs that are stored individually are also more accessible by a larger number of document developers, and it's easier to ensure that those developers are all working from the same version of the DTD. You'd have to send out notices to all the developers each time you made a change to the DTD to make sure that the developers' documents contained the most current version of the DTD. Knowing why it's often best to store a DTD in its own file external to the documents written for it raises yet another set of questions: What should you include in an external DTD, and what should you include in the internal DTD?

What Goes Outside

The external DTD holds the general element declarations, attribute-list definitions, content models, and general entity descriptions. Any structure that all the documents working with the DTD need to have access to should live in the external DTD. I showed you how `library.dtd` could be defined as either an external or an internal DTD. If I were using `library.dtd` in a real-world application, I would use it as an external DTD. I have too many books to describe them all in a single document, so I'd divide them up by some means, probably alphabetically or by type. In the end, I'd feed the documents to an application that allowed me to search my records by any type of information included in the record, from author or cover type to ISBN number. Because I'd have a collection of documents working together, I'd want to make sure that they were all working from the same DTD. If for some reason I made a change to the DTD, I'd want it to affect all my documents equally. An externally stored DTD is the only method that guarantees consistency.

What Goes Inside

Internal DTDs are used to store document-specific processing instructions and entity declarations for any document-specific entities. If `library.dtd` supported a reference to a scan of a book's cover in GIF format (a binary format), the cover would have to be referenced as a binary entity. All entities have to be declared before they can be used in a document, so I'd declare the entities for each document in the internal DTD subset of each document.

In theory, I could put them in the general DTD, but I'd have to add a new entity declaration to the external `library.dtd` each time I added a book record to a document. After the first 50 or so book's records, the external DTD would become cumbersome. The entities would be difficult to maintain and the DTD would be larger than necessary. With the entities stored in the internal DTD subsets of the documents that reference them, they are easier to maintain, sort, and keep track of.

The internal DTD subset can also be used to add new elements, attribute lists, and content models. These additions are tacked onto the external DTD as if they were part of it and processed right along with the structures in the external DTD.

In addition to reading regular fiction, I also collect rare and old books. If I wanted to catalog those books along with those in my personal library, I might add three new elements to the DTD just for those books—`PUBDATE`, `CONDITION`, and `VALUE`—to catalog when the book was published, its condition, and its value. These elements are specifically to describe rare books, and I know I'll keep the descriptions of all the rare books in a single XML file. Knowing that, I may want to add the element and any attribute-list specifications to the document's internal XML file rather than to the general `library.dtd` file. To do so, I would add this code to the prolog of the rare-books file:

```
<DOCTYPE library SYSTEM "library.dtd"> [
<!ELEMENT book (title, author, publisher, cover, category, isbn,
rating, comments?, pubdate, condition, value)>
<!ELEMENT category EMPTY>
     <!ATTLIST CATEGORY
     CLASS (FICTION | FANTASY | SCIFI | MYSTERY | HORROR |
     NONFICTION | HISTORICAL | BIOGRAPHY | RARE) "RARE" #REQUIRED>
<!ELEMENT pubdate (#PCDATA)>
<!ELEMENT condition (#PCDATA)>
     <!ATTLIST CONDITION
     STATE (POOR | FAIR | GOOD | EXCELLENT)#REQUIRED>
<!ELEMENT value (#PCDATA)>
     <!ATTLIST VALUE
     SOURCE CDATA #REQUIRED>
]
```

This adds to the document DTD the three new elements `PUBDATE`, `CONDITION`, and `VALUE`. None of the elements are empty, and two have attributes. The `PUBDATE` element takes regular data content to allow for the entry of the book's publication date. The `CONDITION` element can contain regular data content for a description of the book's condition and also has a required `STATE` attribute that can take one of four values: `POOR`, `FAIR`, `GOOD`, or `EXCELLENT`. This approach allows the document developer to include a detailed description of the book's condition but also requires that she include an attribute that uses one of four predefined values to describe the condition. Finally, the `VALUE` element can contain regular data that describes the book's current value. The value also requires a `SOURCE` attribute that uses a string value to describe the source of the valuation.

Notice that the `BOOK` element has been redefined for the document to require the presence of these three new elements in a book's description as well as the required elements already found in all the other books described by the DTD. The internal subset also adds a new value to the list of possible values the `CLASS` attribute for the `CATEGORY` element can take: `RARE`. The default value for the `CLASS` attribute is also changed to `RARE` because the books described by this modified DTD are rare. A document including this external DTD subset, internal DTD subset, and a single rare book description might be set up as the following code:

```
<?XML VERSION="1.0" RMD="ALL" ?>
<?XML ENCODING="UTF-8" ?>

<DOCTYPE library SYSTEM "library.dtd"> [
<!ELEMENT book (title, author, publisher, cover, category, isbn,
rating, comments?, pubdate, condition, value)>
```

```
<!ELEMENT pubdate (#PCDATA)>
<!ELEMENT condition (#PCDATA)>
     <!ATTLIST CONDITION
     STATE (POOR | FAIR | GOOD | EXCELLENT)#REQUIRED>
<!ELEMENT value (#PCDATA)>
     <!ATTLIST VALUE
     SOURCE CDATA #REQUIRED>
]

<LIBRARY>
<BOOK>
     <TITLE>The Iliad</TITLE>
     <AUTHOR>Homer</AUTHOR>
     <PUBLISHER>MacMillan</PUBLISHER>
     <COVER TYPE="HARDBACK" />
     <CATEGORY CLASS="RARE" />
     <ISBN>none</ISBN>
     <RATING NUMBER="3" />
     <COMMENTS>Translated by Lang, Leaf, and Myers. Not my
     favorite translation of this wonderful story but does
     serve as a good source for comparing interpretations of
     certain Greek grammatical structures.
     </COMMENTS>
     <PUBDATE>1930</PUBDATE>
     <CONDITION STATE="GOOD">Binding is still good but some
     pages are beginning to become loose. Could stand to be
     rebound. Has some writing in the margins and on the
     front pages.</CONDITION>
     <VALUE SOURC="BUYER">$150 US</VALUE>
</BOOK>

</LIBRARY>
```

Now you see how the internal DTD subset can be used to add to or carefully modify a document's DTD. As I mentioned earlier, there are lots of reasons why you don't want to go around modifying DTDs and why, if you do, you'll need to keep certain things in mind. Read more about this topic in Skill 19, "Creating Documents for XML Applications."

Designing Flawless Documents

There's a lot to be said about DTDs and documents, and I've only really touched the tip of the iceberg. In this skill, you learned a great deal about the roles DTDs and documents play in describing information. You also probably know more about what your author reads in her spare time than you really wanted to know.

Understanding the intricacies of DTDs and documents is important, but it's also important that you know how to create usable XML documents. If your documents don't play by the general rules laid down by XML and, more often than not, by the specific rules of the DTD, they could be malformed or even invalid. Yuck. Malformed and invalid are two pretty nasty words, and they can mean the documents you've worked hard to develop are totally useless. In Skill 7, I show you how to avoid the malformed and invalid pitfalls and, instead, how to design well-formed and valid documents any XML processor will gobble up with delight.

TIP

Even the most seasoned DTD developer is human and can miss the little mistakes in a DTD and document that render it unusable. To check (or validate) your XML, visit the RUWF? (Are You Well Formed?) XML checker at `http://www.xml.com/`.

Are You up to Speed?

Now you can...

- ☑ **Describe the structures of XML DTDs and documents**
- ☑ **Discuss how DTD components are invoked in XML documents**
- ☑ **Explain the difference between internal and external DTD subsets**

SKILL 7

Creating Well-Formed and Valid XML Documents

- The difference between well-formed and valid documents
- Why all XML documents must be at least well formed
- When a document must be well formed instead of valid

XML documents must follow the rules. I've said it over and over, and I'll probably say it many more times before we part. In Skills 5 and 6, I briefly described both well-formed and valid documents. Because these concepts are central to the successful design and implementation of any XML document, this skill explores the topic of well-formed and valid XML documents in depth. I'll show you how to convert an HTML document to a well-formed XML document as well as how to determine whether you need a well-formed or valid document to begin with. I have also included a well-formed and valid documents FAQ, highlighting key concepts.

The Difference between Well-Formed and Valid Documents

Unlike many things in XML, the difference between well-formed and valid documents is relatively cut-and-dry. A well-formed document adheres to all XML's basic rules for document design. Whereas all XML documents must be well formed, they don't necessarily have to be valid. A valid document not only is well formed but is required to play by the DTD's rules. This isn't to say that a well-formed document might not be written for a specific DTD; many are, but a document doesn't have to adhere to any of the rules of the DTD to retain its well-formed stamp of approval. If all that went by a bit fast, don't worry; I'm about to thoroughly dissect well-formed and valid documents so you can see every exquisite detail. To get you started, the following sidebar answers the most common questions about well-formed and valid documents.

Well-Formed and Valid Documents FAQ

What is a well-formed document?

A well-formed document is one that adheres to all of the basic rules of XML. A well-formed document exhibits all of these characteristics:

- It is an XML declaration that includes a required markup declaration.

continued

- It is a single DOCUMENT element in which all of the other elements, and their content, are nested.
- All entities used within the document must be declared in the document-level DTD.
- All elements, attributes, and entities within the document must use the correct syntax.

What is a valid document?

A valid document is a well-formed document that also adheres to the rules established by the DTD it references. Valid documents contain only elements defined by their DTD, include all required elements and attributes, and follow the nesting guidelines set up in the DTD.

How do I decide whether my document needs to be well formed or valid?

If you are working with a document that doesn't have an associated DTD beyond its internal entity definitions, the document only needs to be well formed. The documentation written for an XML vocabulary and any associated processor will often let you know whether you need to create valid documents or just well-formed ones.

NOTE This skill is designed to be an overview of what it takes to create well-formed and valid documents. I realize that I haven't covered some of the XML constructs discussed in the chapter, and you may not be 100 percent familiar with them and how they work specifically in XML. These rules of syntax will become clearer as we go along, trust me.

A Well-Formed Document Plays by XML's Rules

Every XML document you create must adhere to all of XML's basic rules; a well-formed document adheres to all of XML's basic rules. So, every XML document you create must be a well-formed document. The question then becomes what are the rules you have to follow to create a well-formed document? XML isn't as harsh a taskmistress as you might think. A well-formed document must always possess these characteristics:

- An XML declaration that includes a required markup declaration.
- A single document element in which all of the other elements and their content are properly nested.
- All entities used within the document must be declared in the document-level DTD.
- All elements, attributes, and entities within the document must use the correct syntax.

See, that wasn't so bad. All you have to do is make sure your documents meet these four simple requirements, and they'll be well-formed and useable XML documents. To make sure your documents always conform to these basic well-formed standards, let's look at each one of them in more detail.

An XML Declaration that Includes a Required Markup Declaration

As I described in Skill 6, "Understanding the Basics of XML DTDs and Documents," every XML document must begin with an XML declaration that looks like this:

```
<?XML VERSION="1.0"?>
```

In addition to the version information, the XML declaration must include a special attribute, called the Required Markup Declaration (RMD), that specifies whether the processor needs to read and process a DTD along with the document.

Even though a document may not have a specific external DTD associated with it, it will most likely have an internal subset that defines the document's entities. The `RMD` attribute takes one of these three values:

`ALL` This value indicates to the processor that it should read and process all DTDs, internal and external, associated with the document. The majority of well-formed documents will not use this `RMD` attribute value, but if you don't include an `RMD`, the value automatically defaults to `ALL`.

`INTERNAL` This value indicates to the processor that it should read and process only the document's internal DTD. This is often the value for the `RMD` attribute because a document's internal DTD may include information vital to successfully processing the document, such as entity definitions, default values for some attributes, and important information about nesting elements within elements.

NONE This value indicates to the processor that it doesn't need to worry about either an internal or external DTD. This is the value assigned to the RMD attribute when the document may be processed correctly without any DTD information. This means the document doesn't have any predefined entities or attributes with default values and isn't affected by any nesting rules.

An XML declaration with the RMD attribute added takes this form:

```
<?XML VERSION="1.0" RMD="INTERNAL"?>
```

The default value for the RMD attribute is ALL; if you don't include the attribute within the XML declaration, the XML processor will automatically attempt to process all the DTDs associated with the document. More often than not, well-formed documents need only an RMD value of INTERNAL or NONE. Whether a document's DTD(s) needs to be processed or not affects the processing time as well as the type of parser required. Skill 14, "Processing XML Documents," focuses on the various types of processors and how they deal with both well-formed and valid documents.

A Single Document Element in Which All of the Other Elements and Their Content Are Nested

As I discussed in Skill 6, every XML document must have a single document, or ROOT, element. This element contains the rest of the document's other elements and their content. For example, the ROOT element for an HTML file is <HTML>... </HTML>. The ROOT element for a Channel Definition Format (CDF) file is <CHANNEL> ...</CHANNEL>.

Generally, the ROOT element is defined by the document's DTD. Even if you're working toward only a well-formed document and not a valid one, when you're writing the document for a specific DTD, you'll want to use the document element specified by the DTD. If, however, you're creating a document that doesn't have a DTD (on very rare occasions), you'll still need to have a document element within which all of your other elements are nested. Basically, your document element's START tag begins the markup portion of your document, and its END tag ends it. Make sure you don't put any other markup after the document element or your document will be malformed.

All Entities Used within the Document Must Be Declared in the Document-Level DTD

I haven't discussed entities in depth yet, although they were introduced in Skill 5, "Investigating XML," and discussed again in Skill 6, "Understanding the Basics of XML DTDs and Documents." Skill 12, "Employing Entities in DTDs and Documents," is devoted entirely to entities. As a refresher, an entity is a block of binary or text data. Entities can represent non-ASCII text, such as accented characters, graphics, and other non-XML files referenced by an XML document, as well as chunks of XML markup and content stored elsewhere and embedded in an XML document.

What you need to know about entities for the purposes of this discussion is that they all have to be defined in the document's DTD, internal or external, in order for them to be referenced within the document. Usually entities for non-ASCII characters are referenced in the external DTD. Entities for document-specific images and other non-XML documents, as well as text-based entities embedded in the document, are referenced in the internal DTD. Although this is the way it is usually done, it's not required.

Regardless of where an entity is declared in a document's DTD, it must be declared. So, if you plan to embed any graphics in your document or include any non-ASCII characters, you'll have to include entity declarations in your internal DTD. If you include these declarations, you'll need to set your `RMD` attribute in your XML declaration to `INTERNAL` to make sure that the processor recognizes your entities when it comes across them in the document.

If you're still a bit confused about entities, don't worry. I'll explain it all in good time. Just don't forget that you always have to declare an entity before you can use it. Do this and your documents will always be well formed.

All Elements, Attributes, and Entities within the Document Must Use the Correct Syntax

Once you've defined the document as an XML document—including an `RMD` attribute and value—declared all of your entities, and set up your document element, it's time to add the meat of the XML document: the elements, their attributes and content, and the entity references. The first three items on this list are relatively easy to include in a document, but the last requirement is trickier.

All of your elements, attributes, and entities must be formed using the correct XML syntax. This means that

- All elements that are not EMPTY elements must have both a START and END tag. If I were creating a well-formed HTML document (which I will be doing in a few pages), every <P> would need a </P> and every <LI> would need a </LI>. Regardless of the specific vocabulary being used, every element in a well-formed XML document must have a companion closing tag. Remember that Web browsers are forgiving; XML processors are not.
- Empty elements must have a slash at the end of the tag before the greater-than sign. The HTML IMAGE tag would appear as <IMG SRC="myimage.gif" /> in a well-formed XML document. Note the slash at the end of the tag. That's a signal to the processor that the element is empty and that the processor doesn't need to look for a close tag.
- Every (and yes, I mean every) attribute value must be enclosed in quotation marks. This isn't an option with XML; it's a requirement. Even one missing quotation mark before or after an attribute value can render the entire document malformed. Because the attributes in this tag are missing quotation marks, it is malformed: <TABLE WIDTH=100% CELLPADDING=10 CELLSPACING =10>. Once you add quotation marks around the values, the document is well formed: <TABLE WIDTH="100%" CELLPADDING="10" CELLSPACING="10">.
- All nonbinary entity references must begin with an ampersand (&) and end with a semicolon (;), as these two character entities do: < and >. This is nothing new to HTML developers, but unlike forgiving Web browsers that render an entity for you even if you forget the semicolon, an XML parser hangs on an incomplete entity and labels the document malformed.
- All nested elements must be nested correctly. The rule of thumb is always close first what you opened last. Remember that when you're nesting an element within another element, you want the nesting to be complete. This is the wrong way to nest elements: <P><B>This is wrong</P></B>. This is the right way: <P><B>This is correct</B></P>. Notice that the BOLD tag is completely opened and closed within the PARAGRAPH tag. A Web browser might let you get away with incorrectly nested tags; an XML parser definitely won't.

You don't need to know everything about entities to understand well-formed and valid documents. In fact, it's better to have these requirements firmly in mind before you learn about elements, attributes, and entities in detail. Knowing that you'll have to abide by a certain set of rules from the outset will help prevent you from picking up bad habits along the way.

Converting an HTML Document into a Well-Formed XML Document

Whew! We've finally completed our survey of the basic rules of XML—for the time being, anyway. To take a break from rules and as an exercise in creating well-formed documents, let's take a few minutes to convert a real-life HTML page into a valid XML document. Keep in mind that this is just an exercise; you can't actually use this XML document on a Web server because Web browsers don't speak XML yet. This is, however, a good indication of the way HTML pages may look in the future, especially if HTML becomes an XML vocabulary, as many experts believe it may.

The guinea pig document for this conversion is the LANWrights, Inc., "What's New" page, found on the Web at `http://www.lanw.com/new.htm`. I've snipped a bunch of the text out to save a few trees and to help focus on the task at hand: converting this valid HTML document into a valid XML document.

First, here's the page, sans some text:

```
<HTML>
     <HEAD>
             <META HTTP-EQUIV="content-type"
                 CONTENT="text/html;charset=iso-8859-1">
             <TITLE>LANWrights - Writing and Consulting - What's
                 New</TITLE>
             <LINK HREF="lanwstyle.css" TYPE="text/css"
                 REL="STYLESHEET">

        </HEAD>

<BODY BGCOLOR=#FFFFFF LINK=#800000 VLINK=#000080>

<CENTER>
<P>
<IMG SRC="graphics/wn_logo.gif" ALT="What's New @ LANWrights"
ALIGN=CENTER BORDER="0">
</P>
</CENTER>
<BR><BR>
```

```
<H3>Test Prep Core Four Pack Number 6 at Ingram, and TCP/IP Booms!</H3>
For the past 16 weeks, at least two Test Prep titles (including the
Core Four Pack) have been on the Ingram Top 50 Computer books in the
Networking/Communicatons category. On some weeks, we've had as many as
five titles on that list, on several others three or four. We've also
had our Windows 95 and Windows NT Workstation titles make intermittent
appearances on the Operating Systems Top 50 at Ingram. Top that off
with a few appearances on the Amazon Bestseller list and you've got
evidence of some pretty good sales.<P>

[snip]

<UL>
<LI><A HREF="books/hphtml4.htm"> HTML 4.0 Quick Guide</A>) <BR><BR>
<LI><A HREF="books/html4d4.htm">HTML 4.0 For Newbies</A> <BR><BR>
<LI><A HREF="books/xml4dum.htm">XML For Newbies</A>  <BR><BR>
<LI><A HREF="books/epntw.htm">Windows NT Workstation Test Prep</A>
<BR><BR>
</UL>

[snip]

<CENTER>
<P>
<IMG SRC="graphics/navigbar.gif"  ALT="Navigtion Image, see text links
below" USEMAP="#navigbar" ISMAP BORDER="0">
</P>
</CENTER>
<P><BR>
<IMG SRC="graphics/line.gif" WIDTH="100%" HEIGHT="2" USEMAP="#">
</P>
</CENTER>

[snip]

</BODY>
</HTML>
```

Where to start, where to start? I'll look at each of the characteristics of a well-formed document and check our sample document to see if it exhibits each one. If the document doesn't, I'll fix things so it does.

Does the document have an XML declaration that includes a required markup declaration?

The answer to this all-important question is "No." Before I remedy the situation and add an XML declaration to the document, I'll need to figure out what the value of my RMD attribute should be. A quick glance through the document shows me that there are several graphics embedded in it. Because graphics are binary entities that have to be declared in the DTD before they can be referenced, I know I need to create an internal DTD for this document to declare the entities. For this document to process correctly, its internal DTD will have to be processed. Knowing that the RMD attribute value will have to be INTERNAL, I'll add this XML declaration to the document:

```
<?XML VERSION="1.0" RMD="INTERNAL">
```

Does the document contain a single document element in which all of the other elements and their content are nested?

The answer to this question is yes. The <HTML>...</HTML> tags serve as the document element.

Are all the entities used within the document declared in the document-level DTD?

Because HTML does not require entities to be predefined before they can be referenced, the answer to this question is a resounding "No." It's easy enough to fix this problem, however. By adding the following entity declarations to the document, I'm one step closer to a well-formed XML document:

```
<!ENTITY new.logo SYSTEM "graphics/wn_logo.gif" NDATA GIF>
<!ENTITY navbar SYSTEM "graphics/navigbar.gif" NDATA GIF>
<!ENTITY line SYSTEM "graphics/line.gif" NDATA GIF>
```

Without going into the details about entities, I can tell you a few things about these three entity declarations without totally confusing you. The entity declaration (beginning with <!ENTITY) assigns an alias (such as new.logo) to an entity (such as graphics/wn_logo.gif) stored either on your local system (hence the SYSTEM notation) or a public server (indicated by PUBLIC instead of SYSTEM). The NDATA GIF portion of the declaration lets the processor know the entity's type so the processor will know what to do with it.

Because binary entities are referenced in documents by the alias you assign them in the entity declaration rather than by their actual file names, I'll have to change all the SRC= values in the IMAGE tags to match the alias names. Once that's done and I'm sure there aren't any text or character entities to worry about (which there aren't), it's time to move onto the last, and most complex, question.

Do all of the document elements, attributes, and entities within the document use the correct syntax?

To answer this question I'll have to look at each line of the document to verify that the elements and attributes are coded with the proper XML syntax. The first thing to look for is missing CLOSE tags. I see several, including a missing </P> in the first full paragraph of the document and a slew of missing </LI> tags in the list farther down. The open paragraph is missing a CLOSE tag because it's being used as a singleton in this document, a technique supported by Web browsers, instead of a tag pair. To make the document XML-compliant, I'll move the OPEN tag to the beginning of the document and add a CLOSE tag where the current OPEN tag is. The new code looks like this:

```
<P>For the past 16 weeks, at least two Test Prep titles (including the
Core Four Pack) have been on the Ingram Top 50 Computer books in the
Networking/Communicatons category. On some weeks, we've had as many as
five titles on that list, on several others three or four. We've also
had our Windows 95 and Windows NT Workstation titles make intermittent
appearances on the Operating Systems Top 50 at Ingram. Top that off
with a few appearances on the Amazon Bestseller list and you've got
evidence of some pretty good sales.</P>
```

I'll also go through and add </LI> tags in the document's unordered list. The resulting code looks like this:

```
<UL>
<LI><A HREF="books/hphtml4.htm"> HTML 4.0 Quick Guide</A> <BR><BR></LI>
<LI><A HREF="books/html4d4.htm">HTML 4.0 For Newbies</A> <BR><BR></LI>
<LI><A HREF="books/xml4dum.htm">XML For Newbies</A> <BR><BR></LI>
<LI><A HREF="books/epntw.htm">Windows NT Workstation Tst Prep</A>
<BR><BR></LI>
</UL>
```

A quick scan of the rest of the document shows that every OPEN tag has a corresponding CLOSE tag. Now it's time to add the slash (/) to all the empty IMAGE (<IMG>) and LINE-BREAK (<BR>) tags, as well as the <META> and <LINK> tags at the beginning of the document, to identify them to an XML processor as empty rather than missing a CLOSE tag. There are several instances of both the IMAGE and LINE-BREAK tags, so look for them in the final XML version of the code at the end of the "Conversion" section.

The next step in the process is to check for missing quotation marks around attribute values. A few values without quotation marks appear here and there—in fact, there aren't any around the attributes of the BODY element at all—but they are easy enough to fix. Once that's done, I will check for malformed entity references and find none. A final check for incorrectly nested elements comes up empty, so it looks like I'm ready to unveil the new and improved XML version of my company's "What's New" page.

```
<?XML VERSION="1.0" RMD="INTERNAL">
<!ENTITY new.logo SYSTEM "graphics/wn_logo.gif" NDATA GIF>
<!ENTITY navbar SYSTEM "graphics/navigbar.gif" NDATA GIF>
<!ENTITY line SYSTEM "graphics/line.gif" NDATA GIF>

<HTML>
    <HEAD>
          <META HTTP-EQUIV="content-type"
             CONTENT="text/html;charset=iso-8859-1" />
          <TITLE>LANWrights - Writing and Consulting - What's
             New</TITLE>
          <LINK HREF="lanwstyle.css" TYPE="text/css"
             REL="STYLESHEET" />

</HEAD>

<BODY BGCOLOR="#FFFFFF" LINK="#800000" VLINK="#000080">

<CENTER>
<P>
<IMG SRC="new.logo" ALT="What's New @ LANWrights" ALIGN="CENTER" BOR-
DER="0" />
</P>
</CENTER>
<BR /><BR />
<H3>Test Prep Core Four Pack Number 6 at Ingram, and TCP/IP Booms!</H3>
<P>For the past 16 weeks, at least two Test Prep titles (including the
Core Four Pack) have been on the Ingram Top 50 Computer books in the
Networking/Communicatons category. On some weeks, we've had as many as
five titles on that list, on several others three or four. We've also
had our Windows 95 and Windows NT Workstation titles make intermittent
appearances on the Operating Systems Top 50 at Ingram. Top that off
with a few appearances on the Amazon Bestseller list and you've got
evidence of some pretty good sales.</P>

[snip]

<UL>
<LI><A HREF="books/hphtml4.htm"> HTML 4.0 Quick Guide</A>
<BR /><BR /></LI>
<LI><A HREF="books/html4d4.htm">HTML 4.0 For Newbies</A>
<BR /><BR /></LI>
<LI><A HREF="books/xml4dum.htm">XML For Newbies</A>
<BR /><BR /></LI>
<LI><A HREF="books/epntw.htm">Windows NT Workstation Test Prep</A>
```

```
<BR /><BR /></LI>
</UL>

[snip]

<CENTER>
<P>
<IMG SRC="navbar"  ALT="Navigtion Image, see text links below"
USEMAP="#navigbar" ISMAP BORDER="0" />
</P>
</CENTER>
<P><BR />
<IMG SRC="line" WIDTH="100%" HEIGHT="2" USEMAP="#" />
</P>

[snip]

</BODY>
</HTML>
```

Isn't it lovely? All in all, it wasn't that difficult to convert my HTML document to XML, but that may be because I'm careful when I design HTML documents and try to adhere to the rules of markup as closely as HTML will allow. Skill 17, "Turning Existing HTML Documents into Valid XML Documents," further explores the issues of turning HTML documents into well-formed XML documents and working with HTML as an XML vocabulary. Now that you know all about well-formed documents, let's move on to the subject of valid documents and the more stringent sets of rules that govern them.

A Valid Document Plays by XML's and the DTD's Rules

A valid document is simply a document that adheres to the rules of a declared DTD in addition to being well formed. A valid document has all the virtues of a well-formed document—and then some. Because every DTD is different, I can't go through a set of characteristics every valid document displays, but I can highlight some of the things you'll have to watch out for when creating valid documents. You should always be sure to

- Use the document element specified by the DTD as your document element. The document element is listed in your DTD declaration in the prolog of your document. Remember a DTD declaration looks like this:

  ```
  <!DOCTYPE document SYSTEM "doc.dtd">
  ```

The document element for documents created with this DTD is `<DOCUMENT>`.

- Include any attributes marked as required with their elements. Skill 10, "Assigning Attributes to Elements," discusses both optional and required attributes in detail. For now, just keep in mind that to create a valid document, you have to supply those attributes marked as required each time you use the elements associate with them.
- Adhere exactly to the content model described for each and every element. Remember that the content model describes which elements can be nested within other elements. The content model also dictates which elements *must* be nested within a given element. Skill 11, "Defining Content Models for Elements," describes content models in general terms. Once you can read a content model, always make sure to follow it.

That's it, really. However, always including all the required attributes and nested elements may be more difficult than you think if the document and DTD are long and complex. Before you begin working with any DTD, make sure you're familiar with it and understand each element's definition and requirements completely. When you finish this book, reading a DTD will be almost second nature to you, so the task won't be as difficult as you might think.

Tools Make Life Easier

You're probably wondering how it's possible to create valid or even well-formed documents when so much as a missing quotation mark or semicolon can throw the whole thing out of whack and stop your document dead in its tracks. A good quality XML editor will be your best ally in your quest to create well-formed and valid documents. An XML editor should warn you when you make a basic mistake, such as leaving out a quotation mark or semicolon. Even better editors will have advanced interfaces that will add most of the easy but required syntax to your document for you.

If you're working on a document that must be valid, an XML editor will be able to read the document's DTD and present you with a drop-down menu of element choices limited to those listed in the DTD. In addition, the editor should either warn you when you leave out a required tag or attribute or simply not allow you to omit them at all.

Because XML is a version of SGML, a wide variety of XML tools are already beginning to appear on the market, and most are from established SGML editor developers. Don't look for the WYSIWYG HTML editors that seem to proliferate like bunnies in the current market. Remember that the whole point of XML is to separate markup from display. It's not about what you see; it's about what you describe.

Skill 27, "Choosing the Right XML Tool," is given over to a survey of the current XML tool offerings. I wanted to mention tools here, however, to show you that creating both well-formed and valid usable XML documents is not as onerous a task as earlier discussions in the skill might have made it seem.

Time to Type Your Markup

You probably think I mean it's time to key your tags and content into an editor of some kind. It's not the time for that just yet. Before you start hacking XML, you need to know what type of markup and content you're working with: content-based or presentation-based? Confused? In Skill 8, "Working with Different Types of Markup," you'll meet the two distinct types of markup and learn when to use one or the other.

Are You up to Speed?

Now you can...

- ☑ **Explain why a document must be well formed**
- ☑ **Describe what makes a document well formed**
- ☑ **Know when a document must be valid in addition to well formed**

SKILL 8

Working with Different Types of Markup

- What content-based and presentation-based markup are
- How to choose the right kind of markup for your content
- Examples of content-based and presentation-based DTDs

Markup describes content, and the content itself dictates what kind of markup you use to describe it. You wouldn't use the Chemical Markup Language to describe a memo, and you certainly wouldn't use HTML to describe the components of a software package for installation. In addition to having a unique set of goals and characteristics, most XML vocabularies can be categorized as either content-based or presentation-based markup. The category that a vocabulary falls into says quite a bit about the markup itself, the content it describes, and how its documents will be used. If you are a document developer, you'll want to know what type of markup you're working with to make sure it fits your content. If you're designing a DTD, knowing what type of markup you want to create can be an advantage as you begin the design process.

This skill examines both content-based and presentation-based markup, including examples of each type of markup and a guide to choosing the right type of markup for your documents and DTDs. A FAQ covering markup types ends the skill, highlighting all the key concepts you'll need to understand about content-based and presentation-based markup.

Why Two Categories of Markup?

You're probably wondering why there is a need to categorize XML vocabularies at all. The whole point of XML is to give developers a variety of markup languages, allowing for a virtually unlimited range of vocabularies. So are categories, or types, of markup added into the mix to make things even more complicated? Actually, the categorization of markup as content- or presentation-based is really driven by the different types of content the markup is called upon to describe. An example will help clear things up.

Imagine that you have two different documents to describe. The first is a marketing brochure for a software product; the other, a set of specifications for installing the same software product over a network. How are the contents of the two documents different? A marketing brochure is a visual entity. The content will most likely be disseminated to users as a print brochure, as part of a demonstration, or on a Web page. An automated program to install the software on user computers over a network will most likely use the installation specifics.

When you choose a markup language to describe each document, your requirements would be different in each case. To describe the marketing brochure, you would need a markup language similar to HTML, with `PARAGRAPH`, `HEADING`, `LIST`, and other similar tags. Even though you're not concerned with which application will ultimately display, print, or project your document, you know the final results will be presented to users in one media or another. The markup requirements for the installation specifics are a bit different, though. The contents of the installation document aren't meant for human consumption but will be read and interpreted by a computer. The markup that describes the document will include tags for identifying the operating system on which the software runs, the amount of hard-disk space and RAM required by the application, and other technical specifics. The markup for this document will identify important content that the installation application needs to complete its mission.

Two different types of content require two different types of markup. Which is which? If you don't know by now, keep reading.

Content-Based Markup

Content-based markup is concerned primarily with pinning down the important information in a document so the processing application can do something fun or interesting with it. The Resource Description Format (RDF) vocabulary is a perfect example of a content-based markup language. RDF isn't interested in how the resources it describes are displayed on the screen. Instead, it wants to know important facts about the resources, such as the author, media type, URL, title, and description. Applications that process RDF data can take this information and create searchable databases that are far more effective than the Web search engines of today.

The Open Software Description (OSD) vocabulary is the markup language that describes software packages for installations over a network, to which I referred to in my earlier example. OSD doesn't want to display information about the software on a Web page as part of a marketing spiel. Its primary purpose is to describe the important technical specifications of the software package to facilitate a hands-off installation across a network.

The elements found in the RDF and OSD specifications are indicative of their focus on use of document content by applications for an express purpose rather than the display of the document's content for the benefit of users. A brief look at the OSD specification finds this sampling of elements:

> `CODEBASE` This element identifies the location of the actual files to be installed as part of the software package. It takes the `HREF` attribute to point to the file's location using the standard Web addressing system or the `FILENAME` attribute to point to another file in the same folder as the OSD document. The `SIZE` attribute can also be used with this element to indicate the size of the file to be installed.

`OS` This element is used to specify what operating system the software package can run on. The `VALUE` attribute takes one of several predefined values to name the actual operating system. By working from a list of predefined values rather than allowing the user to type in their own text string, the DTD ensures that the processing application will recognize the operating systems referred to by this element. The document developer can use as many individual `OS` elements as necessary to list all the operating systems the software package supports.

`PROCESSOR` Similar to the `OS` element in both form and function, the `PROCESSOR` element specifies what kind of processor a computer using the software package must have. This element also uses the `VALUE` attribute with a list of predefined values to help document developers avoid creating OSD documents that the processing application can't understand.

There are several other elements in the OSD DTD, as discussed in Skill 22, "Installing Software with OSD," but these three provide a good example of how content-based markup specifically describes the particular content the processing application needs to complete its job. Leaving nothing to chance, OSD even provides developers with a list of operating system and processor values from which to choose. To the human eye, Windows 95, Windows95, and Win95 may all mean the same thing, but they are three completely different entities to a computer program.

As you can see, content-based markup languages are designed to describe the information in a document that is going to be most useful to the processing application in the completion of some task. Very little, if any, of the content described by a content-based vocabulary will be seen by users. You could say that content described with content-based markup is meant for computer consumption, whereas content described with presentation-based markup is meant for human consumption. The upcoming discussion of presentation-based markup explains why.

Presentation-Based Markup

As a general rule, computers are more concerned with the accuracy of information than with its presentation. The same cannot be said for people. For human beings, the presentation of a document conveys as much about the document as its content does. And while markup is supposed to be separate from display in XML—and any other markup language—those markup languages that describe information that will be eventually presented in some format or another for human consumption are labeled as presentation-based.

A perfect example of a presentation-based markup language is HTML. In fact, HTML is a monument to presentation-based markup language that got out of control. HTML is not alone in the presentation-based markup category. The Tutorial Markup Language (TML) and the Precision Graphics Markup Language (PGML) are both presentation-based XML vocabularies. Whereas HTML attempts to describe a wide variety of documents for presentation on the Web, both TML and PGML are limited in scope. TML focuses on tutorial, training, and assessment content while PGML is a graphics description and display language. Regardless of what kind of content they are describing, all three markup languages—HTML, TML, and PGML—are examples of presentation-based markup.

The applications that process documents described by presentation-based markup aren't nearly as concerned with doing something with the information contained in the document as they are with displaying the document's contents for a user. The document may be displayed in print, on the Web, or by projection. Presentation isn't limited to only visual display; it can include Braille output or audio output from a text-to-speech reader. Regardless of how it's disseminated, content described by a presentation-based markup language is geared for human consumption rather than computer consumption.

Hybrid Markup

There are a few instances where a markup language may be categorized as both content-based and presentation-based. Those markup languages are really hybrids that include elements for describing content to be processed by a computer or program to accomplish a task as well as elements that describe content to be presented to users. Hybrid markup languages tend to be broader in scope, defined by more complex DTDs, and meant for processing by a specific type of browser or application. A perfect example of a hybrid markup language is the Chemical Markup Language (CML). CML includes elements for describing molecules for display as well as for describing molecular compounds and other chemical formulae to be computed by an application.

In reality, the majority of XML vocabularies will fall into either one category or the other. For a markup to address both content and presentation issues, it has to be vast and more than a little complex. To see for yourself, visit the CML home page at `http://www.venus.co.uk/omf/cml/`. The list of new additions alone is enough to make you see why CML can wear both kinds of markup hats simultaneously.

Real-World Examples

It always helps to look at real-world examples when working your way through a particular concept. Although the languages I've chosen as examples of content-based and presentation-based markup languages are discussed elsewhere in the book (CDF even has its own skill), the focus on them in this skill is as examples of a particular kind of markup. I didn't include an example of a hybrid markup language because they are by nature intricate and difficult to explain, even at this level. Besides, if you understand how content-based and presentation-based markup each function alone, you'll certainly be able to recognize them when they are working in concert.

The majority of the XML vocabularies currently under development are content-based simply because HTML has already been developed as the standard presentation-based markup language of the Web. Why reinvent the wheel when there are other fish to fry? (How's that for a mixed metaphor?) The following examples examine the Channel Definition Format (CDF) as a content-based markup language and the Tutorial Markup Language (TML) as a presentation-based markup language. Don't worry if you don't understand everything about each language; the important thing to focus on is why each language is assigned to a specific content type. Learning to recognize content- and presentation-based markup is an important XML skill.

Content-Based Markup: CDF

The Channel Definition Format (CDF) vocabulary was created by Microsoft to describe channels. A channel delivers Web-based information directly to the user's desktop using server push technology. Server push is a Web technology that allows Web content to be sent directly to the user without the usual Web page request (or pull) associated with accessing a Web site. Information is delivered to channel subscribers on a schedule defined by a CDF document. The actual content is HTML-based and just like the content found on regular Web pages, but the document that controls the delivery is XML-based.

TIP CDF is currently a note under review by the W3C and may possibly become a standard. To view the current CDF specification at the W3C, visit `http://www.w3.org/TR/NOTE-CDFsubmit.html`.

CDF is considered a content-based markup language because it describes a set of parameters used by the Web server sending out channel information to subscribers. The parameters identify the location of the channel's home page, set a schedule for sending updates to the subscriber's desktop, and provide a mechanism for setting up subchannels within a main channel. About the only thing described by CDF that the user actually sees is the logo added to the browser's Active channel guide that identifies the channel. All the other content described by CDF is used by the server sending out the data. As I said earlier, content described by content-based markup is meant for computer consumption. The CDF file controls a server sending out files described by HTML, a presentation-based markup, for human consumption. A look at some CDF elements illustrates why it's aptly categorized as content-based markup:

`SCHEDULE` This element sets the schedule for the initiation of a channel and contains other elements that establish the channel's update schedule. The `STARTDATE` attribute assigns a specific launch date for the channel. To specify an update schedule for the channel, these three elements can be nested within the `SCHEDULE` element:

`INTERVALTIME` The time interval between updates is defined with this element and its `HOURS` attribute.

`LATESTTIME` The latest time an update can begin is defined with this element and its `HOURS` attribute.

`EARLIESTTIME` The earliest time an update can begin is defined with this element and its `HOURS` attribute

`ITEM` This element identifies a section within the channel, or a *subchannel*. By including several `ITEM` elements within a single channel, a developer can set up pointers to a hierarchy of information inside a single channel. The `HREF` attribute points to the actual HTML file that serves as the subchannel's home page. Remember that the `ITEM` element simply sets up the subchannel, while an HTML file provides the actual presented content.

Although there's quite a bit more to creating a channel, the CDF file provides the control mechanisms needed to establish and regulate the channel. CDF is considered a content-based markup language because it provides information to a computer application—the Web server—to help it complete a task. Skill 20, "Channeling Data with CDF," discusses all CDF elements in more detail and includes a tutorial on creating Active channel content.

Presentation-Based Markup: TML

The Tutorial Markup Language (TML) is designed to describe different types of questions for presentation in a variety of media. By separating the actual question from its final form, entire question banks can be created on any topic. When an instructor needs a set of questions, he or she simply pulls them from the question bank and uses whatever display mechanism is required or preferred. The same questions can be printed for a paper-based test or output to a source file for a computer-based test.

Although questions described by TML aren't designed to be presented by a particular application or software package—or in any specific format—they are nevertheless meant to be presented to students in some way or another. Documents created with TML are intended almost entirely for human consumption. This makes TML a presentation-based markup language.

TML contains some HTML elements, technically making it a superset of HTML, and also includes a group of tags specifically designed to describe different types of questions. The current 4.0 version of TML is written in SGML but is being ported to XML to take advantage of the development of XML as a Web technology.

The TML specification is found online at `http://www.ilrt.bris.ac.uk/netquest/liveserver/TML_INSTALL/lib/ETS/dtd/TML_4.0` and includes many familiar HTML elements as well as the new elements for describing questions. The following is a sampling of those elements:

`QUESTION` This element describes a question; each individual question can contain a whole host of other elements that describe it, its possible solutions, hints, and of course, answers.

`SCORE` This element displays the student's score when a computer-based testing environment administers tests.

`CHOICE` This element describes answer options for questions.

`HINT` This element allows developers to provide hints for test takers.

TML is a good example of the kind of presentation-based markup you can expect to see in XML's future. Instead of reinventing the wheel, DTD developers will continue to make it better, adding onto and refining HTML to meet their specific needs. Of course, this means at some point that HTML may have to become an actual XML vocabulary, but that's not such a great leap to make.

Choosing the Right Kind of Markup for the Job

So now the question becomes how do you choose the right type of markup for your document or DTD? The answer is actually quite simple: Let your content be your guide. Ask yourself these two questions (which are really variations on the same theme):

- What is the content's purpose? Is it supposed to provide information to people, or is it to be used by a computer for accomplishing a task?
- Will the results of parsing your document be designed for computer or human consumption?

After answering these two questions, you should have a good idea of what type of markup language you'll need to describe your content. If you're describing information to be processed by a computer, you'll need a content-based markup language. However, if your final audience is made up of skin and bones ("wetware") rather than silicon, you'll want to use a presentation-based markup. If your information seems to call for a hybrid, you might want to reevaluate your content to see if it can't be divided along content- and presentation-based lines and described by two markup languages instead. If a division of content isn't a workable solution, you'll need to find a hybrid. You'll be in for a fun ride once you jump on that train.

Once you've chosen which type of markup you need, the job is still not quite done. You still need to narrow the choices within each category to the specific XML vocabulary that best fits your content. Chapter 19, "Creating Documents for XML Applications," includes a how-to section on that very topic.

Even if you're developing DTDs rather than designing documents, you'll need to ask yourself the same questions to help decide what kind of markup language to create. The majority of XML vocabularies are, or will be, developed to provide a solution to a specific content-description need. The content drives the creation of DTDs in the same way it drives the creation of documents. If you know what kind of content you're creating the DTD for, you'll know what kind of DTD to create. It really is that simple.

Markup Types FAQ

Why are markup languages categorized by type?

Markup languages are categorized by type because most information falls into one of two categories: content-based and presentation-based. As XML vocabularies are developed to meet a specific information-description need, they naturally fall into one of these categories.

What is content-based markup?

Content-based markup is used to describe information that will be processed by an application toward the completion of a certain task. Information described by content-based markup is usually intended solely for use by a computer and isn't presented to users at all. Examples of content-based markup include vocabularies that describe metadata (information about information resources) and Active channels, those that describe software packages for installation over a network, and other information not intended for presentation. The majority of new XML vocabularies are content-based because HTML is a presentation-based markup language that has often been unsuccessfully pressed into service as a content-based markup language.

What is presentation-based markup?

Presentation-based markup is used to describe information that will eventually be displayed for users using one or more media. HTML is an example of presentation-based markup, as is the Tutorial Markup Language (TML).

What is hybrid markup?

Hybrid markup includes both presentation- and content-based markup elements. Those markup languages that fall into the hybrid category are usually complex and extensive because they must account for both types of information. Few markup languages can be described as hybrid, but the Chemical Markup Language is an example of a truly hybrid XML vocabulary.

continued ➧

How do I choose the right kind of markup?

Let your markup choice be driven by your content, whether you're creating documents or DTDs. If your content will be used primarily by a computer to accomplish a specific task, use content-based markup to describe it. If your content will be disseminated to users in any medium at all, use presentation-based markup.

Ready, Set, Build

The first eight skills of this book have been an XML primer. You've met many key XML concepts along the way, and you're familiar enough with all of them now to really get your hands dirty. Skill 8 is the first of five chapters that detail the building blocks of XML DTDs and documents. Now that we're finished with the fundamentals, it's time to start building a real DTD. It'll be fun, I promise. Roll up your sleeves, and let's get to work.

Are You up to Speed?

Now you can...

- ☑ **Explain the difference between presentation-based and content-based markup**
- ☑ **Decide what type of markup best fits your content**

PART II

The Building Blocks of XML

SKILL 9

Engineering Elements for a DTD

- The purpose of elements in DTDs and documents
- What the different element types are and when to use them
- The syntax for declaring elements in a DTD
- How to include elements in an XML document
- Element design tips

Elements are the main ingredients in any XML DTD; the tags you use to describe content are the direct result of element definitions. Without elements, there would be no way to label your content so XML processors can read and render it usefully. This skill is the first of five that take a detailed look at the building blocks of XML. In the next few pages, you will learn about the two different types of elements found in any XML DTD or document and the role of elements in a DTD. When you finish, you will know all there is to know about how to declare elements in a DTD and how to use them in a document. We also provide a collection of tips and tricks that make planning effective and well-organized elements for your own DTDs as easy as pie.

The Role of Elements in a DTD

Tags are the heart of any markup language, and elements define what tags make up that markup language. As you saw in the earlier discussion of HTML and in the many examples of markup languages since, tags and elements are a major part of XML. It is safe to say that elements are the primary building block of any XML DTD or document and that all of the other building blocks—attributes, content models, entities, and links—are formed with the elements in mind.

The elements defined in a DTD determine what kind of content a markup language can describe. If a DTD doesn't provide some sort of an element for identifying paragraphs (the case with many of the newly developed XML vocabularies), that markup language can't be used to describe paragraphs. It is as simple as that.

It's impossible to design one DTD that provides every element anyone might need. Trying to meet the demands of providing descriptions for every possible type of content is like tilting at windmills with a lance (and Don Quixote found out the hard way why that's a bad idea). Instead, elements for describing similar kinds of information are grouped into individual DTDs with a closely focused purpose—which is why the list of XML vocabularies is growing like the proverbial weed with each passing day.

In short, elements are the meat of any DTD, and the tags defined by those elements are the major tool employed for the description of content with markup. All of the other markup components are tied in one way or the other to elements. When you're designing a DTD, you typically begin with the elements, and when you're describing a document with markup, you almost always begin with tags.

Learning by Example

Maybe it's all of my college education classes coming back to haunt me, but I've found that examples are often the best teachers, especially when working with precise syntax. As with anything in XML, elements are described in DTDs and referenced by tags in documents in a very specific way. There's also the matter of how individual elements are used in various DTDs to support the DTD's form and function. Examining why a particular DTD employs certain elements to achieve its goal can be very telling.

Throughout this and the next four skills, I'll be using two example DTDs and related documents to illustrate the creation and implementation of the various components of XML. The first example DTD is the Precision Graphics Markup Language (PGML). PGML was developed to describe two-dimensional, scalable graphics to provide graphic designers with a more powerful Web-based tool for describing graphics. The PGML DTD is used to describe in great detail the common structures used in graphic design, such as lines, arcs, rectangles, and circles, as well as provide mechanisms for describing more advanced graphical structures, such as animations and gradients. PGML is a good teaching DTD because it makes use of every XML component, it isn't as long and arduous as with many other XML vocabularies, and it describes content with which many people have some familiarity. My dissection of the PGML DTD and step-by-step creation of a PGML document is intended to give you some insight into how to read and interpret someone else's DTD, a crucial skill in this new XML world.

The second example is the Online Training Markup Language (OTML). Don't bother looking for this DTD on the Web; the only place it exists is in my mind. The OTML is going to be my example of a DTD in development. Through the next several skills, I'll build the OTML DTD and an example document from the ground up. When I'm finished, you will have witnessed firsthand the development of an XML DTD and along the way learned a few things about developing your own DTDs, another crucial XML skill.

Identifying Elements for PGML

The Precision Graphics Markup Language (PGML) includes a variety of elements for describing the various pieces and parts of an image or graphic. The elements in PGML provide a mechanism for describing the following:

- A PGML file that contains drawing objects
- A header with information that describes the graphic
- A group of objects that have common attributes
- A path, its start and end points, and its curve and arc
- A rectangle
- A circle
- An ellipse
- A pie wedge
- An imported image (equivalent to HTML's `<IMG>` tag)
- Text that spans the graphic
- Scripts for controlling the graphic
- Application specific information
- An animation
- A Java animation
- Servers that contain objects, colors, patterns, and filters to be applied to the graphic
- Reusable graphic objects
- A gradient

If it's a graphic and you want to describe it, PGML has every element you'll need.

NOTE The PGML DTD, authored by employees of Adobe, IBM, Netscape, and Sun Microsystems, is currently listed as a note to the W3C and copyrighted by the W3C. You can find the full text of the note online at `http://www.w3.org/TR/1998/NOTE-PGML`.

Identifying Elements for OTML

The Online Training Markup Language (OTML) will be used to describe content for training materials of any kind to be delivered online and to create a document that represents an entire set of training materials. I'm currently using HTML to describe my online training content, but I don't need all of HTML's elements, and there are a few things HTML is missing that I'd like to be able to describe. Currently, each section of material in any given training session is saved as an individual HTML document named `m##p##.html` where `m` stands for module and # is a number from 0 to 9. Page eight of module one is referred to as `m01p08.html`. This is a cumbersome way to work with and save content. If I want to add a new slide in the middle of my training I have to renumber each successive slide after it, and that is no walk in the park.

Although my training sessions are all offered online and the module material is meant to be read on the screen, I've had several users ask me if they can print out the module materials. Because the content is stored in so many different files, they have to print out each page individually from their Web browser. Some modules are over 50 pages long, so this isn't the best solution. I could compile all the materials into a Rich Text Format (RTF), Microsoft Word, or text-only document for printing purposes. This is a time-consuming task, and if I make a change to a slide, I have to remember to change the print document, as well—not an efficient or consistent system.

A final issue that will affect the elements used in OTML is that I often teach in the classroom the same courses I teach online. I need to cover the same material but don't want classroom students to see paragraphs of text on the overhead screen as online students do. Instead, I need a collection of bullet points that illustrate each slide's key content for in-class presentations. I could (and currently do) maintain two separate documents for online and in-class sessions, but a change to one requires a change to the other, and once again, I'm faced with issues of efficiency and consistency. Better to work from one set of files for all instances of the training, regardless of how the content is presented.

My ultimate goal for OTML is to be able to describe an entire training course in one document, using markup to denote each new slide. I'll worry about processing and displaying the document content later on; the most important thing now is designing an XML application that meets my needs.

OTML will need to describe

- A specific training session, such as "Introduction to the World Wide Web and HTML"
- The training session's title, general description level, and prerequisites

- Authorship and copyright information
- Individual slides
- Slide titles
- Slide headings
- Slide paragraphs
- Slide exhibits
- Boldface and italicized text
- Code samples
- Ordered lists
- Unordered lists
- An in-class version of each slide's content (a bulleted list of key topics used offline and hidden online)
- Bullet points for the in-class version

These elements will provide me with all the tags I need to describe a training in a single document for both online and in-class use. I've thrown out all of the extra HTML elements I don't use, such as `TABLES` and `FORMS`, to make my DTDs and documents as clean and compact as possible. (The "Building a Better DTD: Element Planning" section of this skill describes why more elements are not always better.)

Now that you know what role an element plays in both an XML DTD and document, you've met our two example DTDs, and you know what kind of elements they employ, roll up your sleeves and get ready to dig into the guts of XML elements.

Different Types of Elements

There are two different kinds of elements used in XML DTDs and documents: those that can contain text and other elements (`CONTAINERS`), and those that can't (`EMPTY`). Each kind of element has its uses, and you'll find that the majority of XML DTDs employ both.

CONTAINER Elements

A CONTAINER element can hold both regular text and other elements (provided its content model allows it). CONTAINER elements are found throughout HTML. The <HTML>...</HTML> elements are the fundamental CONTAINER elements (called the DOCUMENT element in XML). In fact, the majority of HTML elements are CONTAINER elements. Examples include all of the text-formatting elements, such as the BOLD (<B>...</B>) and ITALICS (<I>...</I>) tags, as well as the ORDERED (<OL>...</OL>) and UNORDERED (<UL>...</UL>) LIST tags. Table markup uses TABLE DATA tags (<TD>...</TD>) nested within TABLE ROW tags (<TR>...</TR>) nested within TABLE tags (<TABLE>...</TABLE>) to create the basic structure of any HTML table.

In both XML and HTML, the START and END tags in CONTAINER elements are like switches: the START tags turns the description on, and the END tag turns it off. Everything in between is assigned the tag's label. Presentation-based markup makes heavy use of CONTAINER elements to describe user content for eventual display. Content-based markup often makes less use of CONTAINER elements.

TIP For a quick refresher on presentation-based and content-based markup, revisit Skill 8, "Working with Different Types of Markup."

EMPTY Elements

EMPTY elements can't contain any text or other elements. In fact, any EMPTY element makes use of only one tag rather than two. What good is an EMPTY element? An EMPTY element alone is usually pretty limited, but an EMPTY element with the right set of attributes can work wonders. EMPTY elements generally rely on their attributes and attribute values to provide the bulk of the information. Content-based markup that requires a high degree of precision makes use of EMPTY elements and attributes with predefined values to closely control what content users can include in their documents. As we work through our PGML and OTML examples, you'll see both CONTAINER and EMPTY elements at work. An example of EMPTY tags used in HTML are <IMG> and <BR>. These tags don't contain text but rather insert objects (images and line breaks) into a Web page.

Declaring Elements in a DTD

So how exactly do you define an XML element? Every DTD has a set of *element declarations* that describe an element and indicate whether it is a CONTAINER or EMPTY element. The syntax for declaring an element is

```
<!ELEMENT name>
```

The *name* portion of the syntax identifies the element's name and indicates which set of characters will be included within the less-than and greater-than signs when the element is invoked by a tag in a document.

TIP

The exclamation point (!) before the ELEMENT notation is very important, so don't leave it out, and don't put a space between ! and ELEMENT.

To create an element called title, use this declaration:

```
<!ELEMENT title>
```

Element declarations often include content models for the given element. Content models can be complex creatures that play by their own rules; I'll discuss them in detail in Skill 11, "Defining Content Models for Elements."

All elements are CONTAINER elements by default. EMPTY elements have the additional string EMPTY added to their element declarations. An EMPTY TITLE element is described by this declaration:

```
<!ELEMENT title EMPTY>
```

That's really all there is to it. Let's take a look at the element declarations that make up the PGML and OTML DTDs.

PGML's Element Declarations

The PGML element declaration list shown below creates elements to describe all the different parts of an image listed earlier in the skill.

```
<!ELEMENT pgml>
<!ELEMENT head>
<!ELEMENT group>
<!ELEMENT path>
<!ELEMENT moveto EMPTY>
<!ELEMENT lineto EMPTY>
<!ELEMENT curveto EMPTY>
```

```
<!ELEMENT arc EMPTY>
<!ELEMENT closepath EMPTY>
<!ELEMENT rectangle EMPTY>
<!ELEMENT circle EMPTY>
<!ELEMENT ellipse EMPTY>
<!ELEMENT piewedge EMPTY>
<!ELEMENT img EMPTY>
<!ELEMENT text>
<!ELEMENT textspan>
<!ELEMENT drawobject>
<!ELEMENT script>
<!ELEMENT private>
<!ELEMENT animation>
<!ELEMENT extension EMPTY>
<!ELEMENT objectserver EMPTY>
<!ELEMENT paintserver EMPTY>
<!ELEMENT colorspaceserver EMPTY>
<!ELEMENT filterserver EMPTY>
<!ELEMENT graphic>
<!ELEMENT lineargradient>
```

These element declarations include a healthy mix of CONTAINER and EMPTY elements. The majority of these elements, both CONTAINER and EMPTY, rely heavily on attributes to provide additional information about the content they describe. If you've looked at the PGML code, you've probably noticed that I removed all the content models from the declarations. I'll put them back later, but for now, I want to highlight the elements.

OTML's Element Declarations

The OTML element declaration list is similar in form but different in function from the PGML list.

```
<!ELEMENT training>
<!ELEMENT head>
<!ELEMENT title>
<!ELEMENT description>
<!ELEMENT level EMPTY>
<!ELEMENT prereq EMPTY>
<!ELEEMNT author>
<!ELEMENT copyright>
<!ELEMENT body>
<!ELEMENT slide>
<!ELEMENT h1>
<!ELEMENT h2>
<!ELEMENT h3>
```

```
<!ELEMENT p>
<!ELEMENT exhibit>
<!ELEMENT b>
<!ELEMENT i>
<!ELEMENT code>
<!ELEMENT ol>
<!ELEMENT ul>
<!ELEMENT li>
<!ELEMENT classroom>
<!ELEMENT bullet>
```

OTML doesn't have nearly as many EMPTY elements as PGML, but remember that the goal of the markup language is to describe content for display on a computer screen or overhead as well as in print. You'll see a few familiar HTML elements such as P, OL, and UL (if it ain't broke don't fix it) along with the new elements. This group of element declarations forms the foundation around which the remaining parts of the DTD will be built.

Referencing Elements in an XML Document

If you've ever used HTML, you've referenced a markup element in a document. XML works in the same way. Tags invoke elements in an XML document. This element declaration defines a TITLE element:

```
<!ELEMENT title>
```

To use the element in an XML document, use this markup:

```
<TITLE>Title text goes here</TITLE>
```

Once again, it's that simple. If the element declaration defines the element as empty, the reference in the element would look like this:

```
<TITLE />
```

The slash (/) before the greater-than sign (>) indicates the element is an EMPTY element.

You must use every element in the manner defined by the element declaration. If an element is a container, it must have both START and END tags. If an element is empty, it can have only one tag and must include the slash before the greater-than sign. Forgetting to close a container, not adding a slash to an EMPTY tag, or trying to use a CONTAINER tag as an EMPTY tag results in an invalid XML document.

Although defining and using XML elements is as easy as it looks, there is a catch (you knew there had to be). The attributes you can use with an element, as well as the text and other elements you can nest within an element, are tightly controlled by attribute and content model declarations (the subjects of the next two skills). You need to bear in mind that we've only just begun our look at how DTDs and documents are formed. By the time we finish, there will be many rules you'll need to know about that affect how you create and reference elements in your DTDs and documents. The following examples of elements at work in PGML and OTML documents rely on rules you haven't met yet, so don't be alarmed if everything you see doesn't make complete sense—all will be revealed in time. Concentrate on the technical aspects of how the tags are formed and on how they describe different types of content.

Elements in a PGML Document

Borrowing a sample from the PGML note, this bit of markup creates a blue circle drawn on top of a red rectangle, which is then placed over a green rectangle. I've added comments to help you dissect the markup.

```
<pgml>
<group fill="1">
    <rectangle fillcolor="green"
               x="100" y="100" width="500" height="500"/>
<!- creates 500 x 500 green rectangle placed 100 pixels down
     and 100 pixels across on the screen ->

    <group opacity=".25">
<!- sets the opacity for the next two objects to 25% ->

      <rectangle fillcolor="red"
                 x="200" y="200" width="200" height="200"/>
<!- creates a 200 x 200 red rectangle placed 200 pixels down
     and 200 pixels across on the screen ->

      <circle fillcolor="blue"
              cx="300" cy="300" r="50"/>
<!- creates a blue circle 300 pixels in diameter with the
     radius at 50 pixels ->

    </group>
  </group>
</pgml>
```

The two RECTANGLE elements and the CIRCLE element are used to describe shapes and are EMPTY elements. The purpose of the RECTANGLE and CIRCLE elements is to provide specifics about shapes. Specifying the shape information can be accomplished with attributes alone, so these elements are empty. However, the group elements are designed to contain other elements and label them as a single group, so the group element has to be a CONTAINER tag.

When interpreted by a processor that knows what to do with it, the previous markup creates an actual graphic, something previously accomplished only with drawing tools such as Adobe Illustrator and Paint Shop Pro. These kinds of programs can produce grand and spectacular effects, but the graphics they generate are rendered in a format that is not Web compatible. PGML can produce the same effects and work on the Web. This definitely isn't your mama's HTML.

Elements in an OTML Document

Remember that OTML is designed to describe a single training and all its content in one document. The next bit of sample code shows how OTML elements might be used to describe the "Introduction to the World Wide Web and HTML" online training material and its first slides. Because I'm building this DTD and its associated document from scratch, this example may appear incomplete. Never fear; I'll flesh it out into a fully valid and viable document by the end.

Using the OTML elements I defined earlier, the start of an OTML document looks like this:

```
<TRAINING>

  <HEAD>
     <TITLE>Introduction to the World Wide Web and HTML</TITLE>
     <DESCRIPTION>Designed to introduce students to the technologies
                  and mechanisms of the Web and HTML. Begins with an
                  overview of the Internet and Web followed by a
                  discussion of HTML and Web page creation. Covers all
                  basic HTML markup.
     </DESCRIPTION>
     <LEVEL />
     <PREREEQ />
     <AUTHOR>Natanya Pitts-Moultis</AUTHOR>
     <AUTHOR>William Brogden</AUTHOR>
     <COPYRIGHT>LANWrights, Inc.</COPYRIGHT>
  </HEAD>
<BODY>
     <SLIDE>
```

```
<TITLE>Introduction to the Internet
      and the World Wide Web
</TITLE>
<P>The Internet is the world's premier global communications net-
work; it's not a monolithic network. Instead, it's a combination of
many programs and functions all working together. Today, the most visi-
ble and important portion of the Internet is the World Wide Web (Web or
W3). The graphics-rich Web is often used as a source of static
(unchanging) data, but its real excitement comes from its interactive
qualities. That is, when you ask it something or input data, it reacts
based on your questions and data. It is a very personal place. One of
the Web's greatest features is that anyone can create and publish Web
documents, usually called Web pages. They are created using a simple
language called HTML (HyperText Markup Language). However, before we
rush off and help you create your own Web offerings, we need to take a
good look at the Internet. In this module, we'll explore the visible
and invisible parts of the Internet. Knowing what is under the hood
will make creating your own Web pages quicker and easier.</P>
<CLASSROOM>
     <BULLET>A worldwide network</BULLET>
     <BULLET>Web is the most visible</BULLET>
     <BULLET>HTML is used to create Web pages</BULLET>
     <BULLET>Understanding the Web is key to creating
           good Web pages</BULLET>
</CLASSROOM>
</SLIDE>
</BODY>
</TRAINING>
```

While OTML's elements alone do a pretty good job of describing the training and its slides, just wait until I add the attributes and entities. Every element in every XML DTD and document is designed and invoked in exactly the same way, regardless of the goal or design of the individual XML vocabulary to which the element belongs. When you're working with someone else's DTD, your main concern is interpreting the DTD and using the elements correctly. When you're designing your own DTD, you're responsible for designing your own elements and using them correctly, which is not always as easy at it may sound.

Building a Better DTD: Element Planning

DTD design is a high art form practiced by many but truly mastered by few. If you've never designed your own DTD, you're in for an interesting time. This is not to say that writing your own DTD and developing your very own XML vocabulary isn't rewarding and well worth the challenges it presents. However, you don't want to stumble into your design quickly or blindly, or you'll find yourself rebuilding your DTD from the ground up several times before you're happy with it.

In the next five skills, you'll find special sections like this one that focus on tips and tricks designed to make your DTD building adventures more fun and rewarding. Although they certainly aren't the definitive guides to DTD building, they contain some good ideas and important caveats.

In this section, I address some important organizational and efficiency issues that are related to the definition of elements in a DTD. Because elements are the foundation of any DTD, you want to make sure that the elements you define will serve their intended purpose without stepping on each other's toes or making document design cumbersome. To that end, there are some general organizational issues you need to address and a couple of interesting tricks that you can use.

Planning Ahead Saves Time Later On

It seems as if all our lives we've been admonished to make a plan and be prepared. While spontaneity can be fun and adventurous, there is no room for it in DTD design. A DTD should work like a well-oiled machine, providing document developers with the highest quality tools for describing content in the best way possible. That kind of quality and efficiency is achieved only through careful planning and well thought out execution. Even when armed with all the syntactical information you need to create element declarations in your DTD, there's quite a bit of work to do before you type your first `<!`.

Why are you creating a DTD in the first place? The answer to this question will drive your element design in a significant way. A one- or two-line answer here won't serve you very well. Instead, you need to dissect the motives, needs, and final expectations for your DTD before you can begin writing it. To help get you started, I've compiled a list of questions.

1. How can I best describe the information that will be defined with the markup from my DTD?
2. Is the information content- or presentation-based?
3. What established XML vocabularies are already available to describe my content?
4. What are these vocabularies missing that make me feel that I have to define my own vocabulary?
5. How can I break my content down into its individual pieces?

Once you've satisfactorily answered these questions, you might want to sit down with a knowledgeable friend or coworker to discuss your answers further. Encourage your partner to play the devil's advocate, pointing out omissions and challenging your assertion that you have to write your own DTD. Figuring out what's missing from currently available DTDs helps you decide what to put in your own. Finally, examine closely the individual pieces of your content. These pieces will eventually serve as the blueprint for your individual elements. Make sure that the pieces aren't so large that they can be ambiguous or encompass too much information. At the same time, you don't want them to be too small, or you'll have a million elements in your DTD (see the "Why More Isn't Always Better" section).

To show you what the question and answer process is like and the results it can produce, here's a transcript of the answers I gave to these key questions when I began the design process for the OTML DTD.

1. *How can I best describe the information that will be defined with the markup from my DTD?*
   This DTD will be used not only to describe the particulars about any given online training but also to contain all of the training's content in a single document. The DTD needs to include standard mechanisms for describing the training's categorization and authorship information as well as the "guts" of the training. The markup language will need to work with our current online training Java/JavaScript environment.

2. *Is the information content- or presentation-based?*
   The initial information that categorizes the training is content-based, but the slide information (the majority of the content) is presentation-based and meant to be displayed on a computer screen or an overhead projector or to be printed out by students.

3. *What established XML vocabularies are already available to describe my content?*
   HTML and the Tutorial Markup Language (TML).

4. *What are these vocabularies missing that make me feel like I have to define my own vocabulary?*
   Although HTML has a plethora of elements for defining the slide content, it doesn't have any mechanisms for identifying training particulars or individual slides. TML's focus is more on an evaluation system for training content rather than a way of displaying the actual content. In addition, TML doesn't provide a way to define individual slides or sections for an individual training. Because we already have our own evaluation system, TML is a bit redundant.

5. *How can I break my content down into its individual pieces?*
   The two main sections of the content are the head and body. The head should contain

- Title, description, authorship, and copyright information
- Course difficulty specifics and prerequisites

  The body will need to include

  - A mechanism for identifying slides
  - Heading levels and paragraphs
  - Graphics
  - Bold, italic, and code formatting at the text level
  - Lists
  - A way to identify bulleted items for a classroom version of each slide

This is representative of the kind of information you need to have before you begin designing your DTD. It's often helpful when a team of developers working together on a single DTD create a design document that answers these five basic questions. Pass the document around, and allow everyone to put in his or her two cents. You'll find that the design for your DTD begins to emerge rather quickly, as your design document becomes more detailed. When you're done answering these questions, you should have a good idea of not only where you're going with your DTD but how you're going to get there.

Learn from What Already Works

In this and the previous skills, I've used a number of examples of real-life XML vocabularies and DTDs at work because there is much to learn from what already works. XML vocabularies are emerging almost daily, and many of them are the result of work by some of the industry's biggest and best developers, including the likes of Microsoft, IBM, Sun, Adobe, and Netscape. These organizations have the resources and motivation to put together quality, functioning, well-designed vocabularies. It makes sense to pay attention to the mechanisms they use in their own DTDs.

TIP

One of the best sources of information on developing XML vocabularies is `http://www.schema.net`, maintained by James Tauber. You'll find links to all the key information relating to most XML DTDs conveniently grouped for easy access. Bookmark this page, and visit it often to see what others are doing with XML.

When HTML first appeared on the scene, before all the books and Web sites about creating Web pages began to multiply like rabbits, early Web developers learned a great deal from each other by making use of the View Source button common to all Web browsers. Often the answer to "How'd they do that?" provided an answer to "How can I do that?" Although learning HTML from other people's Web pages may not have been 100 percent reliable, it was definitely a place to start.

XML is a stickler for standards, and the majority of XML DTDs under development today are well documented, so learning from others is a safe and reliable way to master good DTD design. The best way to understand why a certain DTD uses certain elements is to read the documentation for the DTD and answer the five key planning questions. This examination process will quickly turn you into a student of DTD design, which is the whole point of this little exercise in the first place.

Learning by example and using other DTDs as models are perfectly acceptable and fall under the fair-use category of copyright law. You can glean all you want from other people's work, and imitation is still considered the highest form of flattery. However, taking someone else's work and calling it your own is a flagrant violation of international copyright law and could land you in serious trouble. Learn all you can from what others have done, but always remember that in the act of creating those DTDs and documents the designer automatically retains copyright.

Don't Reinvent the Wheel

Before you create your own DTD, make sure all that effort is really necessary. Because XML can't just be displayed in all of its glory as HTML can, you'll need to worry about processing and browsing your XML DTDs and documents in addition to creating them. It may be that one or two DTDs out there meet most, but not all, your needs. Feel free to write complementary DTDs designed to work with existing DTDs. The processing and browsing software designed for those DTDs may not work seamlessly with your new DTD, but it's a place to start.

The Web wouldn't exist without the collaborative efforts of many individuals around the world. Vendors and developers have been working together for the last several years on projects of mutual interest and benefit. You may want to contact those developers who are working on the DTDs that almost meet your needs and see what their future plans are. Offer constructive feedback, and let them know how you or your organization might use an expanded version of the

DTD. If you've written your own companion DTD, show them what you've done. (You still retain copyright.) You or your organization might even want to form a partnership to further the interests of everyone involved.

Reinventing the wheel is a time-consuming task that eats away at resources that could be used in more fruitful pursuits. However, improving the wheel or creating your own unique wheel based on basic wheel design can be gratifying and productive.

The Friendly Flash Card

Okay, this is going to sound a bit strange, but I'm going to say it anyway. Use flash cards in your planning stages to identify the elements you plan to include in your DTD. Give each element its own card and you can use the cards later to help add attributes and create content models. Lay your flash cards out on a table to see what elements you've already designed and picture how they might all work together. This can help you avoid redundancies and keep your elements organized. I've used this method a time or two myself, especially when I was first experimenting with DTD design. I know it sounds a bit archaic, but if you try it, you'll be pleasantly surprised with the results.

To Contain or Not to Contain?

One of the important decisions you have to make when developing elements in a DTD is whether each individual element will be a standard `CONTAINER` or an `EMPTY` tag. Of course, the information the element is intended to convey will drive in large part the type of element you choose to use. Content-based markup makes frequent use of `EMPTY` elements, whereas presentation-based markup uses more `CONTAINER` elements. Review Skill 8 for a guide as to when you should use content-based or presentation-based markup.

In general, if you need to tightly control the way content is worded or specified, you'll want to use `EMPTY` elements with lots of attributes and carefully controlled values. The `LEVEL` and `PREREQ` elements in the OTML DTD are empty, so I can use attributes and their respective values to achieve consistency among level and prerequisite information.

When you are designing markup to describe content that will eventually be displayed in some way, you'll find that traditional `CONTAINER` elements will suit your needs best. It doesn't make any sense to use an empty P element with a CONTENTS= attribute to hold the guts of the paragraph, when a paragraph CONTAINER tag with a START and END tag will work just as well. The more you work with DTDs, the easier it will be to decide what type of element to use for each type of information. Experiment with each type of element for a particular type of content until you're satisfied with the results.

Why More Isn't Always Better

More elements aren't always better. One of the big problems with HTML is that vendors keep expanding it to meet developer's demands. The whole idea behind XML is to create focused DTDs that work with a specific type of information. If you try to create a single, comprehensive DTD you soon discover that it will become unruly and difficult to organize and maintain. Keep your list of elements concise, and don't create gratuitous elements just because you've seen them in other DTDs or in HTML.

Keep At It

The last bit of advice I can offer about defining elements in a DTD and for working with DTDs in general is to keep working until you're satisfied. Don't settle for a DTD that "will do"; keep testing and refining your DTD until it meets your needs in an effective and efficient way. As you work on your DTD, you'll learn a great deal about XML and DTD design, and you'll find that development gets easier with time.

Getting Specific with Attributes

While elements are the foundation of any XML DTD or document, attributes provide more specific information about elements and their contents. In Skill 10, we'll examine this next building block of XML.

Are You up to Speed?

Now you can...

- ☑ Explain what an XML element is
- ☑ Describe the difference betwee container and empty elements
- ☑ Define an element in a DTD
- ☑ Use tags to invoke an element in an XML document
- ☑ Describe tricks and tips that help you create well-organized and well-designed elements in a DTD

SKILL 10

Assigning Attributes to Elements

- The role attributes play in DTDs and documents
- The syntax for specifying attributes in a DTD
- The syntax for including attributes with elements in a document
- Attribute-specific DTD design tips

Attributes are the icing on the XML element cake. Whereas elements describe content in general, attributes provide more specific information about the element's content. In this skill, you'll learn how to define element lists for individual elements in DTDs, add attributes to tags in documents, and plan attributes for a DTD. Once again, the PGML and OTML DTDs will serve as working examples of this all-important XML construct.

The Role of Attributes in a DTD

XML uses elements to describe content in a general way. Paragraphs are different from headings, which are different from lists; therefore, each different type of content gets its own tag or set of tags. However, just because all paragraphs are labeled as paragraphs doesn't mean that they are all 100 percent alike. Instead, each paragraph is an instance of content that carries a paragraph label, but the paragraph may have its own unique characteristics and role in the document. The first paragraph of a document is different in location and function than the last paragraph. For example, a sidebar paragraph is different from a main body paragraph. A PARAGRAPH element alone can't make the distinction between these many different types of paragraphs. This tag just labels them as paragraphs, and it has done its duty.

When you want to get more specific about particular content described by an element, you have a couple of choices. The first choice is to use other elements to describe it in more detail. For example, a sidebar paragraph could be described using <P> elements nested within <SBAR> elements, like this:

```
<SBAR>
     <P>
          This is a paragraph in a sidebar.
     </P>
<SBAR>
```

Or, the first paragraph in a document might be described using <FIRST> elements nested within <P> elements, like this:

```
<P>
     <FIRST>
          This is the first paragraph of the document.
     </FIRST>
</P>
```

While this simple nesting method may be just fine for adding one level of specification to a content's description, it starts to break down after a while. Let's elaborate.

Imagine if each image in HTML were described using a series of tags nested within each other. The definition for one image might look something like this:

```
<IMG>
     <SRC>http://www.mysite.com/graphics/image3.gif</SRC>
     <ALIGN>LEFT</ALIGN>
     <VALIGN>MIDDLE</ALIGN>
     <ALT>A sample image</ALT>
     <BORDER>0</BORDER>
     <WIDTH>150</WIDTH>
     <HEIGHT>100</HEIGHT>
</IMG>
```

Not very effective is it? This is a glimpse of what an attribute-free markup world would look like. Element nesting would go on and on and on, level upon level. And because XML isn't as forgiving as HTML, it would take only one missing closing tag to break the entire page. Not a pretty sight (or Web site for that matter)!

Luckily, attributes exist as mechanisms for providing more specific information about any given instance of an element in a document. Attributes allow you to create top-level elements that describe all of the major pieces and parts of a document. You can also define attribute lists to go with those elements that will provide more detail as needed.

The attributes defined for each element in a DTD are just as important as the elements they work with. Attribute definitions can also include specific information that shows which attributes are required each time a tag is used and which attributes are optional. The user can type the values of attributes in, or the user can choose from a predefined set of values. Some attributes even have fixed values that you can't change. To successfully create valid XML documents, you must know whether an attribute is required or optional and know which type of value it takes. Your document will break if you leave out a required attribute, use a value that's not in the predefined list, or change the value of a fixed attribute.

From a DTD designer's standpoint, attributes are powerful tools used to tightly control how document developers include information in documents and to control the type of information developers include in documents. With attributes, you can require that certain information is included each time an element is used and set fixed values to assure that the XML processor has what it needs to successfully process documents written for the DTD. The correct attribute definitions can also help avoid problems caused by data inconsistencies, which are all too prevalent among documents created by human authors.

Skill 10

Attributes consist of an attribute name and an associated value. For example, in HTML, `SRC` is an attribute for the `IMG` tag, and the location of the image is the attribute's value. `VALIGN` is another `IMG` tag attribute, and its value can be `LEFT`,

MIDDLE, or RIGHT. The combination of the name and the value makes up the entire attribute unit.

As you saw in Skill 8, "Working with Different Types of Markup," attributes can be used in many different ways, depending on the goals and purposes of each individual DTD. In the next couple of sections, I'll examine how attributes are used in my two sample DTDs, the Precision Graphics Markup Language (PGML), which is under development by Adobe and several other organizations, and my own Online Training Markup Language (OTML), which is currently in the works as an alternative solution to HTML for describing content for Web-based training.

The Role of Attributes in PGML

For the most part, attributes in PGML are used to provide specific information about the properties of a unique graphic object described by PGML. The FONT attributes supply text size and word- and character-spacing specifics. Even HANDLER attributes link specific functions (defined using a scripting language such as JavaScript) to certain user actions, such as moving a mouse over or off an object (onmouseover and onmouseout) or clicking on an object (onclick).

None of the attributes in PGML have predefined value lists, because the goal of the language is to define unique objects with their own specific properties. Lists of predefined values wouldn't work because there's no realistic way to determine all of the possible values a graphical object could use to describe itself. Trying to generate such lists would be not only an exercise in futility but also a DTD design nightmare. Instead, PGML concentrates on providing a mechanism for describing all the properties of any given object and leaves the actual value assignments up to the document developer. Consequently, PGML contains a wide variety of attributes but virtually no predefined values.

The Role of Attributes in OTML

Because my goals for OTML aren't the same as those of PGML's developers, I use attributes in the OTML DTD differently. The attributes in the OTML DTD serve several purposes:

- A unique identification code must be assigned to each training that is independent of the TITLE element already included in the DTD. This helps catalog and identify various versions of the same training.

- I also want to ensure that all level and prerequisite description information is entered in the same way, so I use attributes with predefined values for those elements to restrict document developers' choice of descriptors.
- It's important that the `COPYRIGHT` element include the year each training was copyrighted, so the `COPYRIGHT` element includes a required `DATE` attribute.
- The `EXHIBIT` element describes a graphic or picture used in the training, so an attribute provides a mechanism for including an alternative text description of the exhibit.
- An ordered list may be numerical or alphabetical. A numerical list may require Roman or Arabic numerals, and an alphabetical list may require either upper- or lowercase letters. Taking a cue from HTML, my ordered list includes a `TYPE` attribute to further specify what kind of ordered list it is.
- There may be more than one level of bullets in a slide used for classroom presentation. Rather than nest bullets within bullets, I use a `LEVEL` attribute to define where a particular bullet is in the hierarchy of a slide. Although the same effect could be achieved by nesting bullets within bullets, the attribute method allows me to group and identify all of the bullets in a side-by-side level.

OTML doesn't use as many attributes as PGML, but OTML is also designed to describe a great deal of original user content that is primarily text-oriented. I'm not trying to describe the various pieces and parts of an image in detail, but instead, I'm interested in describing large chunks of information. I simply don't need as many attributes. In both XML vocabularies, attributes are used to provide more specific information about an element, but the nature of each type of information is different; therefore, it requires different attributes. You'll find that the same can be said about any two compared XML DTDs.

Different Types of Attributes

XML attributes can be grouped into three different categories:

- Required
- Fixed
- Implied

Each type of attribute has its specific uses in a DTD, and the type assigned to an attribute can greatly affect document developers. It's important for both DTD designers and document developers to know how and why each type is used. I'll discuss these types of attributes in the following sections.

Required

Required attributes are just that: required. If an element's attribute is labeled in the DTD as required, it must appear each time the element does. If the required element is missing, the document will be invalid.

NOTE Only validating XML parsers check the DTD for required attributes.

Required attributes are useful tools for DTD developers because they help guide document developers and ensure that the information necessary for the successful processing of a document is always included in the document. Required attributes aren't necessarily a bane to document developers, but as a developer, you do need to be on the lookout for required attributes. A good XML document-editing tool will help remind you that an attribute is required, and it will flag elements that are missing required elements.

The PGML DTD doesn't include any required elements, but my OTML DTD does. The unique training identification, the level and prerequisite specifics, and the copyright date must all be present in any OTML document.

Fixed

Fixed attributes are (like their required sibling) exactly what they sound like: fixed. A fixed attribute has a value that can't be changed by the document developer. This unchangeable value is defined as the attribute's default value (discussed in the "Defining the Default Value for an Attribute" section), and each time the attribute appears, its value must match the default.

WARNING If you change the value of a fixed attribute, your document will be invalid. Nonvalidating parsers won't catch this error, but validating ones will.

Fixed attributes are not required attributes, so a document developer doesn't have to include the attribute and its fixed value with every instance of the element's value. However, when developers do choose the fixed attribute, they can't use any other value with it.

Fixed values provide a way for DTD developers to include necessary information and prevent document developers from changing it. You'll find fixed values more often in content-based markup than in presentation-based markup. Content-based markup is meant mostly for computer consumption and usually must be accurate to process correctly.

As they do with required attributes, document developers need to be aware of fixed attributes. Care should be taken to use the correct default value each time they include the attribute with its element. Once again, a good authoring tool should flag fixed attributes and either not allow their values to be changed or (at least) object strenuously when they are.

Neither the PGML nor OTML DTDs use fixed attributes. PGML needs to be flexible enough to describe a wide range of objects, and fixed values aren't conducive to that goal. OTML is designed to describe a wide variety of training information, and I simply haven't found a need for fixed attributes.

Implied

If an attribute isn't required or fixed, it is implied. An implied attribute doesn't even have a default value, and it doesn't have to be used each time its associated element is used. Values for implied attributes are always text strings, and implied attributes never have predefined lists of possible values.

The `SRC` and `ALT` attributes of the HTML `IMG` tag are examples of attributes whose values are implied. The unique address of an image or the alternative text used to describe it will be different every time, so there's no reason to try to predict each possible address. Almost all of the attributes in the PGML DTD are implied because they provide user-specified information about a unique graphic. There's no basic default graphic from which all other graphics are built, so there's no need to have a default value for the attributes used to describe a graphic.

> **TIP** Also note that according to the HTML 4.0 recommendation, the `SRC` and `ALT` attributes for the `IMAGE` tag are required, and your HTML documents are invalid if you don't include both attributes for each and every instance of the `<IMG>` tag.

The only implied attributes you'll find in the OTML DTD are the `SRC` and `ALT` attributes for the `<EXHIBIT>` tag. These attributes are designed to allow users to define a unique Web address and text alternative to an exhibit shown in the training. I can't anticipate every exhibit's URL or its description, so there's no need for defaults or predefined value lists.

The different types of attributes are designed to both control document developer content and give developers the freedom to include unique information as attribute values. DTD designers should use the right kind of attribute for the job, as discussed in the "Best Attribute for the Job" section you'll find further on in this skill.

Different Types of Attribute Values

Just as there are different types of attributes, there are different types of attribute values. Both an attribute's type and its role in the DTD and the documents created for the DTD drive an attribute to take one of four different types of values:

- Plain text
- A unique ID
- A predefined list of values
- A nontext entity

In addition, most attributes have a default value that is automatically assigned to the attribute if the document developer doesn't assign one. Each different type of value contributes significantly to the role the associated attribute plays in both DTDs and documents.

Plain Text

Plain text values, also known as `CDATA`, are simply strings of text specified by the document developer. The majority of implied attributes have plain text as their value type because the purpose of an implied attribute is to give the user the flexibility to define their own values. This is the simplest form of attribute value you'll find.

Unique ID

An ID value is used to assign a unique `IDENTIFICATION` tag to each element in a document. Traditionally used with an attribute named `ID`, this attribute value cannot be the same for any two elements in the same document without rendering the document both malformed and invalid. By assigning a unique `IDENTIFICATION` tag to each element in a document, the element is made available to both style sheets and scripting languages for easy manipulation. Although you can describe an element to a script or style sheet as "the third paragraph in the second first-level heading," the description changes the second you add another paragraph or first-level heading.

XML doesn't include any specific rules about how you should assign IDs to elements, other than mandating that the ID should begin with an alphanumeric character. You are free to create your own ID system, but don't use the same ID twice.

NOTE

It's customary to assign the name `ID` to the attribute that takes a unique ID value. Although this is not required, it does help keep track of your attributes and their functions and is intuitive to document developers.

Predefined

If you've worked with HTML even a little bit, you're familiar with attributes that have predefined values. Instead of supplying their own attribute values, document developers choose from a list of values preset by the DTD designer. The ability to predefine the values for any given attribute gives DTD designers an added measure of control and helps ensure that document developers provide the exact attribute value necessary for the document's content to be processed correctly. In addition, the combination of a required attribute with a list of predefined values can be a powerful one for the DTD designer. This ensures that the attribute is present and has the correct type of value.

WARNING

If you assign a value other than a predefined value to an attribute that has a set of predefined values, your document will be invalid when checked against its DTD.

You'll find that predefined values are abundant in both presentation-based and content-based markup. In presentation-based DTDs, predefined value lists help provide a list of parameters developers can use to define content in a consistent way. Imagine that the `ALIGN=` attribute for the HTML `IMG` tag did not have a set of predefined values. Soon you'd find values like middle-right, top-left, top-middle, and other interesting descriptors of alignment. While these different values may be comprehensible to humans, a computer wouldn't know what to do with them. There's no way for the processor designer to anticipate every possible value for `ALIGN=` and instruct the display device how to interpret and render those alignments. Providing a list of predefined values solves many of the problems inherent in the way different people describe the same value.

Content-based markup makes use of predefined value lists for the same reasons presentation-based markup does: to control developer input. Because content-based documents are primarily for computer consumption, a list of predefined values helps avoid errors.

Nontext Entity

If you want to include nontext entities, such as graphics and multimedia files, you first have to declare them using an entity declaration (discussed in depth in Chapter 12, "Employing Entities in DTDs and Documents"). To reference the entity in your document, you'll need to use an attribute that is defined to take an entity value. The SRC= attribute for the HTML IMG tag is an example of an attribute that takes an entity value.

NOTE If you don't declare an entity with an entity declaration before you include it as a value for a given attribute, your document will be both invalid and malformed.

Default Values for Attributes

Many attributes have default values that are automatically assigned to them if the document developer doesn't stipulate a value. Default values are most commonly assigned to attributes with a predefined list of values. Fixed attributes also employ a default value; the default value is the only possible value for this type of attribute. Attributes that take plain text, unique IDs, and entity values generally don't have default values.

If an attribute with a default value isn't included in a document by a document developer, the parser automatically acts as if the attribute and its default value have actually been included. This is a nice shortcut for document developers. If the default value of an attribute works for you, there's no reason to even type in the attribute and its value. Let the parser do the work for you.

HTML makes extensive use of default values, especially for the ALIGN= attributes defined for the PARAGRAPH, HEADING, IMAGE, and TABLE tags. Web page developers generally include an attribute that has a default value with a tag only when they want to change the value. As a DTD designer, you'll want to make sure to include defaults for every element that has a predefined list of values.

Defining Attributes in a DTD

So now you know all about the role attributes play in a document as well as the different types of attributes and values you'll be working with in your DTD and document design and development. The next step to mastering attributes is learning how to define them in a DTD and reference them in an XML document.

Attributes are defined in a DTD with attribute-list declarations. Any given declaration specifies the element to which the list of attributes is assigned, the individual attributes themselves, a type for each attribute in the list, and a default value if there is one. You can have multiple attribute-list declarations for any one element or combine all your attribute definitions into one list declaration. In general, it's better to have only one declaration per entity to make organization and maintenance of a DTD's elements easier.

The syntax for an attribute-list declaration is

```
<!ATTLIST element-name
     attribute-name value-type attribute-type "default">
```

The `attribute-name value-type attribute-type "default"` section of the list may be repeated as often as necessary to create multiple attributes for any given element. Each attribute definition may or may not include all of the components shown in the syntax (i.e., the name, value-type, attribute-type, and default). Each definition must include at least the attribute name and value type. The attribute type and default value are present only when necessary. A simplified version of the attribute list for the HTML `IMG` tag takes this form:

```
<!ATTLIST img
     SRC #CDATA #IMPLIED
     ALIGN (left | right | center) "left" >
```

A specific label identifies each type of attribute and value type. Table 10.1 lists the attribute types and their associated labels, while Table 10.2 lists the attribute value types and their associated labels.

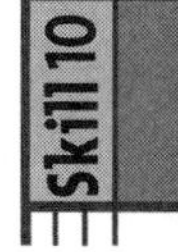

TABLE 10.1: Attribute Types and Their Labels

Type	Label
Required	#REQUIRED
Fixed	#FIXED
Implied	#IMPLIED

NOTE Each attribute-type label is prefaced with a pound (#) sign, which must be present in an attribute-list definition for the parser to be able to recognize the attribute-type label.

TABLE 10.2: Attribute Value Types and Their Labels

Type	Label
Plain text	`CDATA`
Unique ID	`ID`
Nontext entity	`ENTITY`
Predefined	`(value | value | … | value)`

NOTE You'll notice that the plain text, ID, and entity-value types are all identified by name, whereas a predefined list is indicated by a list of values enclosed within parentheses.

In earlier sections I described attribute and value types, and you know that each attribute type typically has a specific value type that it can take. Table 10.3 brings everything together and illustrates how different attribute types and value types may be combined for different purposes.

TABLE 10.3: Pairing Attribute Types and Values

Attribute Type	Value Type	Use	DTD Syntax
Implied	Plain text	To allow users to enter their own text-string values	`<!ATTLIST img border CDATA #IMPLIED>`
Required	Plain text	To require that users enter their own text-string values	`<!ATTLIST img alt CDATA #REQUIRED>`
Required	Unique ID	To require that users assign a unique identifier to each instance of an element	`<!ATTLIST img id ID #REQUIRED>`

TABLE 10.3 CONTINUED: Pairing Attribute Types and Values

Attribute Type	Value Type	Use	DTD Syntax
Required	Nontext entity	To require that users include the attribute with an entity value each time the element is used	<!ATTLIST img src ENTITY #REQUIRED>
Required	Predefined	To require that users include an attribute with a value chosen from a predetermined list of choices each time the element is used	<!ATTLIST img align (left|right|center) #REQUIRED "left"
Fixed	Plain text	To permanently attach a value to an attribute	<!ATTLIST img valign CDATA FIXED "middle"

NOTE

Any of the attributes formed with the required attribute label may also be used without the required label as regular attributes to be included at the developer's discretion.

You can mix and match attribute types and value types to meet your needs, although you'll discover that the combinations shown in Table 10.3 are the ones most commonly used.

PGML's Attribute-Definition Lists

PGML has some fairly extensive attribute-definition lists because it makes frequent use of attributes to allow document developers to define specifics for a unique graphical object. The whole list of attribute-definition lists is a bit too lengthy to include here, but I've included two lists from the DTD so you can see how attributes are used in PGML.

```
<!ATTLIST img
     %event_handler_attributes;
     %gs_general_attributes;
     x CDATA #IMPLIED
     y CDATA #IMPLIED
     width CDATA #IMPLIED
     height CDATA #IMPLIED
     src CDATA #IMPLIED
>
```

This first attribute-definition list is for the `IMG` element and includes the following attributes:

`x` Defines the *x* coordinate of the image's upper left-hand corner and is used to place the image on the page.

`y` Defines the *y* coordinate of the image's upper left-hand corner and is used to place the image on the page.

`width` Defines the width of the image.

`height` Defines the height of the image.

`src` Defines the source of the image.

All of these attributes take plain text values and are neither required nor fixed. Each is designed to solicit specific information from the developer about an external image to be imported into the document. The attribute-definition list also makes use of two parameter entities, and I'll discuss the very flexible and useful parameter entities in Skill 12.

The attribute-definition list for the `ANIMATION` element includes a wide variety of attributes for describing and controlling an animation. Once again, all of these attributes take text-only values and don't have default or predefined values, because they are designed to provide the developer with a way to define a unique animation.

```
<!ATTLIST animation
     target CDATA #IMPLIED
     starttime CDATA #IMPLIED
     duration CDATA #IMPLIED
     repetitions CDATA #IMPLIED
     motion CDATA #IMPLIED
     motionspeed CDATA #IMPLIED
     autorotate CDATA #IMPLIED
     scale CDATA #IMPLIED
     scalespeed CDATA #IMPLIED
     rotate CDATA #IMPLIED
     rotatespeed CDATA #IMPLIED
```

```
        xtranslate CDATA #IMPLIED
        xtranslatespeed CDATA #IMPLIED
        ytranslate CDATA #IMPLIED
        ytranslatespeed CDATA #IMPLIED
        xshear CDATA #IMPLIED
        xshearspeed CDATA #IMPLIED
        yshear CDATA #IMPLIED
        yshearspeed CDATA #IMPLIED
        opacity CDATA #IMPLIED
        opacityspeed CDATA #IMPLIED
        red CDATA #IMPLIED redspeed
         CDATA #IMPLIED
        green CDATA #IMPLIED
        greenspeed CDATA #IMPLIED
        blue CDATA #IMPLIED
        bluespeed CDATA #IMPLIED
        hue CDATA #IMPLIED
        huespeed CDATA #IMPLIED
        saturation CDATA #IMPLIED
        saturationspeed CDATA #IMPLIED
        brightness CDATA #IMPLIED
        brightnessspeed CDATA #IMPLIED
>
```

OTML's Attribute-Definition Lists

The attribute-definition lists I've created in the OTML DTD are a bit more concise and different in scope and use than those found in the PGML DTD. The complete set of attribute-definition lists for OTML includes

```
<!ATTLIST training
     id ID #REQUIRED>

<!ATTLIST level
     classification
     (intro | intermediate | advanced) #REQUIRED "intro">

<!ATTLIST prereq
     classification
     (none | computer-basic | computer-advanced | web-basic |
      web-intermediate | web-advanced) #REQUIRED "none">

<!ATTLIST copyright
     date CDATA #REQUIRED "1998">

<!ATTLIST exhibit
     src ENTITY #REQUIRED
     alt CDATA #IMPLIED>
```

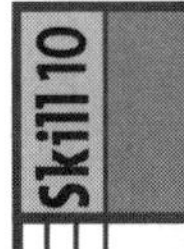

```
<!ATTLIST ol
     type (alpha-lower | alpha-upper | number-arabic |
     number-roman) "number-arabic">

<!ATTLIST bullet
     level CDATA #IMPLIED>
```

Because I use attributes to describe several different types of content—from training identification to list type—the OTML attribute-definition lists run the gamut of attribute and value types. The flexibility of the XML attribute mechanism is one of the most powerful tools a DTD designer has at their disposal.

Adding Attributes to Tags in a Document

Once a designer has harnessed the power of attributes in a DTD, it's up to the document developer to employ attributes correctly and consistently. Even if your document just needs to be well formed and not valid, it's best to get used to using attributes as directed by the DTD. As HTML users know, you can assign an attribute to an element using this syntax:

```
<ELEMENT ATTRIBUTE="value">
```

You can include as many attributes within the less-than and greater-than signs of an element as the DTD provides.

Attribute values must always be included within quotation marks, or your document will be malformed.

Be careful not to include any attribute twice within the same element—especially if each instance has a separate value—or your document will be malformed. And, of course, don't forget to include required attributes as necessary, and don't change the value of fixed elements.

You can't mix and match attributes from one element with another. Attributes work only with the elements they are defined for, so if you want to use an attribute with more than one element, you'll have to define it for each element independently. In addition, just because two or more elements share attributes that have the same name doesn't mean those attributes have to have the same type or take the same values.

That's really all there is to adding attributes to an element. The HTML IMG tag with several of its attributes looks like this (using proper XML syntax, of course):

```
<IMG SRC="graphics/nav-gif1.gif" ALIGN="center" VALIGN="top"
     ALT="Navigation image" BORDER="0">
```

Regardless of type or purpose, all XML elements and attributes are formed in the same way.

Attributes in a PGML Document

You've seen that attributes are used in the PGML document to provide specific information about a unique graphic. Here is the same bit of sample PGML code I showed you in Skill 9, complete with attributes:

```
<pgml>
<group fill="1">
    <rectangle fillcolor="green"
               x="100" y="100" width="500" height="500"/>
<!- creates 500 x 500 green rectangle placed 100 pixels down
     and 100 pixels across on the screen ->

    <group opacity=".25">
<!- sets the opacity for the next two objects to 25% ->

      <rectangle fillcolor="red"
                 x="200" y="200" width="200" height="200"/>
<!- creates a 200 x 200 red rectangle placed 200 pixels down
     and 200 pixels across on the screen ->

      <circle fillcolor="blue"
              cx="300" cy="300" r="50"/>
<!- creates a blue circle 300 pixels in diameter with the
     radius at 50 pixels ->

    </group>
  </group>
</pgml>
```

Skill 10

By simply changing a few attribute values I can create a completely different graphic:

```
<pgml>
<group fill="1">
    <rectangle fillcolor="teal"
               x="100" y="100" width="350" height="350"/>
<!- creates 350 x 350 teal rectangle placed 100 pixels down
     and 100 pixels across on the screen ->
```

```
    <group opacity=".15">
<!- sets the opacity for the next two objects to 15% ->

      <rectangle fillcolor="yellow"
                x="300" y="300" width="200" height="200"/>
<!- creates a 200 x 200 red rectangle placed 200 pixels down
     and 200 pixels across on the screen ->

      <circle fillcolor="green"
             cx="300" cy="300" r="50"/>
<!- creates a green circle 300 pixels in diameter with the
     radius at 50 pixels ->

    </group>
  </group>
</pgml>
```

The first rectangle is now teal rather than green and 350 pixels by 350 pixels in size. The rectangle-circle group has an opacity of 15 percent, the rectangle is yellow instead of red, and the circle is green rather than blue. The markup is very similar, but a few simple changes in attribute values generate a completely different graphical object.

Attributes in an OTML Document

In OTML, attributes provide more specific information about a training and its contents. You'll recall this code sample from Skill 9:

```
<TRAINING >

  <HEAD>
     <TITLE>Introdcution to the World Wide Web and HTML</TITLE>
     <DESCRIPTION>Designed to introduce students to the technologies
                  and mechanisms of the Web and HTML. Begins with an
                  overview of the Internet and Web followed by a
                  discussion of HTML and Web page creation. Covers all
                  basic HTML markup.
     </DESCRIPTION>
     <LEVEL />
     <PREREEQ />
     <AUTHOR>Natany Pitts-Moultis</AUTHOR>
     <AUTHOR>William Brogden</AUTHOR>
     <COPYRIGHT>LANWrights, Inc.</COPYRIGHT>
  </HEAD>
<BODY>
     <SLIDE>
     <TITLE>Introduction to the Internet and the World Wide Web
```

```
        </TITLE>
        <P>The Internet is the world's premier global communications net-
        work; it's not a monolithic network. Instead, it's a combination
        of many programs and functions all working together. Today, the
        most visible and important portion of the Internet is the World
        Wide Web (Web or W3). The graphics-rich Web is often used as a
        source of static (unchanging) data, but its real excitement comes
        from its interactive qualities. That is, when you ask it something
        or input data, it reacts based on your questions and data. It is a
        very personal place. One of the Web's greatest features is that
        anyone can create and publish Web documents, usually called Web
        pages. They are created using a simple language called HTML
        (Hypertext Markup Language). However, before we rush off and help
        you create your own Web offerings, we need to take a good look at
        the Internet. In this module, we'll explore the visible and invis-
        ible parts of the Internet. Knowing what is under the hood will
        make creating your own Web pages quicker and easier.</P>
        <CLASSROOM>
             <BULLET>A worldwide network</BULLET>
             <BULLET>Web is the most visible</BULLET>
             <BULLET>HTML is used to create Web pages</BULLET>
             <BULLET>Understanding the Web is key to creating
                     good Web pages</BULLET>
        </CLASSROOM>
        </SLIDE>
</BODY>
```

The addition of attributes makes the description of the content even more precise:

```
<TRAINING ID="iww01">

  <HEAD>
     <TITLE>Introduction to the World Wide Web and HTML</TITLE>
     <DESCRIPTION>Designed to introduce students to the technologies
                  and mechanisms of the Web and HTML. Begins with an
                  overview of the Internet and Web followed by a
                  discussion of HTML and Web page creation. Covers
                  all basic HTML markup.
     </DESCRIPTION>
     <LEVEL CLASSIFICATION="intro" />
     <PREREEQ CLASSIFICATION="computer-basic"/>
     <AUTHOR>Natany Pitts-Moultis</AUTHOR>
     <AUTHOR>William Brogden</AUTHOR>
     <COPYRIGHT DATE="1998">LANWrights, Inc.</COPYRIGHT>
  </HEAD>
<BODY>
     <SLIDE>
     <TITLE>Introduction to the Internet and the World Wide Web
```

```
        </TITLE>
        <P>The Internet is the world's premier global communications net-
        work; it's not a monolithic network. Instead, it's a combination
        of many programs and functions all working together. Today, the
        most visible and important portion of the Internet is the World
        Wide Web (Web or W3). The graphics-rich Web is often used as a
        source of static (unchanging) data, but its real excitement comes
        from its interactive qualities. That is, when you ask it something
        or input data, it reacts based on your questions and data. It is a
        very personal place. One of the Web's greatest features is that
        anyone can create and publish Web documents, usually called Web
        pages. They are created using a simple language called HTML
        (Hypertext Markup Language). However, before we rush off and help
        you create your own Web offerings, we need to take a good look at
        the Internet. In this module, we'll explore the visible and invis-
        ible parts of the Internet. Knowing what is under the hood will
        make creating your own Web pages quicker and easier.</P>
        <CLASSROOM>
             <BULLET LEVEL="1">A worldwide network</BULLET>
             <BULLET LEVEL="1">Web is the most visible</BULLET>
             <BULLET LEVEL="2">HTML is used to create Web
                  pages</BULLET>
             <BULLET LEVEL="2">Understanding the Web is key to creating
                     good Web pages</BULLET>
        </CLASSROOM>
        </SLIDE>
   </BODY>
```

In many ways the code speaks for itself. Attributes provide a unique IDENTIFICATION tag to the training, add specific copyright-date information, and distinguish level-one and level-two bullets.

Building a Better DTD: Attribute Planning

The syntax for creating attributes isn't any more complex than what you use for defining elements. The most difficult part of adding elements to a DTD is planning attributes that will serve your purposes in the most efficient and effective ways. In addition, you'll need to decide when to include predefined values and when to leave document developers to their own devices. Once again, I'm going to suggest you think about using flashcards to help you plan and organize your attributes.

Planning Doesn't End with Elements

Once you've established the elements that compose your DTD, you are on your way to a functioning DTD; however, there's still plenty to do. You'll need to assign to each element attributes that further the purpose of the element. The best way to go about this is to consider the role each element will play in the document and how you can use attributes to help accomplish the document's goals.

You may also find along the way that an individual element might be better as an attribute for another element. For example, the `LEVEL` and `PREREQ` elements in the OTML DTD might be just as effective, if not more effective, as attributes for the `TRAINING` element. Carefully think your way through your elements and their prospective attributes before you start making assignments. And, of course, the more you test your DTD by applying it to different content the better you'll be able to work out the kinks.

Predefined Values Ensure Accuracy

The decision as to whether to leave developers to their own devices when assigning values to an attribute or to limit them to a list of values is often a tough one. If you let developers supply their own values, you run the risk of getting a value your processor can't deal with. If you supply your own list, it might be too narrow or specific and make your DTD less usable.

If you let users supply their own values, you'll want to include plenty of documentation with your DTD, explaining the purpose of the DTD and the appropriate types of values. If you create a predefined list of values for your users, be sure to test your DTD carefully and get feedback from others about their needs.

Flash Cards Revisited

I'm going to get on the flash card soapbox again for a second. If you're new to DTD design, you'll be surprised how useful this particular technique can be. By listing the attributes you propose to assign to an element on each element's flash card, you'll be able to organize your elements, see if their attributes are redundant, and identify missing pieces in your DTD. Try it—you'll be amazed.

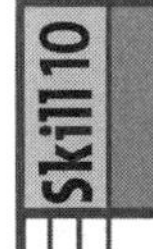

The Rules of Nesting: Content Models

Once you've got elements and attributes down, you're roughly half way through the DTD and document-design process. The rules of nesting (officially known as content models), or how elements may be contained within other elements, direct the structure of your documents. In Skill 11, you'll learn why content models are necessary, how they're specified in a DTD, and how to create a document that adheres to the content models defined in a given DTD.

Are You up to Speed?

Now you can...

- ☑ **Explain the role attributes play in XML DTDs and documents**
- ☑ **Create an attribute-definition list in a DTD**
- ☑ **Include attributes in an XML document**
- ☑ **Describe better techniques for designing attributes for a DTD**

SKILL 11

Defining Content Models for Elements

- How content models drive document structure
- The different types of content
- Defining and referencing content models
- Tips and tricks for content model planning

Elements and attributes are a powerful combination, but elements nested within elements can be just as powerful. As useful as element combinations can be, they can cause problems if they aren't carefully controlled. This skill explores the rules of nesting elements in XML documents and how DTD designers can best employ element combinations.

The Power of Nesting: Lessons Learned from HTML

The ability to nest elements within elements is key to the success of a markup language. A single element used alone may provide only part of the total description of a block of content. A perfect example of nesting is HTML table markup. Alone, the TABLE element only describes a block of content as a table, but it isn't designed to provide specific information about the rows and cells of the table or what those cells may contain. Groups of <TR> (TABLE ROW) and <TD> (TABLE DATA) tags complete the markup that describes the physical structure of the table. These tags also create the cells that contain text and other elements, known as *cell content*.

This set of nested elements is required to create a single-cell table:

```
<TABLE>
     <TR>
     <TD></TD>
     </TR>
</TABLE>
```

To include a paragraph inside of the table, yet another nested tag is added to the collection:

```
<TABLE>
     <TR>
     <TD>
          <P>This is a paragraph</P>
     </TD>
     </TR>
</TABLE>
```

To make the table look like a table on a Web page, I'll have to throw in a few attributes for good measure, as shown in the next bit of code. The final results are shown in Figure 11.1.

```
<TABLE BORDER=1 CELLPADDING=5>
     <TR>
     <TD>
          <P>This is a paragraph</P>
     </TD>
     <TR>
</TABLE>
```

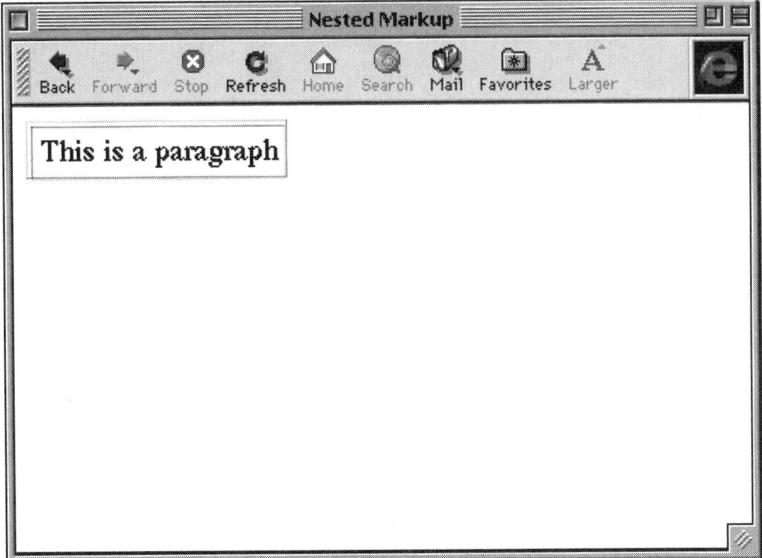

FIGURE 11.1: Nesting markup elements creates a one-cell table.

The final visual isn't the most spectacular, but from a purely structural point of view, this simple document is rather significant. It demonstrates how elements can be combined to provide a detailed description of content in a way that a single element, even with the best attributes, could not.

NOTE That last bit of table code was for example only. In the real Web world, HTML table markup should only be used for tabular data (as it's name implies), not strictly for layout.

HTML list markup is another good example of how nesting markup elements can generate a more accurate description of content. By themselves, LI (list) elements indicate that their content is a list item. The inclusion of items in either an OL (ordered list) or UL (unordered list) element not only groups list items together as a unit but also describes the items as part of an ordered or unordered list.

The Role of Content Models in a DTD

As you've seen, nesting elements within one another can be beneficial in many ways. However, the best and most effective combinations of elements, as well as the order they should be nested in, need to be carefully controlled so nesting doesn't get out of hand. Content models serve as the rules of nesting in a DTD.

A content model for any given element can dictate

- Whether other elements may be nested within the element
- Which other elements may be nested within the element
- Which elements must be nested within the elements
- How many times another element may or must be nested within the element
- In what order other elements must be nested within the element

Careful design of content models for individual elements can ensure that document developers include necessary elements and are prevented from creating troublesome combinations of elements. For many of you, it may be difficult to imagine a table without rows or cells or a list in which the items come before the list-type identifier, so the rules of nesting seem almost intuitive (a nine on a "Duh!" scale of ten). Still, as a DTD designer, you can never be sure what others are thinking, what's intuitive to them, or even if they've read and understood the documentation about your DTD. Besides, XML won't let you get away with creating DTDs without content models, so you're stuck with them anyway.

Believe it or not, HTML actually uses content models extensively, but Web browsers aren't that rigorous about enforcing them. For example, did you know that you're not supposed to enclose your entire document inside of <FONT>... </FONT> tags? FONT elements should be nested within individual paragraphs, headings, blockquotes, and list items. In addition, you shouldn't nest paragraphs inside of paragraphs or include any markup within ANCHOR elements. List items should only be nested within ORDERED or UNORDERED LIST elements.

TIP To see how many rules of HTML your pages violate, including nesting rules, point your Web browser at the W3C's validation service at `http://validator.w3.org`. You can test entire HTML pages or just a line or two of code.

The role of a content model is fairly simple: it guides document developers through the nesting of tags. Still, the ability of a DTD designer to require that certain elements are nested within others—or to prevent elements from being nested within others—provides yet another avenue for closely controlling the way documents are described to ensure consistency and ease of processing.

NOTE An element's content model only applies to the first level of elements nested within it (CHILD elements). The rules of nesting for elements contained within an element's children are dictated by the children's content models. For example, the content model for an unordered list states that it can only contain list items as CHILD elements. Their own content models, not the unordered-list content model, govern what the list items may contain.

The Role of Content Models in PGML

PGML contains a base content model that allows for the general nesting of PGML, GROUP, PATH, IMG, TEXT, RECTANGLE, CIRCLE, ELLIPSE, PIEWEDGE, SCRIPT, PRIVATE, DRAWOBJECT, and ANIMATION elements within the GROUP element. This establishes the major CONTAINER elements and allows them to be combined within groups.

Many of these major CONTAINER elements have their own content models that carefully define which elements they can contain. The content model for the PATH element specifies that it may contain elements that describe where the path moves to, lines to, or curves to as well as its arc and the point where the path ends. The PATH element and these subelements work together to describe a particular path in detail. The PATH subelements were created specifically to augment the PATH element, and they shouldn't be used with any other elements. The content models of the other elements prevent this by not including the PATH subelements in their respective content models.

The Role of Content Models in OTML

In the OTML DTD, I use content models to accomplish three different things:

- To ensure that important information about the training session, such as its title, description, level, prerequisite, author, and copyright information, are included in every OTML document.
- To make sure every slide in a training session has a `TITLE` element.
- To carefully govern how `SLIDE` elements may be nested to ensure accuracy of the description of content.

By designing solid content models for my elements, I can make sure that every training session is correctly documented and that the descriptions of `SLIDE` content make sense and will work well with the system designed to process OTML documents.

Content Types

Any given element (except `EMPTY` elements of course) can hold one of four types of content:

- Elements only
- Text
- Elements and text
- Any content

Content that consists of only elements is called *element content*, whereas content that is either text or both elements and text is called *mixed content*. Any content is called just that. The following three sections discuss each type of content in detail.

Element Content

Element content consists entirely of elements. This means that an element with element content can't contain text. This may seem a bit strange at first (creating elements that can't contain text), but if you examine it further, you'll see that element content can be useful.

The `TABLE` and `TR` elements' content models contain only element content. The `TABLE` element can only contain `TR` elements, and the `TR` element can only contain

TD elements. Limiting these two elements' content models to element content helps guide document developers in the construction of tables and prevents them from including text content within the wrong elements. A Web browser doesn't expect or really know what to do with text inside of TABLE or TR tags, and the use of element content ensures that it won't have to.

I've mentioned a couple of times that an element's content model can be used to control how many times and in what order other elements can be nested within the element. This control can only be exerted over element content. Text is the wildcard in the content world, and once it's included in the content model, all bets are off. Although a DTD designer can impose guidelines for the specific nesting of other elements, they can't do the same with text. Elements are preset entities, and the designer knows exactly which elements he or she has to work with. Text can be any number of characters long and is an unknown quantity. The bottom line is if you want to have tight control over the number and order of nested elements, your content will have to be strictly element content. The "Declaring Content Models in a DTD" section later in the skill describes the syntax for creating content models that contain element, mixed, and any content.

Mixed Content

Mixed content is a bit of a misnomer because it implies that a content model with mixed content always includes both element and regular text content. What it really indicates is that the content model includes just regular text or both text and element content. When dealing with mixed content, you can still specify which other elements may be nested within a given element, along with text, but you can't control the order or frequency in which those elements appear.

The content model for an HTML paragraph contains mixed content. In addition to the paragraph text, other text-level markup elements, such as BOLDFACE, ITALIC, and SUBSCRIPT, can be contained within an HTML paragraph. In this case, mixed content is a necessity. Not only does a paragraph need to contain regular text but it also needs other elements that users might want to nest within the paragraphs to further describe some or all of the paragraph's contents.

Of course, there are some elements that shouldn't be nested within a paragraph, such as other paragraphs, headings, or tables (to name a few), and the DTD can keep these inappropriate elements out by simply not including them in the mixed content model. A mixed content model is far from being a free-for-all, but it certainly isn't as rigidly controllable as an element content model.

Any Content

This label accurately describe its type. Any content means any content. An element whose content model includes any content will be able to contain any and all elements in the DTD as well as plain text. Any content is truly a free-for-all and allows the document developer to do as they darn well please. Although this may be a good thing while a DTD is under development, it's not necessarily the best method for defining content in a fully functional and final DTD. You won't find many DTDs with content models that include any content. It's just too risky.

Declaring Content Models in a DTD

Declaring a content model for an element is just as easy as declaring the element itself or defining its attribute list. The content model is included inside of the element's definition and takes the following syntax:

```
<!ELEMENT element-name (content model)>
```

The content model between the parentheses contains the elements and/or text that can be nested within the element. See, that wasn't so bad now, was it?

The form a content model takes is different depending on the type of content an element can take. The next three sections look at the syntax specifics for including each type of content in a content model.

Declaring Element Content

As I've already indicated, you have the most control over element content. To that end, XML provides some specific mechanisms that allow you to define the order elements must be nested in as well as how many times they may occur. Element content uses a series of punctuation marks to describe the elements in a content model. Table 11.1 lists each punctuation mark and describes it role in specifying an element content model.

TABLE 11.1: Punctuation Used to Describe Element Content

Name	Symbol	Description
comma	,	separates element types in a list or sequence
vertical line	|	separates elements in a list of alternatives
plus	+	indicates that an element will occur one or more times

TABLE 11.1 CONTINUED: Punctuation Used to Describe Element Content

Name	Symbol	Description
question mark	?	indicates that an element will occur zero or one time
asterisk	*	indicates that an element will occur zero or more times

As you can see, the punctuation mark that follows an element goes a long way in describing whether an element must occur and how many times it will occur. If an element is followed by a plus sign, it must appear at least one time but can appear as many other times as necessary. If the element is followed by a question mark, it doesn't necessarily have to appear, but if it does, it can only appear once. Elements followed by an asterisk don't have to appear, but they can appear as many times as possible. If an element isn't followed by any punctuation, it must be nested exactly once within its PARENT element. When you see content models at work in the PGML and OTML DTDs, the role each punctuation mark plays will become even clearer.

The order in which the elements appear inside the parentheses defines the content model and is also relevant when you're working with element content. The order inside of the parentheses defines the order in which the elements must appear when nested.

The content model for the HTML OL element looks something like this:

```
<!ELEMENT ol (li+)>
```

This content model contains only element content, and the plus sign (+) after the LI element means that the LI element can occur one or more times within the OL element.

The order in which the elements appear inside the parentheses defines the content model and is also relevant when you're working with element content. The order inside of the parentheses defines the order in which the elements must appear when nested.

The content model for the HTML DL (DEFINITION LIST) element takes this form:

```
<!ELEMENT dl (dt, dd+)+>
```

Note the two plus signs: one inside the parentheses after the DD element and one outside of the parentheses. This particular combination of elements and punctuation marks means that a DL element may contain one or more instances of a DT element followed by one or more instances of a DD element. Because the plus sign is outside of the parentheses, it marks the DT followed by one or more DD elements as a unit and then indicates that the unit may occur more than once.

The punctuation syntax is relatively simple, but the more complex the combinations of punctuation and elements become, the more complex the content model is. On the simpler side, the content model for the HTML element looks something like this:

```
<!ELEMENT html (head, body)>
```

This content model indicates that the HEAD and BODY elements must each occur once in that order within the HTML element.

Declaring Mixed Content

If mixed content contains just text, it is described by this syntax:

```
<!ELEMENT name (#PCDATA)>
```

#PCDATA is XML's notation for plain text. If, however, the mixed content is truly mixed and includes both text and elements, it is described by this syntax:

```
<!ELEMENT name (#PCDATA | element | element | element)*>
```

Note the asterisk at the end of the parentheses. Although this bit of punctuation is carried over from the element-content syntax, this doesn't mean you can substitute a question mark or plus sign here. Instead it simply means the regular text as well as the other element alternatives listed may appear zero or more times within the element.

As I mentioned earlier, the XML P element takes mixed content, so an abbreviated version of the element's content model might look something like this:

```
<!ELEMENT P (#PCDATA | B | I | CODE | SUB | SUP )*
```

Remember that this is a very abbreviated version of the entire content model as listed in the HTML DTD, but it's enough to make my point.

Declaring Any Content

The declaration for any content is as simple as the content itself:

```
<!ELEMENT name ANY>
```

How much simpler can you get? To assign any content to the element TEST, use this element declaration:

```
<!ELEMENT test ANY>
```

Got it? Got it. Good.

PGML's Content Models

PGML's base content model is actually defined by a parameter entity instead of a regular element content model. Because parameter entities are the subject of Skill 12, "Employing Entities in DTDs and Documents," I'll wait until then to get into the particulars of defining a content model with a parameter entity. PGML does contain other, regular content models that serve as good examples of content models in action.

The content model for the HEAD element indicates that the EXTENSION, OBJECTSERVER, PAINTSERVER, COLORSPACESERVER, FILTERSERVER, SCRIPT, PRIVATE, GRAPHIC, LINEARGRADIENT, and ANIMATION elements may occur zero or more times within the HEAD element:

```
<!ELEMENT HEAD (EXTENSION | OBJECTSERVER | PAINTSERVER |
     COLORSPACESERVER | FILTERSERVER | SCRIPT | PRIVATE |
     GRAPHIC | LINEARGRADIENT | ANIMATION)*>
```

Vertical lines separate the elements, which means they are alternative elements, not elements in a sequence. The HEAD element may contain any or all of these elements, as many times as necessary, in any given order.

PGML combines element and mixed content in the TEXT element declaration:

```
<!ELEMENT text      (private?,(#PCDATA | textspan )*) >
```

This content model nests mixed content within an element content to make use of the strengths of both types of content. The content model first indicates that a PRIVATE element may occur zero or one time within a TEXT element. If the PRIVATE element exists, it can only be used once within each given TEXT element, and it must be nested first. Text and the TEXTSPAN element may then follow the PRIVATE element as needed. This clever combination of element content and mixed content provides the DTD designer with the ability to direct the number and order of elements and still include mixed content within an element.

TIP If you're going to nest mixed content within element content, always include the mixed content as the last option in the list.

OTML's Content Models

I used content models in the OTML DTD to make sure developers include important information in every document and don't nest elements where they shouldn't be nested. The following code listing shows the complete list of OTML elements with their content models (except the EMPTY elements, of course):

```
<!ELEMENT training (head, body)>
<!ELEMENT head (title, description, author+, copyright, level, prereq)>
<!ELEMENT title (#PCDATA)>
<!ELEMENT description (#PCDATA)>
<!ELEEMNT author (#PCDATA)>
<!ELEMENT copyright (#PCDATA)>
<!ELEMENT body (slide+)>
<!ELEMENT slide (title (#PCDATA, h1| h2 | h3| p | exhibit |
          ol | ul | classroom)*>
<!ELEMENT h1 (#PCDATA | b | i )*>
<!ELEMENT h2 (#PCDATA | b | i )*>
<!ELEMENT h3 (#PCDATA | b | i )*>
<!ELEMENT p (#PCDATA | b | i | code)*>
<!ELEMENT b (#PCDATA |i )*>
<!ELEMENT i (#PCDATA | b )*>
<!ELEMENT code (#PCDATA | b | i )*>
<!ELEMENT ol (li+)>
<!ELEMENT ul (li+)>
<!ELEMENT li (#PCDATA | p | b | i | code | ol | ul)*>
<!ELEMENT classroom (bullet+)>
<!ELEMENT bullet (#PCDATA | b | i | code)>
```

So, what do all of these content models mean for the OTML document? In short, they indicate that

- The TRAINING element must include exactly one HEAD element and one BODY element, in that order.
- The HEAD element must include one TITLE element, one DESCRIPTION element, one or more AUTHOR elements, one COPYRIGHT, one LEVEL, and one PREREQ element, in that order.
- The TITLE, DESCRIPTION, AUTHOR, and COPYRIGHT elements can only contain text.
- The BODY element must contain at least one or more SLIDE elements.
- Each SLIDE element must have exactly one TITLE element that is listed first, and may contain any number of H1, H2, H3, P, EXHIBIT, OL, UL, and CLASSROOM elements as well as regular text.
- The H1, H2, and H3 elements may all contain regular text as well as B and I elements.

- The P element may contain regular text, B, I, and CODE elements.
- The OL and UL elements must contain one or more LI elements.
- The LI element may contain plain text as well as P, B, I, CODE, OL, and UL elements.
- The CLASSROOM element must contain one or more BULLET elements.
- The BULLET element may contain regular text as well as B, I, and CODE elements.

The content models ensure that proper header information is contained in training documents, that each slide has a title and a set of classroom bullets, that paragraphs can't be nested within paragraphs, and that other important rules of OTML document creation are followed.

Adhering to Content Model Guidelines in an XML Document

For the document developer, the most difficult thing about content models is following the rules. The DTD designer created content models for each element with a specific purpose in mind. If, as a document developer, you want to create a document that adheres to the spirit of the DTD and that will work with the DTD document processor, you'll want to follow the content model guidelines closely.

WARNING Documents that don't abide by the rules defined in the DTD's content models will be invalid when processed by a parser.

Structuring Documents According to PGML Content Models

A couple of sections back I showed you these two content models from the PGML DTD:

```
<!ELEMENT HEAD (EXTENSION | OBJECTSERVER | PAINTSERVER |
     COLORSPACESERVER | FILTERSERVER | SCRIPT | PRIVATE |
     GRAPHIC | LINEARGRADIENT | ANIMATION)*>
<!ELEMENT text      (private?,(#PCDATA | textspan )*) >
```

Markup that abides by the rules set up by these two content models might look something like this:

```
<!- example 1 ->
<HEAD>
     <EXTENSION ?>
     <SCRIPT>Here's some script text</SCRIPT>
     <FILTERSERVER />
</HEAD>

<!- example 2 ->
<TEXT>
     <PRIVATE>Application specific private data</PRIVATE>
     Here's some regular text
     <TEXTSPAN>
          <PRIVATE>Application specific private data</PRIVATE>
          Here's some regular text
     <TEXTSPAN>
</TEXT>
```

In the first example, I can use any one of several elements listed in the content model for the HEAD document, and the elements can be listed in any order. I know the SCRIPT element can contain regular text, not from the content model for the HEAD element, but rather from the content model for the SCRIPT element.

TIP Remember that content models only apply to the first level of CHILD elements.

In the second example, I use a PRIVATE element inside of the TEXT element, and it's listed first according to the TEXT element's content model. I can then follow with regular text and the TEXTSPAN element as necessary. Note the PRIVATE element and regular text nested within the TEXTSPAN element. Again, I had to look at the content model for the CHILD element (TEXTSPAN in this case) to find out what it could contain. You'll find as you work with content models that nesting is usually several layers deep, so to make sure your markup is 100 percent valid, you'll have to check the content models for several elements and not just one.

Structuring Documents According to OTML Content Models

Because I'm rather familiar with the OTML DTD, the example I first showed you in Skill 9 adheres to the content models defined in the DTD:

```
<TRAINING>

  <HEAD>
```

```
        <TITLE>Introduction to the World Wide Web and HTML</TITLE>
        <DESCRIPTION>Designed to introduce students to the technologies
                  and mechanisms of the Web and HTML. Begins with an
                  overview of the Internet and Web followed by a discussion
                  of HTML and Web page creation. Covers all basic HTML
                  markup.
        </DESCRIPTION>
        <LEVEL />
        <PREREEQ />
        <AUTHOR>Natanya Pitts-Moultis</AUTHOR>
        <AUTHOR>William Brogden</AUTHOR>
        <COPYRIGHT>LANWrights, Inc.</COPYRIGHT>
   </HEAD>
<BODY>
        <SLIDE>
        <TITLE>Introduction to the Internet
              and the World Wide Web
        </TITLE>
        <P>The Internet is the world's premier global communications network;
it's not a monolithic network. Instead, it's a combination of many pro-
grams and functions all working together. Today, the most visible and
important portion of the Internet is the World Wide Web (Web or W3). The
graphics-rich Web is often used as a source of static (unchanging) data,
but its real excitement comes from its interactive qualities. That is,
when you ask it something or input data, it reacts based on your questions
and data. It is a very personal place. One of the Web's greatest features
is that anyone can create and publish Web documents, usually called Web
pages. They are created using a simple language called HTML (Hypertext
Markup Language). However, before we rush off and help you create your own
Web offerings, we need to take a good look at the Internet. In this mod-
ule, we'll explore the visible and invisible parts of the Internet.
Knowing what is under the hood will make creating your own Web pages
quicker and easier.</P>
        <CLASSROOM>
             <BULLET>A worldwide network</BULLET>
             <BULLET>Web is the most visible</BULLET>
             <BULLET>HTML is used to create Web pages</BULLET>
             <BULLET>Understanding the Web is key to creating
                   good Web pages</BULLET>
        </CLASSROOM>
        </SLIDE>
</BODY>
```

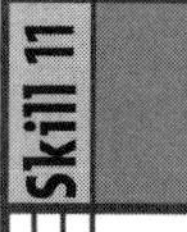

Notice that the HEAD contains all of the required elements, the SLIDE has a title, the PARAGRAPH doesn't have any other paragraphs nested inside of it, and the classroom section has several bullets (not just the single bullet it's required to have). The better acquainted you are with a DTD, the easier it will be to create documents that follow the content model rules. When you're first learning about a particular DTD, pay close attention to its documentation and sample markup to get the feel for how elements and text are nested within other elements.

Building a Better DTD: Content Model Planning

Once again, long-range planning is the key to creating content models for a DTD that not only work but are also efficient and easy to use. Because the content model for one element may rely on the content model for another element to build a structure or define a particular type of content (as with HTML table markup), you'll want to think carefully about how your elements should nest within each other for several levels down—not just on the first level. Imagine if the HTML `LI` element couldn't contain `OL` and `UL` elements. There wouldn't be any way to nest tables within tables to create a hierarchy of information.

The more complex your DTD is, the longer it's going to take to work the kinks out of your content models. However, once the kinks are out, the DTD will be even better than it was before and much more usable by document developers. The next few sections point out some important things to think about when planning your DTD. These sections should also help get you started down the right road to successful content model creation.

Identify Key Element Combinations

The first and most important step in planning your content models is to identify those elements that are designed to work together. List types and list items are just two examples of elements that will be combined to describe a set of content. Keep in mind that one element may be part of several different combinations and because of that, its content model must be designed with care to ensure that it functions well in every combination it is a part of.

The process of identifying key element combinations will go a long way in the planning for content models. A picture of how elements are going to interact to describe content will begin to form in your mind. Once you've decided which elements must work together, the next important step is to identify those that won't work together.

Identify Incompatible Elements

It is just as important to define elements that shouldn't be combined as it is to define elements that should. Paragraphs nested within paragraphs is an example of this key issue. You'll want to identify those combinations of elements that will cause more harm than good and keep them firmly entrenched in your mind as you begin to create your content models. Jot down particularly lethal combinations so when you're reviewing your first attempts at content model creation, you can immediately locate and dispose of those havoc-causing combinations.

Test, Test, Test

In the end, testing your DTD will reveal the bugs in your content models and help you exterminate them. Testing may also reveal new and better ways to define content models that will enhance your DTD and make it easier to use. Enlist the help of as many testers as you can and be ready to listen closely to their suggestions. Developers shouldn't have to force their content to fit into your content models. Instead your content models should fit their content like a glove. Take the time to massage your content models and you'll wind up with a solid DTD.

Entities: XML Containers

Elements, attributes, and content models make up a large part of any XML DTD and document. However, entities are the containers that make DTDs more efficient and allow developers to include nontext content as well as non-ASCII characters in their documents. In Skill 12, I'll take you to the wonderful world of entities and show you how to create and access your own virtual storage units.

Are You up to Speed?

Now you can...

- ☑ **Explain the role content models play in a DTD**
- ☑ **Describe the different types of content**
- ☑ **Define a content model**
- ☑ **Create a document that abides by document model rules**
- ☑ **Plan the content models that will appear in your DTDs**

SKILL 12

Employing Entities in DTDs and Documents

- Using entities in XML DTDs and documents
- Employing different kinds of entities to contain different kinds of content
- Declaring entities in DTDs
- Referencing entities in XML documents

An entity is a virtual storage unit that can hold anything from a text string to a graphics file to a list of frequently used attribute definitions. Even veteran Web page developers haven't had much interaction with entities because HTML doesn't use them very often. In XML, entities are commonly used tools that give both document developers and DTD designers a way to better organize and maintain their DTDs and documents.

The Role of Entities in a DTD

If you've worked with HTML, you've already worked with character entities: combinations of characters that represent non-ASCII characters, such as the ampersand (&) in `&`. You may also have encountered numeric entities, which are similar in form and function to character entities and use a series of numbers and letters to define a non-ASCII character. The numeric entity `©` represents the copyright symbol (©). Character and numeric entities are just the tip of the entity iceberg. While HTML only uses entities to describe special characters, XML uses entities in a much broader range of capacities.

Entities can hold four different kinds of content:

- A block of text
- A text string
- A set of nontext (binary) data, such as an audio or graphics file
- A non-ASCII character

Regardless of its type, an entity must be declared in a document's internal or external DTD subset before it can be referenced in the document. XML also makes use of parameter entities, a special kind of entity found only in a DTD, to contain frequently used groups of attributes or content modes and make them easy to reference over and over in the DTD.

In the remaining pages of this skill you'll learn about the different types of entities, when you should use each one, and how to declare and reference each type. Entities are powerful tools that you can use to store and reference frequently used strings and blocks of text. Entities also play a crucial role in the inclusion of non-text data and in the organization of DTDs, so you will very rarely find a DTD or document that doesn't include an entity of some kind.

Different Types of Entities

All entities are virtual storage units, but an entity can contain one of several types of content, and the content determines the way the entity is referenced in a document. Entities are generally referred to by their content type: text entity, binary entity, parameter entity, character entity, or numeric entity. The type of entity you use depends entirely on what you're trying to store.

Text Entities

Text entities can contain either frequently used phrases and text strings or entire chunks of text. You can store the string "Hypertext Markup Language" inside an entity named HTML. Each time the entity is referenced, the stored string will replace the entity. You can even store entire chunks of frequently used text within an entity to make it easier to include the chunk in another document later on. You can reference the stored block of text in as many documents as you like; any change you make to the entity's content is automatically made in every document that references the entity.

TIP

Text entities can contain just text or a combination of text and markup in any quantity. However, they cannot include their own `<!doctype>` declarations. More than one internal DTD in a document will cause the document to be malformed, and a processing application won't be able to read or parse it.

Binary Entities

Binary entities contain all data other than plain text and markup. Store all graphics, multimedia files, and other special nontext files in binary entities. The contents of text entities are considered XML-encoded and are treated like all the other text and markup in a document. Binary entities are not treated as XML-encoded but as a special file type that needs to be handled in a particular way.

Every binary entity must have a notation that describes the entity's file type, and every DTD must include notation descriptions that indicate what non-XML file types will be included in the document and how they should be treated. The actual non-XML file types supported by the processing application may vary from application to application. HTML browsers support only GIF, JPEG, and PNG graphics even though graphics may be saved as TIFF, BMP, and other file formats. When you include binary entities in your documents, you'll need to be sure the application that's going to process a document supports the binary entities you intend to include.

Parameter Entities

Parameter entities are a special entity type reserved for use in a document's DTD, and they are designed to hold lists of attributes and content models. Parameter entities can help you to organize your DTD and make DTD creation faster, more consistent, and more efficient. If several different elements in your documents have the same list of attributes, you can store that list once in a parameter entity and reference it as many times as necessary throughout your DTD rather than re-create the same list over again for each element. If you need to modify the list, you have to change it only once—in the parameter entity—and it's as if you changed the attribute-definition lists for all the elements that reference that parameter entity.

You can use a parameter entity as part of an attribute-definition list or a content-model declaration. Larger DTDs make frequent use of parameter entities to contain a base list of attributes or a content model that several or all of the elements in the DTD have in common. They also add on other attributes or content information as necessary on a case-by-case basis. You'll see this technique employed heavily in the PGML DTD.

Character and Numeric Entities

As I noted at the beginning of the skill, character and numeric entities are a regular part of Web page development with HTML. They provide a mechanism for describing non-ASCII characters, such as accented letters or special symbols. A character entity uses a string of characters in its description of the non-ASCII character, while a numeric entity uses numbers. To be compatible with HTML—and because the system makes sense—XML supports, but is not limited to, the same character entity sets as HTML.

Character and numeric entities are usually grouped into sets of like characters. Some examples of character sets include

- The ISO-Latin-1 character set
- The mathematical character set
- The Greek letter character set
- The miscellaneous technical character set
- The miscellaneous symbol character set

This list doesn't begin to come close to listing all the available character sets that can be used with XML, but it does show how different those character sets can be. XML supports ISO-Latin-1 by default, but you'll have to declare the other character sets in a document's DTD (either internal or external) if you want to represent the characters in them. This is described later in the skill.

All about ISO and Unicode (and Why You Should Care)

As you work with XML and character and numeric entities, you'll often come across the acronym *ISO* and the term *Unicode*. So what do they actually mean, and what do they have to do with XML?

ISO-Latin-1: The Basic Character Set

ISO stands for the International Standards Organization, the body officially responsible for managing international standards for everything from computer protocols to character sets. The ISO-Latin-1 character set (officially known as ISO 8859-1) is the default character set that XML and HTML both use. Table 12.1 later in the skill provides a complete listing of the characters in the ISO-Latin-1 character set and their equivalent character and numeric entities. "Latin" references the Roman alphabet that so many languages use. The first character set in the ISO-Latin character series is indicated by a "1."

The majority of special characters and symbols that you'll need can be found in the ISO-Latin character set. Because XML supports this character set by default, you can always use its character and numeric entities in your documents. However, if you're working with non-Latin characters, such as those found in Chinese and Russian languages, you'll have to use other entity sets to represent your characters, and for that, you'll need Unicode.

Unicode: All the Characters Known to Man (and Then Some)

XML also supports ISO 10646, a system of defining characters known as Unicode, of which ISO-Latin-1 is a subset. The characters defined in ISO-Latin-1 are just a drop in the Unicode bucket. Unicode was created to

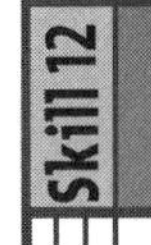

continued

describe every known language character and a large collection of special characters using unique bit patterns that computers can recognize and display. Unicode encompasses virtually every kind of glyph or typographical element you'll find in any language around the world. Needless to say, it's huge.

The entire Unicode character set also goes by the name UCS-2 (Universal Character Set, version two). It's a pretty big character set (to say the least) and can be difficult for computers and people to work their way through. To make Unicode easier to digest for all parties involved—carbon- or silicon-based—Unicode has been divided into manageable subsets like ISO-Latin-1.

These subsets are often referred to as UTFs (Universal [Character Set] Transformation Formats), and each subset uses a different encoding scheme to describe a character. ISO-Latin-1 is an 8-bit character set that can describe 256 unique characters. In comparison, ASCII is a 7-bit character set that allows for only 128 unique characters. The whole Unicode character set uses 16-bit encoding and can create over 65,000 unique characters. The more bits used in a character set, the more unique characters it can describe.

Although it might be nice to have 65,000 characters at your disposal, the larger the character set, the longer it takes for an application to process—which is why XML uses an 8-bit character set by default. But what if you need to access a single character that's not in the 8-bit set? Do you have to include the entire 16-bit set to get to it? The answer is a resounding "No!" Because XML fully supports all of Unicode, you can reference the character in an entity by using its Unicode character number.

How do you find out which Unicode subset you need to use or what an individual character's Unicode number is? The ultimate authority on the subject is the Unicode Web site at `http://www.unicode.org/`. Because XML supports characters in exactly the same way as HTML, document developers who have had to work with non-Latin and special character sets in HTML will be able to use all they already know about character encoding in XML.

continued

> **Why Should You Care?**
>
> All this talk about 8-bit and 16-bit encoding may be interesting, but you're probably still wondering why you should care. For the most part, XML has all the character entities the majority of developers will ever need built right in, just as HTML does. However, there may come a day when you'll have to translate your site into Sanskrit or some other non-Latin language, and (in addition to learning Sanskrit) you'll need to figure out how to represent the Sanskrit alphabet in a way that your XML browser will understand. When that day comes, you'll be prepared.

The Role of Entities in PGML and OTML

PGML primarily makes use of parameter entities to hold frequently used attribute definitions and content models. PGML also provides for the inclusion of external graphics files in its documents. Before an external binary file—even a standard GIF or JPEG—can be included in a PGML document, it must first be declared as an entity in the document's internal DTD.

The role of entities in OTML is limited for the most part to declaring graphics (binary entities) that will be used in conjunction with the `<exhibit>` tag. Because exhibits will change from document to document, most of these entities are defined in each individual document's internal DTD subset rather than in the general OTML DTD. The OTML DTD is sufficiently simple that I really don't need to make use of parameter entities. I've also found that text entities are great for creating and including footer information in pages, so every slide in a given training described by OTML ends with a text entity that contains standard footer information.

Declaring Entities in a Document

All entity declarations use the same basic syntax:

```
<!ENTITY name "content">
```

A variety of different components are added to this foundation syntax depending on the type of entity you're describing. In addition, an entity is either an *internal*

entity or an *external* entity. Internal entities include their content directly inside the entity declaration, while external entities reference an external file. Binary entities are almost always external entities, whereas parameter entities are always internal entities. Text entities and character entities may be either. The following sections describe the specific syntax for declaring each type of entity.

NOTE Regardless of the number or type of entities you're using in your XML document, they must all be declared before you can reference them. An entity can be declared in either the internal or external DTD. Generally, those entities that will be used in a wide variety of documents, such as character entities, are stored in the external DTD, and entities specific to a document, such as graphics, are stored in the document's internal DTD.

Declaring Text Entities

A text entity may be either internal or external. An internal text-entity declaration is probably the simplest entity declaration you'll ever create or come across. This text declaration describes an entity named `ISO` with a content of `International Standards Organization`:

```
<!entity iso "International Standards Organization">
```

This entity is an internal entity because the entity's content is contained directly within the declaration.

An external entity replaces the actual entity content with the location of a file that holds that content. A `public` or `system` identifier is also added to the entity declaration. `system` indicates that the file is saved somewhere on the local file system; `public` indicates that the file is widely available and doesn't have to be stored on the system. Examples of public files are widely used DTDs and specifications. If you're concerned that your XML processor won't know where to find a public file, you can always save a local copy to your system and identify the entity as a system file instead of a public file.

This declaration describes an external entity named `footer` whose content is saved in a system file called `footer.xml`:

```
<!entity footer "footer.xml" SYSTEM>
```

Declaring Binary Entities

Most binary entities are external entities stored on your local system. You should declare a binary entity in the same way you declare a text entity, but you must add the identifier NDATA and a notation name to the entity declaration that describes the entity's type. The syntax is

```
<!entity name "filename" system ndata filetype>
```

This entity declaration assigns the name `logo` to the external binary file `logo.gif` of type `GIF`:

```
<!entity logo "logo.gif" system ndata gif>
```

Declaring Notations in Document

A binary file type must be described with a notation declaration for an XML processor to be able to recognize it and know what to do with it. The notation declaration assigns a name to the file type and tells the processor something about how to process the non-XML file type. This notation declaration identifies the TIFF format and indicates that it should be processed by PhotoShop:

```
<!notation tiff system "\apps\graphics\photoshop.exe">
```

For a document with this notation in its DTD to be processed correctly, the application described in the notation must actually be available to the processor. This doesn't mean that the processor must use the referenced application as a helper application to process the file. If the processor already knows how to deal with the binary file format, it may choose to use its own internal mechanisms instead of the specified application. However, if the processor doesn't know what to do with the file type, the notation declaration is there to help it along.

Declaring Parameter Entities

Because parameter entities can be used only in the DTD, they have a special marker added to their declarations to label them as parameter entities. This special marker is a percent sign (%), and the following notation declares the parameter entity:

```
<!entity % name "content">
```

Remember that parameter entities are regularly used to store frequently used lists of attributes and content models. This parameter entity assigns the name `block` to a content model that contains the `p`, `blockquote`, `h1`, and `ol` elements:

```
<!entity % block "p | blockquote | h1 | ol">
```

This particular declaration stores a content model in the entity, but it could as easily store a list of attributes as this declaration does:

```
<!entity % common "
     id id #required
     class #cdata #implied
     lang #cdata #implied
     title #cdata #implied">
```

In this entity declaration, the attributes `ID`, `CLASS`, `LANG`, and `TITLE` are assigned to the entity `common`.

Declaring Character Entities

XML has a small set of predefined character entities that you can use when you need to include characters reserved for XML in your documents. They include

- `amp`: ampersand (&)
- `apos`: apostrophe (')
- `gt`: greater than (>)
- `lt`: less than (<)
- `quot`: quotation mark (")

You will usually get your character entities from a predefined entity list that's widely supported by XML processors. Using standard character-entity references ensures that the majority of processors will be able to read and display your documents.

Declaring a Character Entity Set in a Document

You can declare all of the entities in the ISO-Latin-1 character set all at once in your XML documents by including this entity declaration in your internal DTD subset:

```
<!entity % HTMLlat1 public
"ISO 8879-1986//ENTITIES Added Latin 1//EN//XML">
%HTMLlat1;
```

You don't actually have to include the entity declaration in every document because the ISO-Latin-1 character set is the default character set for XML. For other character sets, you will have to include an entity declaration. In addition to using an entity declaration to include a character set in your document, you can use a processing instruction (PI) to indicate which encoding system your document uses with this syntax:

```
<?xml encoding="[scheme-name]" ?>
```

To indicate that your document uses the UTF 8-bit encoding scheme, use this PI:

```
<?xml encoding="UTF-8" ?>
```

The encoding schemes supported by XML are

- UTF-8
- UTF-16
- ISO-10646-UCS-2
- ISO-10646-UCS-4
- ISO-8859-1 to -9
- ISO-2022-JP
- Shift_JIS
- EUC-JP

For a complete description of each of these encoding schemes, visit the Unicode site at `http://www.unicode.org/`.

Table 12.1 shows you how complete the ISO-Latin-1 character set is, including all of the characters in the set, their character and numeric entities, and a brief description of each.

TABLE 12.1: The ISO-Latin-1 Character Set

Character	Character Entity	Numeric Entity	Description
		� -	Unused
			Horizontal tab
Line feed
		-	Unused
	&space		Space

TABLE 12.1 CONTINUED: The ISO-Latin-1 Character Set

Character	Character Entity	Numeric Entity	Description
!	&exclam;	!	Exclamation mark
"	"	"	Quotation mark
#	&hash;	#	Number
$	&dlr:	$	Dollar
%	&pct;	%	Percent
&	&	&	Ampersand
'	'	'	Apostrophe
(	&lparen;	(	Left parenthesis
)	&rparen;	)	Right parenthesis
*	*	*	Asterisk
+	+	+	Plus
,	,	,	Comma
-	&hyph;	-	Hyphen
.	&per;	.	Period (full stop)
/	&fwsl;	/	Slash
0-9	&d0; - &d9;	0 - 9	Digits 0 through 9
:	&colon:	:	Colon
;	&semi:	;	Semicolon
<	<	<	Less than
=	&eq;	=	Equals
>	>	>	Greater than
?	&ques:	?	Question mark
@	&at;	@	Commercial at
A-Z		A - Z	Letters *A* through *Z* (uppercase)
[	&lsq;	[	Left square bracket
\	&bksl;	\	Reverse solidus (backslash)
]	&rsq;	]	Right square bracket
^	&crt;	^	Caret
_	ℏ	_	Horizontal bar

TABLE 12.1 CONTINUED: The ISO-Latin-1 Character Set

Character	Character Entity	Numeric Entity	Description
`	&grav;	`	Grave accent
a-z		a - z	Letters *a* through *z* (lowercase)
{	&lcb;	{	Left curly brace
|	&bar;			Vertical bar
}	&rcb;	}	Right curly brace
~	&til;	~	Tilde
		-	Unused
¡	&ixl;	¡	Inverted exclamation mark
¢	&cnt;	¢	Cent
£	&lbs;	£	Pound sterling
¤	&cur;	¤	General currency
¥	¥	¥	Yen
	&brvb;	¦	Broken vertical bar
§	&sec;	§	Section
¨	¨	¨	Umlaut (dieresis)
″	&coy;	©	Copyright
ª	&for;	ª	Feminine ordinal
«	&glf;	«	Left angle quote, guillemet left
¬	¬	¬	Not
_			Soft hyphen
,	&trd;	®	Registered trademark
¯	&mac;	¯	Macron accent
°	°	°	Degree
±	&plm;	±	Plus or minus
x^2	&s2;	²	Superscript two
x^3	&s3;	³	Superscript three
´	&acc;	´	Acute accent
µ	&mic;	µ	Micro
¶	∥	¶	Paragraph

TABLE 12.1 CONTINUED: The ISO-Latin-1 Character Set

Character	Character Entity	Numeric Entity	Description
·	`&mdt;`	`·`	Middle dot
¸	`&cd;`	`¸`	Cedilla
x^1	`&s1;`	`¹`	Superscript one
º	`&mor;`	`º`	Masculine ordinal
»	`&glr;`	`»`	Right angle quote, guillemet right
1/4	`&f4;`	`¼`	Fraction one-fourth
1/2	`&f2;`	`½`	Fraction one-half
3/4	`&f34;`	`¾`	Fraction three-fourths
¿	`&iqm;`	`¿`	Inverted question mark
À	`À`	`À`	Capital *A,* grave accent
Á	`Á`	`Á`	Capital *A,* acute accent
Â	`Â`	`Â`	Capital *A,* circumflex accent
Ã	`Ã`	`Ã`	Capital *A,* tilde
Ä	`Ä`	`Ä`	Capital *A,* dieresis or umlaut
Å	`Å`	`Å`	Capital *A,* ring
Æ	`Æ`	`Æ`	Capital *AE,* diphthong (ligature)
Ç	`Ç`	`Ç`	Capital *C,* cedilla
È	`È`	`È`	Capital *E,* grave accent
É	`É`	`É`	Capital *E,* acute accent
Ê	`Ê`	`Ê`	Capital *E,* circumflex accent
Ë	`Ë`	`Ë`	Capital *E,* dieresis or umlaut
Ì	`Ì`	`Ì`	Capital *I,* grave accent
Í	`Í`	`Í`	Capital *I,* acute accent
Î	`Î`	`Î`	Capital *I,* circumflex accent
Ï	`Ï`	`Ï`	Capital *I,* dieresis or umlaut
Ñ	`Ñ`	`Ñ`	Capital *N,* tilde
Ò	`Ò`	`Ò`	Capital *O,* grave accent

TABLE 12.1 CONTINUED: The ISO-Latin-1 Character Set

Character	Character Entity	Numeric Entity	Description
Ó	`Ó`	`Ó`	Capital *O,* acute accent
Ô	`Ô`	`Ô`	Capital *O,* circumflex accent
Õ	`Õ`	`Õ`	Capital *O,* tilde
Ö	`Ö`	`Ö`	Capital *O,* dieresis or umlaut
×	`×`	`×`	Multiply
Ø	`Ø`	`Ø`	Capital *O,* slash
Ù	`Ù`	`Ù`	Capital *U,* grave accent
Ú	`Ú`	`Ú`	Capital *U,* acute accent
Û	`Û`	`Û`	Capital *U,* circumflex accent
Ü	`Ü`	`Ü`	Capital *U,* dieresis or umlaut
Ý	`Ý`	`Ý`	Capital *Y,* acute accent
ß	`ß`	`ß`	Small sharp *s,* German (sz ligature)
à	`à`	`à`	Small *a,* grave accent
á	`á`	`á`	Small *a,* acute accent
â	`â`	`â`	Small *a,* circumflex accent
ã	`ã`	`ã`	Small *a,* tilde
ä	`ä`	`ä`	Small *a,* dieresis or umlaut
å	`å`	`å`	Small *a,* ring
æ	`æ`	`æ`	Small *ae,* diphthong (ligature)
ç	`ç`	`ç`	Small *c,* cedilla
è	`è`	`è`	Small *e,* grave accent
é	`é`	`é`	Small *e,* acute accent
ê	`ê`	`ê`	Small *e,* circumflex accent
ë	`ë`	`ë`	Small *e,* dieresis or umlaut
ì	`ì`	`ì`	Small *i,* grave accent
í	`í`	`í`	Small *i,* acute accent
î	`î`	`î`	Small *i,* circumflex accent
ï	`ï`	`ï`	Small *i,* dieresis or umlaut

TABLE 12.1 CONTINUED: The ISO-Latin-1 Character Set

Character	Character Entity	Numeric Entity	Description
ñ	ñ	ñ	Small *n*, tilde
ò	ò	ò	Small *o*, grave accent
ó	gó	ó	Small *o*, acute accent
ô	ô	ô	Small *o*, circumflex accent
õ	õ	õ	Small *o*, tilde
ö	ö	ö	Small *o*, dieresis or umlaut
÷	÷	÷	Division
ø	ø	ø	Small *o*, slash
ù	ù	ù	Small *u*, grave accent
ú	ú	ú	Small *u*, acute accent
û	û	û	Small *u*, circumflex accent
ü	ü	ü	Small *u*, dieresis or umlaut
ý	ý	ý	Small *y*, acute accent
ÿ	ÿ	ÿ	Small *y*, dieresis or umlaut

Entities in the PGML DTD

The PGML DTD is an excellent example of parameter entities at work. PGML uses parameter entities to define several common attribute lists, as shown in this excerpt from the DTD:

```
<!entity % gs_general_attributes
          'concat cdata #implied
           clippath cdata #implied'
>
<!entity % gs_fillstroke_attributes
          'fill (0 | 1)  "1"
           fillrule (nonzero | evenodd)  "nonzero"
           fillcolor cdata "black"
           fillcolorspace cdata "srgb"
           fillpaintserver cdata "color"
           fillparams cdata #implied
           fillname cdata #implied
           stroke (0 | 1)  "0"
```

```
            strokecolor cdata "black"
            strokecolorspace cdata "srgb"
            strokepaintserver cdata "color"
            strokeparams cdata #implied
            strokename cdata #implied
            opacity cdata "1"
            antialias (0 | 1)  "1"'
>
<!entity % gs_stroking_attributes
           'linecap (0 | 1 | 2)  "0"
            linejoin (0 | 1 | 2)  "0"
            miterlimit cdata "10"
            dasharray cdata "solid"
            dashoffset cdata "0"
            linewidth cdata "1"'
>
<!entity % gs_font_attribute 'font cdata #implied' >
<!entity % gs_text_attributes
           '%gs_font_attribute;
            textsize cdata #implied
            charspacing cdata "0"
            wordspacing cdata "0"
            textrise cdata "0"'
>
<!entity % gs_all_attributes
           '%gs_general_attributes;
            %gs_fillstroke_attributes;
            %gs_stroking_attributes;
            %gs_text_attributes;'
>
<!entity % event_handler_attributes
           'onmousedown     cdata #implied
            onmouseup       cdata #implied
            onclick         cdata #implied
            ondblclick      cdata #implied
            onmouseover     cdata #implied
            onmousemove     cdata #implied
            onmouseout      cdata #implied
            onkeydown       cdata #implied
            onkeypress      cdata #implied
            onkeyup         cdata #implied
            onload          cdata #implied
            onunload        cdata #implied'
>
```

PGML also uses parameter entities to define a base content model, base content attributes, and a bounding-box attribute list:

```
<!entity % base_content_model
         '(pgml | group |  path | img | text | rectangle |
           circle | ellipse | piewedge | script | private |
          drawobject | animation)*'
>
<!entity % base_content_attributes
          '%gs_all_attributes;
            name           id    #implied
            description    cdata    #implied
            visibility   (0 | 1)  "1"
            xml:link       cdata #fixed "simple"
            href       cdata #implied
            refx       cdata #implied
            refy       cdata #implied'
>
<!entity % gs_bounding_box_attribute 'boundingbox cdata #implied' >
```

Several of these parameter entities, e.g., `gs_all_attributes`, reference other parameter entities. This technique makes it easier to manage groups of attributes and content models and to create combinations of those groups as necessary throughout the DTD. These attributes and content models can be repeatedly referenced anywhere in the DTD, as the section "Using Entities in PGML DTDs and Documents" will show.

Entities in an OTML Document

I don't use parameter entities in the external OTML DTD, so the primary use of entities in OTML will be in the internal DTDs of the various OTML documents. The `<EXHIBIT>` tag has an `SRC=` attribute that takes an entity value. I have to create an entity declaration for every graphic I want to include as an exhibit using the `<EXHIBIT SRC=>` tag. To specify a binary entity called `net-pict`, which resides in the file `netpicture.gif` in the internal DTD of a training document, I use this code:

```
<!doctype training system "otml.dtd" [
     <!entity net-pict system "\graphics\netpicture.gif" ndata gif>
]>
```

In this particular training document, I'd like to include a footer at the bottom of every page that contains the same information. I could type it in each time, but that would mean changing every instance of the footer when I want to change the information. To make things simpler and more consistent, I choose to store the footer string in an internal text entity defined in the internal DTD (notice that the text entity also has the character entity for the copyright symbol included within it):

```
<!doctype training system "otml.dtd" [
     <!entity net-pict system "\graphics\netpicture.gif" ndata gif>
     <!entity footer "copyright &copy; lanwrights, inc. 1998">
]>
```

Referencing Entities

Regardless of an entity's type, all entities are referenced in the same way:

```
&name;
```

Parameter entities replace the ampersand (&) with a percent sign (%) to indicate that the reference is to a parameter entity rather than a regular entity:

```
%name;
```

This code includes the simple entity `<!entity iso "International Standards Organization">` within a sentence:

```
The &iso; sets the standard for character encoding.
```

When interpreted by an XML parser the result is

```
The International Standards Organization sets the standard
for character encoding.
```

External text entities are referenced in the same way as internal text entities, with the content of the external file referenced by the entity declaration, which replaces the entity reference. Any text entity can be referenced directly within the text of a document, just as any character entity can. The code `Copyright ©` is rendered as "`Copyright ©`".

Although text and character entities can be referenced anywhere within an XML document, binary entities can be referenced only as the value of an element with an attribute that takes an entity value. If you try to reference the entity defined in the following declaration with `&logo;`, your document will be malformed:

```
<!entity logo "logo.gif" SYSTEM NDATA GIF>
```

If, however, you reference the entity using an element and attribute, as shown here, your document will be fine (assuming the element IMG was defined with an attribute of SRC that takes an entity value):

```
<img src="logo" />
```

NOTE Notice that an attribute that references a binary entity uses the entity name as its value and not the actual name of the file. <IMG SRC="logo.gif"> is incorrect because the name of the entity is logo, and the source is logo.gif. This is different from the conventions used in HTML.

Recall these two parameter entities from earlier:

```
<!entity % block "p | blockquote | h1 | ol">

<!entity % common "
     id id #required
     class #cdata #implied
     lang #cdata #implied
     title #cdata #implied">
```

These entities can be used only within the DTD itself. This bit of code references the block parameter entity to define the content model for the BODY element:

```
<!element body %block;>
```

This is equivalent to

```
<!element body (p | blockquote | h1 | ol)>
```

This code creates an attribute list for the BODY element using the common parameter entity:

```
<!element body %block;>
     <!attlist body %common;>
```

To achieve the same element and attribute-list declarations without the use of parameter entities, you would have to use this code:

```
<!element body (p | blockquote | h1 | ol)>
     <!attlist body
     id id #required
     class #cdata #implied
     lang #cdata #implied
     title #cdata #implied>
```

TIP

Referencing any kind of entity is simple. Keep these three rules in mind and you can't go wrong:
1. Text and binary entities can be referenced anywhere in your document with the syntax &name;.
2. Binary entities can be referenced only as attribute values (don't forget to use the entity name and not the source name).
3. Parameter entities can be referenced only in the DTD and use the syntax %name;.

Using Entities in PGML DTDs and Documents

You've already seen that PGML makes frequent use of parameter entities to contain both attribute lists and content models. These parameter entities are used within the DTD to provide base attribute lists or content models to which other attributes or content information is added. The very first element declaration in the DTD describes the PGML element and makes use of four parameter entities, one in the element's content model and three in its attribute-list definition:

```
<!element pgml (head?, %base_content_model;) >
<!attlist pgml %base_content_attributes;
               %gs_bounding_box_attribute;
               %event_handler_attributes;
               preserveaspectratio (0 | 1)  "1"
               x             cdata #implied
               y             cdata #implied
               width         cdata #implied
               height        cdata #implied
               src           cdata #implied
>
```

Notice the base_content_model parameter entity makes up only part of the element's content model, in addition to head?. Also, the base_content_attributes, gs_bounding_box_attribute, and event_handler_attributes parameter entities are joined by other, standard attribute declarations to form the entire attribute-definition list for the element. When the parameter entities are replaced by their contents, the actual element declaration and attribute-definition list for the PGML element looks like this:

```
<!element pgml (head? (pgml | group | path | img | text | rectangle |
                circle | ellipse | piewedge | script | private |
```

```
                drawobject | animation)*) >
<!attlist pgml concat cdata #implied
               clippath cdata #implied
               fill (0 | 1)  "1"
               fillrule (nonzero | evenodd)  "nonzero"
               fillcolor cdata "black"
               fillcolorspace cdata "srgb"
               fillpaintserver cdata "color"
               fillparams cdata #implied
               fillname cdata #implied
               stroke (0 | 1)  "0"
               strokecolor cdata "black"
               strokecolorspace cdata "srgb"
               strokepaintserver cdata "color"
               strokeparams cdata #implied
               strokename cdata #implied
               opacity cdata "1"
               antialias (0 | 1)  "1"
               linecap (0 | 1 | 2)  "0"
               linejoin (0 | 1 | 2)  "0"
               miterlimit cdata "10"
               dasharray cdata "solid"
               dashoffset cdata "0"
               linewidth cdata "1"
               font cdata #implied
               textsize cdata #implied
               charspacing cdata "0"
               wordspacing cdata "0"
               textrise cdata "0"
               boundingbox cdata #implied
               onmousedown     cdata #implied
               onmouseup       cdata #implied
               onclick         cdata #implied
               ondblclick      cdata #implied
               onmouseover     cdata #implied
               onmousemove     cdata #implied
               onmouseout      cdata #implied
               onkeydown       cdata #implied
               onkeypress      cdata #implied
               onkeyup         cdata #implied
               onload          cdata #implied
               onunload        cdata #implied
               preserveaspectratio (0 | 1)  "1"
               x            cdata #implied
               y            cdata #implied
               width        cdata #implied
               height       cdata #implied
               src          cdata #implied
>
```

Although the content model is compact enough to work with even when it's not stored in a parameter entity, the list of attributes is long and unwieldy. Separating the attributes into subgroups makes them easier to manage and change as well as easier to reference. Almost every other element within the PGML DTD also makes use of parameter entities, usually to include the base content attributes or event handler attributes in their respective attribute-definition lists.

TIP

PGML is not alone in its abundant use of parameter entities. Take a look at the HTML 4.0 specification at `http://www.w3.org/TR/REC-html40/strict.dtd` to see a truly masterful use of parameter entities in organizing and managing a DTD. To view the file, save it to your hard drive, and open it with a text editor, or choose View Source from your Web browser's View menu.

Using Entities in OTML DTDs and Documents

Entities don't play as large a role in OTML documents as they do in PGML documents. I make use of entities in OTML only to reference binary files that are to be used as exhibits and to include a base footer in every page. This is the internal DTD from the sample OTML document I've been using:

```
<!doctype training system "otml.dtd" [
     <!entity net-pict system "\graphics\netpicture.gif" ndata gif>
     <!entity footer "copyright &copy; lanwrights, inc. 1998">
]>
```

I can easily add these entities to my sample document (additions are in bold):

```
<!doctype training system "otml.dtd" [
     <!entity net-pict system "\graphics\netpicture.gif" NDATA GIF>
     <!entity footer "Copyright &copy; LANWrights, Inc. 1998">
]>
<training id="iww01">

<!- head content snipped for the sake of brevity in this example ->

<body>
     <slide>
     <title>Introduction to the Internet
            and the World Wide Web
```

```
    </title>
    <p>The Internet is the world's premier global communications net-
work; it's not a monolithic network. ... Knowing what is under the hood
will make creating your own Web pages quicker and easier.</p>

<exhibit src="net-pict">

<!- classroom content snipped ->

<p>&footer;</p>

    </slide>
</body>
```

Notice that when I reference the binary GIF entity, I use the entity's name and not the actual name of the source file as I would have done had this been an HTML file. Also, I enclose the footer entity within a PARAGRAPH element because the content of the entity is just text without any kind of markup. All text content within a document must be described by markup, so the footer entity must always be placed within a markup element of some kind. I could have included the markup in the entity content itself, but in that case, the content would always be a paragraph, and I would be bound by the paragraph content model for placement of the entity. By not adding any markup to the footer entity, I can place its content within any element that can contain regular text.

Although OTML doesn't make use of parameter entities, any set of training materials described by OTML will include binary entities as the source for the EXHIBIT element as well as many text entities. The different uses of entities in PGML and OTML demonstrate that each XML vocabulary and the documents written for it should use the entity mechanism to make both DTDs and documents easier to manage and work with. There is no rule that says a DTD must use parameter entities or that a document must include binary entities. Instead, DTD designers and document developers should make use of entities as best fits their needs and goals.

Bringing It All Together with Links

Your DTD is complete. You've created elements, assigned attributes and content models to them, and declared entities that store everything from frequently used attribute lists to graphics files. You know how to use all of these tools to describe your content and create XML documents. So what's missing?

The Web wouldn't be the Web without hyperlinks, and because XML is very much a Web technology, it needs to have a hyperlinking mechanism. In Skill 13, "Linking Up with XLink and Xpointer," you'll learn all about XLink, the XML linking specification. XLink goes beyond the boundaries of traditional Web hyperlinks to a new level of linking.

Are You up to Speed?

Now you can...

- ☑ **Explain the role entities play in XML DTDs and documents**
- ☑ **Describe the different types of entities and how they are used in DTDs and documents**
- ☑ **Declare entities in both the external and internal DTD subsets of a document**
- ☑ **Reference entities in an XML DTD**

SKILL 13

Linking Up with XLink and XPointer

- Understanding the role of the XLink and XPointer specifications
- Creating simple and extended links out of any document element
- Pointing to specific places in an XML document with XPointer

You can't have hypertext without hyperlinking, and XML certainly couldn't operate within the world of the Web without some sort of hyperlinking mechanism. HTML's hyperlinks are functional and have reliably provided document developers with a standard and nonproprietary way to reference the work of others directly from within their own documents. However, HTML hyperlinks barely begin to harness the full power of hyperlinks. XML hyperlinks are more extensible, and a single link can connect hundreds of documents. In this skill you'll learn about XLink, the XML linking mechanism, and XPointer, the XML referencing mechanism. Together with a set of well-described documents, XLink and XPointer take hyperlinking where no link has gone before.

The Role of XLinks and XPointers in XML

Links on the Web connect documents across hundreds of servers in scores of countries as if they were all part of one document collection residing on a single server. Links transcend the limits inherent in storing files on a localized server and connect the documents of the world via the Internet and Web. Just as XML is a more robust and extensible markup language than HTML, its linking system must be more extensive than HTML's. In this particular case, bigger is better.

The XML linking mechanism is so specialized and extensive that it has two unique specifications that describe its inner workings. The first of these specifications, XLink (formerly known as the Extensible Linking Language, or XLL), details how XML documents should link to one another. It allows you to set up multidirectional links among multiple documents. No more hyperlinking from just point A to point B. You can go from A to B to D and back to A via C, if you'd like. XLink also allows you to store descriptions of all of your links in one document, making management and updating of links easier.

The second specification that governs linking among XML documents, XPointer, details how links should point to the various places inside a document. You use XLink to link up documents and XPointer to reference specific points within the documents themselves. Combined, XLink and XPointer make a powerful team for creating links across collections of XML documents.

An Important Note about the Status of the XLink and XPointer Specifications

Because the XLink and XPointer rulebooks are specifications and are separate from the actual XML specification, they are not officially part of XML version one. Both XLink and XPointer are still in the working draft stage and are far from being standard. This makes describing how linking within XML actually works an interesting challenge, because a lot can, and probably will, change between the current drafts and the final versions of the XLink and XPointer specification. Such is life on the bleeding edge of technology.

The information in this skill is based entirely upon the currently available working-draft specification. Although I know that XLink and XPointer will change as they are developed, I am convinced that the basic mechanisms for creating links and pointers will stay the same.

For the latest and most accurate information about XLink and XPointer (or any other specification, for that matter), you should consult the W3C's Web site. To visit the most current versions of XLink and XPointer, point your Web browser at

- The XML Linking Language (XLink) at `http://www.w3.org/TR/WD-xlink`
- The XML Pointer Language (XPointer) at `http://www.w3.org/TR/WD-xptr`

The goal of XML's developers is to integrate XML documents seamlessly with HTML documents so users don't even realize they're looking at information described by two different markup languages. To that end, XLink is both compatible with the existing `<A HREF=>` link tag used in HTML documents and powerful enough to meet the needs of XML. Using XLink, you can create hyperlinks between XML and HTML documents as well as between XML documents.

Links in XML can be embedded in a document and traversed from one end to the other just like standard HTML links. The document browser, in concert with the developer's style sheet, determines how the link should be rendered for the user. Don't look for blue underlined text to go away any time soon. The user can activate XML links, usually by clicking on them. All of these characteristics should be familiar to you because they apply also to HTML links.

XML links can also

- Be attached to any element, not just the ANCHOR (<A>) element; this fits with XML's initial goal of allowing DTD designers to define their own markup elements. Any element can be a hyperlink with XML.
- Reference a specific point in an XML document by name or based on certain qualifying factors such as their context or location in the document. This is where the XPointer specification comes into play.
- Be displayed or processed in one of several ways as directed by the document developer. Links can be automatically activated rather than relying on the user to click on the underlined text.
- Be described in a document that isn't actually part of the link.
- Be traversed in more than one direction. HTML links are one-way, but XML links can be multidirectional.

XPointer is designed to provide XLink with a way to point to specific places in documents. In its simplest form, XPointer can point to elements based on their unique ID or NAME attributes. In its more robust form, XPointer can pinpoint an element by its location or context. XPointer makes use of a location term to specify exactly where a link should be made. A location term can be defined as an absolute location, a relative location, a spanning location, an attribute location, or a string location. The "Making XLinks More Specific with XPointers" section of this skill provides detailed information about each of these locations and how to use them with XPointer.

As you can see, links in XML are much more advanced than they are in HTML and give you many more options for connecting your documents. In the remaining sections of this skill, you'll meet the various components used to describe XML links and see exactly how to create links in your XML documents.

FROM THE PRACTICAL TO THE THEORETICAL: LEAVING PGML AND OTML BEHIND

Because XLink and XPointer are still in working draft form, they aren't being used to create hyperlinks in either PGML or OTML documents. Until a final version of XML's linking mechanisms is available, the majority of DTD and document developers are sticking to HTML hyperlinks because they are supported by Web software.

So here we leave our friends PGML and OTML behind. This doesn't mean this skill won't have plenty of examples and code, but the majority of both will be examples of how XLink and XPointer will work once they're formalized. In the constantly changing world of XML, it's important to differentiate between what you can realistically implement and what's still under development. In the case of linking, there's still a long way to go before you can begin to use XML's advanced hyperlinks in your documents.

Using URLs in Links

Both the XLink and XPointer specifications use URIs (Uniform Resource Identifiers) to reference documents on the Web. Most Web denizens are familiar with URLs (Uniform Resource Locators); the difference between URIs and URLs is negligible when you're dealing with links in XML documents. The bottom line is that you won't have to learn a new set of rules for describing Web resources. Your old friend `http://www.somesite.com/somepage.html` is here to stay.

NOTE If you'd like a little refresher course in generating URLs, visit `http://www.w3.org/Addressing/rfc1738.txt` for information on creating absolute URLs and `http://www.w3.org/Addressing/rfc1808.txt` for more about creating relative URLs.

Different Types of XLinks

There are two basic kinds of XLinks:

- Simple links
- Extended links

Extended links can further be broken down into

- Out-of-line links
- Multidirectional links

A simple link uses the HREF attribute to point to a single resource somewhere on your local server or out on the Internet. HTML links are simple links, and you can use any element in any XML document to create a simple link using the same syntax you use with the A element in HTML.

Extended links are a bit more complex. An extended link can point to several different resources, and the document that describes the extended link doesn't actually have to be one of the resources to which the link points. Using this linking mechanism, you could catalog all of the links in your entire Web site in one document. A link described by a resource that isn't one of that link's resources is called an *out-of-line link*. An extended link may also be a multidirectional link that joins several documents together in a single link and can be traversed from any one of its resources.

Although simple links may make perfect sense, extended links are an entirely new beast and may be a bit confusing. As you read about the syntax used to describe extended links and the various attributes you can use with them, their role in XML documents will begin to make more sense.

Some Important Terminology

XLink and XPointer have their own vocabulary that they use to describe the components that make up the various types of XML links. I'll be referencing these components over and over in the remaining sections of the skill, so I thought it best to lay them all out for you here to avoid confusion later on:

Link This component describes a connection between two or more resources or subsections of those resources.

LINKING element In an XML document, this is the element that declares and also describes a link. The HTML LINKING element is the ANCHOR tag, but in XML, any element can be a LINKING element.

Locator This component is the URL of a resource.

Resource This component is any document that has a URL and is part of a link. Resources can include XML documents, a part of an XML document, binary and text files, as well as HTML documents, and it includes the following:

Subresource This is a specific part of a resource; XPointers point to subresources.

Participating resource This is any resource that is part of a link; all resources can potentially be part of a link, and a resource becomes a participating resource only when a locator is used to include it as part of a link.

Local resource This is a document that both contains a link and is one of the link's resources.

Remote resource This is a document that is one of the link's resources but that doesn't actually contain the link.

Traversal This component causes a link to access its resource. In HTML links, only a user clicking on anchored text can activate. In XML links, there are several different ways to activate link transversal, including some that don't require any user interaction at all.

Because linking in XML is so different from that in HTML, you'll need to be prepared for your XLinks to do things you never imagined. To help put the definitions into perspective, consider the following:

- Simple links are always inline links that connect the local resource to one remote resource. In the simple hyperlink `<a href="http://www.w3.org/">` saved in the document `example.html`, the local resource is `example.html`, and the remote resource is `http://www.w3.org/`.
- When the linking element isn't a resource in the link, the link is an out-of-line link, and the linking element is contained inside a remote resource; for example, a catalog document describing all of the links on your Web site without actually participating in any of the links. The Web site resources that are part of the links described by the out-of-line link in the remote resource are all participating resources.

That's quite a bit to wrap your mind around, but it will all become clear in time.

Creating XLinks in an XML Document

XLinks are added to any element in an XML document by simply adding a series of attributes to that element. You don't have to include the attributes in an element's attribute-definition list for the element to describe a link. Instead, these attributes are reserved for the linking mechanism and are automatically able to be included with any XML element.

Creating a Simple Link

Use this syntax to turn any element into a simple link:

```
<element href="url" xml:link="simple">...</element>
```

There are two important XLink attributes at work here. The first is `HREF`, the standard attribute you always use to point to a resource in a hyperlink. The second, `XML:LINK`, describes what kind of link you've created for the application that will be processing your document. The value `simple` indicates that this is a simple link. All simple links must have both an `HREF` attribute with a URL value and the `XML:LINK` attribute with a value of `simple`. This is a simple XLink:

```
<site href="http://www.htmlhelp.com" xml:link="simple">...</site>
```

This basic simple link isn't any different from a link in an HTML document, except that it's attached to the `SITE` element instead of the `A` element. XLink includes several other attributes that allow you to better label the link, control its traversal, and decide how its content is displayed, as discussed in the following sections.

The `XML:LINK` attribute can take the following values in addition to `simple`:

`document` Labels the link as one that references a document that describes a set of extended links.

`extended` Labels the link as an extended link, which means it can be an out-of-line link or a multidirectional link.

`group` Labels the link as one in a group of extended links.

`locator` Labels the link as a locator (URL) that points to a resource.

You will use these attributes when creating extended links, and they will be discussed in more depth in the "Creating an Extended Link" section.

Categorizing a Link

The ROLE attribute provides a way for document developers to pass on important information about the link and its resource to the application that is going to process the document. Because every link is different, you can use the ROLE attribute any way you'd like; for instance, as a cataloging mechanism for searching through links. You can assign a role to each link that describes what kind of resource it points to, as in this example:

```
<site href="http://www.htmlhelp.com" xml:link="simple"
     role="general/reference/tutorial">...</site>

<site href="http://www.xmlinfo.com" xml:link="simple"
     role="xml/reference/tutorial">...</site>

<site href="http://www.dhtmlzone.com" xml:link="simple"
     role="dhtml/reference/tutorial">...</site>
```

A search mechanism built into the processing application can use the role you've assigned to each link to help users search for links to sites they're specifically interested in. The ROLE attribute is an optional attribute in an XML link.

While the ROLE attribute is designed to create a machine-readable label for a link, the TITLE attribute allows a developer to assign a human-readable label, as well. In this code, both machine- and human-readable labels are provided for the link to the HTML Help site:

```
<site href="http://www.htmlhelp.com" xml-link="simple"
     role="general/reference/tutorial"
     title="Web Design Group's Excellent Web Guide and
            Tutorial Site">...</site>
```

Activating a Link

The ACTUATE attribute provides developers with a way of specifying how a link should be activated. The values for ACTUATE are

`user` Traversal of the link should be activated by the user.

`auto` Traversal of the link should be automatically activated when the document is processed.

In the following example, the link to the HTML Help site is user-activated, while the link to James Tauber's XML site is activated automatically:

```
<site href="http://www.htmlhelp.com" xml:link="simple"
     role="general/reference/tutorial" acutate="user">...</site>
```

```
<site href="http://www.xmlinfo.com" xml:link="simple"
     role="xml/reference/tutorial" acutate="auto">...</site>
```

HTML links are user-activated; in HTML, you cannot force a hyperlink to activate automatically. You may be wondering why you would want a link to be automatically activated rather than user-activated. As discussed in the next section, XLink provides a way for developers to specify that the contents of a resource should be inserted into the local resource instead of completely replacing the local resource. This means you can build a document from a series of simple links, indicate that their content should be included in the document, and have the links activated automatically. When the user views the document, it looks like a regular document but it will really comprise content from several other documents included via simple links automatically traversed.

Controlling the Resource's Content

Use the `SHOW` attribute to specify how the content of a resource should be displayed. Its values include

`embed` Specifies that the content of the resource should be embedded within the local resource; the content of the linked resource effectively becomes part of the local resource.

`new` Specifies that the content of the resource should be displayed in a new window or frame or another area separate from the one in which the local resource is being displayed. This is similar to the `TARGET="_BLANK"` or `TARGET="FRAME-NAME"` attributes used with the HTML `ANCHOR` element, which causes a linked resource to be opened in a new window or a specific frame in a frameset.

`replace` Specifies that the content of the resource should replace the content of the local resource, as is done with regular HTML links.

The code below indicates that when the user activates links, the HTML Help site should be included within the current document, the XML Info site should be opened in a new window, and the DHTML Zone site should replace the current document contents:

```
<site href="http://www.htmlhelp.com" xml:link="simple"
     role="general/reference/tutorial" acutate="user"
     show="embed">...</site>
```

```
<site href="http://www.xmlinfo.com" xml:link="simple"
     role="xml/reference/tutorial" acuate="user"
     show="new">...</site>

<site href="http://www.dhtmlzone.com" xml:link="simple"
     role="dhtml/reference/tutorial" acuate="user"
     show="replace">...</site>
```

In XML even simple links do more than regular HTML links. And if the added functionality of simple links isn't enough, there are always extended links.

Creating an Extended Link

The out-of-line link mechanism allows a developer to describe a link between resources from within another document that isn't actually part of the link. The syntax for creating an extended link is

```
<element xml:link="extended">
     <element xml:link="locator" href="url">...</element>
     <element xml:link="locator" href="url">...</element>
     <element xml:link="locator" href="url">...</element>
</element>
```

Once again, you can use any element to create an extended link, but notice that an extended link is actually formed by an element or series of elements with the `XML:LINK="LOCATOR"` attribute nested within a `PARENT` element that includes the `XML:LINK="EXTENDED"` attribute. For an extended link to work correctly and not result in an invalid document, the `PARENT` and `CHILD` elements must adhere to the content models established in the document's DTD. Your document will be invalid if you try to create `CHILD` elements as locators for an extended link inside a `PARENT` element they aren't allowed to be nested within.

This example turns our three simple links from the previous section into resources for a single extended link:

```
<resources xml-link="extended">
<site href="http://www.htmlhelp.com" xml:link="locator"
     role="general/reference/tutorial" acutate="auto"
     show="embed">...</site>

<site href="http://www.xmlinfo.com" xml:link="locator"
     role="xml/reference/tutorial" acuate="auto"
     show="new">...</site>
```

```
<site href="http://www.dhtmlzone.com" xml:link="locator"
     role="dhtml/reference/tutorial" acuate="auto"
     show="replace">...</site>
</resources>
```

Locator links can include the ROLE, ACTUATE, SHOW, and TITLE elements just as simple links can. In addition, you can add the following attributes to the EXTENDED LINK element:

INLINE=(true | false) Specifies that the linking element is a resource of the link as well as of the locator links. The default value for this attribute is false, making all extended links out-of-line links unless you specify otherwise.

CONTENT-ROLE Provides a machine-readable role label for the extended link's local resource when it is an inline extended link.

CONTENT-TITLE Includes a human-readable title label for the extended link's local resource when it is an inline extended link.

When these attributes and values are added to the extended link sample, they label the link as an inline extended link (so the local resource is part of the link) and assign it a role and a title:

```
<resources xml:link="extended" inline="true"
     content-role="catalog/reference"
     content-title="Important Online Resources">
<site href="http://www.htmlhelp.com" xml:link="locator"
     role="general/reference/tutorial" acutate="auto"
     show="embed">...</site>

<site href="http://www.xmlinfo.com" xml:link="locator"
     role="xml/reference/tutorial" acuate="auto"
     show="new">...</site>

<site href="http://www.dhtmlzone.com" xml:link="locator"
     role="dhtml/reference/tutorial" acuate="auto"
     show="replace">...</site>
```

If the INLINE attributes are missing, the extended link will be, by default, an out-of-line link, and the local resource that contains the link description will not be part of the link.

You can group together several documents that describe extended links to form an extended link group using this syntax:

```
<element xml:link="group">
     <element xml-link="document" href="url">...</element>
     <element xml:link="document" href="url">...</element>
     <element xml:link="document" href="url">...</element>
</element>
```

A group simply describes a collection of extended link documents and is a highly effective tool for managing large numbers of links on a single site or across multiple sites. Here is an example that uses the RGROUP element to describe the linking group and the RDOC element to describe the documents in the group:

```
<rgroup xml:link="group">
     <rdoc xml-link="document" href="resources1.xml">...</rdoc>
     <rdoc xml:link="document" href="resources2.xml">...</rdoc>
     <rdoc xml:link="document" href="resources3.xml">...</rdoc>
</rgroup>
```

Once processing applications are designed that know how to work with extended XML links and groups of extended links, Web site maintenance will never be the same again.

Making XLinks More Specific with XPointers

XPointers take resource descriptions one step forward by allowing you to reference a subresource within a resource. Use one of these two characters to attach an XPointer to a URL:

- #
- |

The pound sign (#) is the connector used in HTML to link to a specific point within an HTML file and is included in XPointer for compatibility with HTML links. The vertical bar (|) is an XML-specific connector.

If the pound sign connects the URL and the XPointer, the entire resource is downloaded to the processing application, even though the pointer references only a specific point in the document. This is consistent with the way Web browsers deal with links to a specific point in a document. The entire page is downloaded, but the specific spot in the page is brought to the top of the browser window. For example, this link references the LANWrights, Inc., corporate information page in general, but it doesn't reference a certain spot in the document:

```
<a href="http://www.lanw.com/corporat.htm">
```

This link, however, points not only to the corporate information page but also specifically to the development and consulting section of the page:

```
http://www.lanw.com/corporat.htm#Devcon
```

When viewed in a Web browser, the first URL loads the entire document and displays it from the beginning, as shown in Figure 13.1. The second URL loads the entire document, then brings the development and consulting section immediately into view, as shown in Figure 13.2.

By contrast, when you use the XML-specific vertical bar (|) connector, the way the resource and the specific subresource to which the pointer points are handled is entirely up to the processing application. The application may decide to retrieve only the specific subresource rather than the entire document as a Web browser does. XPointer hasn't been implemented by anyone yet, so it's difficult to tell. XML pointers are designed to be more flexible than HTML pointers and should allow DTD and processor designers to determine how subresources need to be treated in a specific application of XML.

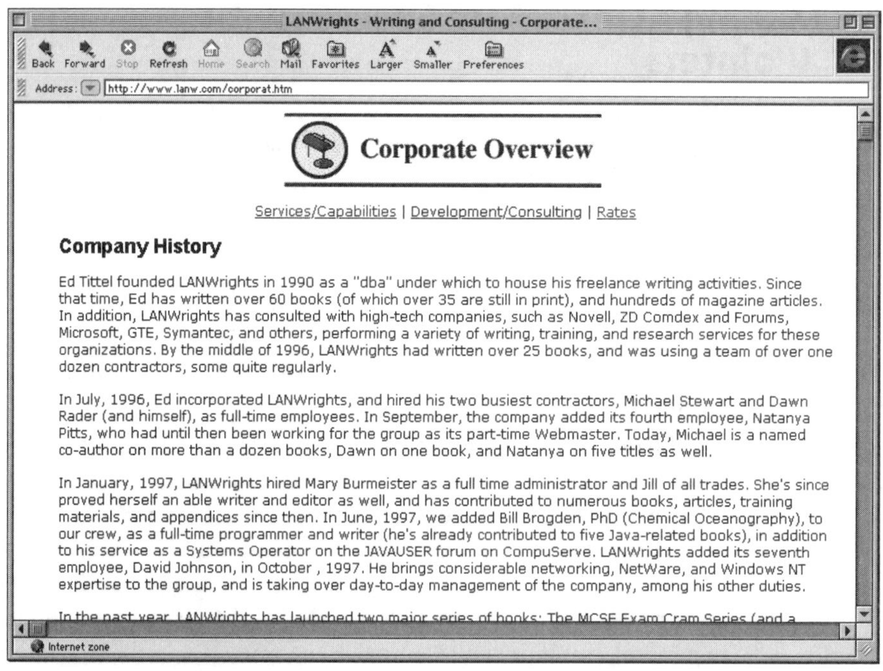

FIGURE 13.1: A Web page without a pointer is displayed from the very beginning of the document.

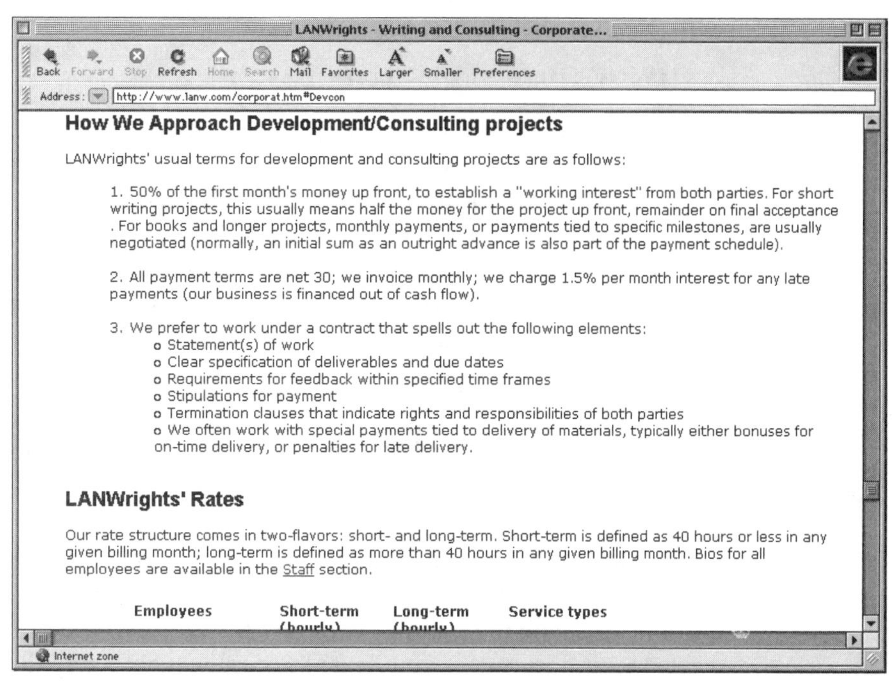

FIGURE 13.2: A Web page with a pointer is displayed from the location of the pointer.

In HTML documents, a specific subresource is identified using the `<a name="string"></a>` attribute. On the LANWrights, Inc. corporate page, the development and consulting section is labeled with this tag:

```
<a name="DevCon">
```

The string that provides the value for the NAME attribute is what follows the pound sign in a pointer to a specific place in an HTML document. XPointers support this method of identifying subresources, but the NAME attribute can be used with any element in the document. XPointer also recognizes unique identifiers assigned to an element with the ID attribute.

Using these two methods, you can point directly to any element in a document by following the document's URL with the pound sign or vertical bar with the element's unique name or ID. If you don't include a URL before the pound sign or vertical bar, XPointer assumes you're referencing a specific point within the local document. This simple link uses an XML connector to point to an element with the ID of `abstract` in the same document:

```
<link xml:link="simple" href="|abstract">
```

XPointer is also designed to provide you with other ways of referencing subresources, including by location and string value. However, the specifics of how this is going to be done are among the most contended parts of the XLink specification. Until the first full version of the specification is out, there's no way to tell exactly what forms these other location devices will take. Even so, the extended abilities of links in XML, combined with XPointers, already provide document developers with an advanced system of hyperlinking unlike any seen before.

When the Description Is Done: Deploying XML Documents

You know all there is to know about describing and linking up your XML documents. You can write your own DTD or use someone else's, and you're on top of the hottest linking mechanism to ever hit the Web. So, what's next? After you've created your documents, you'll want to deploy them for all the world to see, and that's a whole new ball game.

The next skill concentrates on the issues surrounding the deployment of your XML documents, starting with the all-important issue of processing them. In Skill 14, "Processing XML Documents," you'll explore an XML processor from the inside out and get a sneak preview of how XML documents can be disseminated over the Web for viewing with your favorite Web browser.

Are You up to Speed?

Now you can...

- ☑ **Describe the XML linking mechanism**
- ☑ **Create simple and extended XML Links**
- ☑ **Add XPointers to your links**

PART III

Deploying XML Documents

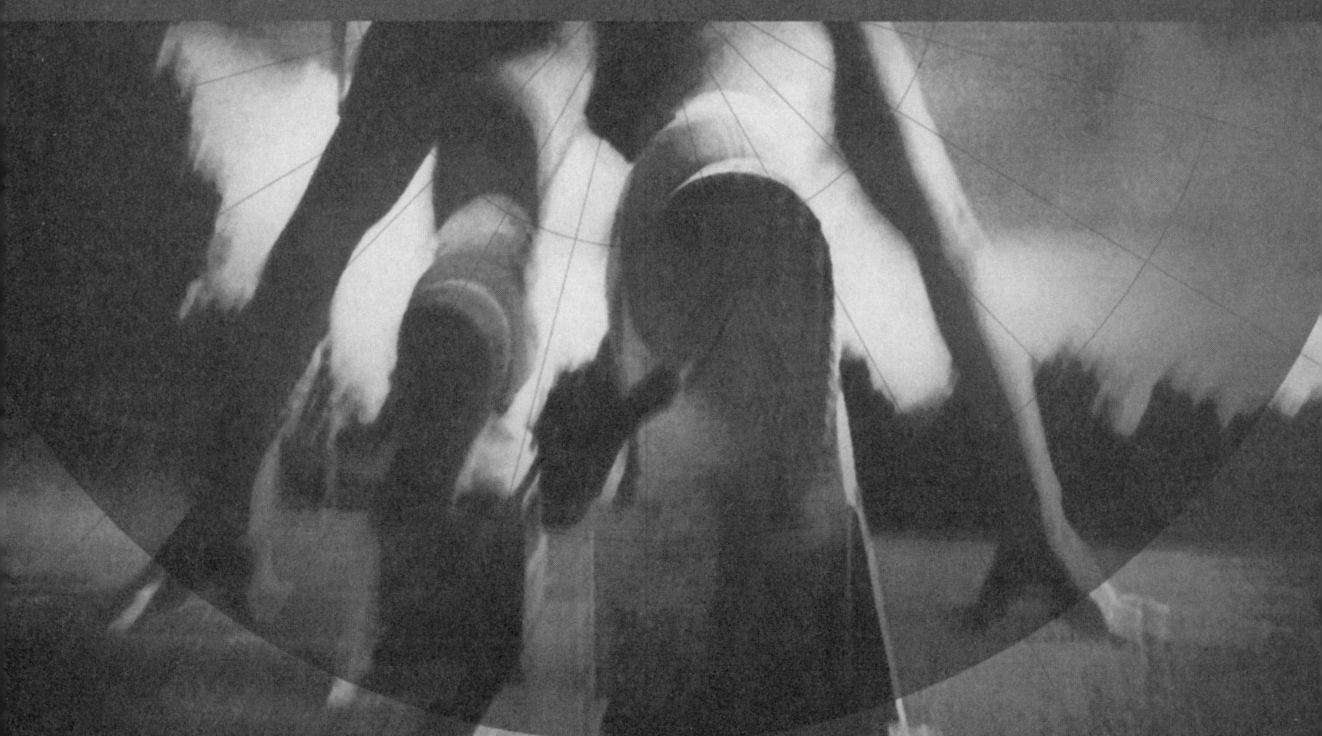

SKILL 14

Processing XML Documents

- How XML documents are processed for display
- The difference between a parser and a display device
- A survey of XML processing tools

You're up to speed on creating both XML DTDs and documents, so now what? After you've built your documents using your own or someone else's DTD, you'll need to deploy those documents—and for that you'll need a processing application. In this skill, I'll introduce you to the inner workings of the applications that process your XML documents, and I'll discuss the difference between validating and non-validating processors. I'll also acquaint you with some of the currently available XML processors and look at how you can use processing instructions to help guide the applications that process your documents.

The Role of an XML Processor

Believe it or not, a Web browser is an HTML processor. It reads the document, sorts through all of the document's elements and their content, and it displays the content accordingly in the browser window. An XML processor works in the same way: reading documents, interpreting their markup, and rendering them on a display device, such as a browser screen or printer. Processors make it possible for XML documents to be deployed and displayed.

Even though all XML processors function in essentially the same way, the end results can be very different. The processor that reads and interprets an Open Software Description (OSD) document will install one or more software packages based on the document's content. A processor that reads and interprets a Precision Graphics Markup Language (PGML) document will render a high-quality vector graphic.

As with all of the other aspects of XML, the final processing and application of an XML document is entirely driven by content. In the pre-XML world of HTML, a Web browser was the only kind of processor. With the introduction of XML, it is possible to create specialized processors that focus on only one kind of content rather than trying to be all things to all documents.

Dissecting an XML Processor

An XML processor can have two distinct parts:

- The parser
- The display device

As you learned in Skill 7, "Creating Well-Formed and Valid Documents," a parser is the tool that reads your document and breaks the document down into its component parts. Usually a parser creates a tree or catalog of all the elements and their content in your document and then passes that information along to a device that knows how to display the content based on the parser's evaluation. All Web browsers have built-in parsers that analyze your HTML documents. The display you see in your browser window is the browser's interpretation of the data supplied to it by the parser. Although you can have a parser without a browser, you generally can't have a browser without a parser because the browser needs parsed data to function properly.

Validating and Nonvalidating Processors

You also learned in Skill 7 that there are two kinds of parsers: validating and nonvalidating. Validating processors check a document against a DTD to make sure that the document strictly adheres to the rules set down in the DTD. If the document violates any part of the DTD, the parser will return an error, and the processing of the document may cease entirely. This is not necessarily a bad thing. You can use a validating processor to check your documents for accuracy before you deploy them. A good validating parser not only will return an error but will elaborate in the error message about the particular source of the error. In the end, a validating processor is one of the best debugging tools you have at your disposal.

A nonvalidating processor checks only to see if a document is well formed. These processors return an error only when there's a problem with the general construction of the document, such as a missing quotation mark around an attribute value or a missing close tag in a tag pair. Nonvalidating processors generally process a document faster because they don't have to check every element and content group against a DTD. Often developers will use a validating processor to test their documents and use a nonvalidating processor for final deployment. Once you know a document is valid, there's no reason to check it each time it's processed.

NOTE A good example of nonvalidating parsers are the ones used in Netscape Navigator and Internet Explorer to parse Web pages. Although this does speed up the parsing time, it doesn't force Web developers to create valid HTML. To see an example of a validating parser at work, visit `http://validator.w3.org/`.

Parsers Dominate the Field

The majority of the processors currently available are simply parsers that aren't responsible for the display of a document. There are a couple of processors that both parse and display documents, and as XML develops, there will definitely be more. Many DTD designers are working on processors engineered to parse and display documents written for their DTDs. At the same time, others in the XML field are developing stand-alone parsers that aren't geared toward one DTD or another but that can be used to process any DTD.

If a full-fledged processor hasn't been created specifically to parse and display your XML documents, you can choose one of the many individual parsers already available and add your own display device to it. Granted, creating a display device isn't as simple as baking a cake, but it's certainly easier than creating both a parser and a display device. You may think that all this theoretical discussion about how a processor behaves is not really applicable to work in the real world. To convince you otherwise, I'd like to introduce you to JUMBO (no, it's not a circus act), the application responsible for processing documents written for the Chemical Markup Language (CML) vocabulary.

A Real-World Example: The CML JUMBO Browser

The developers of CML created their XML vocabulary to describe molecular and chemical formulas. To display and manipulate such complex formulas, they had to develop a specialized browser. To that end, they created JUMBO, a Java-based validating XML processor. This processor includes both a parser and a display mechanism, and when used as an applet, JUMBO will display CML documents inside a Web page. The CML and JUMBO tutorial located at `http://ala.vsms.nottingham.ac.uk/vsms/java/cml/tutorial.html` provides a wealth of information about both the vocabulary and the browser it has spawned.

NOTE The following example and screenshot come from the CML site and are copyrighted by Peter Murray-Rust, 1996, 1997.

I'd be the first to admit that I don't remember much from high school chemistry, but I'm still impressed that JUMBO can take this source code and generate the display you see in Figure 14.1:

```
<!DOCTYPE CML PUBLIC "-//CML//DTD CML//EN">
<CML>
<MOL>
<ATOMS>
<ARRAY BUILTIN="X2">
-1.342 0.137 0.8 -0.1029 -1.3289 -1.882 -1.8799 0.438 0.464 -0.1409
0.163
</ARRAY>
<ARRAY BUILTIN="Y2">
-0.527 -0.905 0.335 1.2439 0.879 -0.8419 -0.878 -1.471 -1.441 1.1049
2.28
</ARRAY>
<ARRAY BUILTIN="ELSYM">
C C O C O H H H H H H
</ARRAY>
<ARRAY BUILTIN="FORMCHARGE">
0 0 0 0 0 0 0 0 0 0 0
</ARRAY>
</ATOMS>
<BONDS>
<ARRAY BUILTIN="ATID1">
1 1 1 1 2 2 2 3 4 4 4
</ARRAY>
<ARRAY BUILTIN="ATID2">
2 5 6 7 3 8 9 4 5 10 11
</ARRAY>
<ARRAY BUILTIN="ORDER">
1 1 1 1 1 1 1 1 1 1 1
</ARRAY>
<ARRAY BUILTIN="STER">
0 0 0 0 0 0 0 0 0 0 0
</ARRAY>
</BONDS>
<FORMULA>
<XVAR BUILTIN="STOICH">
C C O C O H H H H H H
</XVAR>
</FORMULA>
</MOL>
</CML>
```

Skill 14

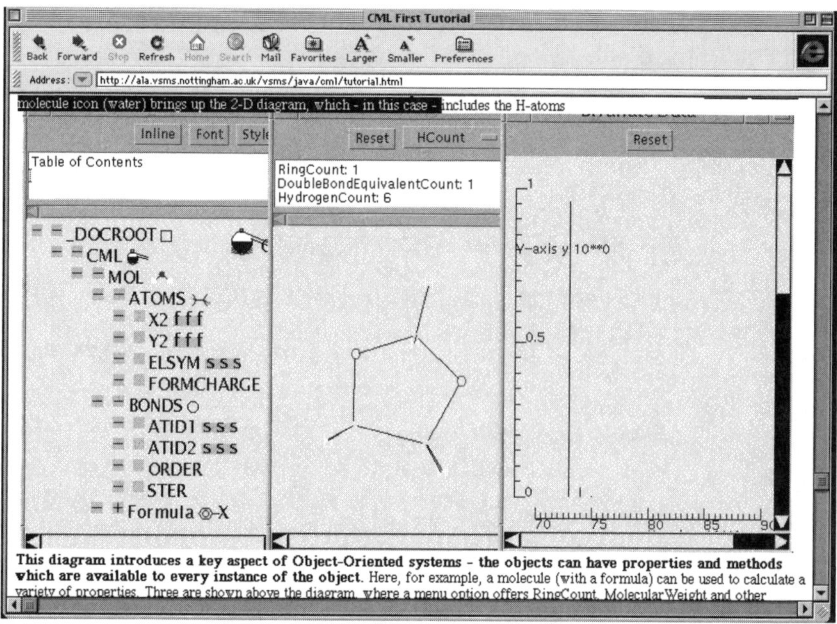

FIGURE 14.1: An example of JUMBO at work, as seen on the JUMBO tutorial Web page

You don't have to know a thing about chemistry to be amazed by what JUMBO and a CML document can accomplish. While you may never create your own CML documents, the fact that JUMBO exists and is a fully functional browser means that others will soon follow.

Utilizing Processing Instructions

XML provides a mechanism that allows document developers to pass important instructions along to the application that processes them. Use this syntax to create processing instructions (PIs):

```
<?name instruction ?>
```

The name portion of the PI indicates which application should read and interpret the PI and is officially called the PI target. XML actually uses PIs for several different purposes, including specifying the XML version for which the document is built. The name XML is reserved for those XML-specific PIs. The PI that indicates the XML version looks like this:


```
<?XML version="1.0" ?>
```

This is the most common XML PI you'll ever use and is the only one mentioned in this book. Even if this state of affairs changes as XML grows, you'll be fine as long as you know what a PI is, what it does, and how to form one.

To pass instructions to JUMBO, use this format:

```
<?JUMBO information goes here ?>
```

In large part, the application and document with which the PI is working determines the kind of PIs a processing application recognizes and knows how to use. You might encounter some problems if you try to pass a JUMBO-specific PI to a PGML processor. The documentation for the DTD or the processor includes information about the PIs that you can use in processing documents for that DTD or with that processor.

A Survey of Available XML Processors

In this section, I'll look at a few of the different stand-alone XML processors currently available or under development. This list is by no means exhaustive; it is intended to provide a sampling of the kind of processors you have at your disposal. The selection of currently available XML processors that display documents is driven in large part by the actual XML vocabularies being used by various organizations and industries. Because many of those organizations are still developing their XML solutions, few display-oriented processors are available, even in beta form. Expect this to change as XML becomes more common. For now, parsers are the most commonly available XML processing tools.

NOTE For a complete discussion of other XML development tools, turn to Skill 27, "Choosing the Right XML Tool." That skill focuses on all the different kinds of tools available to help you create and disseminate your documents, from editors to document management systems.

KEEPING UP WITH PARSER PROGRESS

Because XML is a rapidly growing technology, the list of processors will grow almost on a daily basis. To keep up with all the latest processor developments, visit these three Web sites regularly:

- The W3C's XML page software section at `http://www.w3.org/XML/`
- James Tauber's XML software pages at `http://www.xmlsoftware.com/`
- Robin Cover's XML software list at `http://www.sil.org/sgml/publicSW.html`

The following sections describes an individual processor and includes a list of vital statistics that answer these questions about each:

- Is the processor validating or nonvalidating?
- What language is the parser written in?
- What platforms does the parser run on?
- What author or authors are responsible for the processor?
- What Web resources provide more information about the processor?

In addition, each section includes a brief description of the processor and a discussion of using it as part of an overall XML solution. In general, I've tried to winnow out processors that are currently available and provide a selection of those that are the most dependable, useable, and likely to continue to be developed. All of these processors are freely available for public use. However, if you intend to use them to build your own software suite or XML application, you'll need to license them from the developer.

You'll notice that many of the stand-alone parsers are written in Java to allow them to work in Web browsers as well as across several different platforms without having to be rewritten. The current trend in XML processor development is to use the Java language, and it seems that Java will continue to be the language of choice for the development of XML processors.

DataChannel XML Parser (DXP)

The DXP vital statistics are

- Validating
- Written in Java
- Runs on any platform that is Java-enabled
- Authored by DataChannel and Juergen Modre
- URL: `http://www.datachannel.com/xml_resources/dxp.shtml`

DataChannel was one of the first companies to fully adopt XML and to create tools for developing and deploying XML documents. Their DXP parser is based on Norbert's XML Parser (NXP), one of the earliest XML processors developed. DataChannel just happens to have Norbert Mikula on staff, so this parser is well grounded in the XML tradition. The parser was specifically created as a tool for software developers to use in the development of applications that use XML to achieve a particular purpose. Although DXP is written in Java, all of the bells and whistles that make it such a powerful tool for application developers also make it impractical for use in applets that have to be downloaded across the Web. DXP is truly a parser for the professional.

Expat

The Expat vital statistics are

- Nonvalidating
- Written in C
- Windows 95/98 and NT
- Authored by James Clark
- URL: `http://www.jclark.com/xml/expat.html`

Expat was released as part of Netscape's Mozilla source code and is going to be part of the Netscape Navigator 5 XML support solution. Expat is small and fast and will work well once it is fully integrated into the browser environment. Expat in combination with user-defined style sheets (discussed in Skill 15, "Adding Style with CSS") allows Web users to browse XML documents. Because Expat has been licensed as part of the Mozilla source code, it is subject to the provisions of that license. Most people will use the parser in the context of the Navigator browser, but if you'd like to license it for your own use for other applications, contact James Clark at the previous URL to work something out.

NOTE The implementation of XML in Navigator is explored more fully in Skill 18, "Browsing XML with the Latest Web Clients."

Lark

The Lark vital statistics are

- Nonvalidating
- Written in Java
- Runs on any platform that is Java-enabled
- Authored by Tim Bray
- URL: `http://www.textuality.com/Lark/`

Tim Bray is the chief editor of the XML specification, and his Lark parser was one of the first XML processors to arrive on the scene. Lark began as an experiment in both XML and Java and has turned out to be a nifty little processing tool. As with most stand-alone parsers, Lark can only read and interpret XML documents, not display them. As display tools are developed, you'll find that Lark is the underlying processor that makes them tick. If you're looking for a solid nonvalidating parser to experiment with—or perhaps create your own XML browser—Lark is a good candidate.

NOTE Bray has also written a validating version of the Lark browser called *Larval*. It is available for download at the same URL as Lark.

Microsoft XML (MSXML)

The MSXML vital statistics are

- Validating
- Java or C++

- Should run on any platform that is Java-enabled; works best on Windows 95/98 and NT
- Authored by Microsoft
- URL: `http://www.microsoft.com/xml/parser/jparser.asp`

Microsoft created MSXML specifically for use with Internet Explorer 4 and later. IE 4 for Windows 95/98 and NT come with the C++ version of the parser already installed; the Java version is free for download from the Microsoft site. Although the Java-based parser should run on any platform, it doesn't do well on the Macintosh; however, that will probably change with time. MSXML is part of Microsoft's overall XML solution, but even on its own, it is a great little parser. MSXML will play a large role in bringing XML to the Web as we make the transition from HTML pages to XML documents.

NOTE As of August 20, 1998, Microsoft is partnering with DataChannel for future developments of their XML parser. I shouldn't be surprised if the next iteration includes DXP. An early beta of the IE 5 parser is at `http://www.datachannel.com/xml_resources/index.shtml`.

NOTE Skill 18 includes a more in-depth discussion of how MSXML works with the current version of Internet Explorer (4) and the role it will play in displaying XML documents in IE 5.

XML for Java

The XML for Java vital statistics are

- Validating
- Java
- Runs on any platform that is Java-enabled
- URL: `http://www.alphaworks.ibm.com/formula/xml`

Created by Kent Tamura and Hiroshi Maruyama at the IBM facility in Tokyo, XML for Java is one of the newest parsers to hit the information superhighway. XML for Java is designed to be more than a parser though; it can also be used to generate

XML and includes support for XPointers. IBM is distributing this gem free of charge, even for commercial use; however, you have to license it (for free) if you want to include it in other software applications. This could just be the perfect tool for the developer who is going to be working with XML documents outside the scope of basic Web browsers. It has the development power of IBM behind it, and it seems that Big Blue is going to continue development on the parser as well as develop a tool kit that will make the parser easy to use.

Installing and Using an XML Processor on Your Computer

Java-based processors will run on any computer that has a Java runtime environment stored on it. For the most part, that means you can run a parser from within your Web browser. However, because Web browsers are designed to do more than just display Java, you might want to consider downloading a Java browser whose only job is to run Java class files. If you are working in the Windows or Sun/Solaris platforms, visit `http://java.sun.com/products/jdk/1.1/jre/index.html` to download a Java runtime environment for working with Java-based parsers. If your platform of choice is the Macintosh, visit `http://www.apple.com/macos/java/` to download a Mac OS Runtime for Java.

Processors written in a language other than Java, such the C-based Expat or the C++ version of MSXML, are generally compiled into executable files that automatically run on your computer when you double-click on their icon. These parsers are usually not platform-independent and tend to be developed for delivery in the Windows environment.

Whetting Your Whistle

I hope this look at five of the top XML processors gives you some idea of what kinds of processing tools are out there and what you can expect to do with them. As I mentioned earlier, the group of tools that will both parse and display is very small but seems to be growing. Both major Web browser vendors have licensed XML parsers, so you'll be able to browse your documents in either browser in the not-too-distant future. For the majority of people who want to dabble in XML but don't have the research and development resources necessary to create their own browser software, a Web browser will be all that they'll need as a display device for documents.

Stylin' XML with CSS

You're probably wondering how a Web browser, or any other browser for that matter, knows how to display your XML documents, especially since you can create your own tags. Browser developers obviously can't predict every tag a browser will have to display nor can they program a browser to display the tags and their content. It's up to you, as the developer, to tell the browser how you want your documents displayed. Because XML is a markup language rather than a formatting language, you'll need some sort of tool to provide the formatting information. That tool is called a style sheet. In Skill 15, "Adding Style With CSS," you will learn all about the first of two style-sheet mechanisms, Cascading Style Sheets (CSS), and how to tell a document browser what it needs to know about displaying your XML documents.

Are You up to Speed?

Now you can...

- ☑ **Describe how XML documents are processed for display**
- ☑ **Explain the difference between a parser and a display device**
- ☑ **Describe how a validating parser is different from a nonvalidating parser**
- ☑ **Choose a parser that best fits your needs**

SKILL 15

Adding Style with CSS

- The role of style sheets in the display of markup
- Using CSS with XML
- Creating style sheet rules
- A rundown of all CSS2 specifications

The focus of this book until now has been on markup and accurate description of content. In Skill 2, I told you to forget about display and not to use a markup language as a formatting language. Although you can leave display behind for a while, the time eventually comes when display moves to the forefront. That time is now. Just as markup controls description, style controls display. In this skill, I explore the first of two style mechanisms you can use to describe the final display of your marked-up content.

The Role Style Sheets Play in the Markup World

Even though the idea behind markup is to separate content from display, you can't just leave display hanging out to dry unless you trust someone else to read your mind and decide how you want your content displayed. One of the reasons Web developers go to such lengths to mangle markup is because their unique display is ultimately determined by a browser over which they have little control. In the traditional and structured world of markup, a style sheet is usually written by the document developer to control the final display of a document in any media.

In its simplest form, a style sheet is a list of instructions that tell a display device how to format DTD elements and their content. Several style sheets can exist for one document, allowing that document to be rendered by a wide range of formatting devices, from Web browsers to printers. Multiple style sheets can even be written to provide for different output on the same formatting device.

In my early discussions of markup, I said that a key benefit of separating content from display was that you could write one document and display it anywhere as many times as you liked. This is similar to the "write one, run anywhere" theory at work behind the Java programming language. For markup, "display anywhere" is made possible by style sheets. Granted, for this "write once, display anywhere" theory to work, style sheets have to be fully supported by the browsers, which they are not. Until both Navigator and Internet Explorer support CSS in its entirety and with some consistency, we're not in a much better place display-wise than we were before.

There are two style-sheet languages you can use with your XML documents. The first, and the topic of this skill, is Cascading Style Sheets (CSS), the original style-sheet mechanism created for HTML. The other, and the topic of Skill 16, is the Extensible Style Language (XSL), a special style-sheet mechanism created specifically for XML documents. Of the two, CSS is definitely the easier to learn and implement. XSL is based on the DSSSL style-sheet language written for SGML and is noticeably more complex and extensive than CSS. In addition, CSS is a formal W3C standard, whereas XSL is still under development and won't be released as a standard until at least mid-1999.

CSS will be the primary style language used to direct the display of XML documents on the Web and in other media. Although not as extensive as XSL, CSS is by no means wimpy, and it will provide a solid mechanism for describing the final display of XML documents. In the remaining sections of this skill, I'll introduce you to CSS, its syntax, and the element properties it allows you to define and manipulate as you design the instructions that guide the display of your XML documents.

The Original Style-Sheet Mechanism

The HTML markup language was created without an accompanying style-sheet language. In all of my reading and discussions with HTML gurus, I've never been able to find out why. Maybe it was because they thought HTML was so basic it didn't need one, or maybe they didn't expect HTML to become the major content-delivery system. However, it didn't take long for the powers that be to realize that a style-sheet language was badly needed.

Mangled markup and creative table markup were just two symptoms of a larger problem. Document developers were obviously yearning for more control over the final display of their documents and would do anything—no matter how proprietary or convoluted it might be—to achieve that control. In response to the rapidly growing demand, the W3C began work on a style-sheet mechanism for HTML. The result was CSS.

TIP Links to the full text of the current CSS specification and related resources can be found at the W3C's Web site at `http://www.w3.org/Style/CSS/`.

CSS is a relatively simple tool that allows you to assign styles to HTML elements and instruct any browser that is willing to listen how to display those elements and their contents. Although CSS duplicates some formatting built into HTML, such as the assignment of font colors and styles, it also provides Web developers with access to a large variety of formatting properties, such as margins, line-height, word-spacing, and more. The traditional properties to which page-layout specialists have always had access are now accessible to Web developers.

CSS is easy to learn and style sheets can be included directly in your documents or saved as stand-alone text files. The single biggest drawback associated with using CSS isn't related to the style-sheet language itself but is browser-related. The CSS support in the major browsers could definitely be better. CSS was first implemented in a limited way in Internet Explorer 3. Both Netscape Navigator 4 and Internet Explorer 4 have a more inclusive, but still incomplete, support for CSS. Support also varies from OS to OS, with better support implemented in the Windows versions of the browsers than in those for the Mac.

TIP

The folks at Webreview have put together a list of the safe, questionable, and unsupported CSS properties by the various browsers. To view these informative lists, point your Web browser at `http://www.webreview.com/`, and visit the Style Sheets section of the site.

Both Microsoft and Netscape have promised full CSS support in their version 5 browsers, which are currently in early beta versions. It's impossible to determine what "full CSS support" really means. One thing is for sure: the browser developers know that CSS is the vehicle that allows XML documents to be displayed in Web browsers, and they also know that XML is the future of the Web. These two things combined give me hope for the full implementation of CSS in the version 5 browsers.

Using CSS with XML

As I'm sure you've figured out by now, CSS will work as well with XML as it does with HTML. If you've built CSS style sheets for HTML documents, you'll be able to use the same skills to build CSS style sheets for XML documents. To use CSS with XML, you'll need to fully understand a DTD's purpose and goals and be very familiar with how its elements work together. In all probability, DTD designers will eventually create sample style sheets for their DTDs to give document developers an idea of how the markup and its content might be displayed.

As always with developing technologies, you'll want to play extensively with XML and style sheets. The more you do, the better you will understand how the two technologies work together and how you can use style sheets to create different renditions of the same document on one or more display devices.

Building CSS Style Sheets

A style sheet is just a collection of style rules. Once you know how to build one style rule, you can keep adding others to it to form a style sheet. It really is that simple. The syntax for defining style rules is fairly straightforward, and by the time you've completed this skill, you'll be constructing style sheets like a pro.

NOTE CSS is now in its second version with the current specification labeled CSS2. The specifics for building style sheets in this skill are based on CSS2. However, current 4.0 browsers do not support the additions made to the specification from version one to version two. These changes involve the addition of new properties rather than a change in syntax, so you can still safely create and implement style sheets. Look for alerts throughout the skill that provide important information about how the absence of CSS2 support might affect your XML documents.

Internal and External Style Sheets

A style sheet can be included in your XML or HTML document, or it can be saved to an external file and referenced from the document. HTML provides a clear syntax for doing this, but the jury is still out on exactly how XML will link to external style sheets or even how it will include internal style sheets in documents. All the hints I've received indicate that XML's style sheet referencing will be similar to that of HTML, so the following sections will describe that syntax.

To include style rules within a document, simply place them within STYLE tags, as shown here:

```
<style> type="text/css">
<!-
selector {declaration}
selector {declaration}
->
</style>
```

To create an external style sheet, simply save your style rules to a plain text file and then link to the style sheet using the <LINK> tag:

```
<LINK HREF="MYSTYLE.CSS" REL="STYLESHEET" TYPE="TEXT/CSS">
```

It's not clear yet whether Web browsers will automatically recognize the STYLE and LINK elements in any XML document or whether these elements will have to be included as part of each DTD. Even if they have to be added to the DTD, you'll be fine; you already know how to define elements in a DTD.

Basic Style Rule Syntax

A style rule has two parts:

The selector The element that the rule will affect

The declaration How the element will be affected

The declaration is further broken down into

A property What aspect of the element will be affected

A value How that aspect will be rendered

The syntax for creating a style rule is

```
selector {property: value}
```

So, a style rule that specifies that all third-level headings should be blue takes this form:

```
h3 {color: blue}
```

And you thought this was going to be difficult. There are a few specifics applicable to the process of creating a style rule. First, the selector has to be an element defined in a DTD. If you're writing a style rule for an HTML document, you can use only HTML elements as selectors. If you're writing a style rule for a PGML document, you can use only PGML elements as selectors. This is why you have to know a DTD well before you can create style sheets for it.

Also, you can't make up your own properties or values. The CSS2 specification dictates which properties you can use and which kind of values they take. The majority of this skill is dedicated to a listing of those properties and their associated values. Not every element has every property included in the specification. List-item properties don't work with paragraphs, as well they shouldn't.

Once you define a basic style rule for an element, that style rule is applied to every instance of the element throughout the document. But what if you want to apply the rule only to certain instances of the element? Or what if you want to create a rule that isn't attached to any one element but that can be used with any element in a document? Finally, what if you want to assign the same rule to several selectors or have more than one property-value combination in any given rule?

All of these are valid and important questions. They were also asked by the developers of CSS and have good answers. The following sections address the different variations on the basic style rule as well as when and how they should be used.

Different Types of Selectors

In addition to the basic element selector, you can create a style rule with two other types of selectors:

- Class
- ID

A class selector allows you to link a style rule to a specific instance of an element instead of to every instance of the element. For example, in an HTML document you might have different kinds of paragraphs. One kind might be an abstract, and another might be a plain vanilla paragraph. You might want to have the abstract paragraphs formatted in one way and the regular paragraphs in another. Because HTML doesn't include an ABSTRACT element, you'll have to use the P element to describe both types of paragraphs. To differentiate the types of paragraphs, you can use the CLASS= attribute:

```
<p class="abstract">This is an abstract.</p>
<p>This is a regular paragraph.</p>
```

To create a style rule that applies the style to just the abstract paragraphs and not the regular paragraphs, use this code:

```
p.abstract {font-family: Arial}
```

This style rule will be assigned only to those paragraphs that have a class of abstract. You can also create another style rule for the remaining regular paragraphs using the basic syntax:

```
p {font-family: Verdana}
```

This rule will be applied to all paragraphs that don't have a class of any kind.

By using class as part of your selector, you can create a series of style rules for the same element that are invoked only when the element matches the class of the rule. There's no limit to the number of rules or classes you can have for each element.

TIP The value for the CLASS= attribute must match exactly the string that comes after the period in the style rule's selector, or the style rule won't be applied to the element and its contents.

It is also possible to create a style rule that isn't linked to any individual element but is a free agent that can be assigned to any element in a document. These style rules have unique identifiers that are referenced using an element's `ID=` attribute. To create this kind of style rule, use this code:

```
#abstract {font-family: Arial}
```

This bit of code creates a style rule with the identifier `abstract` that can be invoked by any element in the document using this code:

```
<h1 id="abstract">This is an abstract heading</h1>
```

The same style rule can be applied to a paragraph in the same way:

```
<p id="abstract">This is an abstract paragraph</p>
```

You'll find that you create more style rules for specific elements than you do for generic style rules, but at least you have the mechanism at your disposal.

Class and ID selectors used in addition to regular selectors provide you with a pretty extensive repertoire of options for linking a style rule to an element in a document.

Grouping Selectors and Declarations

You can also group both selectors and declarations to link one style rule to multiple elements or combine several property-value combinations in one style rule. To link a declaration to more than one selector, simply separate the selectors with commas (,):

```
h1, h2, h3 {color: blue}
```

This rule applies one declaration to three separate selectors. You can also mix and match selector types in one style rule:

```
#abstract, p.abstract, h2 {color: blue}
```

To include more than one property-value combination in a style rule, simply separate them with semicolons:

```
#abstract, p.abstract, h2 {color: blue;
                           font-family: Arial}
```

Once again, it really is that simple.

A Review of CSS Punctuation

You've probably noticed that punctuation plays an important role in the style-sheet language. As a review, Table 15.1 lists all of the punctuation marks used in CSS and describes the role each plays.

TABLE 15.1: CSS Punctuation

Punctuation	Name	Description
{ }	curly braces	Contain declarations in a style rule
:	colon	Separates properties from values in a declaration
.	period	Adds a class identifier to a selector
,	comma	Separates multiple selectors in a style rule
;	semicolon	Separates multiple declarations in a style rule

TIP The correct use of punctuation can make or break your style sheet, so when debugging a style sheet, first make sure you didn't accidentally switch your commas and periods or colons and semicolons.

Units in CSS

When you're assigning values to certain CSS properties, such as width, height, and font size, you can use the unit of your choice from a wide variety of options. Table 15.2 lists each unit of measurement and its abbreviation.

TABLE 15.2: Units of Measurement for CSS Properties

Unit Name	Abbreviation
Inches	in
Centimeters	cm
Millimeters	mm
Picas	pi
Points	pt
Pixels	px
Ems	em
Ens	en

My best advice regarding choosing and using different types of units is to work with those units with which you're most comfortable and be consistent. This isn't to say that you have to use one single unit of measurement throughout a style sheet, but if you start defining font sizes with points, stick with points.

The Different Property Families

You know how to create style rules and, by extension, style sheets. All that's left is to examine the style properties and their associated values, which you can use to create your declarations. The following sections describe each property family and then list the properties, their possible values, and a brief description of the property.

NOTE CSS is a pretty broad topic and whole books have been devoted to it. This skill can only touch the tip of the style-sheet iceberg. The Webreview (`http://www.webreview.com`), Webmonkey (`http://www.webmonkey.com`), and HTML Help (`http://www.htmlhelp.com`) sites all have great CSS tutorials and go into more detail about style sheets.

Property Value Syntax

The property value tables in the following sections include information about the types of values that a given property can take. To decode that value information, you'll need to know a bit about the notation used. Table 15.3 tells you all you need to know about reading value descriptions.

TABLE 15.3: The Property Value Notation System

Value	Description	Example
<value>	Identifies a particular type of value	`<length>`
Value*	Specifies that the value is repeated zero or more times	`[[<family-name>| <generic-family>],]*`
Value?	Specifies an optional value	`[/<uri >]?`
Value{X,Y}	Specifies that the value must occur at least *x* times and at most *y* times	`[<percentage>| <length>]{1,2}`
Keyword	Identifies a keyword that must appear exactly as shown	`repeat`
X | Y	Specifies a list of keyword alternatives from which only one may be used	`scroll	fixed	inherit`

TABLE 15.3 CONTINUED: The Property Value Notation System

Value	Description	Example
X || Y	Specifies a list of alternatives from which one or more may be used	<font-style> || <font-variant> || <font-weight>
[items]	Defines a group of items	[border-width || border-style|| <color> | inherit]

Box Properties

Box properties don't describe graphical boxes; they describe how the block of content described by elements is sized and arranged as well as how its borders and other physical attributes are formatted. Every element in a document, along with its content, has its own box, and you can exactly place each element's content on the page by setting the various box attributes for that element.

TABLE 15.4: Box Properties

Property	Description	Syntax	Values
border	Defines the width, color, and style for all of an element's borders	border: <value>	<border-width> || <border-style> || <color>
border-bottom	Defines the width, color, and style of an element's bottom border	border-bottom: <value>	<border-bottom-width> || <border-style> || <color>
border-bottom-color	Defines the color for an element's bottom border	border-bottom: <value>	<color>
border-bottom-style	Defines the style for an element's bottom border	border-bottom-style: <value>	none | hidden | dotted | dashed | solid | double | groove | ridge | inset | outset
border-bottom-width	Defines the width of an element's bottom border	border-bottom-width: <value>	thin | medium | thick | <length>

TABLE 15.4 CONTINUED: Box Properties

Property	Description	Syntax	Values
border-color	Defines the color for all four sides of an element's border	border-color: <value>	<color>{1,4} | transparent
border-left	Defines the width, color, and style of an element's left border	border-left: <value>	<border-left-width> || <border-style> || <color>
border-left-color	Defines the color for an element's left border	border-left-color: <value>	<color>
border-left-style	Defines the style for an element's left border	border-left-style: <value>	none | hidden | dotted | dashed | solid | double | groove | ridge | inset | outset
border-left-width	Defines the width of an element's left border	border-left-width: <value>	thin | medium | thick | <length>
border-right	Defines the width, color, and style of an element's right border	border-right: <value>	<border-right-width> || <border-style> || <color>
border-right-color	Defines the color for an element's right border	border-right-color: <value>	<color>
border-right-style	Defines the style for an element's right border	border-right-style: <value>	none | hidden | dotted | dashed | solid | double | groove | ridge | inset | outset
border-right-width	Defines the width of an element's right border	border-right-width: <value>	thin | medium | thick | <length>
border-style	Defines the style for all four sides of an element's border	border-style: <value>	[none | hidden | dotted | dashed | solid | double | groove | ridge | inset | outset]{1,4}

TABLE 15.4 CONTINUED: Box Properties

Property	Description	Syntax	Values
border-top	Defines the width, color, and style of an element's top border	border-top: <value>	<border-top-width> || <border-style> || <color>
border-top-color	Defines the color for an element's top border	border-top-color: <value>	<color>
border-top-style	Defines the style for an element's top border	border-top-style: <value>	none | hidden | dotted | dashed | solid | double | groove | ridge | inset | outset
border-top-width	Defines the width of an element's top border	border-top-width: <value>	thin | medium | thick | <length>
border-width	Defines the width of all four element borders at one time	border-width: <value>	[thin | medium | thick | <length>]{1,4}
bottom	Defines how far a box's bottom edge is from any other box that contains it	bottom: <value>	<length> | <percentage> | auto
clear	Specifies the sides on which text can be wrapped around an element	clear: <value>	none | left | right | both
float	Allows text to wrap around an element	float: <value>	left | right | none
height	Specifies an element's height	height: <value>	<length> | <percentage> | auto
left	Defines how far a box's left edge is from the right edge of any other box that contains it	left: <value>	<length> | <percentage> | auto
margin	Defines the size of all four element margins at one time	margin: <value>	[<length> | <percentage> | auto]{1,4}

TABLE 15.4 CONTINUED: Box Properties

Property	Description	Syntax	Values
margin-bottom	Defines the size of an element's bottom margin	margin-bottom: <value>	<length> | <percentage> | auto
margin-left	Defines the size of an element's left margin	margin-left: <value>	<length> | <percentage> | auto
margin-right	Defines the size of an element's right margin	margin-right: <value>	<length> | <percentage> | auto
margin-top	Sets the size of an element's top margin	margin-top: <value>	<length> | <percentage> | auto
max-height	Defines the maximum height for the box	max-height: <value>	<length> | <percentage> | none
max-width	Defines the maximum width for the box	max-width: <value>	<length> | <percentage> | none
min-height	Defines the minimum height for the box	min-height: <value>	<length> | <percentage>
min-width	Defines the minimum width for the box	min-width: <value>	<length> | <percentage> | auto
padding	Sets the padding size for all sides of an element at one time	padding: <value>	[<length> | <percentage>]{1,4}
padding-bottom	Sets the amount of space between an element's content and its bottom border	padding-bottom: <value>	<length> | <percentage>
padding-left	Sets the amount of space between an element's content and its left border	padding-left: <value>	<length> | <percentage>

TABLE 15.4 CONTINUED: Box Properties

Property	Description	Syntax	Values
padding-right	Sets the amount of space between an element's content and its right border	padding-right: <value>	<length> | <percentage>
padding-top	Sets the amount of space between an element's content and its top border	padding-top: <value>	<length> | <percentage>
position	Defines how a box is positioned in the browser window	position: <value>	normal | relative | absolute | fixed
right	Defines how far a box's right edge is from the left edge of any other box that contains it	right: <value>	<length> | <percentage> | auto
top	Defines how far a box's top edge is from any other box that contains it	bottom: <value>	<length> | <percentage> | auto
width	Specifies an element's width	width: <value>	<length> | <percentage> | auto

Classification Properties

Classification properties define how an element is classified. An element's classification as inline, block, or a list item greatly influence how it is displayed by a browser. Block elements, like headings and paragraphs, are almost always formatted with a line break and a full space after them. Inline elements, like HTML's bold and italics tags, are generally used within block elements and don't have any special spacing associated with them. Finally, list items are exactly what they sound like—items in a list—and are formatted accordingly. You can use these properties to classify an element and its content.

TABLE 15.5: Classification Properties

<table>
<tr><th>Property</th><th>Description</th><th>Syntax</th><th>Values</th></tr>
<tr><td>display</td><td>Specifies how an element should be displayed</td><td>display: <value></td><td>block | inline | list-item | none | run-in | compact | table | inline-table | table-row-group | table-column-group | table-header-group | table-footer-group | table-row | table-cell | table-caption</td></tr>
<tr><td>list-style</td><td>Specifies the list-style type, position, and marker image URL</td><td>list-style: <value></td><td><list-style-type> || <list-style-position> <list-style-image> || <url></td></tr>
<tr><td>list-style-image</td><td>Specifies an image to be used as a list-item marker</td><td>list-style-image: <value></td><td><url> | none</td></tr>
<tr><td>list-style-position</td><td>Specifies whether text in a list should be displayed inside or outside of the list-item marker</td><td>list-style-position: <value></td><td>inside | outside</td></tr>
<tr><td>list-style-type</td><td>Defines the type of marker to be used within a list</td><td>list-style-type: <value></td><td>disc | circle | square | decimal | lower-roman | upper-roman | lower-alpha | upper-alpha | none</td></tr>
<tr><td>white-space</td><td>Specifies how white space within an element should be rendered</td><td>white-space: <value></td><td>normal | pre | nowrap</td></tr>
</table>

Background and Color Properties

As the name implies, background and color properties specify how an element's background and color will be rendered.

TABLE 15.6: Background and Color Properties

Property	Description	Syntax	Values
background	Specifies an element's background color and image as well as how the image repeats its attachment and its position	background: <value>	<background-color> || <background-image> || <background-repeat> || <background-attachment> || <background-position>
background-attachment	Specifies whether an element's background image is fixed in the browser window or scrolls with the element	background-attachment: <value>	scroll | fixed
background-color	Defines an element's background color	background-color: <value>	<color> | transparent
background-image	Defines an image to be attached as the background for an element	background-image: <value>	<url> | none
background-position	Specifies the position of an element's background image in relation to the element	background-position: <value>	[<percentage> | <length>]{1,2} | [top | center | bottom] || [left | center | right]
background-repeat	Specifies how an element's background image should be repeated	background-repeat: <value>	repeat | repeat-x | repeat-y | no-repeat
color	Defines an element's color	color: <color>	

Skill 15

Browser Properties

The ability to control browser properties is new to CSS2. Currently, the only browser property you can affect with a style rule is the cursor—but it's a start.

TABLE 15.7: Browser Properties

Property	Description	Syntax	Values
cursor	Determines what kind of cursor will be displayed	cursor: <value>	[[auto | crosshair | default | pointer | move | e-resize | ne-resize | nw-resize | n-resize | se-resize | sw-resize | s-resize | w-resize | text | wait | help] || <uri>?]_

Font Properties

Once again, the uses of font properties are pretty intuitive. Use these properties to specify which font the text should be displayed in and other specifics about that display, including style and variant information.

TABLE 15.8: Font Properties

Property	Description	Syntax	Values
font	Specifies all of the font properties in one property/value set	font: <value>	[[<font-style> || <font-variant> || <font-weight>]? <font-size> [/ <line-height>]? <font-family>] | caption | icon | menu | messagbox | smallcaption | statusbar
font-family	Defines the font in which to display an element's text	font-family: [[<family-name> | <generic-family>],]* [<family-name> | <generic-family>]	<family-name> <generic-family> serif (ex: "Century Schoolbook") sans-serif (ex: "Helvetica") monospace (ex: "Courier") cursive (ex: "Zapf-Chancery") fantasy (ex: "Western")
font-size	Defines the size of text	font-size: <absolute-size> | <relative-size> | <length> | <percentage>	<absolute-size> xx-small | x-small | small | medium | large | x-large | xx-large <relative-size> larger | smaller <length> <percentage>
font-style	Specifies an element's font style	font-style: <value>	normal | italic | oblique

TABLE 15.8 CONTINUED: Font Properties

Property	Description	Syntax	Values
font-variant	Defines whether the text should be rendered as normal or small caps	font-variant <value>	`normal	small-caps`
font-weight	Specifies how dark or light text should be	font-weight: <value>	`normal	bold	bolder	lighter	100	200	300	400	500	600	700	800	900`

Paged Media Properties

This group of properties is new to CSS2 and is specifically designed to describe how a document should be rendered in paged media (print). This addition to the CSS specification recognizes that documents that look good in a browser don't necessarily look good in print. Use these properties to create a specific style sheet for when your document is printed.

TABLE 15.9: Paged Media Properties

Property	Description	Syntax	Values
marks	Specifies which type of marks should appear outside of a page box	marks: <value>	`crop		cross	none`
orphans	Identifies the minimum number of lines of a paragraph that must be left at the bottom of a page	orphans: <value>	`<integer>`
page-break-after	Specifies how a page break should be used after a page	page-break-after: <value>	`auto	always	avoid	left	right`
page-break-before	Specifies how a page break should be used before a page	page-break-before: <value>	`auto	always	avoid	left	right`

TABLE 15.9 CONTINUED: Paged Media Properties

Property	Description	Syntax	Values
size	Sets the size and orientation of a page	size: <value>	<length>{1,2} | auto | portrait | landscape
widows	Identifies the minimum number of paragraph lines that must be left at the top of a page	widows: <value>	<integer>

Table Properties

Also new to CSS2, table properties add control over table display to style sheets. Many markup languages make use of tables, and you'll need a way to format them.

TABLE 15.10: Table Properties

Property	Description	Syntax	Values
border-collapse	Determines whether borders are drawn around all sides of each cell in a table or just around the table itself	border-collapse: <value>	collapse | separate
caption-side	Specifies where a table's caption will appear	caption-side: <value>	top | bottom
cell-spacing	Defines the cell spacing in a table	cell-spacing: <value>	none | <length> <length>?
column-span	Specifies how many columns a cell should span	column-span: <value>	<integer>
row-span	Specifies how many rows a cell should span	row-span: <value>	<integer>

TABLE 15.10 CONTINUED: Table Properties

Property	Description	Syntax	Values
table-layout	Determines whether the table layout is controlled by the browser or is fixed based on present widths set for rows and columns	table-layout: <value>	auto | fixed

Text Properties

Text properties control the spacing between letters, words, and lines (to name a few items) as well as set alignment and other text display specifics. The content property, another new addition to CSS2, allows you to define blocks of content and have them automatically inserted wherever the style rule is used.

TABLE 15.11: Text Properties

Property	Description	Syntax	Values
content	Defines a block of content to be inserted in the document	content: <value>	[<string> | <uri> | <counter>]+
letter-spacing	Defines the amount of space between the letters in an element	letter-spacing: <value>	normal | <length>
line-height	Sets the amount of space between lines in an element	line-height: <value>	normal | <number> | <length> | <percentage>
text-align	Defines how text in an element should be aligned relative to its PARENT element and the page	text-align: <value>	left | right | center | justify

TABLE 15.11 CONTINUED: Text Properties

<table>
<tr><th>Property</th><th>Description</th><th>Syntax</th><th>Values</th></tr>
<tr><td>text-decoration</td><td>Defines how the text in an element should be decorated</td><td>text-decoration: <value></td><td>none | [underline || overline || line-through || blink]</td></tr>
<tr><td>text-shadow</td><td>Describes a shadow for a block of text</td><td>text-shadow: <value></td><td>none | [<color> || <length> <length> <length?]* [<color> || <length> <length> <length?]</td></tr>
<tr><td>text-indent</td><td>Defines how much the first line of a block-level element should be indented</td><td>text-indent: <value></td><td><length> | <percentage></td></tr>
<tr><td>text-transform</td><td>Defines the case in which the text in an element should be rendered (regardless of the case in which it is typed)</td><td>text-transform: <value></td><td>none | capitalize | uppercase | lowercase</td></tr>
<tr><td>vertical-align</td><td>Defines how an INLINE element should be positioned relative to its PARENT element</td><td>vertical-align: <value></td><td>baseline | sub | super | top | text-top | middle | bottom | text-bottom | <percentage></td></tr>
<tr><td>word-spacing</td><td>Defines the amount of space between the words in an element</td><td>word-spacing: <value></td><td>normal | <length></td></tr>
<tr><td>z-index</td><td>Identifies the box's horizontal position</td><td>z-index: <value></td><td>auto | <integer></td></tr>
</table>

Visual Effects Properties

The visual effects properties are another product of the CSS2 specification and control the most basic aspects of displaying content.

TABLE 15.12: Visual Effects Properties

Property	Description	Syntax	Values
clip	Specifies which part of an element's content is actually visible	clip: <value>	<shape> | auto
overflow	Indicates how a box should be rendered when its content is bigger than the dimension of the box	overflow: <value>	visible | hidden | scroll | auto
visibility	Specifies whether content is visible or invisible	visibility: <value>	visible | hidden

Moving up the Style-Sheet Ladder

This whirlwind trip through the world of CSS has been a fun one, but you're not finished with style sheets yet. In Skill 16, you'll meet the basic mechanisms of XSL and learn how to change an XML document into an HTML document using XSL. More fun is on the way.

Are You up to Speed?

Now you can...

- ☑ **Explain how style sheets are used to control the display of content**
- ☑ **Create basic style sheet rules**
- ☑ **Identify all of the CSS2 properties and their values**
- ☑ **Use CSS2 to create a style sheet for an XML document**

SKILL 16

Converting XML to HTML with XSL

- Exploring the role of XSL
- Using XSL to translate XML into HTML
- Creating XSL style rules
- Understanding the realities of XSL

Because XML is a more robust and extensible markup language than HTML, yet less complex that its parent SGML, it needs its own style-sheet language that goes beyond the bounds of CSS. However, this style sheet isn't unnecessarily complex. This skill examines XSL, the Extensible Stylesheet Language, which is the style mechanism under development that is specifically for use with XML documents. As XML evolves to become the primary markup tool for the Web, XSL will work in concert with CSS to drive the display of Web documents. In the immediate future, the most used feature of XSL will be its ability to transform documents described by one markup language into documents described by a different markup language. This will make it possible to convert documents described by any XML vocabulary into an HTML document that any Web browser can read.

Introducing XSL: The XML Style-Sheet Mechanism

In Skill 15, you met CSS, the style-sheet tool designed specifically to work with HTML documents. CSS also works with XML and is indeed the easiest and fastest way to develop a style sheet for an XML document. However, in the same way that the Web has outgrown HTML, so will XML quickly outgrow CSS. The developers of XML recognized immediately that it would need its own specialized style-sheet language, capable of supporting the many advanced applications of XML. Once the initial draft of XML was created and the direction XML was going to take was made a bit clearer, the W3C put together a working group charged with developing a style-sheet language for XML, to be called XSL.

XSL was developed from a proposal authored by a group of editors representing Microsoft, Inso, ArborText, and the University of Edinburgh, along with James Clark, a major player in the XML world and one of the editors of the XML standard. Although XML 1.0 is already a formal recommendation from the W3C and is therefore as standard as any Web technology gets, XSL is still under development. A formal draft of XSL was released on August 18, 1998, and the W3C's XML page at `http://www.w3.org/Style/XSL/` indicates that a final recommendation for XSL won't be released until May, 1999, at the earliest.

What all of this means to a developer is that XSL is a moving target. The working draft of XSL released in August is different from the original proposal submitted to the W3C by Microsoft and others. However, all of the XSL tools to date have been developed according to that original proposal, and there's no telling how the final XSL recommendation will compare to either the initial proposal or even this first working draft.

Although it's almost impossible to nail down how XSL will accomplish its goals in the end, the goals themselves are very telling about what you can expect XSL to do. Taken from the official working draft at `http://www.w3.org/TR/WD-xsl`, these design principles describe what XSL is meant to accomplish:

- XSL should support browsing, printing, and interactive editing and design tools.
- XSL should be capable of specifying presentations for traditional and Web environments.
- XSL should support interaction with structured information as well as the presentation of it.
- XSL should support all kinds of structured information, including both data and documents.
- XSL should support both visual and nonvisual presentations.
- XSL should be a declarative language.
- XSL should be optimized to provide simple specifications for common formatting tasks and not preclude more sophisticated formatting tasks.
- XSL should provide an extensibility mechanism.
- The number of optional features in XSL should be kept to a minimum.
- XSL should provide the formatting functionality of at least DSSSL and CSS.
- XSL should leverage other recommendations and standards, including XML, XLL, DOM, HTML, and ECMAScript.
- XSL should be expressed in XML syntax.
- XSL style sheets should be readable and reasonably clear.
- Terseness in XSL markup is of minimal importance.

As you can see, the idea behind XSL is to use XML syntax to write style sheets that will drive the final display of XML documents by any type of device, visual and nonvisual. In addition, XSL style sheets will be somewhat easy to read, once you learn the syntax of the style mechanism, of course, and the mechanism itself will be developed in such a way that it will grow with XML.

The Realities of Implementing XSL in the Here and Now

Although "will do" and "can accomplish" are great in theory, the real question is how can you use XSL style sheets right now? I mentioned earlier that all of the tools that have been developed for XSL up to this point were based on the original XSL submission, but the first working draft of XSL is different in syntax from the original submission. As a developer, how do you resolve the differences and write syntactically correct but usable style sheets?

In the end, you are bound by the processing devices that read and implement XSL, and you have to write style sheets that the devices can read and do something useful with. The "Processing XSL for Display on the Web" section later in this skill discusses what you have to do and what tools you need to use XSL in a real-world application; Skill 28, "Choosing the Right XML Tool," includes detailed descriptions of all of the XSL development and processing tools currently available on the market. However, the stark reality is that the tools that read your XSL style sheets, work with the syntax of the original XSL proposal and will probably continue to do so until a final XSL recommendation is released in the late spring of 1999.

To prepare you to work with XSL in any environment, the remaining sections of this skill theoretically discuss what XSL is designed to do without going into much detail about how it actually does it. You can learn what to expect from XSL without being bound to one version or another of the specification. As XSL becomes more stable, you will be able to apply the theories from this skill using the specific syntactical mechanisms the W3C decides upon.

Creating XSL Style Sheets

XSL style sheets have many applications, including defining how elements in an XML document should be rendered by a display mechanism. However, for this to work, the display mechanism has to understand both XML and XSL. The second and more immediately applicable use of XSL is to convert documents described with one markup language into documents described by a second, different markup language. In the real world, this means you can use XSL to convert XML to HTML for display on the Web.

Until XML support in Web browsers is standardized and becomes more widespread, the use of XSL style sheets to convert XML documents into HTML documents is the most practical way to disseminate XML documents via the Web.

XSL style sheets are actually XML documents themselves, and XSL is technically defined as an XML DTD. This means that any XML processor can read XSL style sheets and treat them like any other XML document. However, the processor must know how to interpret the results of a parsed XSL document and apply them to a standard XML document to create HTML. If the processor isn't XSL aware, it can parse the XSL document but not do much else with it. To generate HTML from an XML document and XSL style sheet, an XSL-aware processor reads both documents, applies the conversion information in the style sheet to the document, and creates HTML, as illustrated in Figure 16.1.

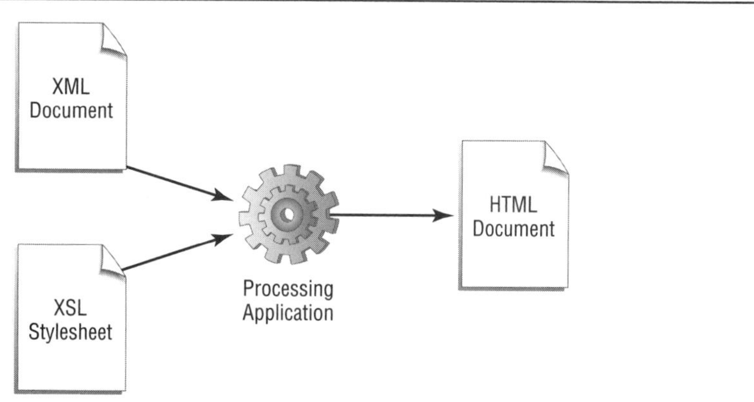

FIGURE 16.1: Processing an XML document and XSL style sheet to create an HTML document

An XSL style sheet that converts an XML document into an HTML document comprises style rules that map patterns of markup in the XML document to a final output in the HTML file. XSL syntax provides a standard way to describe patterns of markup in an XML document as well as to define how that markup should be translated into HTML.

Understanding Key XSL Terminology

Before you dive headlong into XSL, it's helpful to understand some common terms that crop up time and again during any discussion of XSL:

Construction rule The building block of an XSL style sheet; it defines the markup patterns the rule applies to and how that markup should be formatted or changed.

Pattern The part of a construction rule that specifies the markup in a document that will be formatted or translated.

Action The part of a construction rule that specifies how the pattern should be formatted or translated.

Root rule The construction rule that specifies what action should be applied to an XML document's document element.

Default rule A construction rule the specifies what actions should be applied to all markup not governed by other constructions rules.

As you work more with XSL, the definitions of these terms will make a lot more sense, and you'll find yourself speaking XSL in no time.

Construction Rules: The Basic XSL Building Block

A construction rule is the most basic of XSL's components. Just like a CSS style sheet comprises style rules, an XSL style sheet comprises construction rules. A construction rule associates a pattern with an action. Patterns are chunks of markup that an action—or formatting sequence—is applied to. The bulk of the XSL specification focuses on the specific syntax you use to define both patterns and actions.

To make it easier to define how an element and all of its content, including `CHILD` elements and their content, is formatted, XSL includes a convention called a `PROCESSING` element. This processing element directs the style rule to include in the display any `CHILD` elements (and their content) contained within the element whose formatting is described by the pattern. XSL syntax also provides a mechanism for specifying an element based on its context. You can identify an element in a pattern by describing the other elements around it and only have the rule's pattern apply to the element when it is in the exact context described by the pattern.

You may also include attribute specifics in a rule's pattern to identify not only which element in a document should have the rule's action applied to it but also which element with which specific attributes the action should affect. Finally, XSL provides a special syntax for specifying how the document element, also called a `ROOT` element in XSL, should be formatted or translated.

These are all of the basic syntax mechanisms that make up the original XSL proposal and that all of the current XSL development and browsing tools are designed for.

A Sample XSL Style Rule

After reading about the theory of XSL, you're probably chomping at the bit to see what the actual code behind an XSL style sheet looks like.

NOTE Remember that XSL is still very much in development, so the syntax conventions you see in the next example may change before the final XSL specification is released. Visit the book's Web site at www.sybex.com to keep up with the latest developments in XSL.

Before we can create a style rule, we need to have some XML markup and content to style. This chunk of code represents one piece of an XML document that might need a style sheet applied to it for formatting:

```
<heading>My first XSL style sheet</heading>
<body>This is my first XSL style sheet. I've never created one
before but it looks like fun.</body>
```

This bit of code contains two elements, HEADING and BODY, as well as their text content. To describe how the elements' content should be displayed in a browser of some sort, I'll need to create two construction rules (or templates). Each rule will have a pattern (the part of the rule that defines the element the rule is applied to) and an action (the part of the rule that defines how the element should be formatted).

The HEADING element describes a heading for a document or a section of a document, so the font used to display it in a browser should be larger than the size of the font used to display the regular body text. This construction rule specifies that the HEADING element and its content should be displayed in a 24-point font :

NOTE Be sure to read the comments within the style sheet carefully to see what each syntax convention does.

```
<xsl:stylesheet>
      <!- identifies this information as an XSL style sheet ->

     <xsl:template match= "heading">
          <!- specifies the pattern (the XML element) the style
           rule should be applied to ->
```

```
        <fo:block font-size="24 pt">
             <!- the action part of the rule that creates a
             block level flow object (includes a line break
             both before and after the element content) whose font size
             is 24 point ->

             <process-children/>
                 <!- specifies that all child elements and content
                  within the element should have the formatting action
                 applied to it as well ->
               </fo:block>
        </xsl:template>
   </xsl:stylesheet>
```

As the comments indicate, the style sheet first identifies the pattern, or XML element, that the rule's action should be applied to. The following addition to the code specifies that the BODY element should be formatted in 12-point type:

```
   <xsl:stylesheet>
        <xsl:template match= "body">
        <fo:block font-size="12 pt">
             <process-children/>
        </fo:block>
        </xsl:template>
   </xsl:stylesheet>
```

Both of these style rules employ the most basic XSL conventions but should give you a good idea of how XSL will work once the specification is nailed down. To find a complete listing of all the flow objects and properties (font size, color, margins, etc.) that you can use in XSL, visit the W3C's XSL Web site at **http://www.w3.org/Style/XSL**.

Writing a Style Sheet to Convert XML to HTML

Regardless of its syntax or structures, XSL is still a style-sheet language designed to determine how a document described by markup should be displayed by a browser. Even when XSL is used to convert a document written by one XML vocabulary into HTML, it is still governing how that document should be displayed because it is converting the document into a markup format viewable by a particular browser. It is entirely possible that once XSL is used to convert an XML document into HTML, there might be a separate CSS style sheet that governs how the HTML document is displayed in a Web browser.

As you know, the beauty of separating display from content is that one document may be displayed in several different ways, depending on the style sheet that is applied to it. XSL style sheets are the key to displaying an XML file in a regular HTML-based Web browser in any number of formats. Currently, Web browsers do not understand XSL, so an XSL ActiveX control is an important component in the display of an XML file as an HTML file. The control (available only for Internet Explorer 4 or later on the PC) interprets the results of the processing of both the XSL style sheets and the XML documents by Internet Explorer's built-in XML processor and displays them on the Web browser screen.

Conceivably, you could write several XSL style sheets to be applied to a single document written with one DTD, with each designed to display certain parts of the document (such as a table of contents or abstract information) or the entire document in a different display (full text or full text in large print). Using XSL to convert XML documents to HTML will be the first step in displaying documents described by XSL within regular Web browsers.

The Future of XSL

XSL is very unstable right now. With the release of a first working draft that is vastly different from the original proposal, the future of XSL is unclear. It is safe to say that XSL will be a formal specification in the late spring or early summer of 1999, but the form its syntax and structures will take is ambiguous. The initial release of the working draft has sparked a great deal of conversation and controversy, more than usually associated with the release of a working draft, so there will definitely be a large number of changes to the specification before it is released in final format.

The feeling I get from conversations and research is that tool vendors won't change their tools until the final version of XSL is out next year because they aren't any clearer about its syntax and structures than I am. As with all working drafts and other bleeding-edge technologies, the best thing for you as a developer to do is watch the W3C's XSL page closely as well as several other solid resources of XSL information. These resources include the following Web sites:

- The W3C XSL page
  `www.w3.org/Style/XSL/`
- Extensible Style Sheet Jumpstart
  `http://www.jeremie.com/JS/XSL/all.html`

- The ArborText XSL Tutorial
  `http://www.arbortext.com/xsl/frames.html`
- The Microsoft XSL pages
  `http://www.microsoft.com/xml/xsl/`
- XMLInfo XSL page
  `www.xmlinfo.com/xsl/`

Many of these resources include in-depth and advanced tutorials that are up-to-date with the current specification. They may change several times in the next few months, but then again, so will XSL.

NOTE Check out the Sybex Web site at `www.sybex.com` for further, up-to-the-minute information on XSL.

The Next Step: When HTML Is an XML Vocabulary

In this skill, you learned how to use XSL to convert XML documents to HTML documents for display in a Web browser. However, the day will come when HTML is itself an XML vocabulary, and the need to translate XML documents into it will be gone. Although that day is probably a year or so away, it's good to get into the habit of thinking of HTML as an XML vocabulary. Skill 17, "Turning Existing HTML Documents into Valid XML Documents," addresses all of the key differences between the way you use HTML now and the way you will use it in the future.

Are You up to Speed?

Now you can...

- ☑ **Describe how XSL works with XML to drive document display**
- ☑ **Explain how XSL can be used to convert XML documents into HTML**
- ☑ **Discuss the realities of XSL as a developing specification**

SKILL 17

Turning Existing HTML Documents into Valid XML Documents

- Using HTML as an XML vocabulary
- Forming good markup habits
- Creating a well-formed XML document from an existing HTML document
- Validating an HTML document against the HTML DTD

Time after time, the preceding skills of this book have stated that XML is the markup language of the future, here to take us to the next millennium and beyond. So the question now is what will happen to the markup language of today (HTML)? As you learned in Skill 1, "Learning About XML," XML is designed to work with HTML, and HTML will eventually be integrated with XML as one of its many vocabularies. This means that in the future, HTML documents will have to follow the same rules other XML documents do and that means you'll have to change the way you write HTML. To help you prepare for the future of Web design, this skill highlights the difference between the HTML of today and HTML versions to come by showing you how to convert an existing HTML document into a valid XML document.

Thinking of HTML as an XML Vocabulary

HTML as we now know it will not be the same in a year, but that's to be expected. HTML version 4.0 is vastly different from HTML version 2.0, which took the world by storm a few years ago. However, the differences between the two versions of HTML are entirely tag-related. HTML 4.0 works exactly like its 2.0 and 3.2 predecessors; it just includes more tags and attributes. The same will not be true of the coming versions of HTML. Instead of standing alone as an individual markup language with its own rules and regulations, look for HTML to become an XML vocabulary.

When this change in status for XML finally happens (probably within a year), Web designers will have to change the way they look at HTML. When HTML becomes an XML vocabulary, documents described by HTML will have to play by the same rules as other documents written for an XML vocabulary. HTML documents of the future will have to be at least well formed, and most likely valid, to function correctly.

The key to using HTML as an XML vocabulary is to not throw everything you know about XML and the proper uses of markup out the door the second you start to create a Web page. Instead, treat HTML as any other vocabulary and a Web browser as just another browser written for a specific XML vocabulary. The good news for all Web designers involved, both veteran and freshman, is that Web browsers will continue to support the HTML we're all so fond of. This means you won't have to convert all of your current Web pages to valid XML documents. And, because you can't expect HTML to become an official XML vocabulary for at least another year, you can continue to use HTML in its present format to create Web pages.

The question then becomes, why bother to learn how to create HTML documents that are valid XML documents and to think about HTML as an XML vocabulary? Because HTML will be absorbed into XML, it's best to be aware of which HTML structures and syntaxes will change when this happens. Also, breaking bad HTML habits can take a while, so a bit of practice now will pay off in the long run. Finally, because HTML is the markup language most of us are familiar with, it's a good teaching tool (because you don't have to stumble over tag descriptions and usage issues to work with it). The steps you'll take to create a valid HTML document are the same ones you'll take to create a valid document for any other XML vocabulary.

The next two sections of this skill focus on the bad HTML habits you'll need to break (or avoid forming) to use HTML as an XML vocabulary. The remaining sections of this skill focus on converting an HTML document into a valid XML document, to show you first hand how HTML will change as it begins to conform to XML standards. Even with the invention of a variety of XML vocabularies, HTML is still the simplest and most well known way to describe everyday content. Therefore, it will play an active role in the development of future Web pages, even though it'll just be one of many available vocabularies. What you'll learn in this skill will be valuable to you now as you use XML and later, when you have to use HTML as an XML vocabulary.

Unlearning Bad HTML Habits

If you're new to the world of Web design and markup languages, in many ways, you're lucky because you won't be saddled with the bad habits some experienced Web developers have acquired. But if you're a veteran HTML developer new to the XML scene, you'll have to unlearn some of those bad habits and pick up some new good ones. Not such a difficult thing to do once you've made your mind up to do it.

As you continue to learn about or work with HTML, you'll want to make sure you don't do any of the following:

- Ignore the rules just because the Web browsers do
- Mangle the markup to achieve a desired display effect
- Design pages for display specifically in only one browser or on only one platform
- Force content into markup that doesn't describe it accurately

Most Web browsers don't require your Web documents to be well formed or valid. Instead, they are very forgiving of broken rules and often reward designers by displaying technically broken HTML in a desirable way. For example, according to every HTML specification from version 2.0 to the current version 4.0, list-item markup (<LI>) must always be contained within ordered-list or unordered-list markup (<OL> or <UL> tags). So, this markup is invalid:

```
<li>Item 1
<li>Item 2
<li>Item 3
<li>Item 4
```

In case you hadn't noticed, this markup is also malformed because the <LI> tag is not an EMPTY tag, and each instance in the code sample is missing a close tag. However, despite the fact that this code is both invalid and malformed, both Internet Explorer and Netscape Navigator display this markup as an unordered list, as shown in Figures 17.1 and 17.2.

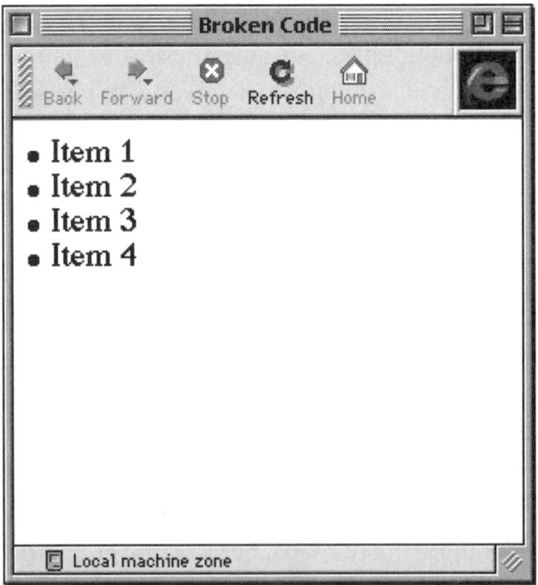

FIGURE 17.1: Malformed and invalid HTML is still displayed by Internet Explorer.

FIGURE 17.2: Malformed and invalid HTML is still displayed by Netscape Navigator.

There are literally hundreds of other examples of both invalid and malformed markup that will be displayed just fine by most available Web browsers. The willingness of Web browsers to forgive mistakes often leads to markup that has been intentionally mangled to achieve a specific effect that can't be achieved with correct markup.

Did you notice that both IE and Navigator displayed the broken list code as an unindented unordered list? Browsers regularly indent both ordered and unordered lists, so a designer looking for a way to display an unindented unordered list might fall back on broken code to arrive at that display. Even though it works, the code is still broken. Once HTML becomes an XML vocabulary, such techniques won't work. Instead, developers can specify how elements and their content should be displayed by a browser the correct way—with style sheets.

Because HTML is a markup language and the final display is left up to the Web browser, the same document may look different, depending on the browser or the platform. For example, the Web page at `http://www.microsoft.com/xml/default.asp` looks very different in Internet Explorer and Netscape Navigator on both the PC and Mac platforms, as Figures 17.3 through 17.6 show.

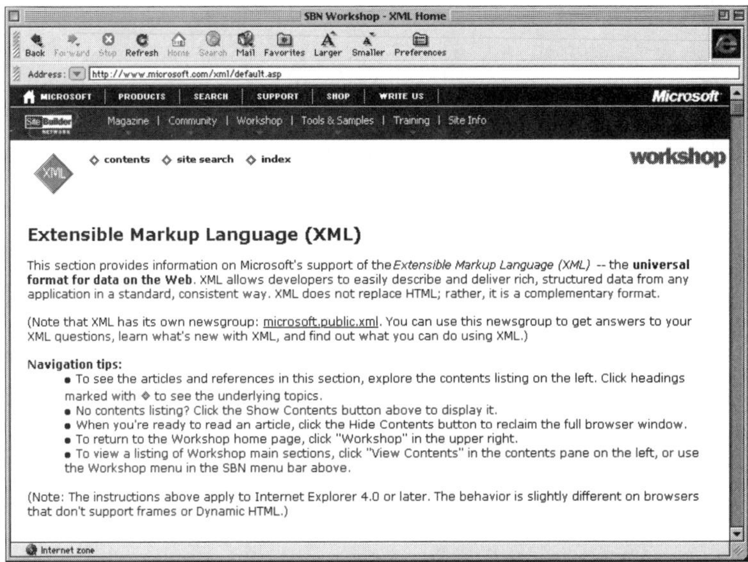

FIGURE 17.3: The Microsoft XML resources page displayed by IE 4 on a Mac

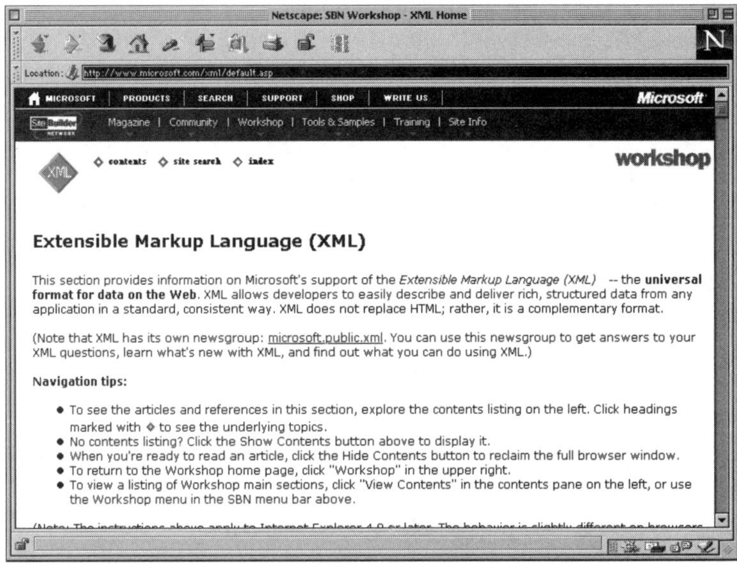

FIGURE 17.4: The Microsoft XML resources page displayed by Navigator 4 on a Mac

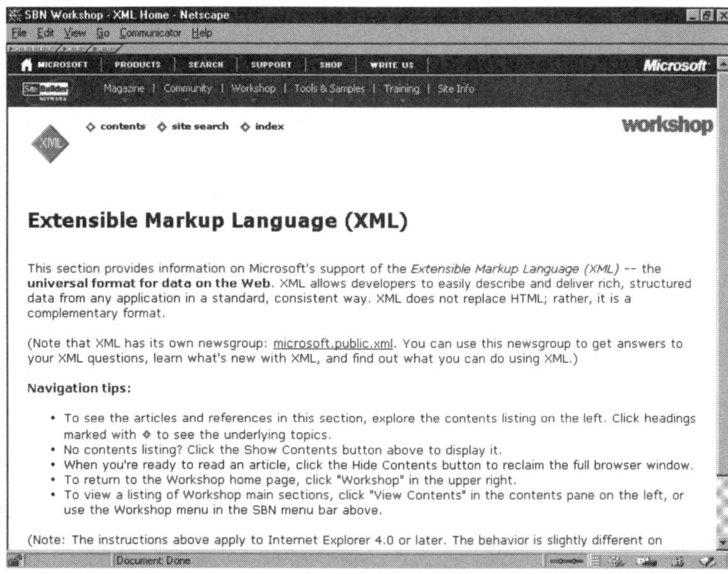

FIGURE 17.5: The Microsoft XML resources page displayed by Navigator 4 on a PC

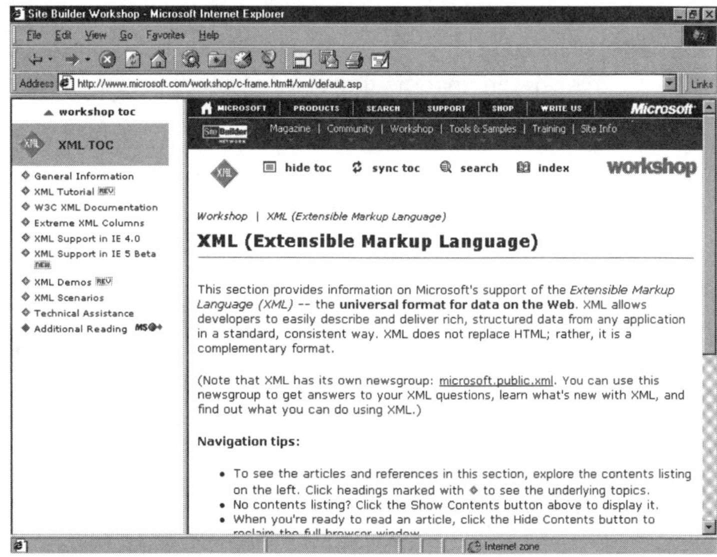

FIGURE 17.6: The Microsoft XML resources page displayed by IE 4.5 on a PC

The Microsoft XML resources page was designed to be viewed with the latest version of Internet Explorer on a PC running a Windows operating system. This may not surprise you considering it is Microsoft Web page, but there are literally thousands of other pages on the Web optimized for one browser or another or one operating system or another. The reason for the differences in display and optimizing pages for just one environment is that it's almost impossible to make mangled markup work consistently from computer to computer.

As you learned in Skill 2, "Making Sense of Markup," the basic premise of any markup language is that it separates content from display and focuses on describing the content of a document as accurately as possible. By forcing round content into a square markup hole (i.e., trying to describe airplane parts with HTML), developers are forced to mangle markup and do all types of interesting things to make their content presentable on the Web. Because XML will bring a wide variety of markup languages to the Web, each with its own specific purpose, there's no reason for content to fit into a particular markup anymore.

By breaking (or just not picking up) bad markup habits, you'll almost automatically acquire good markup habits. Good markup habits lead you to

- Choose the right markup for your content
- Create documents that are always well formed and create valid documents when necessary
- Use the markup language you've chosen to describe your content as accurately as possible
- Keep the final display of your document separated in your mind from its description

Now that I've covered the dos and don'ts any Web developer will need to know, it's time to put them to work to convert an existing HTML document into a valid XML document.

Turning an Existing HTML Document into a Valid XML Document

Skill 7, "Creating Well-Formed and Valid Documents," included a short section on making an existing HTML document well formed. At that point, you had to believe me when I said the document wasn't well formed and what it would require to make it so. Now that you're well versed in all of XML's structures and rules, it's time to revisit the idea of making an existing HTML document XML-compliant. This time you won't have to take my word for it, all that you know about XML will be proof enough. In addition, this skill includes a section on checking your HTML document against a DTD to make sure that it is not only well formed but also valid.

The following code shows a basic HTML page:

```
<html>
<head>

   <title>
      LANWrights - Writing and Consulting - MCSE Resources
   </title>

   <link href="lanwstyle.css" type="text/css" rel="stylesheet">

   <style>
      p, ul, blockquote {font-family: verdana, sans-serif}
   </style>

</head>


<body bgcolor="#ffffff" link="#800000" vlink="#000080">

<center><p>
   <img src="../../graphics/mcselogo.gif" align=bottom
    alt="mcse resources" border="0">
</p> </center>

<center><p>
<a href="#patch"> Core Four Pack Patch</a>
| <a href="#discuss">Discussion Boards</a>
| <a href="#prep">Exam Preparation</a>
| <a href="#contact">Contact</a>
</p></center>

<p>The MCSE Exam Preparation book series from PubHouse are designed to
provide networking professionals seeking the MCSE, or other Microsoft
Certification, with quality exam-prep materials. Ed Tittel is the series
editor for the MCSE Exam Preparation series and LANWrights' staff and
contractors have created quite a collection of Exam Preparation titles
to help budding Microsoft Certified Professionals prepare for and pass
the requisite tests.</p>
```

```
<h2><a name="ep-errata"></a>Exam Preparation</h2>
<p>The table below includes a complete listing of all the LANWrights'
MCSE Preparation titles. Click on a book title to read more about each
Exam Preparation title and even link to Amazon.com to order your own
copy of the book. </p>

<p>In our effort to provide you with the most accurate and up-to-date
information, we have reviewed the entire manuscript of several of the
books and created errata sheets to address the typos, mistakes, and
errors that unfortunately made it into print. Book titles marked with
an asterisk (<b>*</b>) indicate their errata sheets contain details
that are essential to successfully passing the certification exam. To
view the errata for any Exam Preparation book visit our
<a href="../errata/default.htm">errata</a> page.</p>


<dl>
   <dt><b><a href="../epne.htm">
      *Networking Essential Preparation Guide</A></B>
         <DD>(Test #70-058) <br><br>
   <dt><b><a href="../eptcpip.htm">
      *TCP/IP Preparation Guide</a></b>
         <dd> (Test #70-059) <br><br>
   <dt><b><a href="../epwin95.htm">
      Windows 95 Preparation Guide</a></b>
         <dd>(Test #70-063) <br><br>
   <dt><b><a href="../epnts.htm">
      *Windows NT Server 4 Preparation Guide</a></b>
         <dd>(Test #70-067) <br><br>
   <dt><b><a href="../epntse.htm">
      *Windows NT Server in the Enterprise Preparation Guide</a></b>
         <dd> (Test #70-068) <br><br>
   <dt><b><a href="../epntw.htm">
      *Windows NT Workstation Preparation Guide</a></b>
         <dd>(Test #70-073)<br> <br>
   <dt><b><a href="../epps2.htm">
      Proxy Server 2 Preparation Guide</A></B>
         <dd>(Test #70-088) <br><br>
   <dt><b><a href="../epfour.htm">
       MCSE Core Four Pack</a></b><br><br>
       <dd><a name="patch"></a>
           <a href="../examprep/ep4patch398.exe">
           Patch (308Kb)</a> for the 1997 printing of
           Part:198-3 (3/11/98)<br><br>
        <dd>Online version of the
           <a href="../examprep/cdsite/examprep.htm"
           target="_blank">Four Pack CD-ROM</a>
</dl>
```

```
<h3><a name="discuss"></a>Exam Preparation Discussion Boards</h3>
<p>Please visit our
<a href="http://www.lanw.com/webboard/webboard.dll/~2">online discus-
sion forums</A> for each of the Exam Preparation titles. Feel free to
ask questions, share information, and help your peers master the mate-
rials necessary to become an MCP or MCSE! LANWrights promises to
respond to new questions promptly, so be sure to check in regularly.
Note that these forums will be moderated, so don't be disappointed if
repeat questions don't appear, or if we respond privately to queries,
rather than publicly. All submissions will be acknowledged, at least by
e-mail, so be sure to give us your e-mail address when you sign up.</p>


<h2><a name="contact"></a>Contact Us</h2>

<p>For feedback, questions, or errata related to the Exam
Preparation books please send e-mail to
<a href="mailto:examprep@lanw.com">examprep@lanw.com</a>. For
comments or questions about the Web site, or to report
broken links please e-mail the LANWrights'
<a href="mailto:webmaster@lanw.com">Webmaster</a>.</p>

<br><br>

<p><center>
<A HREF="mcse.htm">
<img src="../../graphics/cert_mcse.gif" alt="mcse resources"
   align=bottom border="0"></a>
<a href="java.htm"><img src="../../graphics/cert_java.gif"
   alt="java resources" align=bottom border="0"></a>
<a href="../errata/default.htm"><img
   src="../../graphics/cert_errata.gif" alt="master errata
   list" align=bottom border="0"></a>
<a href="order.htm"><img src="../../graphics/cert_order.gif"
   alt="order practice tests" align=bottom border="0"></a>
</center>


<center>
<p><img src="../../graphics/navigbar.gif"  alt="navigtion image, see
text links below" usemap="#navigbar" ismap border="0">
<map name="navigbar">
<area shape="rect" coords="344, 0, 401, 56"
   href="http://www.lanw.com/overview.htm">
<area shape="rect" coords="287, 1, 345, 56"
   href="http://www.lanw.com/lanw.htm">
<area shape="rect" coords="228, 1, 287, 56"
   href="http://www.lanw.com/showcase.htm">
```

Skill 17

```
<area shape="rect" coords="172, 0, 229, 55"
   href="http://www.lanw.com/exam.htm">
<area shape="rect" coords="114, 1, 172, 55"
   href="http://www.lanw.com/training.htm">
<area shape="rect" coords="55, 1, 115, 56"
   href="http://www.lanw.com/books.htm">
<area shape="rect" coords="0, 1, 55, 55"
   href="http://www.lanw.com/default.htm">
</map></p></center>

<center><p class=textnav>
| <a href="../../default.htm">Home</a>
| <a href="../../books.htm">Book Nook</a>
| <a href="../../training.htm">Training Center</a>
| <a href="../../exam.htm">Certification Central</a>
| <a href="../../showcase.htm">Technology Showcase</a>
| <a href="../../lanw.htm">Corporate HQ</a>
| <a href="../../overview.htm">Site Overview</a>
|</p></center>

<p><br>
<img src="../../graphics/line.gif" width="100%" height="2"></p>

<p class="address">
<img src="../../graphics/css.gif" align=right border="0">

<font face="arial">URL:
<a href="mcse.htm">
http://www.lanw.com/books/examprep/mcse.htm</a><br>
Layout, design &amp; revisions &copy; 1997, 1998
<a href="../../default.htm">LANWrights</a>, Inc. <br>
<a href="mailto:webmaster@lanw.com">Webmaster:</a>
Natanya Pitts <BR>
Revised - August 17, 1998 <i>[NP]</i>
</font></p>

</body>
</html>
```

Two steps are required to turn this HTML document into a valid XML document. The first is to ensure that the document is well formed, and the second is to check it against the HTML 4.0 DTD for validity.

Step 1: Create a Well-Formed XML Document

As you'll recall from Skill 7, a well-formed XML document must

- Include XML and document type declarations
- Declare all entities used in the document within an internal DTD
- Be contained within a single document element
- Include open and close tags for all regular CONTAINER elements
- Identify EMPTY tags with a slash (/) before the closing greater-than sign (>)
- Nest tags correctly
- Enclose all attribute values in quotation marks
- Use entity names instead of actual file locations as values for attributes

By now you've seen enough well-formed XML code to recognize malformed code when you see it. To ensure that the sample HTML document is well formed, there are several changes that will have to be made to it. To demonstrate each of the following snippets of code from the HTML document, additions and changes to the original code are shown in bold italics, and those changes and additions are discussed immediately afterwards.

```
<?xml version="1.0" rmd="internal" ?>
<!doctype html public "-//w3c//dtd html 4.0 transitional//en"
"http://www.w3.org/tr/rec-html40/loose.dtd" [
<!entity mcselogo "../../graphics/mcselogo.gif" system gif>
<!entity cert_mcse "../../graphics/cert_mcse.gif" system gif>
<!entity cert_java "./../graphics/cert_java.gif" system gif>
<!entity cert_errata "../../graphics/cert_errata.gif" system gif>
<!entity cert_order "../../graphics/cert_order.gif" system gif>
<!entity navigbar "../../graphics/navigbar.gif" system gif>
<!entity line "../../graphics/line.gif" system gif>
<!entity css_logo "../../graphics/css.gif" system gif>
]>

<html>
<head>

   <title>
      LANWrights - Writing and Consulting - MCSE Resources
   </title>
```

```
   <link href="lanwstyle.css" type="text/css" rel="stylesheet">

   <style>
      p, ul, blockquote {font-family: verdana, sans-serif}
   </style>

</head>
```

The major changes to this section include the addition of an XML declaration and a DTD. The DTD includes a reference to the HTML 4.0 specification the document is written for as well as an internal DTD that includes entity declarations for all the binary entities used in the document.

```
<body bgcolor="#ffffff" link="#800000" vlink="#000080">

<center><p>
   <img src SRC="mcselogo" align=bottom
    alt="mcse resources" border="0">
</p> </center>

<center><p>
<a href="#patch"> Core Four Pack Patch</a>
| <a href="#discuss">Discussion Boards</a>
| <a href="#prep">Exam Prep</a>
| <a href="#contact">Contact</a>
</p></center>

<p>The MCSE Exam Preparation book series from
PubHouse are designed to provide networking professionals
seeking the MCSE, or other Microsoft Certification, with
quality exam-prep materials. Ed Tittel is the series editor
for the MCSE Exam Preparation series and LANWrights staff and
contractors have created quite a collection of Exam Prepration titles
to help budding Microsoft Certified
Professionals prepare for and pass the requisite tests.</p>


<h2><a name="ep-errata"></a>Exam Preparation</h2>
<p>The table below includes a complete listing of all the LANWrights'
MCSE Preparation titles. Click on a book title to read more about each
Exam Preparation title and even link to Amazon.com to
order your own copy of the book. </p>

<p>In our effort to provide you with the most accurate and up-to-date
information, we have reviewed the entire manuscript of
several of the books and created errata sheets to address
the typos, mistakes, and errors that unfortunately made it
```

```
into print. Book titles marked with an asterisk (<b>*</b>)
indicate their errata sheets contain details that are
essential to successfully passing the certification exam. To
view the errata for any Exam Preparation book visit our
<a href="../errata/default.htm">errata</a> page.</p>
```

There aren't many changes to this section of the document at all. The changes that do need to be made focus entirely on adding in quotation marks around attribute values, slashes at the end of EMPTY elements, and changing SRC= attributes for <IMG> tags to the name assigned to the GIF file in its entity declaration.

```
<dl>
   <dt><b><a href="../epne.htm">
      *Networking Essentials Exam Preparation Guide</a></b>
         <dd>(Test #70-058) <br /><br /></dd>
   </dt>
   <dt><b><a href="../eptcpip.htm">
      *TCP/IP Exam Preparation Guide</a></b>
         <dd> (Test #70-059) <br /><br /></dd>
   </dt>
   <dt><b><a href="../epwin95.htm">
      Windows 95 Exam Preparation Guide</A></B>
         <DD>(Test #70-063) <br /><br /></dd>
   </dt>
   <dt><b><a href="../epnts.htm">
      *Windows NT Server 4 Exam Preparation Guide</a></b>
         <dd>(Test #70-067) <br /><br /></dd>
   </dt>
   <dt><b><a href="../epntse.htm">
      *Windows NT Server in the Enterprise Exam Preparation
Guide</a></b>
         <dd> (Test #70-068) <br /><br /></dd>
   </dt>
   <dt><b><A HREF="../epntw.htm">
      *Windows NT Workstation Exam Preparation Guide</a></b>
         <dd>(Test #70-073)<br /> <br /></dd>
   </dt>
   <dt><b><a href="../epps2.htm">
      Proxy Server 2 Exam Preparation Guide</a></b>
         <dd>(Test #70-088) <br /><br /></dd>
   </dt>
   <dt><b><a href="../epfour.htm">
       MCSE Core Four Pack Preparation Guide</a></b><br /><br />
       <dd><a name="patch"></a>
           <a href="../examprep/ep4patch398.exe">
           Patch (308Kb)</a> for the 1997 printing of
           Part:198-3 (3/11/98)<br /><br /></dd>
```

```
        <dd>Online version of the
           <a href="../examprep/cdsite/examprep.htm"
           target="_blank">Four Pack CD-ROM</a></dd>
   </dt>
</dl>
```

This unordered list is typical of the type of list markup found in conventional HTML pages. Without exception, the close tags for the <DT> and <DD> tags are missing. Because these are not EMPTY elements, close tags have to be added to make the document well formed.

```
<h3><a name="discuss"></a>Exam Preparation Discussion Boards</h3>
<p>Please visit our
<a href="http://www.lanw.com/webboard/webboard.dll/~2">online
discussion forums</A> for each of the Exam Preparation titles. Feel
free to ask questions, share information, and help your
peers master the materials necessary to become an MCP or
MCSE! LANWrights promises to respond to new questions
promptly, so be sure to check in regularly. Note that these
forums will be moderated, so don't be disappointed if repeat
questions don't appear, or if we respond privately to
queries, rather than publicly. All submissions will be
acknowledged, at least by e-mail, so be sure to give us your
e-mail address when you sign up.</p>


<h2><a name="contact"></a>Contact Us</h2>

<p>For feedback, questions, or errata related to the Exam
Preparation books please send e-mail to
<a href="mailto:examprep@lanw.com">examprep@lanw.com</a>. For
comments or questions about the Web site, or to report
broken links please e-mail the LANWrights'
<a href="mailto:webmaster@lanw.com">Webmaster</a>.</p>

<br /><br />
```

Once again, the changes to this section of the page are the addition of closing slashes to EMPTY tags, especially the commonly used <BR> tag.

```
<p><center>
<a href="mcse.htm">
<img src="cert_mcse" alt="mcse resources"
   align="bottom" border="0"></a>
<a href="java.htm"><img src="cert_java"
   alt="java resources" align="bottom" border="0"></a>
```

```
<a href="../errata/default.htm"><img
   src="cert_errata" alt="master errata
   list" align="bottom" border="0"></a>
<a href="order.htm"><img src="cert_order"
   alt="order practice tests" align="bottom "border="0"></a>
</center>


<center>
<p><img src="navigbar"  alt="navigtion image, see text links below"
usemap="#navigbar" ismap border="0">
<map name="navigbar">
<area shape="rect" coords="344, 0, 401, 56"
   href="http://www.lanw.com/overview.htm">
<area shape="rect" coords="287, 1, 345, 56"
   href="http://www.lanw.com/lanw.htm">
<area shape="rect" coords="228, 1, 287, 56"
   href="http://www.lanw.com/showcase.htm">
<area shape="rect" coords="172, 0, 229, 55"
   href="http://www.lanw.com/exam.htm">
<area shape="rect" coords="114, 1, 172, 55"
   href="http://www.lanw.com/training.htm">
<area shape="rect" coords="55, 1, 115, 56"
   href="http://www.lanw.com/books.htm">
<area shape="rect" coords="0, 1, 55, 55"
   href="http://www.lanw.com/default.htm">
</map></p></center>

<center><p class=textnav>
| <a href="../../default.htm">Home</a>
| <a href="../../books.htm">Book Nook</a>
| <a href="../../training.htm">Training Center</a>
| <a href="../../exam.htm">Certification Central</a>
| <a href="../../showcase.htm">Technology Showcase</a>
| <a href="../../lanw.htm">Corporate HQ</a>
| <a href="../../overview.htm">Site Overview</a>
|</p></center>

<p><br />
<img src="line" width="100%" height="2"></p>

<p class="address">
<img src="css" align=right border="0">

<font face="arial">url:
<a href="mcse.htm">
http://www.lanw.com/books/examprep/mcse.htm</a><br />
Layout, design &amp; revisions &copy; 1997, 1998
```

```
<a href="../../default.htm">LANWrights</a>, Inc. <br />
<A HREF="mailto:webmaster@lanw.com">Webmaster:</a>
Natanya Pitts<br />
Revised - August 17, 1998 <i>[NP]</i>
</font></p>

</body>
</html>
```

As with the previous sections of the document, this one required a few quotation marks and closing slashes and changes to the SRC= attribute of several `IMAGE` elements. This document is now well formed, but that's only half of the battle.

Step 2: Validate Your Document against the DTD with a Validating Parser and Correct

The easiest and quickest way to check and see whether your HTML document is valid is to use one of the several HTML validators available on the Web. The majority of these validators are based on SGML, so they do a real good job of validating your document against a DTD. My personal favorite was written and is maintained by Mark Gaither at `http://valsvc.webtechs.com/index.htm`.

When I run my well-formed document through the Webtechs validator the first time, these are the results:

```
line 10: required attribute "TYPE" not specified
line 65: end tag for element "DT"  which is not open
line 69: end tag for element "DT"  which is not open
line 73: end tag for element "DT"  which is not open
line 77: end tag for element "DT"  which is not open
line 81: end tag for element "DT"  which is not open
line 85: end tag for element "DT"  which is not open
line 89: end tag for element "DT"  which is not open
line 99: end tag for element "DT"  which is not open
line 174: required attribute "ALT" not specified
line 176: required attribute "ALT" not specified
line 178: required attribute "ALT" not specified
line 180: required attribute "ALT" not specified
line 182: required attribute "ALT" not specified
line 184: required attribute "ALT" not specified
line 186: required attribute "ALT" not specified
line 200: required attribute "ALT" not specified
line 203: required attribute "ALT" not specified
```

NOTE

For faster results, I only validated my HTML markup and not the DTD portion of my document.

The results from the validator break the document error down by lines. A good XML or text editor will show you line numbers, or you can count for yourself. This is line 10:

```
<style>
```

According to the validator, this line is missing a TYPE attribute. The corrected markup is

```
<style type="text/css">
```

The errors on lines 65 through 99 that indicate a close DEFINITION tag (</DT>) where there isn't an open tag probably mean there's an extra close or open tag somewhere. A bit of examination reveals it's in this line:

```
<dl>
   <dt><b><a href="../ecne.htm">
      *Networking Essential Exam Preparation Guide</a></b>
         <dd>(Test #70-058) <br /><br /></dd>
   <dt>
```

The corrected markup is

```
<dl>
   <dt><b><a href="../ecne.htm">
      *Networking Essential Exam Preparation Guide</a></b>
         <dd>(Test #70-058) <br /><br /></dd>
   </dt>
```

The errors on lines 174 through 203 indicate that an ALT= attribute is required for each instance of the <AREA> tag inside of a <MAP> tag. The correct markup looks like this:

```
<map name="navigbar">
<area shape="rect" coords="344, 0, 401, 56"
   href="http://www.lanw.com/overview.htm"
   alt="site overview">
<area shape="rect" coords="287, 1, 345, 56"
   href="http://www.lanw.com/lanw.htm"
   alt="corporate hq">
<area shape="rect" coords="228, 1, 287, 56"
   href="http://www.lanw.com/showcase.htm"
   alt="technology showcase">
```

Skill 17

```
<area shape="rect" coords="172, 0, 229, 55"
   href="http://www.lanw.com/exam.htm"
   alt="exam prep resources">
<area shape="rect" coords="114, 1, 172, 55"
   href="http://www.lanw.com/training.htm"
   alt="training center">
<area shape="rect" coords="55, 1, 115, 56"
   href="http://www.lanw.com/books.htm"
   alt="book nook">
<area shape="rect" coords="0, 1, 55, 55"
   href="http://www.lanw.com/default.htm"
   alt="home">
</map></p></center>
```

After making all of these corrections, another pass through the validator results in this message:

```
No errors found
```

Now the document is both well formed, valid, and up to XML standards.

From Theory to Reality

If HTML were an XML vocabulary already, you'd have to create documents similar to the example in this skill. The time will come when HTML will be an XML vocabulary, and all of your HTML documents will also be valid XML documents. The conversion from a regular HTML document to a valid XML document isn't all that hard, as you've seen in this skill.

Now it's time to turn from theory to reality. Let's turn the tables and find out what it takes to browse XML documents with the latest Web browsers. In Skill 18, "Browsing XML with the Latest Web Clients," you'll find out what type of XML support you can expect from the upcoming versions of Internet Explorer and Netscape Navigator as well as the realities of including XML in your Web pages.

Are You up to Speed?

Now you can...

- ☑ Explain how HTML will function as an XML vocabulary
- ☑ Describe the good habits Webmasters should develop to prepare for HTML to be an XML vocabulary
- ☑ Turn an existing HTML document into a well-formed XML document
- ☑ Validate an HTML document against its DTD

SKILL 18

Browsing XML with the Latest Web Clients

- How the industry feels about XML
- The key components of Microsoft's XML implementation
- Netscape's approach to XML and metadata
- A real Web site created with XML and scripting

Many of the skills in this book have addressed the potential of XML and have discussed the types of things XML will be able to do when it is adopted as an industry standard. Although XML has the "potential" and it "will be able" to do things, that's not as useful as learning "what XML can do now." This skill addresses what support for XML looks like in the here and now, focusing on how the primary tools for viewing Web data—Web browsers—implement XML support.

A Look at the Industry's Attitude toward XML

As with any developing technology, the members of the Internet and Web industry view XML with both excitement and skepticism. XML is poised to be the next markup language of the Web and promises to take Web developers and their content to a level that can't be achieved with HTML. While that's all well and good, the implementation realities associated with XML can come crashing down rapidly.

One of the primary driving forces behind the Web and any new technologies developed for it is the browser vendors and toolmakers. They are the ones that determine which technologies will have enough support to have a chance at success and which will not. Of course, the consumers and users have quite a bit to say about the situation, as well. However, if a browser vendor doesn't include support for a certain technology in their product, a user won't have access to the technology to give it a thumbs up or a thumbs down.

In addition to the browser vendors, those companies that build solutions for the storage and dissemination of data from business to business are another important force to consider. If they grab hold of a technology and begin using it as the basis for a number of high-end solutions, the technology eventually filters down to become a part of less-extensive, every-day solutions.

As it stands now, it looks as if XML will indeed succeed as an Internet and Web technology. I'm sure that makes you feel better now that you're almost three-quarters of the way through the book. Both of the major browser vendors have indicated that their next browser releases will include support for XML, although support in Internet Explorer is more extensive than in Netscape Navigator. In addition, providers of business-to-business solutions have begun to include XML in their data dissemination solutions. Granted, XML is to be included in only the highest-level solutions, but you can expect that to change in the near future.

XML isn't designed to be a stand-alone solution, but instead, it is intended to be a way to describe data that will be read and manipulated by an application such as a Web browser or specialty client-side tool. Really, XML can't do anything by itself. HTML can't either, but we're so used to the existence of Web browsers and other HTML-compatible software that we often forget that there was a time when HTML was just as cutting edge as XML. The direction that XML takes and the role it will play in the Web and Internet world is going to depend almost entirely on the tools and software packages built to work with it. Web browsers need to be specialized to work with XML, just as they are already specialized to work with HTML.

You learned in Skill 14, "Processing XML Documents," that an XML vocabulary is only as good as the processor or browser that interprets and displays it. Because Web browsers are the windows to HTML for the majority of Web denizens, it's only natural to turn to them as the windows to XML. As an XML developer, you'll want to know what it's going to take to make your documents available to users via their most trusted and well-used tool—the Web browser.

Understanding the Realities of Browsing XML on the Web

I wish I could tell you that serving XML documents over the Web will be as quick and easy as serving HTML pages. Although that may be true in a year or so, it's simply not the case right now. The bottom line is Web browsers are optimized to work with HTML and other technologies, such as scripting languages, that were designed around HTML. Until Web browsers have integrated XML support to the same level they've integrated HTML support, you're going to have to work a little harder to include XML in your Web pages and to make it accessible to your users.

Because serving XML over the Web is going to require extra work and you'll have to learn a few new skills along the way, this skill is only going to touch on the theories and ideas that the browser vendors have put forth for building Web pages with XML. I'll also include lots of pointers to Web sites with complete XML information and how-to sections. Both vendors have their own methods for using XML in Web pages, and these methods aren't cross-browser compatible. These two things combined mean that a detailed description of the steps it takes to write Web pages with XML is beyond the scope of this book.

Regardless of the browser you're using, incorporating XML into your Web pages will mean learning something about Web scripting and possibly even Java. But before you throw the book across the room and run away, you should know that both vendors have included informative and easy-to-understand white papers and how-to articles about including XML in Web documents. Keep in mind that these instructions are optimized for the vendor's particular browser. For example, here are the system requirements for installing and running an XML-based auction program found at Microsoft Site Builder, `http://www.microsoft.com/xml/parser/auction/auction.asp`:

> Internet Explorer 4.0: The demo requires Internet Explorer 4.0, which you can download from `http://www.microsoft.com/ie/ie40/download/`.
>
> Web Server: You must have Active Server Pages (ASP) running on your server to run the Auction demo. You can use Internet Information Server 3.0 or later or Personal Web Server.
>
> Database: The demo will work with either a Microsoft Access or a SQL Server database. No special setup is required to use the Microsoft Access version (although you must have Microsoft Access 97 installed on your system). (Note that Microsoft Access is not required if you download the latest version of Personal Web Server, which includes the Jet database engine that reads from MDB files.)
>
> Parser: Before you can run this demo, you must install the XML Parser in Java package on your machine.

This solution is obviously designed to work with Microsoft Web technologies, and if you aren't using those technologies, then the solutions won't work for you. However, this isn't a Microsoft-only situation. The solutions described at the Netscape site are no different. This use of XML as part of a proprietary Web browser solution is indicative of the role XML is going to play in the Web world, at least for the next few months.

Browsing XML with Internet Explorer

The folks at Microsoft see XML as the key to creating flexible, extensible, and reusable Web applications. A Web application is more than just a series of Web pages with content. Instead, it is an entity akin to a software package that users interact with over the Web and via a Web browser. In its perfect form, a Web application makes use of standard Web technologies, such as HTML and Java, so users on any platform running any operating system and using any browser can access the application. In their more realistic form, many Web applications are optimized to work with one Web browser or another and often only on one or two platforms. A Web application can, in theory, be used to provide users with access to any type of data, including but not limited to

- Financial and stock information
- Human-resource data
- Sales and marketing data
- Merchandise records

Microsoft envisions XML as the markup language of choice for describing any type of data that can be accessed by a Web application running on a Web server and viewed through a Web browser. Microsoft's Web applications have three different tiers:

Storage tier The base tier, usually a database but possibly a mainframe, that contains raw data.

Data integration tier The middle tier, in which a Web server uses XML to describe data and in which other factors, such as business rules, can be applied to the data.

Display tier The top tier, in which a Web browser running on a client's desktop provides the interface to the data; because the data is XML-based, many different displays of the data are possible, depending on who is interacting with the data at any given time.

This approach to using XML as part of an application solution is not unique to Microsoft. However, it is a good example of how you can expect XML to be implemented in the next few months. XML will be the data description language (like that's a big surprise), and then an interface of some type will provide developers and users with a way to access and manipulate the data.

For this reason, the support for XML in Internet Explorer is largely based on XML as a single piece in a larger Web application solution, such as Microsoft's Web channel technology. Beginning with Internet Explorer 4, Microsoft introduced support for a new technology called Web channels. Channels allow developers to simultaneously send an entire collection of Web pages to users who subscribe to the channel. These collections of pages are called *updates* and comprise regular HTML-based Web pages. The difference between this method of delivery and regular Web surfing is that users don't have to request each page in the collection separately; they receive the updates all at once.

The interface for channels is part of IE 4 and 5, but the documents that describe channels and their updates are all written in the XML vocabulary of CDF (Channel Definition Format). If you think about CDF as a Web application, the HTML data is the storage tier (especially if the data is generated from a database in the first place); the Web server with the HTML files and the CDF files that describe the channel composes the data integration tier; and the IE browser that provides users with access to channel updates is the display tier.

Skill 20, "Channeling Data with CDF," is devoted to a discussion of CDF and channels.

To allow for the development of Web applications and other XML solutions, Microsoft's support for XML in the Internet Explorer Web browser comprises the following:

- Two XML parsers
- The XML data source object
- The XML Object Model

The next several sections take a closer look at how these different components can be used with XML documents for display by Internet Explorer.

XML Parsers

As you learned in Skill 14, "Processing XML Documents," a parser is an application that analyzes an XML document and prepares its data to be interpreted by a browser or other display mechanism. Internet Explorer 4 ships with a built-in, nonvalidating C++ parser. In addition, you may download a Java-based validating parser from the Microsoft site at `http://www.microsoft.com/xml/parser/jparser.asp`. Both parsers are designed to read and interpret XML documents and then pass their contents along to the browser for further processing. Without a parser, the remaining XML components wouldn't have any data to work with because they are designed to work explicitly with parsed data received from either of these two parsers.

The XML Data Source Object

The XML Data Source Object (DSO) is part of Microsoft's proprietary data-binding technology that links databases directly to Web pages. A DSO on a Web page is responsible for describing which content from the associated database the Web page may display and which regular HTML elements (usually `TABLE` and `FORM` elements) will display individual pieces of content. DSOs are created and controlled with a Web scripting language, such as JavaScript or VBScript. DSOs are designed to work with data binding only and not with other XML solutions. To read more about data binding and DSOs, visit the DHTML, HTML, and CSS portions of the Microsoft Site Builder site at `http://www.microsoft.com/workshop/author/default.asp`, and scroll down to the section on data binding.

The XML Object Model

Unlike the proprietary DSO, the XML Object Model (XOM) is most likely to be the aspect of XML implementation that Microsoft has in common with other browser and software vendors. The XOM is a hierarchical picture of the elements and their content in an XML document. By recognizing the elements in the XOM for any given XML document, the browser is able to move from one element to the other and decide how to display the document.

The object model identifies the document's document element as the root, and all of the other elements nested within the root as regular elements. Groups of elements on the same level in the document are called `SIBLING` elements. Figure 18.1 provides a graphical representation of how an XML document is described by the XOM.

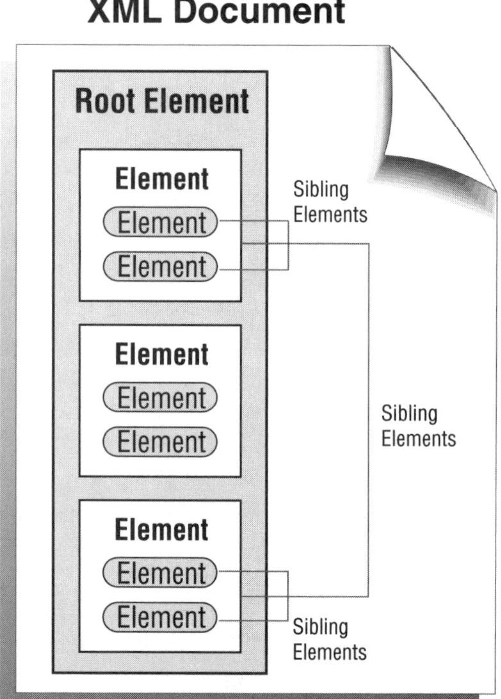

FIGURE 18.1: The XOM describes this document as a collection of elements.

The XOM is not concerned with the contents of the elements, or their attributes for that matter, but rather, it's concerned with where the elements are placed in relation to the document element and the other elements. Scripts written in Microsoft's JScript or VBScript can interpret an individual document's XOM, traverse the document, and do interesting things with its content, including converting it into HTML.

To really make the XOM work and generate Web pages from it, you'll need to use a script similar to this one found at `http://www.microsoft.com/xml/articles/xmlmodel.asp`.

```
<SCRIPT LANGUAGE="JScript" FOR=window EVENT=onload>

  var indent_array = new String("
");
  var str = "";
```

```
var xml = new ActiveXObject("msxml");
xml.URL = "http://Chein/_private/pdcxml.xml";

var docroot = xml.root;

output_doc(docroot,0);

function output_doc(elem,indents)
{
  var i;

   if (elem.type == 0)  // 0 is a tagName
   {
     document.all("results").insertAdjacentText("BeforeEnd",
     indent_array.substring(0,(4 * indents)) +
     "<" + elem.tagName + ">" + "\n");

     if (elem.children != null)
     {
     for (i = 0 ; i < elem.children.length ; i++)
          output_doc(elem.children.item(i),(indents + 1));
     }

     document.all("results").insertAdjacentText("BeforeEnd",
     indent_array.substring(0,(4 * indents)) +
     "</" + elem.tagName + ">" + "\n");
  }
   else if (elem.type == 1) // 1 is a text node
   {
     document.all("results").insertAdjacentText("BeforeEnd",
       indent_array.substring(0,(4 * indents)) +
           "\"" + elem.text + "\"\n");
   }
   else
     alert("unknown element type: " + elem.type);
}
</script>
```

What this script does is take an XML document and display all of the text within elements in the Web page.

This script is written in a version of JScript that can only be processed by the developer's release of Internet Explorer 5 and will not work in other Web browsers or versions of IE.

It's going to take scripts like the previous example and Internet Explorer 5 or later to truly include XML markup and content within a Web page. On a much larger scale, Web page and server scripting will provide the mechanism that drives the manipulation of and interacts with XML data for Web applications.

NOTE The Microsoft Site Builder Web site includes a wide variety of articles and resources for working with XML. Keep in mind that most of them require a working knowledge of both JScript and VBScript. To read more about using XML with Internet Explorer, point your Web browser at `http://www.microsoft.com/xml/contents.htm`.

Browsing XML with Netscape Navigator

Microsoft support for XML focuses mainly on XML as the data descriptor of choice for Web applications, whereas the Netscape implementation of XML focuses almost entirely on XML as a descriptor of metadata. Early in Skill 3, "Forming a Foundation with HTML," you learned that metadata is data used to describe other data, just like XML is a meta–markup language used to describe other markup languages. Metadata information about any given Web document could include the following:

- Authorship information
- Keywords and descriptors
- Recent updates and revisions

One of the reasons searching the Web has become so difficult is that search engines rely on full-text searches of information instead of searches of descriptions of information. Without an effective way to catalog and describe data, there will never be a way to effectively search the Web with any reasonable level of accuracy. Because of this, Netscape has concentrated its efforts in the field of XML on using XML vocabularies to describe metadata in a standard way.

There are several metadata vocabularies already under development, and Netscape has chosen the Resource Description Format (RDF). Netscape's vision is that a metadata browser will be able to integrate RDF descriptions of data on the Web and intranets to create a dynamic navigation tool that allows users to easily navigate the Web.

Netscape Navigator 4 supports RDF in a limited way, and an RDF viewer can be created in a Web page with JavaScript and Java. At Netscape Developer Central, you can view a sample RDF viewer that uses two frames. In Figure 18.2, the one on the right is used to list a set of bookmarks for the site being displayed on the left.

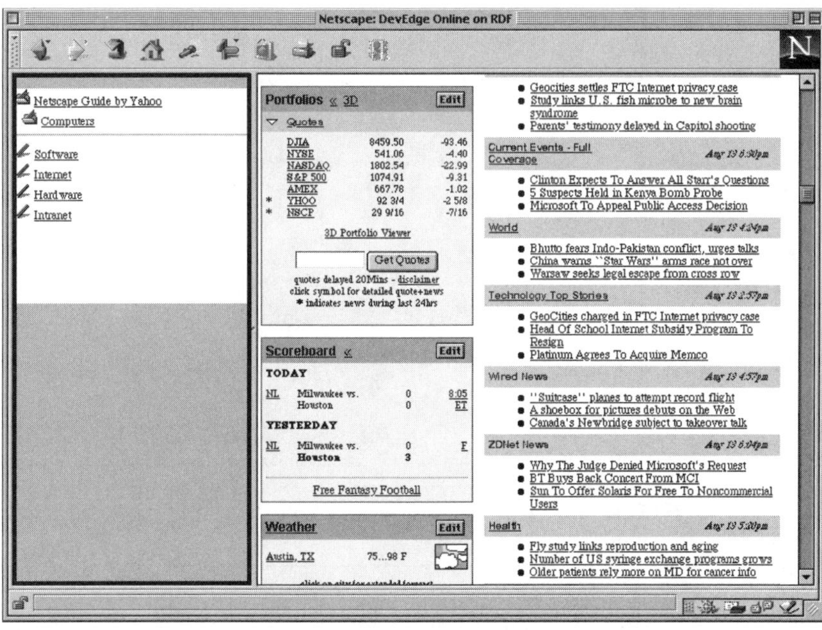

FIGURE 18.2: The Netscape RDF viewer demonstration

NOTE To see and experiment with this viewer, point your Netscape Navigator browser at `http://developer.netscape.com/tech/metadata/demos/demo2.html`.

HTML and JavaScript create the two-framed presentation; however, the navigation links on the right-hand side are the result of an RDF document displayed in a specialized Java browser. Even though this RDF browser uses HTML, JavaScript, and Java—three common Web technologies—it is definitely not designed to work with Internet Explorer, as shown in Figure 18.3.

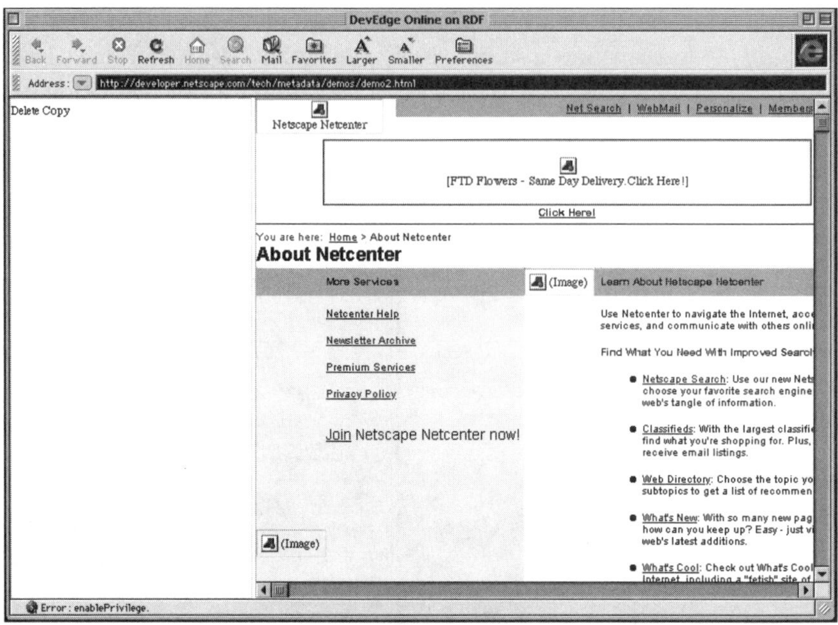

FIGURE 18.3: Internet Explorer can't figure out what to do with the RDF viewer.

Using metadata to improve searching and navigation of Web documents is important, but it's not the only use for XML. However, Netscape's current support for XML is limited to metadata. There's no indication that things will stay this way forever, but that's the current scoop.

TIP To read through Netscape's XML and metadata resources, visit `http://developer.netscape.com/tech/metadata/metadata.html`.

If you are troubled by the news that the Navigator XML implementation is much different and more limited than that found in Internet Explorer, don't despair. Remember that many of the third-party developers who are using XML as part of their solutions are creating XML browsers in Java that function well in both browsers. Instead of expecting the browsers to agree on XML implementations, it may be better to concentrate on created Java-based XML browsers that work well in any browser.

Web Sites Generated from HTML: It Can Be Done

I realize the picture of browser support I've presented so far, although realistic, is a bit discouraging. On a pleasant note, I do have proof that with a bit of effort and energy, as well as a world of patience, you can more or less successfully generate an entire Web site from XML and a database. The XMLInfo site at `http://www.xmlinfo.com/` maintained by James Tauber is generated entirely from a database and XML.

The site's content is described by XML, stored in a database, and then converted to HTML with scripting. However, the display of this site from platform to platform is a bit inconsistent, but that's due in large part to the inconsistency of support for the scripting languages. The conversion of data from XML to HTML is accomplished entirely on the server side, with scripting and CGI programming done before the Web pages are even written.

The site displays perfectly in Internet Explorer 4 and Netscape Navigator 4 on a PC running Windows 95 or NT, and it looks great in Navigator 4 on the Mac, as shown in Figure 18.4.

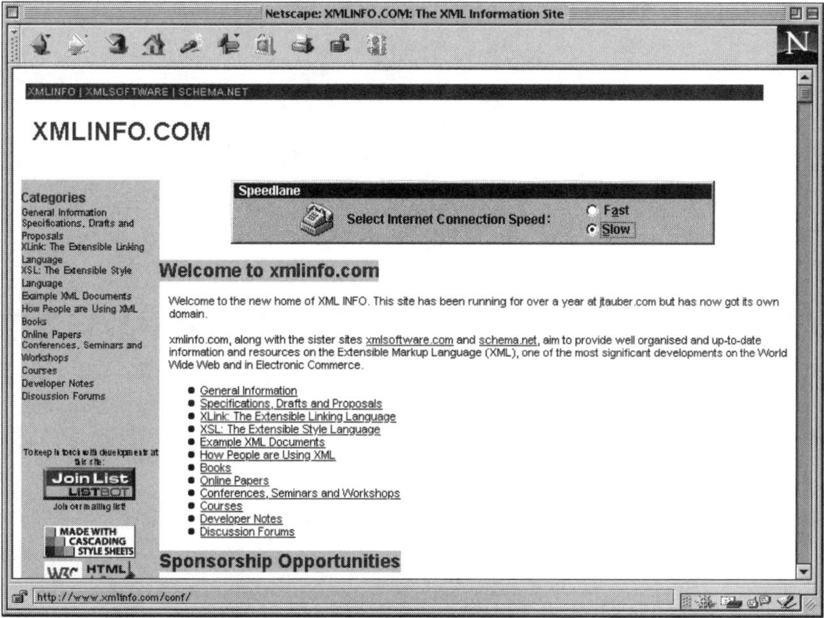

FIGURE 18.4: The XMLInfo site is generated from XML and a database and looks great in Navigator 4 on the Mac.

However, when the site is viewed with Internet Explorer 4 on the Mac, all kinds of interesting scripting errors start to pop up. Luckily, they don't really interfere with the final display of the site's key information, as shown in Figure 18.5.

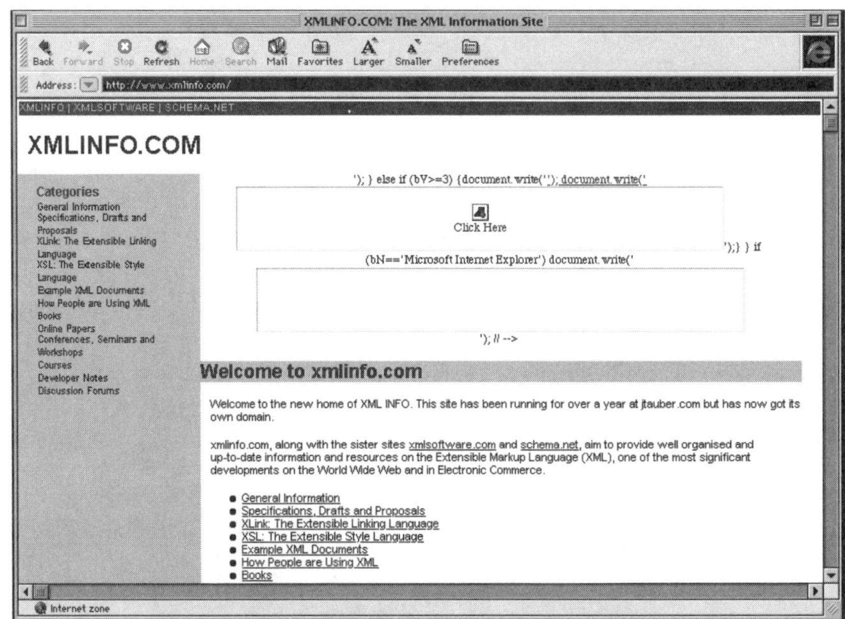

FIGURE 18.5: The XMLInfo site hits a few snags when viewed with Internet Explorer 4 on the Mac.

From General to Specific: Investigating Individual XML Vocabularies

Understanding the basics of XML and creating XML DTDs and documents is different from creating the browsers that will process them or the scripting needed to make them visible in a Web page. In fact, to do both requires two very different skill sets. However, understanding the basics of XML and how DTDs and documents are created is just as crucial to implementing an XML solution as knowing the basics of JavaScript or Java to create a customized browser. As you've read repeatedly from the beginning of this book, XML will be only a part of implementing Web solutions during the next few months and maybe even years, but it will be an important part.

Creating XML documents that can be viewed with the current Web browsers will be a bit of a challenge for innovative Web developers, but as James Tauber proves, it can be done. The largest hurdle you will have to overcome is the difference in support among the Web browsers. Both browser vendors have shown that for the time being, XML will play a large role in their proprietary Web solutions. We can only hope that they will eventually provide better and more standard support for the basic implementation of XML into Web pages without forcing developers to go to extremes or employ other complex technologies.

This is the final skill in Part III of this book. I'll leave the issues of deploying XML documents behind and turn to a discussion of the specific vocabularies written for XML and how they are being implemented as part of larger information dissemination solutions on the Web. Part IV begins with a guide to creating documents for a specific XML application and then follows with a close look at five of the most rapidly developing XML applications. When you're done with Part IV, you'll know how to find out what makes any given application tick, how to decide if it's the right application for your data, and how to go about implementing it as part of a solution.

Are You up to Speed?

Now you can...

- ☑ **Explain what sectors of the industry drive the success or failure of a technology**
- ☑ **Describe the components of Microsoft's XML implementation**
- ☑ **Describe how Netscape is using metadata as a Web cataloging and navigation tool**
- ☑ **Discuss the important issues surrounding the different browser implementations of XML**

PART IV

A Guide to XML Vocabularies

SKILL 19

Creating Documents for XML Applications

- XML applications explained
- Choosing the right XML application to describe your content
- Analyzing an XML application
- Altering an existing XML application

Understanding the pieces and parts of XML DTDs and documents and knowing how to assemble all those pieces into a working and useable document are two very different things. In Part II, you learned everything you need to know about declaring and using the various components of XML. In Part III, you were introduced to the various issues surrounding the deployment of documents. In this first skill of Part IV, you'll learn how to combine what you've learned so far with choosing the right DTD for your content and creating a real, working XML document.

What Is an XML Application?

When you design an XML document, you use markup—tags, attributes, and entities—to describe content. Although the content is the main focus of the document, the markup is the mechanism you use to give the content structure. In many cases, the markup you use to describe your content is directly controlled by a DTD written according to the XML specification.

An XML DTD is officially called an XML application or vocabulary. Early in the book, I said that XML, although a markup language, is designed to be a meta–markup language used to create other markup languages. In Skills 9 through 12, you met the Precision Graphics Markup Language (PGML) and my own Online Training Markup Language (OTML). Both of these DTDs are written according to the XML specification, so they can be officially called XML applications or vocabularies.

For a DTD to be called an XML application, it only has to abide by the rules of XML. It doesn't have to be a formal W3C recommendation or even a note. In fact, a DTD with three elements and two entities can still be considered an XML application, as long as it adheres to the XML specification.

In Skill 14, "Processing XML Documents," and in Skill 18, "Browsing XML with the Latest Web Clients," you learned that the real-world deployment of XML documents will depend mostly on processing applications and browsers developed specifically for individual DTDs or on the style sheets written to allow documents created for a DTD to be displayed by a Web browser. Because an XML DTD is just another word for an XML application or vocabulary, the implementation of documents written for a CML application will depend on the processors and browsers written for the application.

The majority of XML applications have been, or will be, created by organizations and groups of organizations within several different industries to meet very specific needs. Most of these developers see the Internet and Web as the key to disseminating information and collaborating with partners. However, they have been frustrated by the limited abilities of HTML. By creating their own XML applications and associated processors and browsers to interface with the applications and the content they describe, organizations can take advantage of the widespread support of Web and Internet technologies as well as overcome the limitations of HTML.

Chances are that your interactions with XML applications will be part of a larger, total information dissemination solution. It's also possible that you won't know that the tools and technologies you're using are XML-based because you'll be using graphical interfaces to design and deploy documents. If this is so, you're probably wondering why you need to know how to create a document for a DTD from scratch and by hand.

If you're looking to XML as a solution to your own needs or are using a new application that's still in the development stages, you'll need to know how to create a document for that application, using a text editor or a basic XML editor and your knowledge and skills. Finally, the documentation for any given application may not tell you all you need to know about the DTD and the types of content it can describe. You'll want to be able to break down the application, create a test document or two for it, and see if it meets your needs. You already know how to read a DTD and use its components to describe your document, so all you need to learn is how to analyze an application to see whether it meets your needs and how to create a valid and useable document for it. The remaining sections of this skill will teach you how to do that.

Choosing the Right Application for Your Content

The first step toward creating any XML document is choosing the right application to describe your content. HTML is a real-world example of how difficult and crazy things can get when you try to force markup to describe content it wasn't designed to describe. If you choose the wrong application, your document development could be difficult, and the results could be not quite what you wanted. However, before you can choose the right application, you must decide whether you need an application at all.

Deciding Whether You Need an Application

In Skill 7, "Creating Well-Formed and Valid Documents," I mentioned that you don't always have to validate your documents against a DTD, and, in fact, you don't have to have a DTD to create an XML document. Because XML allows you to create your own tags, you can design a document that uses a DTD to just list the entities you'll be using. If the tags you use follow the rules for a well-formed document, your document can be processed by any nonvalidating XML parser and displayed by any browser; however, you must have a style sheet to go along with the document.

If you're just learning XML and are experimenting with combinations of tags, you may not need a strict DTD. In addition, if you're creating XML documents for display via a Web browser only, you won't need to have a DTD for your document to be displayed correctly (assuming your document is well formed, of course) as per your style sheet.

However, the question is how do you know whether you need to write your documents for a particular XML application or not? If the successful processing and display of your document doesn't depend on a DTD (as with an XML-supporting Web browser) or you're learning or experimenting, you may not need to work with a particular application.

However, the job of an XML application is to provide rules and guidelines for document development. If you're going to describe several documents with the same tags, a DTD helps ensure consistency among your descriptions. Also, if the browser or software application that you use to describe your document is looking for or designed to work with markup from a specific application, then you'll want to design documents that are both well formed and valid against the application itself.

Finding the Right Application

Once you've decided that you need an XML application to guide your document development, you'll need to figure out which application fits your content the best. As more XML applications are developed, you'll have a better selection to choose from, and it'll be easier to find one to fit your content. In addition, there are other competing, non-XML solutions that might also meet your needs. So how do you know which XML application is the best choice for describing your content? To answer that question, ask a few of your own:

- What type of content am I describing?
- What XML applications are currently available for describing my content?

- What non-XML solutions might also meet my needs?

Then, compare all of the potential applications in the same way by asking the following questions:

- As indicated by the application's documentation, what type of content is the DTD designed to describe? How similar is that content to my content?
- Is the application an official standard or a proposal under development?
- What type of documentation is available for the application?
- What development tools are available for creating content for the application?
- Have any parsing and browsing tools been designed specifically to process and display documents written for the application?
- Is there any of my content that this application isn't designed to describe?
- Could a total solution that combines XML and other technologies meet my needs better than an XML-only solution? If so, is one application better than another as a part of that solution?

In the following sections, you'll see how asking these questions can help decide whether the Precision Graphics Markup Language (PGML) is the right application to describe the sample graphical content.

What Kind of Content Am I Describing?

The content I want to describe is complex, vector graphics. The graphics need to be sized to scale when displayed by a wide variety of display devices, including high-resolution printers and Web browsers. Each graphical object should have to be described only once, even though it will be displayed in a wide variety of sizes and resolutions. The described graphical data may be line-art illustrations, pictures with a variety of filters applied to achieve different affects, or animations. It should be possible to embed hyperlinks to other Web resources, as well.

What XML Applications Are Currently Available for Describing My Content?

Currently, the only XML application available for describing advanced vector graphics is PGML, an initiative from Adobe. This may change in the foreseeable future.

What Non-XML Solutions Might Also Meet My Needs?

Standard Web graphic formats, such as GIF and JPEG, do not meet the requirements of the content. Graphics saved in these formats cannot be dynamically resized or displayed in different resolutions from the same file. Also, neither of these formats supports vector graphics. Although these are perfectly viable solutions for standard graphics, they do not print well at resolutions higher than 72 dpi. GIF and JPEG can be combined with links and `IMAGE MAP` tags to embed hyperlinks within graphics.

The Portable Network Graphics (PNG) standard for Web graphics is designed specifically for vector graphics and is an official Web graphics standard maintained by the World Wide Web Consortium (W3C). It is supported by version 3 or newer of major browsers (Internet Explorer and Netscape Navigator, for example) and has some support among the major graphic-creation tools. However, PNG was designed specifically as a Web graphics file format and is not supported well outside of the Web environment. In addition, PNG has never caught on like GIF and JPEG as a graphics format, so there's some question about future support for it. As with GIF and JPEG, PNG graphics can be combined with `LINK` and `IMAGE MAP` tags to create clickable images.

Finally, Flash from Macromedia is a proprietary vector-graphics file format that requires a browser plug-in to be viewed from a Web browser. Flash is a powerful format that provides mechanisms for describing complex animations and scaleable vector graphics. Flash animations can include drop-down and expanding menus and can have hyperlinks embedded within them. However, because Flash is a proprietary technology and requires a plug-in, it poses some general accessibility issues. Flash is also designed specifically for distribution over the Web, and there are no other non-Web display tools available for Flash animations. Finally, the tools needed to create Flash animations are expensive to create, even if the plug-in is free. Macromedia, the developer behind Flash, is a major player in the technology world, so Flash is probably not a fleeting phenomena.

As Indicated by the PGML's Documentation, What Type of Content Is the DTD Designed to Describe? How Similar Is That Content to My Content?

As you learned in the skills of Part II, PGML is an XML vocabulary designed to describe complex vector graphics and animations. It provides markup elements for describing shapes, lines, and graphics of all formats. In addition, it provides tags for referencing different filters to be applied to graphics. The goal of PGML is specifically to display vector graphics that are easily scaleable and viewable in a wide variety of resolutions through many different display mechanisms.

PGML was developed by Adobe, the makers of Photoshop and Illustrator graphics creation tools as well as the widely-used Portable Document Format (PDF)—a tool for disseminating highly-formatted documents in many environments. Adobe is also one of the industry's major suppliers of fonts and other display-related technologies. PGML is based largely on PostScript, a programming language for describing a document that will print on any compatible printer (which is almost every printer made these days). Needless to say, Adobe knows graphics, so there's not much in the way of graphics that PGML can't describe well. It meets the needs I outlined for my content easily.

Is the Application an Official Standard or a Proposal Under Development?

PGML is still under development and is currently just a note to the W3C. There's been no indication from either Adobe or the W3C if, or when, PGML will become a standard.

What Type of Documentation Is Available for the Application?

Currently, the only documentation for PGML is the note to the W3C and a white paper from Adobe. Both documentations heavily reference PostScript terminology and basic concepts. There aren't any PGML Web sites or user manuals in the works. Those who want to work with PGML will have to do a bit of research into PostScript—a topic on which there is quite a bit of information—and then combine that knowledge with the limited information contained within Adobe's note and white paper.

It's safe to say that if PGML even looks like it's going to become a standard as well as a realistically useable technology, Web sites, books, and magazine articles will start appearing left and right. Until then, those interested in developing documents for PGML will have to do their best with the two available PGML resources.

What Development Tools Are Available for Creating Content for the Application?

PGML is still a highly theoretical markup language, and although Adobe is a software company, they haven't started making PGML editors yet. So, if an ambitious developer wants to describe a graphic with PGML, they will have to hack their documents by hand or with the assistance of a basic XML editor. If Adobe follows through with PGML, it's reasonable to expect PGML tools from them as well as support for PGML in their current products. Because Adobe is a large organization and has a well-established line of products, development of PGML tools will be business as usual for them.

Have Any Parsing and Browsing Tools Been Designed Specifically to Process and Display Documents Written for the Application?

Once again, because PGML is brand new, there are no processing or browsing tools designed specifically for it. PGML documents will be able to be parsed by any XML parser and displayed by a regular Web browser, as directed by a style sheet. To truly accomplish its goals and describe complex vector graphics for display in any media, PGML will most likely need a special type of browser—most likely implemented as a Java applet or a plug-in Web browser and as a stand-alone tool for non-Web implementations.

Although there aren't any PGML parsing and browsing tools currently available, Adobe does have quite a bit of experience in the application-development business. The Acrobat reader for PDF documents is both a plug-in and a stand-alone browser. Therefore, the task of creating a reader for a new description language would be easy for Adobe. It's safe to assume that if PGML is accepted as a standard, Adobe will create the tools necessary to view PGML documents as they are intended.

Is There Any of My Content That This Application Isn't Designed to Describe?

In the case of my graphics content, the answer is no. PGML is more than equipped to describe any simple or complex graphic.

Could a Total Solution That Combines XML and Other Technologies Meet My Needs Better than an XML-Only Solution? If So, Is One Application Better than Another as a Part of That Solution?

The current non-XML solutions to PGML do not directly involve XML, but there's no rule that says they won't in the future. It may be that Flash will work with PGML one day or that other graphics packages will take advantage of PGML. Currently, the only XML solution is PGML, and PGML isn't designed to work with other technologies.

Drawing Conclusions

Needless to say, the answers to these questions won't always be as simple and straightforward as the ones in my example. You may have several applications to choose from and may have to compare a series of answers to the same questions to find the best application for the job.

Although PGML is the only XML solution to the vector graphics issue, the answers to all of the questions indicate that an XML solution may not be the best one to use right now. Certainly PNG and Flash are the best alternatives to PGML, but they each have their own disadvantages, most notably the lack of industry-wide support for PNG and the proprietary nature of Flash. However, the primary advantage they both have is established development and display tools—something PGML is truly lacking. Although you can describe the same graphic with PNG, Flash, and PGML, you can only deploy the graphic in the real world using PNG or Flash.

When choosing the right application, you must also decide whether an XML application is the right solution at all. Because XML is still in its infancy, you may find yourself choosing non-XML solutions for current needs, but you should remember that XML may replace those solutions in the future. If you'd like to use XML as a solution but are concerned about implementation issues, you may want to choose a non-XML solution that will port easily to XML or that will be easy to combine with XML in the future.

XML Applications Under Development

Table 19.1 gives you an idea of the different types of XML applications being developed and their focus. It includes a listing of a survey of the current XML applications under development.

TABLE 19.1: A sampling of XML vocabularies currently under development

Vocabulary	Description
Channel Definition Format (CDF)	Used to create channels of Web-based information delivered to subscribers over the Internet using server-push technology
Chemical Markup Language (CML)	Used to describe chemical formulas, compounds, and other related data
Conceptual Knowledge Markup Language (CKML)	Used to describe knowledge representation and data analysis content
Genealogical Data in XML (GedML)	Used to describe genealogical data sets
Information & Content Exchange (ICE)	Used to describe online assets in a standard way to facilitate sharing among business partners
Java Speech Markup Language (JSML)	Used to describe text input into Java Speech API speech synthesizers
Mathematical Markup Language (MML)	Used to describes mathematical formulas and data
Meta Content Framework (MCF)	Used to describe information about information (metadata) for cataloging and searching
Open Financial Exchange (OFX)	Used to describe financial data for delivery to client software, such as Microsoft Money or Quicken, from an online server
Open Software Description (OSD)	Used to describe software packages to be installed over a network without the need for hands-on human involvement
Precision Graphics Markup Language (PGML)	Used to describe 2-D scaleable vector graphics
Resource Description Framework (RDF)	Used to described Web-based metadata
Tutorial Markup Language (TML)	Used to describe tutorial content for online delivery and assessment of student understanding
Wireless Markup Language (WML)	Used to describe general content for distribution across a wireless network
XML-Data	Used to describe network-based metadata for cataloging and exchange

As the table clearly illustrates, XML vocabularies come in all flavors and are designed to describe all types of content. As XML becomes a more familiar fixture in the Web world, you'll see new applications emerging on a regular basis.

This means you'll have plenty of candidates to choose from when you need to describe a certain type of content, but it also means that you'll have to do a bit of research into each one, using the techniques described in the previous section.

But what if, after all your research, you discover that none of the available applications are what you're looking for, and you know that you do need an application? The answer is simple—or maybe not so simple: Write your own application.

Deciding to Create Your Own Application

Creating your own XML application can be a rewarding adventure, but it does present some interesting challenges. You already know all you need to know to write a DTD. But you also know that creating the DTD is only part of implementing an application and deploying documents created for it.

When you decide to create your own XML application, you not only have to think about writing a solid DTD but you also have to contemplate how the documents for the application will be processed, disseminated, and displayed. If you're simply looking to display documents in a Web browser, then you're only other consideration, besides the DTD, is creating a style sheet to go with it. If, however, you'd like to create an application that interacts with data stored in a database or that works with software applications other than Web browsers, your task will be a bit more difficult.

In addition to writing the DTD and possibly a style sheet to go with it, you'll need to find a parser to read your DTDs and documents as well as a browser or other rendering device to interpret the parser's results and make them available to a user. There are several freeware parsers available today. Several are written in Java, and others are written in C or C++. Some are validating; others are not.

You'll want to pair your parser with some type of rendering device, and if you're not going to use a Web browser, you'll have to create your own. A large number of XML developers are using Java to create interfaces for their XML applications. These interfaces can be run on any system that has a Java runtime environment, or they may be embedded in Web pages with the <APPLET> or <OBJECT> tag. If you're not a Java programmer, you can probably hire one; although a good one will be a bit costly, it's well worth the expense.

When you choose to write your own application, there are other factors you'll need to take into account, including how you'll parse and process the documents written for the application. Once again, as XML becomes a more popular solution among developers, there will be more examples to look to for guidance in developing XML applications.

Preparing to Create a Document for an Existing Application

You already know how to use tags, attributes, and entities to describe content, but there's more to creating a document for an XML application than tagging text. The fundamental skills of applying markup are of little use to you if you don't take some planning time to analyze the DTD from which you're working. By not rushing headlong into markup and by taking some time to investigate your DTD and plan your document, you'll find that your documents will have fewer flaws and errors and will work better with the software package responsible for processing them.

Analyzing the Application

When you're getting ready to create a document for a specific XML application (especially when you're creating with a simple text or basic XML editor, instead of with a special development tool) take a good long look at the application itself and make a few notes. Your analysis and notes will make your document development much easier than if you dove right into the business of document creation. Analyzing the DTD is sort of like testing the water in a pool with your toe and working your way in little by little. It might be a bit on the safe side, but it saves you from a nasty shock later.

When you're analyzing an application, you want to take note of the following:

- The elements included in the DTD. If an element isn't in the DTD, you can't use it (unless you add it yourself, as discussed in the next section).
- What the element's content models say about the rules of nesting. Check for elements that must be included within others and in what order they must appear. Also, make note of the elements that can contain only element content and the ones that can contain only text content so you don't accidentally nest the wrong kind of content within them.
- Identify those elements with required or fixed attributes. This will help ensure that you provide necessary attributes and don't change fixed ones.
- Identify the character sets supported by the DTD. If you need additional character or numeric entities, you'll have to declare them yourself in the document's internal DTD.

- Read through any documentation for the application. Documentation is designed to provide you with instruction and guidance, so use it. Good documentation will include descriptions of the DTD's elements, attributes, and entities as well as sample documents and important notes from the applications developers. Reading the documentation ahead of time can help you avoid mistakes and processing problems later.

Declaring Entities

As you learned in Skill 12, "Employing Entities in XML DTDs and Documents," entities can be declared in either the internal or external DTD subsets of a document. Those entities that are used in any document written for an application will be included in the external DTD subset. However, entities specific to a document—especially binary entities such as graphics and other embedded objects—are declared in the document's internal DTD subset.

By carefully analyzing the application, you'll know which entities are defined in the external DTD. After you consider your own document needs, you'll then be able to add your own entity declarations to the internal DTD. Remember, if you add a binary entity to the document's internal DTD whose type is different from those in the external DTD, you'll need to add a notation declaration for that type, as well.

Also, it's best to check the documentation of the browser displaying your document to see which binary entities it's capable of supporting. Even though Web browsers will be able to read well-formed XML documents, they won't necessarily support every type of binary entity for inline display. Think twice before using a TIFF or BNP graphic in a document designed for the Web. Stick to GIFs and JPEGs because you know they are supported. The same is true for audio and video formats.

Finally, make sure the application includes support for all the non-ASCII characters you'll need in your document. If it does not, declare your own character sets using a processing instruction or a regular entity declaration. Once again, you'll need to read the documentation for the browser designed to display your document and make sure it knows what to do with any special characters you define as entities.

Checking for Validity

Tagging content isn't the first step in document creation, nor is it the last. Once you've analyzed your XML application and written your document, you'll want to validate the document against the application. You can do this simply and easily with a validating parser or an XML editor that includes a validating tool. If you've gone through all the trouble of creating a document for a particular application, you don't want to waste the effort by not checking for accuracy.

You also need to validate your documents on your own, because the browser designed to display them may include only a nonvalidating parser. As you'll recall from our discussion in Skill 7 of when to use a validating or nonvalidating parser, parsers that don't have to validate documents process documents faster. Although you know a well-formed document will be parsed correctly, a document that is well formed but not valid may not display correctly even though it parses correctly. Rather than take a chance that your document may be displayed incorrectly, it's best to get into the habit of validating all of your documents against their applications as a final step in the creation process.

Modifying an XML Application

You know that most documents have both an internal and external DTD. Although convention dictates that the external DTD includes the element, attribute, and content-model declarations, as well as general entity declarations, and the internal DTD contains entity declarations specific to the document, there's no specific rule that says it has to be that way. Declarations of any type can be included in either the internal or external DTD subset. In fact, you don't even have to have an external DTD subset. You can store the entire DTD right in the document.

Because every document is guided by both subsets of the DTD, you can supplement an existing XML application with your own element, attribute, and entity declarations. After all, XML is all about writing your own tags. However, just because you can do something doesn't mean you should.

If you're working with an XML application designed by someone else—especially one with companion development and processing tools or one that is part of a larger solution—you'll want to think twice before you alter the DTD. Generally, the declarations in a DTD have been designed to work together and have been carefully tested as a unit. When you add new declarations into the fray, the results are unpredictable at best and chaotic at worst. So if it ain't broke, don't fix it.

If you find yourself wanting to add new elements and attributes to an application, you should probably revisit the answers to the questions about the applications I outlined earlier in this chapter. It's entirely possible that the application isn't a good match for your content, and you'll need to reevaluate choosing it to describe your content. Of course, if you feel you have to modify every available existing XML application to meet your needs, it may be a good sign that you need to create your own.

Avoid Conflicts

If you do choose to add your own elements to the internal DTD of a document (which would modify the XML application), be careful to avoid conflicts with the existing declarations. If you redefine an element or create a content model that is in conflict with one that's already established in the application, you'll have problems creating a valid document. The effects of conflicts won't be apparent until the document is validated or processed by a browser of some type.

When declarations conflict, the declaration in the internal DTD takes precedence over the one in the external DTD. Therefore, if you include an element declaration for an element already defined in the application in your document's internal DTD, your new declaration will override the one in the external DTD. This rule applies to all declarations in a DTD, not just element declarations.

I really recommend that you don't alter XML applications, especially those that have associated tools. The unpredictable results will give you plenty of grief. If you do alter an application, test it several times in several different environments to make sure your document can be successfully deployed. Also, if you're writing a document for an application that is standard and you alter the DTD in the internal DTD subset, the document isn't written to a standard DTD anymore. Don't expect it to work as well, if at all, with those processing applications designed to work with documents written for the standard.

Some XML DTDs Up Close and Personal

All of the techniques in this skill for finding the right application and writing a document for it depend upon a certain understanding and familiarity with the application. The next several skills are devoted to in-depth discussions of specific XML applications. These skills will introduce you to some of the emerging XML applications and help you learn how to effectively evaluate an application. In Skill 20, "Automating Web Sites With WIDL," you'll meet the Web Interface

Definition Language (WIDL), which is a neat little application designed to allow any number of business applications to interface with Web data.

Are You up to Speed?

Now you can...

- ☑ **Define an XML application**
- ☑ **Explain techniques for choosing the best application for your content**
- ☑ **Analyze an XML application in preparation for creating documents for it**
- ☑ **Discuss the pros and cons of altering an XML application**

SKILL 20

Automating Web Sites with WIDL

- Introducing WIDL
- Using WIDL to automate the Web
- A look at the major WIDL elements
- Creating a WIDL document

The Web Interface Definition Language (WIDL) is an XML vocabulary that facilitates the exchange of data between business applications over an intranet or the Internet. WIDL provides the foundation for Web Automation, a technology that allows applications other than Web browsers to interact directly with a Web server and the data stored on it. With WIDL, businesses can make direct connections between a wide range of business applications and the company's Web server. This approach takes advantage of the standard protocols of the Web and allows a large number of applications to access and share the same resources stored in one location.

What Is WIDL?

Imagine a world in which business applications from spread sheets to custom databases can communicate with each other and exchange data over the Internet or an intranet. These days, this type of data exchange and communication among non-Web applications is made possible by thousands of lines of programming code and a wealth of Webmaster and programmer ingenuity. The result is a somewhat convoluted process that converts data from one application to Web information, transfers the data across an intranet or the Internet, and converts to the data type of the receiving application. This is definitely not the easiest nor the best way for business applications to share data.

The majority of database software now offer tools that connect the data stored in them to a Web page. In addition to calling up Web pages that include data from the database, Web pages can often be used to automatically update the database. You see this all the time on Web pages that use forms to collect information. WIDL extends this functionality to all business applications and allows them to communicate with data stored on a Web server in a standard and consistent way.

Documents developed for the WIDL DTD describe a series of services or functions, such as tracking a package or defining a personnel profile. Any software package that can understand and process WIDL can perform a service and display the results for the user. The bottom line is that with WIDL, you don't need a Web browser to browse the Web any more. Any WIDL-compliant software package can access and display Web data.

Implementing WIDL

WIDL is not a solution for the individual Web developer, but instead, it is designed specifically for those businesses (large and small) that need to share data internally and with other organizations. WIDL can be used to link customer databases and supplier lists, connect human-resource information across a large company, and provide a standard way of describing financial data for electronic commerce.

The idea behind WIDL isn't to reinvent the wheel and provide a new way to store and display data but rather to take advantage of existing software to allow a wide variety of applications to share the same data. For example, there are several competing home-financial software packages on the market today, including Microsoft's Money and Intuit's Quicken. Both of these packages describe the same types of information (account records and the like) but use different and proprietary formats for data. Short of importing and converting the data from one application type to another, Money can't read Quicken files, and Quicken can't read Money files in their native format.

If a bank wants to provide its customers over the Web with account records that can be read and processed by both Money and Quicken, it has to provide two different types of files, one for each application, in addition to its Web version of the records. This is how my bank does things, and after talking to its Webmaster, I found out it's a difficult way to do business. But, the bank doesn't really have a choice if it wants to support the two major financial packages its customers use.

If my bank implemented WIDL support in Money and Quicken and adopted the vocabulary, its problems would be solved because both software packages could read data from a single source. In addition, because WIDL is designed to allow any application to read and display Web data, customers could use Money or Quicken to survey their online financial data directly instead of having to use a Web browser.

The potential for widespread WIDL implementation is huge. There are hundreds of thousands of proprietary data-management systems in place around the world, and the majority of those systems can't talk to each other. What if one company buys out another and all of their human resource and customer data is stored in two disparate systems? Some unlucky person or team of people would have to convert the data from one of those systems to the other. This is, needless to say, not a very effective way to do business.

If you think that WIDL might be a possible solution for a need that you have for sharing data in a standard way within your organization or with other organizations in your field, then you'll definitely want to visit the webMethods WIDL home site at http://www.webmethods.com/. The creator of WIDL and Web Automation, webMethods includes a variety of demos and white papers that discuss the business-to-business implementation of WIDL. The Web Automation Toolkit is webMethods's WIDL development tool and is an excellent application for implementing Web automation.

Even if you think WIDL is too advanced for your needs, it is still a good example of what XML vocabularies will be called on to do for both industries and individuals. There is obviously a need for a better and more effective way of sharing data across the Web by a variety of software packages, and WIDL provides the foundation for one solution that meets that need. The majority of XML vocabularies under development today are designed to meet a specific need. As a developer, it's up to you to find the best vocabulary for your needs.

The WIDL DTD

WIDL was submitted to the W3C as a note on September 22, 1997. WIDL is not a standard yet, but it does have a fair chance of becoming one. Keep your eye on the W3C's XML page, at http://www.w3.org/XML/, for any news about the status of WIDL.

NOTE You can find the entire contents of the WIDL note on the W3C's Web site at http://www.w3.org/TR/NOTE-widl.

The WIDL DTD is short and sweet—it only has six elements. You may be wondering how such an abbreviated DTD can do all of the things I said it could but remember that WIDL is designed to work with compatible applications. The majority of the functionality of WIDL will be built into those applications. WIDL just describes a service. The application knows what to do with it.

```
<!ELEMENT WIDL ( SERVICE | BINDING )* >
<!ATTLIST WIDL
     NAME       CDATA   #IMPLIED
     VERSION (1.0 | 2.0 | ...) "2.0"
     TEMPLATE   CDATA   #IMPLIED
     BASEURL    CDATA   #IMPLIED
     OBJMODEL (wmdom | ...) "wmdom"
>

<!ELEMENT SERVICE EMPTY>
<!ATTLIST SERVICE
     NAME       CDATA   #REQUIRED
```

```
    URL         CDATA   #REQUIRED
    METHOD (Get | Post) "Get"
    INPUT       CDATA   #IMPLIED
    OUTPUT      CDATA   #IMPLIED
    AUTHUSER    CDATA   #IMPLIED
    AUTHPASS    CDATA   #IMPLIED
    TIMEOUT     CDATA   #IMPLIED
    RETRIES     CDATA   #IMPLIED
>

<!ELEMENT BINDING ( VARIABLE | CONDITION | REGION )* >
<!ATTLIST BINDING
    NAME        CDATA   #REQUIRED
    TYPE (Input | Output) "Output"
>

<!ELEMENT VARIABLE EMPTY>
<!ATTLIST VARIABLE
    NAME        CDATA   #REQUIRED
    FORMNAME    CDATA   #IMPLIED
    TYPE (String | String[] | String[][]) "String"
    USAGE (Default | Header | Internal) "Function"
    REFERENCE   CDATA   #IMPLIED
    VALUE       CDATA   #IMPLIED
    MASK        CDATA   #IMPLIED
    NULLOK              #BOOLEAN
>

<!ELEMENT CONDITION EMPTY>
<!ATTLIST CONDITION
    TYPE  (Success | Failure | Retry) "Success"
    REF         CDATA   #REQUIRED
    MATCH       CDATA   #REQUIRED
    REBIND      CDATA   #IMPLIED
    SERVICE     CDATA   #IMPLIED
    REASONREF   CDATA   #IMPLIED
    REASONTEXT  CDATA   #IMPLIED
    WAIT        CDATA   #IMPLIED
    RETRIES     CDATA   #IMPLIED
>

<!ELEMENT REGION EMPTY>
<!ATTLIST REGION
    NAME        CDATA   #REQUIRED
    START       CDATA   #REQUIRED
    END         CDATA   #REQUIRED
>
```

The next section of this skill describes each of these elements in detail, including a discussion of the type of content each one is designed to describe.

WIDL's Primary Constructs in Detail

WIDL's five elements can be used to describe a service or set of services of any type, from an account record to a supplier's merchandise list. WIDL is definitely a content-based markup language and is designed to describe content to be read and processed by a computer. To show what a WIDL document might look like, I'll create a running example that shows how each element could be used to describe an individual account at a bank.

This section provides a brief overview of the elements in the WIDL DTD; however, for a complete description and in-depth discussion of the many aspects of WIDL, review the WIDL note or the white papers on the webMethods site.

The WIDL Element

The `WIDL` element is the document element for any WIDL document. The element's content and attribute specifics include

- Content: one or more instances of the `SERVICE` and `BINDING` elements
- Attributes: `NAME`, `VERSION`, `TEMPLATE`, `BASEURL`, and `OBJMODEL`

The two elements, `SERVICE` and `BINDING`, and their `CHILD` elements should be nested within the `WIDL` element. The `WIDL` element can take the following five attributes.

`NAME` Declares a name for the interface

`VERSION` Identifies the `WIDL` version used to describe the interface

`TEMPLATE` Identifies a particular specification or set of instructions to which the service should adhere

`BASEURL` Identifies the main URL that describes the interface and its service(s)

`OBJMODEL` Identifies the object model that will govern the way the document's elements are identified and displayed by the application

Of these attributes, the two most important are the NAME and VERSION attributes, as shown by this code sample:

```
<WIDL NAME="Account Information" VERSION="1.0">
</WIDL>
```

The SERVICE Element

The SERVICE element describes a specific service (a request or a response) for the interface. The element's content and attribute specifics include

- Content: empty
- Attributes: NAME, URL, METHOD, INPUT, OUTPUT, AUTHUSER, AUTHPASS, TIMEOUT, and RETRIES

Many interfaces may have more than one service, whereas others may have only one. The actual number of services is determined entirely by the goals of the interface. The attributes for the SERVICE element include the NAME attribute for identifying the service's name; the URL attribute, which points to the location on the Web where the service and its information reside; and the METHOD attribute, which indicates whether the service is accessed by a GET or POST method. The INPUT and OUTPUT attributes specify bindings, or the methods and variables needed for the service to interact (send and receive data) with the data on the Web server. The needs of the interface and the data types will determine the bindings for each service. The AUTHUSER and AUTHPASS attributes store user name and password information, which the client will most likely prompt the user for. The TIMEOUT attribute indicates how long the client should try to connect to a server before it gives up, whereas the RETRIES attribute indicates how many times the client should attempt to connect with the server.

Of these attributes, the most important are the URL, INPUT, and OUTPUT; although this new version of the account interface sample code includes all of the possible attributes (except for the user identification attributes because they change on a user-by-user basis) for the service:

```
<WIDL NAME="Account Information" VERSION="1.0">
   <SERVICE NAME="Checking" METHOD ="GET"
      URL="http://www.mybank.com/accounts/online_banking"
      INPUT="GetAccountInfo"
      OUTPUT="PubAccountInfo"
      TIMEOUT="30"
      RETRIES="4" />
</WIDL>
```

The BINDING Element

The BINDING element contains other elements that provide specific information about the bindings and variables required for a service to do its job. The element's content and attribute specifics include

- Content: one or more instances of the VARIABLE, CONDITION, or REGION elements
- Attributes: NAME and TYPE

The NAME attribute assigns a name to the binding information, and the TYPE attribute indicates whether the binding is an input or output binding. The account service is very simple, and the Web server can provide all of the information to the application based on the simple service description.

The VARIABLE Element

The VARIABLE element is nested within the BINDING element and provides specific content or information for a service to use when it communicates with the Web server. The element's content and attribute specifics include

- Content: empty
- Attributes: NAME, FORMNAME, TYPE, USAGE, REFERNCE, VALUE, MASK, and NULLOK

The VARIABLE element can take the following key attributes:

NAME Identifies the variable's name

FORMNAME Provides a value to be submitted to the server using the GET or POST method specified in the SERVICE element

TYPE Identifies the variable's data type and dimension

USAGE Specifies whether the variable should be passed to the server as header information and whether it should be used inside of the WIDL application

VALUE Identifies the variable's value

A BINDING element may contain as many VARIABLE elements as required by the application or the service. Because the account service doesn't have BINDING tags, it doesn't need VARIABLE elements either.

The CONDITION Element

The CONDITION element defines what happens when a binding is successful or fails. The element's content and attribute specifics include

- Content: empty
- Attributes: TYPE, REF, MATCH, REBIND, SERVICE, REASONREF, REASONTEXT, WAIT, and RETRIES

The attributes provide specifics about what should happen in the event of the success or failure of a service. The TYPE attribute indicates whether the condition should be applied in the event of a success or failure of the service. Its possible values are SUCCESS, FAILURE, and RETRY. In the event of a failure or retry, the REBIND attribute can be used to redirect the service to another version of the binding, whereas the REASONTEXT attribute provides a text string to be returned when the service fails. Once again, because the account service doesn't have BINDING elements, it won't have CONDITION elements either.

The REGION Element

The last element in the WIDL DTD is the REGION element. This element is designed to embed the output of a WIDL binding into another XML or HTML document. This means that WIDL doesn't have to work alone and can be designed to work with other tools and documents that rely on both HTML and XML. The element's content and attribute specifics include

- Content: empty
- Attributes: NAME, START, and END

The NAME attribute provides an easily identifiable name for the region, and the START and END attributes specify where the inclusion of the binding output should be embedded in the document. Region information is specified on a binding-by-binding basis, along with variable and condition information. The account service is designed to work alone, so it won't include region information.

Onward to Channeling

Although the accounts example is a simple one and it's obvious that the more you want to do with WIDL the more complex its documents will be, you've now had a taste of what this rising star XML vocabulary can do. WIDL is designed to extend the functionality of Web servers to allow their data to be browsed by a wide variety of applications; therefore, the subject of the next skill is designed to expand the way Web content is delivered to users. In Skill 21, "Channeling Data with CDF," you'll meet CDF, the Channel Definition Format, which is an XML vocabulary used to deliver Web content on a regular schedule to users across Web channels.

Are You up to Speed?

Now you can...

- ☑ **Define WIDL**
- ☑ **Describe how WIDL can be used to provide access to Web data to a variety of applications**
- ☑ **Identify the primary WIDL elements**
- ☑ **Describe a Web service using WIDL**

SKILL 21

Channeling Data with CDF

- Understanding CDF
- Viewing an Active channel
- Creating an Active channel
- Creating a CDF file

In 1997, the folks at Microsoft thought it might be nice to create a mechanism that would provide Web developers with a way to send new and updated Web pages to their users automatically. This thought lead the way for the first real-world implementation of an XML vocabulary, the Channel Definition Format (CDF).

What Is CDF?

CDF is the XML vocabulary that describes Web channels. What are Web channels? A Web channel, or Active channel in Microsoft-speak, is a virtual link between a client's Web browser and a Web server through which data can be sent automatically. To fully understand channels and, by extension, CDF, there are a couple of new terms and concepts you'll need to understand.

Client-Pull and Server-Push

Client-pull is the fancy name for how Web pages are accessed currently. The user agent on the client machine (the Web browser on your computer) requests a document from a Web server when you want to see it. This request is also called pulling the document from the server, hence the name client-pull. On the other side of the spectrum, there's *server push*. The Web server, instead of the Web client (browser), initiates the act of transferring information to the client, and the content is sent, or pushed, directly to the browser on the client machine. Although the end result is the same—you still view Web pages in your Web browser—how you get those pages is different. *Channels* use server-push to send automatic updates to users.

You may be wondering why it matters how you get your Web pages, or perhaps you don't much like the idea of a Web server sending you pages randomly. After all, that does open you up to all kinds of unsolicited information, and e-mail spam is bad enough. Never fear, server-push isn't set up to send unsolicited Web pages. Before you can receive information from a channel, you must subscribe to it first. There is an advantage to having your content automatically updated by the server: you receive fresh information when it's available, not when you decide to go looking for it. The whole idea behind a channel is that users can receive the latest and greatest information without having to initiate the actual transfer of information.

The Concept behind a Channel

The way a channel actually works is that the Web developer creates a channel using CDF, and users subscribe to it. The developer then creates new HTML (or XML) Web content, with no limit to the number of pages, and alters the CDF file to indicate that new content is available. The user's browser automatically checks the channel, or the user initiates the check, and all of the new content is downloaded to the user's browser automatically, regardless of the number of pages involved. The user gets all of the new information in one fell swoop, without having to surf through old and new information to find the latest updates.

The user controls when the channel is checked for new content through browser settings or by activating the channel manually, but instead of pulling each document in the update individually, the server pushes the entire batch of new files to the client computer. The user can even browse the new content offline because all of the content has been pushed to the client computer.

A Web developer can set up one or more channels of information on a Web site, each with a different content focus. Not all of a Web site's information should be served using channels. Static information that doesn't change very much, such as contact information and white papers, isn't the best choice for channel content. Daily news updates, new product information, bug fixes, and technical reports are all good candidates for channel content because they are updated regularly. In short, anything on a Web site that doesn't change every couple of weeks or so shouldn't be served through a channel, whereas content that changes on a daily basis might be best served to users via a channel.

So where does CDF come into play in the whole channel system? CDF describes the channels themselves, providing specifics about the goal of the channel, which Web resources make up the channel's content, when the channel should be updated, and what logo should be used to identify the channel in the user's Web browser. Later in this skill, in the section "CDF's Primary Constructs in Detail," you'll learn about each element in the CDF DTD and see a CDF document constructed from the ground up.

Implementing CDF

The most mainstream implementation of CDF right now is from Microsoft. Internet Explorer 4 has support for Microsoft's Active channels built directly into the browser. This support is limited to the Windows platform in the IE 4 browser but is extended to the Macintosh in version 4.01. Viewing and creating channels are two different activities, but Microsoft has tools for both that are easy to use.

Viewing Channel Content

To view a channel and its updates, users must first show the channels menu by clicking on the channel icon in the standard toolbar (as shown in Figure 21.1) or by selecting the Channels option from the Explorer Bar submenu of the View main-menu, as shown in Figure 21.2.

FIGURE 21.1: Show the channel menu by clicking the channel icon in the toolbar.

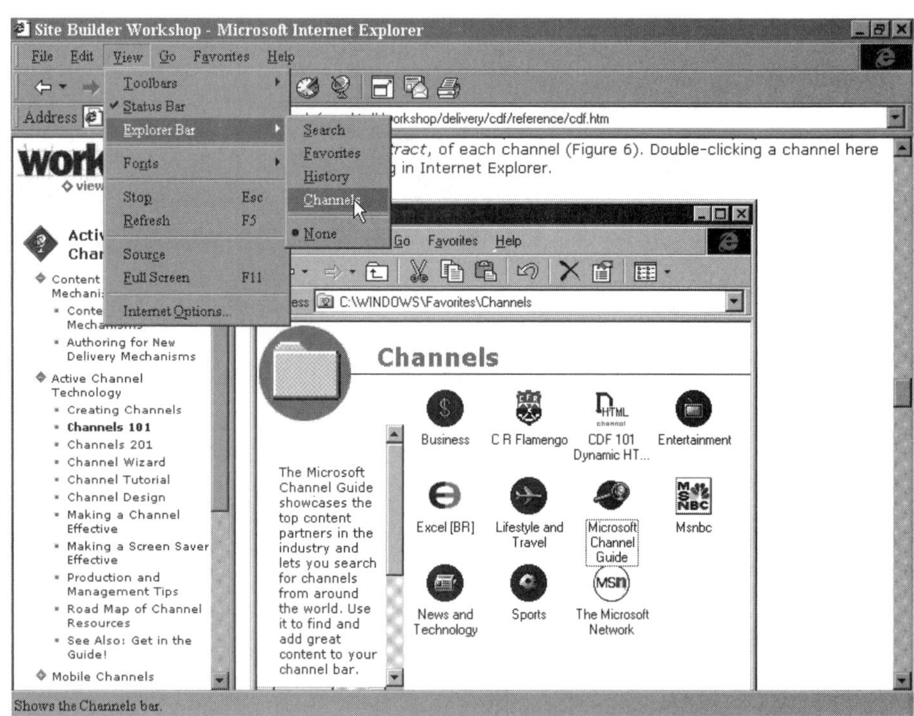

FIGURE 21.2: Show the channel menu by choosing channels from the View menu.

Once the menu is in place, the user simply has to choose a channel icon from the menu. IE comes with several icons already included in the menu bar, such as the Disney icon selected in Figure 21.3.

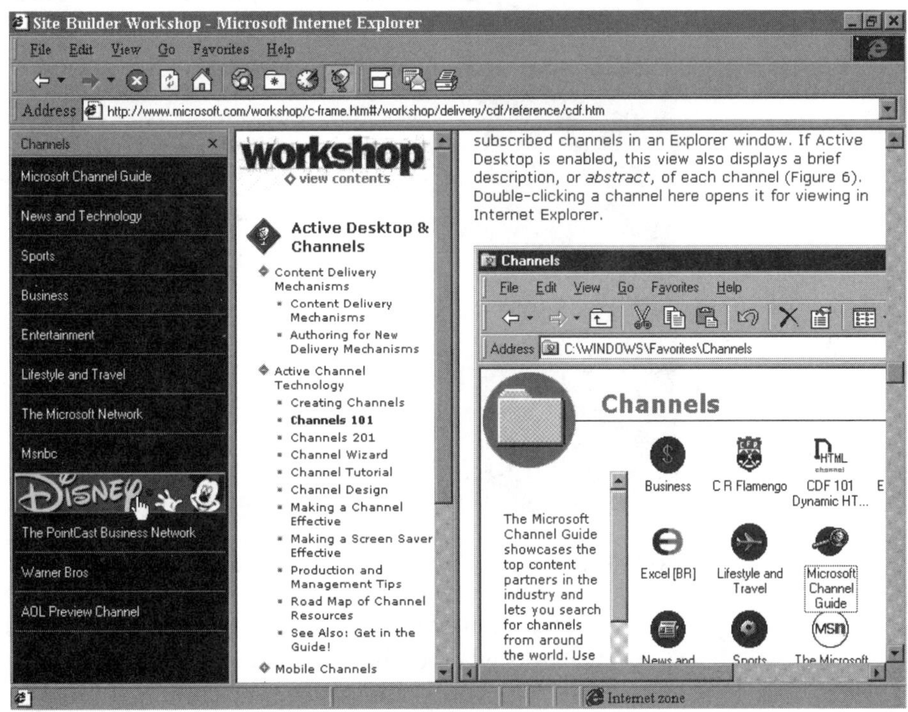

FIGURE 21.3: Select a channel from the channel menu to view its updates.

TIP

Other channel icons don't show up on the menu bar until the user subscribes to the channel.

The updates from the channel are downloaded to the user's computer automatically so the user can surf them at leisure. If a user hasn't subscribed to a channel, he or she can do so easily by clicking the subscribe button on any site that includes an Active channel, as shown in Figure 21.4.

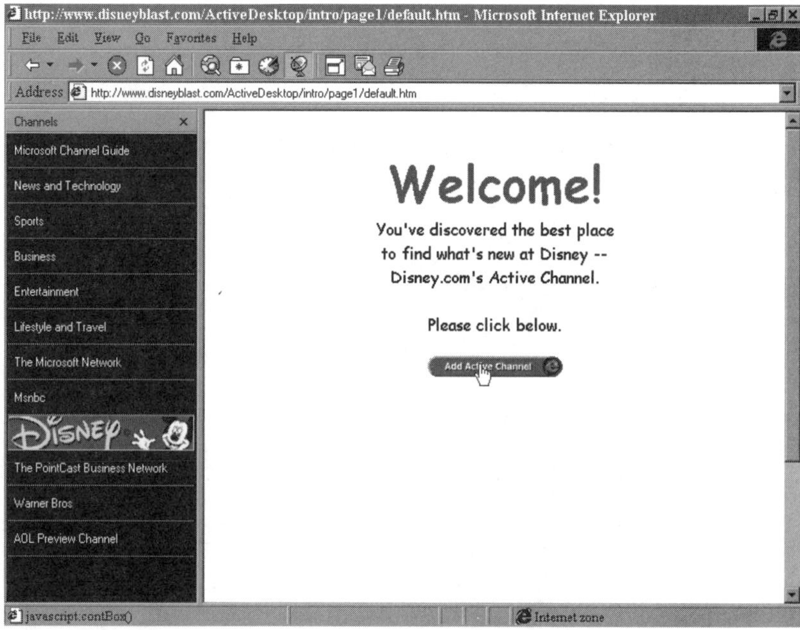

FIGURE 21.4: Subscribe to an Active channel by clicking a button.

When the subscription starts, the user is prompted by a dialog box, shown in Figure 21.5, that asks whether they would like to subscribe to the channel and how they would like the updates handled. The user has the option to not subscribe but to include the channel's icon on the toolbar, subscribe and only be notified of changes, or subscribe and have all changes downloaded to the client's computer automatically.

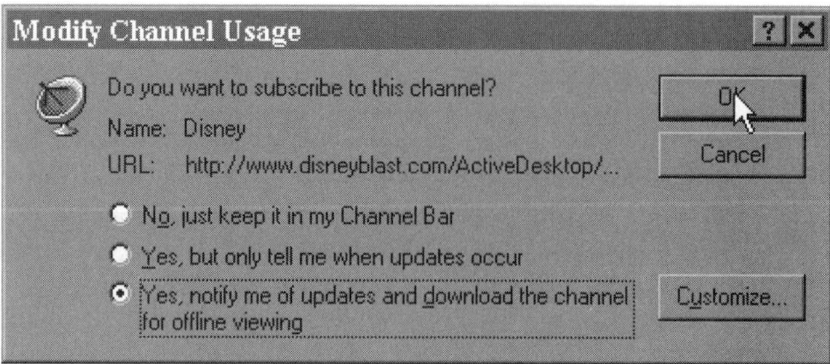

FIGURE 21.5: Specify how a channel and its content should be handled when subscribing to the channel.

As a final touch for controlling channels, users can choose Manage Subscriptions from the Favorites menu to see what channels they are subscribed to and even alter their subscription using the options window, as shown in Figure 21.6.

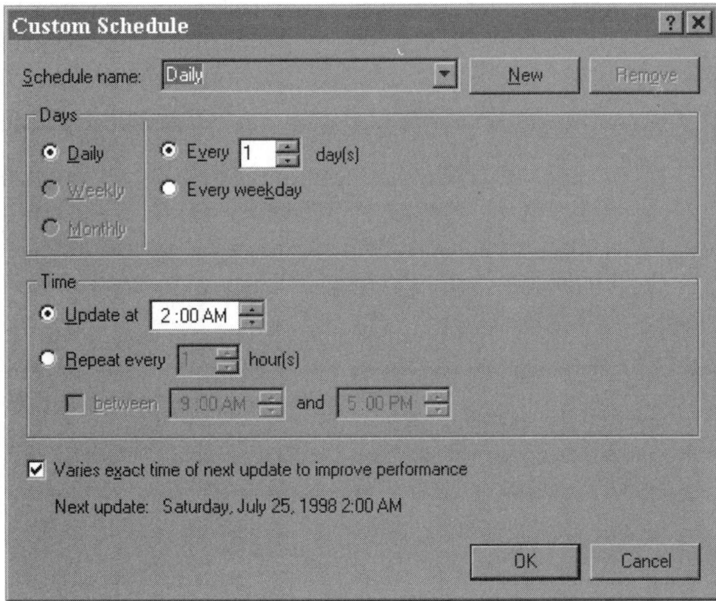

FIGURE 21.6: Control individual channel subscriptions through the channel options window.

Creating Channel Content

All things considered, creating a channel is relatively easy. First, you must create your channel content, which is nothing more than regular Web page creation. You create content for a channel in the same way you would for a regular Web site, using your favorite tools and techniques. To actually define the channel, you must create a CDF file that defines the channel. Once that's done, all you have to do is add a link to a Web page that points to the CDF file. The subscribe button you saw in Figure 21.4 is simply an `IMAGE` element nested inside of an `ANCHOR` tag that points to the CDF file that describes the channel.

The hardest part of creating and managing a channel is keeping your content regularly updated. Users will expect new information frequently. Also, because CDF and channels are only supported by Internet Explorer, you need to provide an alternative method for Netscape and IE 3 users to view your channel content.

Because channel content is regular Web content, you can easily post the content to your site in a What's New or Updates section for those channel-challenged users.

TIP

Microsoft has a host of good resources for creating and managing channel content. There's a channel wizard (no surprise there) and CDF generator you can download and use for free. Point your Web browser at `http://www.microsoft.com/workshop/c-frame.htm#/workshop/delivery/default.asp`.

Other mechanisms and technologies are involved in creating a channel, as the description of viewing and creating channels indicates, but in the end, Web content without CDF is just another Web page, not a channel. To use channel technology, you must create CDF files, and that's what the remainder of this skill is devoted to.

NOTE

To learn more about high-end, business-to-business implementations of CDF, visit the DataChannel Web site at `http://www.datachannel.com/`.

The CDF DTD

CDF was created by the folks at Microsoft and submitted to the W3C as a note. The official submission is available at `http://www.w3.org/TR/NOTE-CDFsubmit.html`. Here's your first peek at the innerworkings of CDF:

```
<!ELEMENT Channel
   ( LastMod | Title | Abstract | Author | Publisher |
    Copyright | PublicationDate | Keywords | Category |
    Rating | Channel | Item | Schedule | IntroURI |
    Authorization | IsClonable | MinStorage | Tracking )* >
<!ATTLIST Channel HREF CDATA #IMPLIED>
<!ATTLIST Channel IsClonable (YES | NO) "NO">

<!ELEMENT Item
   ( LastMod, Title, Abstract, Author, Publisher,
     Copyright, PublicationDate, Keywords, Category, Rating,
     Schedule, Usage )* >
<!ATTLIST Item HREF CDATA #REQUIRED>
<!ATTLIST Item MIMEType CDATA #IMPLIED>
<!ATTLIST Item IsVisible (YES, NO) "YES">
<!ATTLIST Item Priority (HI, NORMAL, LOW) "NORMAL">
<!ATTLIST Item Precache (YES, NO, DEFAULT) "DEFAULT">
```

```
<!ELEMENT LastMod EMPTY>
<!ATTLIST LastMod VALUE CDATA #REQUIRED>

<!ELEMENT Title EMPTY>
<!ATTLIST Title VALUE CDATA #REQUIRED>

<!ELEMENT Abstract EMPTY>
<!ATTLIST Abstract VALUE CDATA #REQUIRED>

<!ELEMENT Author EMPTY>
<!ATTLIST Author VALUE CDATA #REQUIRED>

<!ELEMENT Publisher EMPTY>
<!ATTLIST Publisher VALUE CDATA #REQUIRED>

<!ELEMENT Copyright EMPTY>
<!ATTLIST Copyright VALUE CDATA #REQUIRED>

<!ELEMENT PublicationDate EMPTY>
<!ATTLIST PublicationDate VALUE CDATA #REQUIRED>

<!ELEMENT Keywords EMPTY>
<!ATTLIST Keywords VALUE CDATA #REQUIRED>

<!ELEMENT Category EMPTY>
<!ATTLIST Category VALUE CDATA #REQUIRED>

<!ELEMENT Rating EMPTY>
<!ATTLIST Rating PICS-Label CDATA #REQUIRED>

<!ELEMENT IntroURI EMPTY>
<!ATTLIST IntroURI VALUE CDATA #REQUIRED>

<!ELEMENT Authorization EMPTY>
<!ATTLIST Authorization VALUE CDATA #REQUIRED>

<!ELEMENT MinStorage EMPTY>
<!ATTLIST MinStorage VALUE CDATA "0">

<!ELEMENT Usage ANY>
<!ATTLIST Usage VALUE CDATA #REQUIRED>

<!ELEMENT UserSchedule EMPTY>
<!ATTLIST UserSchedule VALUE
   (DAILY, WEEKLY, HOURLY) #REQUIRED>

<!ELEMENT Schedule
  ( StartDate?, EndDate?, IntervalTime?, EarliestTime?,
    LatestTime? ) >
```

```
<!ELEMENT StartDate EMPTY>
<!ATTLIST StartDate VALUE CDATA #REQUIRED>

<!ELEMENT EndDate EMPTY>
<!ATTLIST EndDate VALUE CDATA #REQUIRED>

<!ELEMENT IntervalTime EMPTY>
<!ATTLIST IntervalTime DAY CDATA "0">
<!ATTLIST IntervalTime HOUR CDATA "0">
<!ATTLIST IntervalTime MIN CDATA "0">
<!ATTLIST IntervalTime SEC CDATA "0">

<!ELEMENT EarliestTime EMPTY>
<!ATTLIST EarliestTime DAY CDATA "0">
<!ATTLIST EarliestTime HOUR CDATA "0">
<!ATTLIST EarliestTime MIN CDATA "0">
<!ATTLIST EarliestTime SEC CDATA "0">

<!ELEMENT LatestTime EMPTY>
<!ATTLIST LatestTime DAY CDATA "0">
<!ATTLIST LatestTime HOUR CDATA "0">
<!ATTLIST LatestTime MIN CDATA "0">
<!ATTLIST LatestTime SEC CDATA "0">

<!ELEMENT Logo EMPTY>
<!ATTLIST Logo HREF CDATA #REQUIRED>
<!ATTLIST Logo TYPE (BIG WIDE SMALL REGULAR) "REGULAR">

<!ELEMENT PostURL EMPTY>
<!ATTLIST PostURL HREF CDATA #REQUIRED>

<!ELEMENT Tracking (PostURL?)>
<!ELEMENT PostURL EMPTY>
<!ATTLIST PostURL HREF CDATA #REQUIRED>
```

Creating usable channels requires that you create accurate CDF files. To that end, the next section of this skill looks at each CDF element in detail and defines a CDF document along the way.

NOTE The CDF DTD and the submission itself are copyrighted by the W3C.

CDF's Primary Constructs in Detail

CDF uses a variety of elements to describe a channel and subchannels (items) within that channel. For example, a channel for a specific software package might include subchannels that focus on product updates, implementations of the product, and technical notes. In addition, CDF can describe how often a channel should be updated. CDF has these major elements:

- CHANNEL
- ITEM
- SCHEDULE
- LOGO

All the other elements in the CDF DTD are designed to provide support for these main elements. The following sections outline the most important elements in the CDF DTD, including content and attribute specifics for each. Along the way, to further explain the role of each element and show you how to build a CDF file, a code sample that describes the technical updates and bug reports channel for a product called Web Widget will be created from the ground up.

NOTE For a look at the complete CDF submission, point your Web browser at http://www.w3.org/TR/NOTE-CDFsubmit.html.

The CHANNEL Element

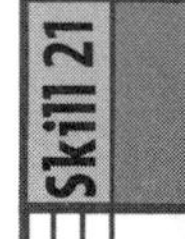

The CHANNEL element serves as the document element for every CDF file you create. The element's content and attribute specifics include

- Content: one or more instances of the LASTMOD, TITLE, ABSTRACT, AUTHOR, PUBLISHER, COPYRIGHT, PUBLICATIONDATE, KEYWORDS, CATEGORY, RATING, CHANNEL, ITEM, SCHEDULE, INTROURI, AUTHORIZATION, ISCLONABLE, MINSTORAGE, or TRACKING elements
- Attributes: HREF, ISCLONABLE

The CHANNEL element can contain one of several elements that provide more information about the channel, including the ITEM element that describes subchannels within the channel. The HREF attribute takes a URL value that points to the CDF file that describes the most recent update for the channel, and the ISCLONABLE attribute takes a YES or NO value that indicates whether the channel can be copied and moved to act as a subchannel for another channel. Each time a new update is created for the channel, the HREF attribute changes to reflect the location of the file that describes the latest update. This is the first element in the description of the Web Widget Tech Channel:

```
<CHANNEL HREF="http://www.mysite.com/channels/wwnew01.cdf"
    ISCLONABLE="NO">
</CHANNEL>
```

The LASTMOD Element

The empty LASTMOD element identifies when the channel was last updated. The element's content and attribute specifics include

- Content: empty
- Attribute: VALUE

The VALUE attribute takes a date value of the format *YYYY.MM.DD*. In these terms, July 22, 1998 would be 1998.07.22. The Web Widget Technical Channel was last modified on May 3, 1998, as the following CDF code shows:

```
<CHANNEL HREF="http://www.mysite.com/channels/wwnew01.cdf"
    ISCLONABLE="NO">
   <LASTMOD VALUE="1998.05.03" />
</CHANNEL>
```

The TITLE Element

The empty TITLE element provides a friendly title for the channel. The element's content and attribute specifics include

- Content: empty
- Attribute: VALUE

You should always title your CDF files as shown in this code:

```
<CHANNEL HREF="http://www.mysite.com/channels/wwnew01.cdf"
       ISCLONABLE="NO">
   <LASTMOD VALUE="1998.05.03" />
```

```
    <TITLE VALUE="The Web Widget Tech Channel" />
</CHANNEL>
```

The ABSTRACT Element

Yet another EMPTY element, the ABSTRACT element provides a more detailed description of the channel and its content. The element's content and attribute specifics include

- Content: empty
- Attribute: VALUE

An ABSTRACT is useful for reminding yourself and others what the purpose and scope of the channel are, as in this bit of code:

```
<CHANNEL HREF="http://www.mysite.com/channels/wwnew01.cdf"
       ISCLONABLE="NO">
    <LASTMOD VALUE="1998.05.03" />
    <TITLE VALUE="The Web Widget Tech Channel" />
    <ABSTRACT VALUE= "A channel that provides the latest
         technical notes and bug reports for the Web Widget
         software application" />
</CHANNEL>
```

The AUTHOR Element

As its name suggests, the AUTHOR element is a mechanism for supplying authorship information for the channel and its content. The element's content and attribute specifics include

- Content: empty
- Attribute: VALUE

According to this CDF code, I'm the author of the Web Widget Tech Channel content:

```
<CHANNEL HREF="http://www.mysite.com/channels/wwnew01.cdf"
       ISCLONABLE="NO">
    <LASTMOD VALUE="1998.05.03" />
    <TITLE VALUE="The Web Widget Tech Channel" />
    <ABSTRACT VALUE="A channel that provides the latest
         technical notes and bug reports for the Web Widget
         software application" />
    <AUTHOR VALUE="Natanya Pitts-Moultis" />
</CHANNEL>
```

The PUBLISHER Element

Although the AUTHOR element assigns authorship to the channel content, the PUBLISHER element provides information about the individual or organization responsible for the publication of the channel and its contents. The element's content and attribute specifics include

- Content: empty
- Attribute: VALUE

In the case of the Web Widget Tech Channel, the publisher is LANWrights, Inc., as reflected in this code:

```
<CHANNEL HREF="http://www.mysite.com/channels/wwnew01.cdf"
      ISCLONABLE="NO">
   <LASTMOD VALUE="1998.05.03" />
   <TITLE VALUE="The Web Widget Tech Channel" />
   <ABSTRACT VALUE="A channel that provides the latest
        technical notes and bug reports for the Web Widget
        software application" />
   <AUTHOR VALUE="Natanya Pitts-Moultis" />
   <PUBLISHER VALUE="LANWrights, Inc." />
</CHANNEL>
```

The COPYRIGHT Element

CDF also includes the COPYRIGHT element to provide information about whoever holds the copyright on the channel's content. The element's content and attribute specifics include

- Content: empty
- Attribute: VALUE

The author, publisher, and copyright holder of a channel's content may or may not be the same individual or organization, so to make it very clear, always include this information, as shown in this code:

```
<CHANNEL HREF="http://www.mysite.com/channels/wwnew01.cdf"
      ISCLONABLE="NO">
   <LASTMOD VALUE="1998.05.03" />
   <TITLE VALUE="The Web Widget Tech Channel" />
   <ABSTRACT VALUE="A channel that provides the latest
        technical notes and bug reports for the Web Widget
        software application" />
```

```
    <AUTHOR VALUE="Natanya Pitts-Moultis" />
    <PUBLISHER VALUE="LANWrights, Inc." />
    <COPYRIGHT VALUE="LANWrights, Inc." />
</CHANNEL>
```

The PUBLICATIONDATE Element

The PUBLICATIONDATE element defines when the channel was first published. The element's content and attribute specifics include

- Content: empty
- Attribute: VALUE

The Web Widget Tech Channel debuted on January 1, 1998, as the newest version of the CDF code reflects:

```
<CHANNEL HREF="http://www.mysite.com/channels/wwnew01.cdf"
       ISCLONABLE="NO">
    <LASTMOD VALUE="1998.05.03" />
    <TITLE VALUE="The Web Widget Tech Channel" />
    <ABSTRACT VALUE="A channel that provides the latest
         technical notes and bug reports for the Web Widget
         software application" />
    <AUTHOR VALUE="Natanya Pitts-Moultis" />
    <PUBLISHER VALUE="LANWrights, Inc." />
    <PUBLICATIONDATE VALUE="1998.01.01" />
    <COPYRIGHT VALUE="LANWrights, Inc." />
</CHANNEL>
```

The KEYWORDS Element

To provide a set of terms that describes the channel, CDF includes the KEYWORDS element. The element's content and attribute specifics include

- Content: empty
- Attribute: VALUE

When this element and its content are added to the description of the Web Widget Tech Channel, the markup looks like this:

```
<CHANNEL HREF="http://www.mysite.com/channels/wwnew01.cdf"
       ISCLONABLE="NO">
    <LASTMOD VALUE="1998.05.03" />
    <TITLE VALUE="The Web Widget Tech Channel" />
    <ABSTRACT VALUE="A channel that provides the latest
```

```
        technical notes and bug reports for the Web Widget
        software application" />
    <AUTHOR VALUE="Natanya Pitts-Moultis" />
    <PUBLISHER VALUE="LANWrights, Inc." />
    <PUBLICATIONDATE VALUE="1998.01.01" />
    <COPYRIGHT VALUE="LANWrights, Inc." />
    <KEYWORDS VALUE="Web Widget, technical information, bug
        reports, software updates" />
</CHANNEL>
```

The INTROURI Element

The INTROURI element describes a Web page that provides an introduction to the channel and allows users to subscribe to it. The element's content and attribute specifics include

- Content: empty
- Attribute: VALUE

When users visit the channel for the first time, they are directed to this page. With this element added to it, the sample CDF code looks like this:

```
<CHANNEL HREF="http://www.mysite.com/channels/wwnew01.cdf"
       ISCLONABLE="NO">
    <LASTMOD VALUE="1998.05.03" />
    <TITLE VALUE="The Web Widget Tech Channel" />
    <ABSTRACT VALUE="A channel that provides the latest
        technical notes and bug reports for the Web Widget
        software application" />
    <AUTHOR VALUE="Natanya Pitts-Moultis" />
    <PUBLISHER VALUE="LANWrights, Inc." />
    <PUBLICATIONDATE VALUE="1998.01.01" />
    <COPYRIGHT VALUE="LANWrights, Inc." />
    <KEYWORDS VALUE="Web Widget, technical information, bug
        reports, software updates" />
    <INTROURI VALUE=
        "http://www.mysite.com/channels/ww-intro.html" />
</CHANNEL>
```

The ITEM Element

The ITEM element describes subchannels of a CHANNEL element. The element's content and attribute specifics include

- Content: one or more instances of LASTMOD, TITLE, ABSTRACT, AUTHOR, PUBLISHER, COPYRIGHT, PUBLICATIONDATE, KEYWORDS, CATEGORY, RATING, SCHEDULE, or USAGE elements

- Attributes: HREF, MIMEType, IsVisible, Priority, Precache

These ITEM and CHANNEL elements have similar content models, and you can describe an item in the same way that you would describe a channel. The HREF attribute takes a URL value that points to the latest channel information. The Web Widget Tech Channel is a simple channel and doesn't have any sub-channels, so its description doesn't include any ITEM elements.

The SCHEDULE Element

The SCHEDULE element is designed to contain a group of other elements that describes the schedule for updating the channel's information. The element's content and attribute specifics include

- Content: zero or single instance of the STARTDATE, ENDDATE, INTERVALTIME, EARLIESTTIME, or LATESTTIME elements
- Attribute: none

A schedule is only activated if the user specifies that the channel information should be updated automatically. Otherwise, the user must request channel updates. The Web Widget Tech Channel does have an update schedule, so this element is needed in the channel's description:

```
<CHANNEL HREF="http://www.mysite.com/channels/wwnew01.cdf"
       ISCLONABLE="NO">
   <LASTMOD VALUE="1998.05.03" />
   <TITLE VALUE="The Web Widget Tech Channel" />
   <ABSTRACT VALUE="A channel that provides the latest
        technical notes and bug reports for the Web Widget
        software application" />
   <AUTHOR VALUE="Natanya Pitts-Moultis" />
   <PUBLISHER VALUE="LANWrights, Inc." />
   <PUBLICATIONDATE VALUE="1998.01.01" />
   <COPYRIGHT VALUE="LANWrights, Inc." />
   <KEYWORDS VALUE="Web Widget, technical information, bug
        reports, software updates" />
   <INTROURI VALUE=
        "http://www.mysite.com/channels/ww-intro.html" />

   <SCHEDULE>
   </SCHEDULE>
</CHANNEL>
```

The STARTDATE Element

The empty STARTDATE element specifies the first day the schedule should be applied to the channel. The element's content and attribute specifics include

- Content: empty
- Attribute: VALUE

The current schedule for the Web Widget Tech Channel began on May 1, 1998, as indicated in the CDF markup:

```
<CHANNEL HREF="http://www.mysite.com/channels/wwnew01.cdf"
       ISCLONABLE="NO">
   <LASTMOD VALUE="1998.05.03" />
   <TITLE VALUE="The Web Widget Tech Channel" />
   <ABSTRACT VALUE="A channel that provides the latest
        technical notes and bug reports for the Web Widget
        software application" />
   <AUTHOR VALUE="Natanya Pitts-Moultis" />
   <PUBLISHER VALUE="LANWrights, Inc." />
   <PUBLICATIONDATE VALUE="1998.01.01" />
   <COPYRIGHT VALUE="LANWrights, Inc." />
   <KEYWORDS VALUE="Web Widget, technical information, bug
        reports, software updates" />
   <INTROURI VALUE=
        "http://www.mysite.com/channels/ww-intro.html" />

   <SCHEDULE>
        <STARTDATE VALUE="1998.05.01" />
   </SCHEDULE>
</CHANNEL>
```

The ENDDATE Element

The opposite of the STARTDATE element, the ENDDATE element specifies when the schedule should stop being applied to the channel. The element's content and attribute specifics include

- Content: empty
- Attribute: VALUE

The last effective date for the Web Widget Tech Channel's current schedule is June 1, 1998, as shown in this code:

```
<CHANNEL HREF="http://www.mysite.com/channels/wwnew01.cdf"
       ISCLONABLE="NO">
```

```
    <LASTMOD VALUE="1998.05.03" />
    <TITLE VALUE="The Web Widget Tech Channel" />
    <ABSTRACT VALUE="A channel that provides the latest
         technical notes and bug reports for the Web Widget
         software application" />
    <AUTHOR VALUE="Natanya Pitts-Moultis" />
    <PUBLISHER VALUE="LANWrights, Inc." />
    <PUBLICATIONDATE VALUE="1998.01.01" />
    <COPYRIGHT VALUE="LANWrights, Inc." />
    <KEYWORDS VALUE="Web Widget, technical information, bug
         reports, software updates" />
    <INTROURI VALUE=
         "http://www.mysite.com/channels/ww-intro.html" />

    <SCHEDULE>
         <STARTDATE VALUE="1998.05.01" />
         <ENDDATE VALUE= "1009.06.01" />
    </SCHEDULE>
</CHANNEL>
```

The INTERVALTIME Element

To describe how often the channel content is updated, use the INTERVALTIME element, using the DAY, HOUR, MIN, or SEC elements and a number value. The element's content and attribute specifics include

- Content: empty
- Attribute: DAY, HOUR, MIN, SEC

The Web Widget Tech Channel is updated every five days, as this markup shows:

```
<CHANNEL HREF="http://www.mysite.com/channels/wwnew01.cdf"
       ISCLONABLE="NO">
    <LASTMOD VALUE="1998.05.03" />
    <TITLE VALUE="The Web Widget Tech Channel" />
    <ABSTRACT VALUE="A channel that provides the latest
         technical notes and bug reports for the Web Widget
         software application" />
    <AUTHOR VALUE="Natanya Pitts-Moultis" />
    <PUBLISHER VALUE="LANWrights, Inc." />
    <PUBLICATIONDATE VALUE="1998.01.01" />
    <COPYRIGHT VALUE="LANWrights, Inc." />
    <KEYWORDS VALUE="Web Widget, technical information, bug
         reports, software updates" />
    <INTROURI VALUE=
         "http://www.mysite.com/channels/ww-intro.html" />
```

```
    <SCHEDULE>
         <STARTDATE VALUE="1998.05.01" />
         <ENDDATE VALUE="1009.06.01" />
         <INTERVALTIME DAY="5" />
    </SCHEDULE>
</CHANNEL>
```

The EARLIESTTIME Element

The EARLIESTTIME element indicates the earliest time the channel can be updated. The element's content and attribute specifics include

- Content: empty
- Attribute: DAY, HOUR, MIN, SEC

The Web Widget Tech Channel shouldn't be updated before 1 A.M., as directed by this markup:

```
<CHANNEL HREF="http://www.mysite.com/channels/wwnew01.cdf"
       ISCLONABLE="NO">
    <LASTMOD VALUE="1998.05.03" />
    <TITLE VALUE="The Web Widget Tech Channel" />
    <ABSTRACT VALUE="A channel that provides the latest
         technical notes and bug reports for the Web Widget
         software application" />
    <AUTHOR VALUE="Natanya Pitts-Moultis" />
    <PUBLISHER VALUE="LANWrights, Inc." />
    <PUBLICATIONDATE VALUE="1998.01.01" />
    <COPYRIGHT VALUE="LANWrights, Inc." />
    <KEYWORDS VALUE="Web Widget, technical information, bug
         reports, software updates" />
    <INTROURI VALUE=
         "http://www.mysite.com/channels/ww-intro.html" />

    <SCHEDULE>
         <STARTDATE VALUE="1998.05.01" />
         <ENDDATE VALUE="1009.06.01" />
         <INTERVALTIME DAY="5" />
         <EARLIESTTIME HOUR="1" />
    </SCHEDULE>
</CHANNEL>
```

The LATESTTIME Element

To set the time frame during which the channel should be updated, the LATEST-TIME element identifies the latest time the channel may be updated after the time specified in the EARLIESTTIME element. The element's content and attribute specifics include

- Content: empty
- Attribute: DAY, HOUR, MIN, SEC

This bit of code shows that the Web Widget Tech Channel shouldn't be updated after 5 A.M. in the morning, a four hour window after the 1 A.M. earliest time setting:

```
<CHANNEL HREF="http://www.mysite.com/channels/wwnew01.cdf"
       ISCLONABLE="NO">
   <LASTMOD VALUE="1998.05.03" />
   <TITLE VALUE="The Web Widget Tech Channel" />
   <ABSTRACT VALUE="A channel that provides the latest
        technical notes and bug reports for the Web Widget
        software application" />
   <AUTHOR VALUE="Natanya Pitts-Moultis" />
   <PUBLISHER VALUE="LANWrights, Inc." />
   <PUBLICATIONDATE VALUE="1998.01.01" />
   <COPYRIGHT VALUE="LANWrights, Inc." />
   <KEYWORDS VALUE="Web Widget, technical information, bug
        reports, software updates" />
   <INTROURI VALUE=
        "http://www.mysite.com/channels/ww-intro.html" />

   <SCHEDULE>
        <STARTDATE VALUE="1998.05.01" />
        <ENDDATE VALUE="1009.06.01" />
        <INTERVALTIME DAY="5" />
        <EARLIESTTIME HOUR="1" />
        <LATESTTIME HOUR="5" />
   </SCHEDULE>
</CHANNEL>
```

The LOGO Element

The LOGO element identifies a source for a logo to be placed in the user's channel menu after subscribing to a channel to represent the channel or a subchannel. The element's content and attribute specifics include

- Content: empty
- Attribute: HREF, TYPE

The HREF attribute points to the source of the file, usually a GIF or JPEG, and the TYPE attribute defines the logo as BIG, SMALL, WIDE, or REGULAR. You'll most often want to use the REGULAR value, as in this code:

```
<CHANNEL HREF="http://www.mysite.com/channels/wwnew01.cdf"
       ISCLONABLE="NO">
   <LASTMOD VALUE="1998.05.03" />
   <TITLE VALUE="The Web Widget Tech Channel" />
   <ABSTRACT VALUE="A channel that provides the latest
        technical notes and bug reports for the Web Widget
        software application" />
   <AUTHOR VALUE="Natanya Pitts-Moultis" />
   <PUBLISHER VALUE="LANWrights, Inc." />
   <PUBLICATIONDATE VALUE="1998.01.01" />
   <COPYRIGHT VALUE="LANWrights, Inc." />
   <KEYWORDS VALUE="Web Widget, technical information, bug
        reports, software updates" />
   <INTROURI VALUE=
        "http://www.mysite.com/channels/ww-intro.html" />

   <SCHEDULE>
        <STARTDATE VALUE="1998.05.01" />
        <ENDDATE VALUE="1009.06.01" />
        <INTERVALTIME DAY="5" />
        <EARLIESTTIME HOUR="1" />
        <LATESTTIME HOUR="5" />
   </SCHEDULE>

   <LOGO HREF=
         "http://www.mysite.com/channels/logos/ww.gif" />
</CHANNEL>
```

Using CDF to Install Software over the Internet

That's all she wrote (well, not quite), but that's all about CDF anyway. Creating a channel is relatively simple, and Microsoft's tutorials and software make it easier. But even without those tools, you still know all you need to know to create and deploy a CDF document. CDF can do more than just deliver server-push Web content. When combined with the Open Software Description (OSD), an XML vocabulary for describing software packages, CDF can help you install software to client computers over an intranet or the Internet. Skill 22, "Installing Software with OSD," discusses this and many other interesting facts about OSD in detail.

Are You up to Speed?

Now you can...

- ☑ Describe CDF and channel technologies
- ☑ View an Active channel with Internet Explorer
- ☑ Describe the components of the CDF DTD
- ☑ Write a CDF document

SKILL 22

Installing Software with OSD

- Understanding and applying OSD
- Combining OSD and CDF for automatic software installation
- Creating an OSD document

Microsoft and Marimba created the Open Software Description (OSD) XML vocabulary as a companion for the Channel Definition Format (CDF) XML vocabulary. Together with CDF, OSD provides a mechanism for the installation of software packages via the Internet or a local intranet. This skill examines the potential implementations and components of OSD and shows you how to build an OSD document, step-by-step.

What Is OSD?

Imagine being able to offer software updates to your customers over the Internet that are automatically initiated and completed with little or no assistance from you or the user. Take the idea one step further, and consider how nice it would be to install a single software package, or even multiple packages, across your company's intranet with a simple XML document and the click of a button. The developers of the OSD imagined both of these scenarios, as well as others, and harnessed the power of XML to make these scenarios a reality.

OSD is the result of collaboration between Marimba and Microsoft. It is a mechanism for installing software across a network without requiring the direct supervision of a network administrator or anyone else. Because OSD is an XML application, it can be used on any network that supports Internet protocols, and that's just about every network around. OSD can also be used outside local networks and across the Internet to make it much easier to provide automatic software updates to customers.

Essentially, OSD documents describe one or more software packages that need to be installed on client computers on an intranet or over the Internet. The description of a software package includes important bits of information, such as its name, version, platform and operating system requirements, and other software components that have to be installed on a client computer for the package to load successfully and function correctly. An OSD document is then delivered to users via a channel described with CDF.

The concept of OSD is a good one, and as it becomes better supported by a variety of tools, expect to see this particular XML vocabulary at work on networks around the world. As an XML vocabulary, OSD is platform and operating-system independent, although the tools and utilities that use it may not be. Currently, the only available implementations of OSD are from Microsoft, so they only work on a PC running Windows 95/98 or NT. Microsoft's utility for processing and using OSD documents is Internet Explorer 4 or 4.01, once again for the PC only.

Therefore, all of the current implementations of OSD will only work on computers running a Microsoft operating system and Internet Explorer. Finally, support for OSD is better in Internet Explorer 4.01 than it is in IE 4. Mac and Netscape users can take heart in knowing that as OSD becomes more popular and useful, it won't be as strictly confined to the Windows world as it is now.

Implementing OSD

The current implementations of OSD involve Internet Explorer 4 and a server (usually Microsoft's Internet Information Server) that can process and initiate a push of content from the server to the client computer, as described in a CDF file. In addition, the application that is described by OSD must be altered. In this section, I'll briefly describe the steps involved in setting up an application to be automatically updated across any network that uses Internet protocols.

NOTE

The Microsoft Web site provides extensive documentation that covers all the specifics of using OSD to install software over a network using Microsoft software and technologies. Although this section of the skill is intended to give you a good idea of how OSD is actually implemented, if you would like to use Microsoft's tools to make OSD part of your Internet and intranet solution, point your Web browser at `http://www.microsoft.com/msdn/sdk/inetsdk/help/itt/osd/overview/publishing.htm`. This Web site provides you with the complete details on the ins and outs of implementing OSD.

There are three things that have to happen before you can use OSD to automatically update an application:

1. The application itself must be prepared in a special way to work with OSD.
2. An active channel has to be defined to deliver the application to the client.
3. The application has to be described in an OSD file.

To automatically update a software application using OSD, the application itself must be configured to work with the user's security settings for Internet Explorer. Even after the application is configured properly, the user's security must still be set to either medium or low. If the user's security is set to high, they won't be able to take advantage of automatic installations directed by OSD.

To automatically notify users when an update is available for a particular software package, the shortcut that is created for the application when the application is installed or run for the very first time has to be modified. To make this process easier, Microsoft's InstallShield Pro can make the modifications using a special script, as discussed in detail at `http://support.installshield.com/resource/is5_wh_paper.htm`.

The next step in implementing OSD after the application is prepared is creating a CDF document that describes the software. This document provides all of the key information about the installation channel, as described by CDF. For a refresher on CDF, turn back a few pages to Skill 21, "Channeling Data with CDF."

Embedded in markup that describes the installation channel is the OSD markup that describes the application that will be installed via the channel. CDF and OSD are combined in a single document that describes both the channel and the package that will be delivered across as well as the package itself. At the end of the "Creating an OSD Document" section, later in the skill, you'll see a sample of such a document.

And that's really it. The server and Internet Explorer take care of the rest. Although this is an example of using OSD the Microsoft way, it's a good indicator of the steps you'll have to go through when working with any OSD utility, regardless of the vendor. Now that you know what OSD is and how it can work with CDF to complete a hands-free installation of software across a network, it's time to examine the nuts and bolts of OSD—it's DTD and documents.

The OSD DTD

For all of its advanced functionality, the OSD specification is actually quite compact. Considering all that you know about the various components of an XML DTD, reading the OSD document should be a piece of cake. Without further ado, here it is:

```
<!ELEMENT ABSTRACT (#PCDATA)>

<!ELEMENT CODEBASE EMPTY>
<!ATTLIST CODEBASE FILENAME CDATA #IMPLIED>
<!ATTLIST CODEBASE HREF CDATA #REQUIRED>
<!ATTLIST CODEBASE SIZE CDATA #IMPLIED>

<!ELEMENT DEPENDENCY (CODEBASE|SOFTPKG)* >
<!ATTLIST DEPENDENCY ACTION (Assert|Install) "Assert">

<!ELEMENT DISKSIZE EMPTY>
<!ATTLIST DISKSIZE VALUE CDATA #REQUIRED>

<!ELEMENT IMPLEMENTATION (CODEBASE | DEPENDENCY | DISKSIZE |
  IMPLTYPE | LANGUAGE | OS | PROCESSOR | VM)*>

<!ELEMENT IMPLTYPE EMPTY>
<!ATTLIST IMPLTYPE VALUE CDATA #REQUIRED>
```

```
<!ELEMENT LANGUAGE EMPTY>
<!ATTLIST LANGUAGE VALUE CDATA #REQUIRED>

<!ELEMENT LICENSE EMPTY>
<!ATTLIST LICENSE HREF CDATA #REQUIRED>

<!ELEMENT MEMSIZE EMPTY>
<!ATTLIST MEMSIZE VALUE CDATA #REQUIRED>

<!ELEMENT OS (OSVERSION)*>
<!ATTLIST OS VALUE CDATA #REQUIRED>

<!ELEMENT OSVERSION EMPTY>
<!ATTLIST OSVERSION VALUE CDATA #REQUIRED>

<!ELEMENT PROCESSOR EMPTY>
<!ATTLIST PROCESSOR VALUE CDATA #REQUIRED>

<!ELEMENT SOFTPKG (ABSTRACT | IMPLEMENTATION | DEPENDENCY | LICENSE |
  TITLE)*>
<!ATTLIST SOFTPKG NAME CDATA #REQUIRED>
<!ATTLIST SOFTPKG VERSION CDATA #IMPLIED>

<!ELEMENT TITLE (#PCDATA) >

<!ELEMENT VM EMPTY>
<!ATTLIST VM VALUE CDATA #REQUIRED>
```

OSD is very much a content-based markup language. All of its elements and attributes are designed to describe a software package in detail so it can be installed over a network. OSD isn't designed to provide instructions to a human technician for installing the software package, but instead OSD describes it to a machine (i.e., software application) that will take care of the installation on its own.

Because documents created for this vocabulary are for consumption by machines and not people, it's important that your descriptions of software are detailed and accurate.

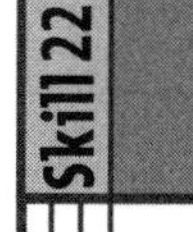

OSD's Primary Constructs in Detail

As I mentioned in Skill 19, "Creating Documents for XML Applications," the key to using an XML vocabulary correctly is understanding what each of its elements is meant to describe. Believe it or not, a software package needs a bit more to define it than just its name and location on a server. The following sections describe each

OSD element, outline its attributes and content model, and discuss what particular aspect of a software package each is designed to describe. Along the way, I'll construct an OSD document that describes a software package called Web Widget so you can see exactly how OSD is used.

NOTE The full OSD specification is available at http://www.microsoft.com/standards/osd/default.asp.

The SOFTPKG Element

The SOFTPKG element is always the document element in any OSD document and contains all of the other elements used to describe the software package. The element's content and attribute specifics include

- Content: one or more instance of ABSTRACT, IMPLEMENTATION, DEPENDENCY, LICENSE, and TITLE
- Attributes: NAME, VERSION, HREF

SOFTPKG takes the NAME, VERSION, and HREF attributes. These attributes provide a unique identifier to the individual distribution of the software package, information about which version of the distribution the document describes, and a link to a Web page or other resource that provides more information or documentation about the installation, respectively. Keep in mind that these attributes describe the individual distribution of the software package and not the software package itself. Begin and end every OSD document with this element, as in this code sample:

```
<SOFTPKG NAME="WW001" VERSION="1" HREF="/install/WW01.htm">
</SOFTPKG>
```

The ABSTRACT Element

The ABSTRACT element is one of the few OSD elements intended for human consumption and is designed to describe or summarize the distribution of a software package. The element's content specifics include

- Content: text only

Include, in the content of the ABSTRACT information, notes to yourself or other developers about the particular distribution of a piece of software that the OSD document defined, as in this newest version of the Web Widget description:

```
<SOFTPKG NAME="WW01" VERSION="1" HREF="/install/WW01.htm">
   <ABSTRACT>This is distribution 01 of the Web Widget
        application. This beta run should help work out
        any bugs in our distribution system. </ABSTRACT>
</SOFTPKG>
```

The IMPLEMENTATION Element

The IMPLEMENTATION element describes a specific execution of a software package. The element's content and attribute specifics include

- Content: one or more instances of CODEBASE, DEPENDENCY, DISKSIZE, IMPLTYPE, LANGUAGE, MEMSIZE, OS, PROCESSOR, or VM
- Attributes: none

Windows 95 and Macintosh versions of the same software are actually two executions or implementations of the same package. You can describe one or more implementations of a package by nesting the IMPLEMENTATION element and its CHILD elements within the SOFTPKG element, as shown here:

```
<SOFTPKG NAME="WW01" VERSION="1" HREF="/install/WW01.htm">
   <ABSTRACT>This is distribution 01 of the Web Widget
        application. This beta run should help work out
        any bugs in our distribution system. </ABSTRACT>
   <IMPLEMENTATION>
   </IMPLEMENTATION>
</SOFTPKG>
```

The CODEBASE Element

CODEBASE is the first of several elements that describe an individual implementation of an application, and it specifies where the actual source file for the implementation is stored. The source file is the data that will be transferred and installed on a client computer. The element's content and attribute specifics include

- Content: empty
- Attributes: HREF, SIZE, FILENAME

The HREF attribute points to the source file, and the SIZE attribute defines the maximum size (measured in K) the source file may be. Several HREF attributes and values may be listed for the same source file if there are several locations or mirrors for the file. If the file pointed to with the HREF attribute is larger than the value given for the SIZE attribute, the file will not be downloaded. After adding the CODEBASE element, our sample code looks like this:

```
<SOFTPKG NAME="WW01" VERSION="1" HREF="/install/WW01.htm">
   <ABSTRACT>This is distribution 01 of the Web Widget
        application. This beta run should help work out
        any bugs in our distribution system. </ABSTRACT>
   <IMPLEMENTATION>
        <CODEBASE HREF="/apps/webwidget.exe" SIZE="500K" />
   </IMPLEMENTATION>
</SOFTPKG>
```

The DEPENDENCY Element

The DEPENDENCY element describes other software components or packages that must be distributed along with the current application being installed. Administrators can ensure that all the client computers that receive an application also have other applications that the client needs to run. When an OSD document includes dependency descriptions, the processor checks the client computer to see whether the required dependent software or components is already installed. The element's content and attribute specifics include

- Content: one or more instances of CODEBASE and SOFTPKG
- Attribute: ACTION

The ACTION attribute lets the processor know what to do if the dependency isn't installed. The ASSERT value causes the processor to skip the installation of all applications entirely when a dependency is missing, whereas the INSTALL value causes the dependent application to be downloaded and installed. Each dependency is described as another software package, using the SOFTPKG element nested within the DEPENDENCY element. The Web Widget doesn't have any dependencies, so there's no need to include it in the sample code.

The DISKSIZE Element

The DISKSIZE element uses the VALUE attribute to describe the approximate amount of disk space the client computer must have free for the implementation of the software package to be installed. The element's content and attribute specifics include

- Content: empty
- Attribute: VALUE

The VALUE attribute's value is measured in K. The Web Widget requires 800K, so the sample code now looks like this:

```
<SOFTPKG NAME="WW01" VERSION="1" HREF="/install/WW01.htm">
   <ABSTRACT>This is distribution 01 of the Web Widget
        application. This beta run should help work out
        any bugs in our distribution system. </ABSTRACT>
   <IMPLEMENTATION>
        <CODEBASE HREF="/apps/webwidget.exe" SIZE="500K" />
        <DISKSIZE VALUE="800" />
   </IMPLEMENTATION>
</SOFTPKG>
```

The IMPLTYPE Element

The IMPLTYPE element is designed to describe, in human-readable terms, the implementation's type. The element's content and attribute specifics include

- Content: empty
- Attribute: VALUE

The VALUE attribute takes a text string value that holds the description. This labeling system can help an OSD document developer keep their implementation descriptions straight. The implementation of the Web Widget I'm describing is a Windows 95 version, as the new addition to the sample code indicates:

```
<SOFTPKG NAME="WW01" VERSION="1" HREF="/install/WW01.htm">
   <ABSTRACT>This is distribution 01 of the Web Widget
        application. This beta run should help work out
        any bugs in our distribution system. </ABSTRACT>
   <IMPLEMENTATION>
        <IMPLTYPE VALUE="Windows 95" />
        <CODEBASE HREF="/apps/webwidget.exe" SIZE="500K" />
        <DISKSIZE VALUE="800" />
   </IMPLEMENTATION>
</SOFTPKG>
```

The LANGUAGE Element

If an implementation of a software package requires a special language, such as Java, to function properly, the LANGUAGE element describes it. The element's content and attribute specifics include

- Content: empty
- Attribute: VALUE

If a LANGUAGE element isn't included for the implementation, then the assumption is that the application runs using the native code of the operating system on which it's installed. The Web Widget doesn't require a special language. It runs using the native Windows 95 language, so there's no reason to add the LANGUAGE element to the growing code sample.

The MEMSIZE Element

Just as the DISKSIZE attribute specifies how much hard-disk space the implementation of the application needs for a successful install, the MEMSIZE element indicates how much RAM is needed to run the application. The element's content and attribute specifics include

- Content: empty
- Attribute: VALUE

The VALUE attribute indicates, in K of course, what the RAM requirements are for the implementation. The Web Widget needs 12MB of RAM to run, so that specification is added to the code sample like this:

```
<SOFTPKG NAME="WW01" VERSION="1" HREF="/install/WW01.htm">
   <ABSTRACT>This is distribution 01 of the Web Widget
        application. This beta run should help work out
        any bugs in our distribution system. </ABSTRACT>
   <IMPLEMENTATION>
        <IMPLTYPE VALUE="Windows 95" />
        <CODEBASE HREF="/apps/webwidget.exe" SIZE="500K" />
        <DISKSIZE VALUE="800" />
        <MEMSIZE VALUE="12000" />
   </IMPLEMENTATION>
</SOFTPKG>
```

The OS Element

The OS element specifies which operating system has to be installed on the client computer for the implementation to run correctly. The element's content and attribute specifics include

- Content: one or more instances of OSVERSION
- Attribute: VALUE

The values the VALUE attribute can take are

AIX	DOS	Linux	SCO	Win95
BSDi	HPBLS	MacOS	Solaris	WinNT
CMW	HPUX	ODT	SunOS	
DECAlpha	IRIX	OS/2	UnixWare	

This implementation of the Web Widget application requires the Win95 OS, as shown in this addition to the code sample:

```
<SOFTPKG NAME="WW01" VERSION="1" HREF="/install/WW01.htm">
   <ABSTRACT>This is distribution 01 of the Web Widget
        application. This beta run should help work out
        any bugs in our distribution system. </ABSTRACT>
   <IMPLEMENTATION>
        <IMPLTYPE VALUE="Windows 95" />
        <CODEBASE HREF="/apps/webwidget.exe" SIZE="500K" />
        <DISKSIZE VALUE="800" />
        <MEMSIZE VALUE="12000" />
        <OS VALUE="Win95"></OS>
   </IMPLEMENTATION>
</SOFTPKG>
```

The OSVERSION Element

The OSVERSION element is nested within the OS element and provides specific information about which version of the operating system the implementation requires. The element's content and attribute specifics include

- Content: empty
- Attribute: VALUE

Because some of the acceptable OS values, such as Win95, include version information, not every OS element will include an OSVERSION element, as is the case with the OS element in the Web Widget description.

The PROCESSOR Element

If an implementation of an application requires a specific type of processor to be installed in the client computer, describe that processor using the PROCESSOR element. The element's content and attribute specifics include

- Content: empty
- Attribute: VALUE

Possible values for the VALUE attribute are

x86	mips
alpha	ppc
sparc	680x0

This implementation of Web Widget will run using any processor that Windows 95 will, so there's no need to include the PROCESSOR element in the description code.

The VM Element

If an application requires Java or any other specialty language to run, then a virtual machine for that language must be installed on the client machine for the software application to run correctly. The VM attribute describes that virtual machine in the VALUE attribute. The element's content and attribute specifics include

- Content: empty
- Attribute: VALUE

Web Widget doesn't need a special virtual machine, so this element won't be added to the code sample either. VM wraps up the list of elements that describe a specific implementation. The remaining two elements, LICENSE and TITLE, describe the entire software package.

The LICENSE Element

The LICENSE element uses the HREF attribute to point to a document that contains the licensing or copyright information associated with all of the implementations of the software package. The element's content and attribute specifics include

- Content: empty
- Attribute: HREF

The license information for the Web Widget application is stored in the same folder as the information about this particular distribution of the package, as the newly updated code sample indicates:

```
<SOFTPKG NAME="WW01" VERSION="1" HREF="/install/WW01.htm">
   <LICENSE HREF="/install/webwidget-copy.txt" />
   <ABSTRACT>This is distribution 01 of the Web Widget
        application. This beta run should help work out
        any bugs in our distribution system. </ABSTRACT>
   <IMPLEMENTATION>
        <IMPLTYPE VALUE="Windows 95" />
        <CODEBASE HREF="/apps/webwidget.exe" SIZE="500K" />
        <DISKSIZE VALUE="800" />
        <MEMSIZE VALUE="12000" />
        <OS VALUE="Win95"></OS>
   </IMPLEMENTATION>
</SOFTPKG>
```

The TITLE Element

For a final touch, the TITLE element assigns a user-friendly title to the software package, which makes it easily identifiable by administrators and anyone else who might look at the document. The element's content and attribute specifics include

- Content: text only
- Attributes: none

Skill 22

The title for this OSD document is enclosed in the TITLE element in this final version of the code sample:

```
<SOFTPKG NAME="WW01" VERSION="1" HREF="/install/WW01.htm">
   <TITLE>Web Widget Install 1</TITLE>
   <LICENSE HREF="/install/webwidget-copy.txt" />
   <ABSTRACT>This is distribution 01 of the Web Widget
        application. This beta run should help work out
```

```
          any bugs in our distribution system. </ABSTRACT>
     <IMPLEMENTATION>
          <IMPLTYPE VALUE="Windows 95" />
          <CODEBASE HREF="/apps/webwidget.exe" SIZE="500K" />
          <DISKSIZE VALUE="800" />
          <MEMSIZE VALUE="12000" />
          <OS VALUE="Win95"></OS>
     </IMPLEMENTATION>
</SOFTPKG>
```

This code sample is a fully developed and valid OSD document. To disseminate the Web Widget over a network, OSD description has to be embedded in a CDF file, as described in the next section.

Adding an OSD Description to a CDF File

Including an OSD description in a CDF file is simple. The CDF file still describes a channel in much the same way as you saw in Skill 21, but it also includes the software package description directly inside of the CDF document. Here's the complete code that combines CDF and OSD to automate the installation of the Web Widget software package:

```
<CHANNEL HREF="http://www.mysite.com/software/ww.html">
   <TITLE>Web Widget Channel</TITLE>
   <LOGO HREF="http://www.mysite.com/graphics/ww.ico"
      STYLE="icon"/>
   <USAGE VALUE="SoftwareUpdate"/>

<SOFTPKG NAME="WW01" VERSION="1" HREF="/install/WW01.htm">
   <TITLE>Web Widget Install 1</TITLE>
   <LICENSE HREF="/install/webwidget-copy.txt" />
   <ABSTRACT>This is distribution 01 of the Web Widget
        application. This beta run should help work out
        any bugs in our distribution system. </ABSTRACT>
   <IMPLEMENTATION>
        <IMPLTYPE VALUE="Windows 95" />
        <CODEBASE HREF="/apps/webwidget.exe" SIZE="500K" />
        <DISKSIZE VALUE="800" />
        <MEMSIZE VALUE="12000" />
        <OS VALUE="Win95"></OS>
   </IMPLEMENTATION>
</SOFTPKG>

</CHANNEL>
```

The CHANNEL element points to the Web page that serves as the subscription and information page for the Web Widget tool. The TITLE element assigns a title to the channel, whereas the LOGO element describes a logo that will be added to the user's version of Internet Explorer to make the channel easily accessible. When the user loads the CDF file into their browser, the browser will begin the download or will ask the user whether they want to begin the download.

When you're ready to send users a new version of the software, update the VERSION attribute of the SOFTPKG element as well as the address of the source file for the update. As users access the new CDF file, they will automatically receive the update or be asked if they want to receive the update. It really is that easy!

From Installing Software to Exchanging Money

If you thought installing software across a Web channel was cool, wait until you see what XML does for e-commerce. In Skill 23, "Exchanging Money with OFX," you'll learn all about the Open Financial Exchange (OFX), the XML vocabulary designed to facilitate the exchange of money and financial data in a standard way over the Internet.

Are You up to Speed?

Now you can...

- ☑ **Describe OSD**
- ☑ **Explain how OSD can be used with CDF to automatically install software over a network**
- ☑ **Create an OSD document**
- ☑ **Combine OSD and CDF to form a single document for delivering software via a channel**

SKILL 23

Exchanging Money with OFX

- Using OFX to describe financial data
- OFX as an example of a high-end XML solution
- A survey of the primary OFX components

Electronic commerce (e-commerce)—the exchange of money, goods, and services over the Internet—is a rapidly growing industry. The major stumbling block to the development of e-commerce is a lack of a standardized way to describe and exchange financial data. The Open Financial Exchange (OFX) XML vocabulary is being developed to help speed the progress of e-commerce and its related standards.

What Is OFX?

The Open Financial Exchange (OFX) XML vocabulary is a markup language designed to describe financial data for exchange via the Internet or an intranet. OFX was developed by a group whose members include representatives from Microsoft, CheckFree, and Intuit—three of the heaviest hitters in the financial software and data exchange world. OFX currently supports a wide variety of financial-related services, including

- Consumer and small business banking
- Investments in stocks, bonds, and mutual funds
- Bill invoicing and payment

The goal of OFX is to promote the exchange of data between a financial institution's server and a Web browser or personal financial software package, such as Microsoft Money or Intuit's Quicken. In Chapter 20, "Automating Web Sites with WIDL," I described a real-world scenario in which banks must provide financial data to their customers over the Internet in both Money and Quicken formats because both software packages hold a large portion of the personal financial-software market share. In addition, more and more financial institutions are providing Web-based account access to their users, so they must convert financial data not only into Quicken and Money formats but also into an HTML-based format that a Web browser can read. When you add this to the bank's own system for describing and storing data, any given financial institution may have to store the same data in up to four different formats.

The discussion in Chapter 20 focused on the Web Interface Definition Language (WIDL) as a solution for describing all kinds of data—not just financial data—in a common way to make it more accessible to WIDL-compliant software. Although WIDL is designed to be a more globally accessible vocabulary, OFX focuses specifically on the delivery of financial data. Instead of describing and storing financial data in four different formats (Web-based, Quicken, Money, and the bank's own proprietary format), financial institutions would describe the data using only OFX. The clients accessing the data would be able to read and display OFX-described data. OFX-compliant versions of Quicken and Money would have equal access to the same information in the same format as an OFX-compliant Web browser. It's understood that the bank's own system would also be OFX compliant, and it's entirely possible that a number of financial institutions that switch to OFX will use Web-based clients to access and update their financial data.

From the 10,000-foot view, OFX is simply a markup language that describes financial data. As with every other XML vocabulary we've looked at, OFX can't do much of anything by itself except describe data. For OFX to work successfully in the financial world, there must be software packages, such as Quicken and Money, that support it as well as Web browsers that are at least XML-aware, if not OFX-aware specifically. Because the developers of OFX include the heaviest hitters in the financial software world as well as a major browser vendor (Microsoft), it seems safe to assume that OFX is going to have support in the personal financial world as well as the Web world. Judging from the information on the OFX Web site at `http://www.ofx.net`, many major financial institutions have followed CheckFree's lead and have begun to adopt OFX as a standard for describing and exchanging financial data.

Implementing OFX

The implementations of OFX will be handled by either a financial institution setting up an OFX server or a financial software vendor creating an OFX-compliant software package. Either way, implementing OFX is not your everyday activity like setting up an Active channel with CDF might be. Still, taking a look at how to set up an OFX server is a good way to see the type of high-end solution that XML vocabularies can be.

According to the section of the OFX Web site devoted to getting started with OFX, a typical OFX server takes up to 90 man-months to set up. This means that if you have 90 people working on the development of the server, it will take a month. It's more realistic to say that setting up a Web server will take ten people between nine months and a year to get up and going. In addition to the human resources cost, you'll have to foot the bill for the server software and hardware. The software that runs on an OFX server isn't your run-of-the-mill Web server software. Instead, you'll need to buy the Microsoft Internet Financial Server ToolKit, which starts at a cool $10K, not counting the licensing fee for Microsoft's Windows NT Server that the ToolKit requires to function properly. A single license for NT runs about $800, without the computer. So between the ToolKit and NT Server, you're looking at laying out a nice chunk of change just to get your computer server up and running before you actually configure the server or store your data.

TIP

To read more about the Microsoft Financial Server ToolKit, visit the Microsoft Financial Services Web site at `http://www.microsoft.com/industry/finserv/default4.htm`. To find out more about Windows NT Server, visit `http://www.microsoft.com/ntserver/`.

Setting up the server is only one small part of what a financial institution will have to go through to set up an OFX server. In a nutshell (a very large nutshell at that), an institution will have to complete the following three steps to get an OFX server up and running.

1. Set up a standard Web server that is capable of handling a large number of hits per day and supports other Internet services, such as e-mail and FTP.
2. Connect the Web server to back-end data-storage systems using OFX to send messages and requests to the system, and receive answers and data to be served up to users who have OFX-compliant Web browsers or personal financial software.
3. Set up a human-resource infrastructure for managing the OFX system and Web server as well as a customer support network and a help desk.

Although there are only three steps in the process, the steps each comprise a number of smaller steps and represent a large investment of both human and financial resources.

Building and maintaining an OFX server from scratch may not be practical for a large number of smaller financial institutions. To that end, CheckFree supports OFX and, for a fee, institutions can use CheckFree's servers and services to implement OFX.

TIP

Visit the CheckFree Web site at `http://www.checkfree.com/` to learn more about their implementation of OFX.

In addition, vendors are beginning to offer canned OFX solutions that include server setup and linking to back-end data-storage systems as well as all of the other services needed to set up a fully functional OFX server. These solutions generally begin around $100,000 and higher. Still, if a financial institution isn't sure they have the know-how or resources to establish their own server, but they recognize that OFX is the best solution to meet their needs, then a prebuilt OFX server may be the best answer for them.

As you can see, nothing about implementing OFX is simple. When you use OFX everyday, your interaction with OFX will be limited to accessing your bank data with a Web browser or your favorite financial software package. However, as a student of XML, it's important to understand that XML is robust and extensible enough to support complex data exchanges, such as those associated with financial data. It's also important to remember that the key to a successful XML solution isn't just the DTD or documents, but rather it is the combination of a strong vocabulary and the tools needed to interpret and display the data described by the vocabulary.

In the following section, we'll take a look at some of the elements of the OFX DTD to discover exactly what it takes to develop a vocabulary capable of supporting the high-end solutions for which OFX was designed.

OFX's Primary Constructs in Detail

The OFX DTD is huge. Even in text format it is 135K and takes a minute or so to download over an average speed modem. To see the DTD for yourself, download the text file from `http://www.ofx.net/ofx/spec15.asp`. OFX is probably one of the best-documented XML vocabularies under development today, and the entire specification is also available for download in PDF format from the address just listed. The specification is 369 pages in length and describes in detail every element, attribute, and entity in the OFX DTD.

Messages are a key concept in OFX, and they represent a complete transaction of information between an OFX server and its data source. As with other client-server communications, messages consist of a request for information and a response. OFX's components can be broken down by functionality or the kind of messages they are designed to facilitate. Although it's not possible to examine each component in detail, the following sections look at the different kinds of data that can be described by OFX and how it goes about describing them.

SIGNON Elements

As you might expect, one of the key sets of elements in OFX provides a mechanism for users to securely log on to an OFX server. The following elements make signons possible:

`<SONRQ>...</SONRQ>` Container tag for the signon request sent by the client to the OFX server

`<DTCLIENT/>` Specifies the date and time the request was made

<USERID>...</USERID> Specifies the user ID of the person signing on

<USERPASS/>...</USERPASS> Specifies the password of the person signing on

<LANGUAGE/> Identifies the language that should be used for any text response sent from the server

<APPID/> Identifies the client application accessing the OFX server

<APPVER/> Identifies the version of the client application

<SONRS>...</SONRS> CONTAINER tag for the signon response sent from the OFX server to the client in response to the signon request

<DTSERVER/> Specifies the data and time the response was sent

It's doubtful that anyone would ever have to code an OFX document by hand, especially because requests and response documents will be created on the fly each time a user requests information from a financial institution. Although developers may have to create other XML documents using a text editor or XML editor, the guts of OFX documents will be created by software packages drawing upon the information provided by users in a friendly, easy-to-use interface.

Account Management Elements

A common activity among banking users is setting up and discontinuing services, such as checking and savings accounts. OFX provides these elements that facilitate the easy addition or removal of services by a user over the Web:

<SCVCADD>...</SCVCADD> Adds a new service

<SVCCHG>...</SVCCHNG> Changes an existing service

<SVCDEL>...</SVCDEL> Removes an existing service

<SVC>...</SVC> Defines the kind of service to be added, changed, or removed using these attributes:

BANKSVC Describes a banking service

BPSVC Describes a billing service

INVSVC Describes an investment service

The OFX account management components also include elements that allow new users to set up (or enroll in) an account on an OFX server as well as change important contact information when necessary via the OFX system, using these elements:

<ENROLLRQ> Contains enrollment information

<FIRSTNAME> Specifies the user's first name

<MIDDLENAME> Specifies the user's middle name

<LASTNAME> Specifies the user's last name

<ADDR1> Identifies the user's address

<CITY> Identifies the user's city

<STATE> Identifies the user's state

<POSTALCODE> Identifies the user's postal code

<COUNTRY> Specifies the user's country

<DAYPHONE> Specifies the user's daytime phone number

<EVEPHONE> Specifies the user's evening phone number

<EMAIL> Provides an e-mail address for the user

<USERID> Identifies the user's preferred logon name

<TAXID> Provides an individual identification number (such as a social security number) for the user for tax purposes

<SECURITYNAME> Identifies a secure name, such as a mother's maiden name

<CHGUSERINFORQ> A container tag that allows all of the information provided in the previous enrollment tags to be changed as necessary by the user

Although these elements may seem to describe rather mundane information, they are still key to the successful maintenance of customer and user records.

Banking Elements

The OFX banking elements describe a wide variety of information, from the bank's individual identifier to bank account balances and transaction specifics. Included in the banking elements category are

<BANKID> Specifies a bank using a unique ID number

<BRANCHID> Includes branch-specific information in a bank identification

<ACCTID> Identifies a user's account using a unique ID number

<ACCTTYPE> Identifies the type of account using one of these four attributes:

CHECKING Checking account

SAVINGS Savings account

MONEYMRKT Money market account

CREDITLINE A line of credit

<XFERINFO> Defines a transfer of funds using these elements:

<BANKACCTFROM> Specifies a bank account from which funds should be transferred

<BANKACCTTO> Specifies a bank account to which funds should be transferred

<CCACCTFROM> Specifies a credit card account from which funds should be transferred

<CCACCTTO> Specifies a credit card account to which funds should be transferred

<TRNAMT> Identifies how much money should be transferred from one account to the other

<STMTRQ> Identifies a request for an account statement using these elements:

<DTSTART> Specifies the start date for the account statement

<DTEND> Specifies the end date for the account statement

<LEDGERBAL> Identifies a request for the ledger balance on an account

<AVAILBAL> Identifies a request for the available balance on an account

These elements represent only the tip of the iceberg for banking data that can be described with OFX. There are elements to describe individual transactions, including the data and time they were made as well as the type of transaction (check, ATM, credit card, etc.). OFX can also describe a stop check, statement closings, and wired funds transfers.

OFX also supports the description and exchange of billing statements and payments, investment information and transfers, as well as recurring payments or transfers from one account to another. As you might have guessed when I told you that the OFX specification is 369 pages in length, there's much more to OFX than I have touched on in this skill. I'm not expecting each of you to have your OFX server up and running by the end of next month, but instead, I want you to start thinking about XML on a much larger scale. Financial data is probably some of the most complex and important data floating around in data-space and cyberspace. The fact that the developers of a new financial data standard have turned to XML as their solution should tell you a great deal about the large-scale solutions XML can be a part of.

SMILing on Multimedia

In keeping with the discussion of XML for use with complex types of data, Skill 24, "Presenting Multimedia with SMIL," explores the wonderful world of SMIL, the Synchronized Multimedia Integration Language. Designed to describe complex multimedia data, such as audio and video, SMIL is another example of a high-end solution to a common need that uses XML at its very core.

Are You up to Speed?

Now you can...

- ☑ **Describe OFX**
- ☑ **Explain how OFX is used to describe financial data**
- ☑ **Discuss the uses of XML as part of a high-end data transfer solution**

SKILL 24

Presenting Multimedia with SMIL

- Disseminating multimedia over the Web
- Using SMIL to describe multimedia presentations
- An introduction to the SMIL DTD and elements

One of the fastest growing and most profitable segments of the Internet and Web industry is multimedia. The ability to embed audio and video files in a Web page has been around for quite a while. Developers are now looking toward the Web as a vehicle for real-time audio and video broadcasting to facilitate the sharing of a variety of information contained within a variety of media across the Internet. The Synchronized Multimedia Integration Language (SMIL) has been developed as a W3C standard to further the role multimedia will play in the dissemination of multimedia over the Web. In this skill, you'll learn how multimedia works on the Web, how SMIL helps users overcome many of the problems inherent in the deployment of multimedia over the Web, what vendors already support SMIL, what it takes to implement a SMIL solution, and take a look at the innerworkings of the SMIL vocabulary.

What Is SMIL?

The W3C's SMIL recommendation at `http://www.w3.org/TR/REC-smil/` defines SMIL like this:

> SMIL allows integrating a set of independent multimedia objects into a synchronized multimedia presentation. Using SMIL, an author can describe the following points:
>
> 1. The temporal behavior of the presentation
> 2. The layout of the presentation on a screen
> 3. The association of hyperlinks with media objects

In plain English, this means that SMIL is an XML vocabulary used to describe multimedia content. Before you can truly understand how SMIL works and why it was needed in the first place, you have to know a bit about the state of multimedia as a Web technology.

Multimedia and the Web

Not long after the first simple text and graphics HTML pages were created and posted to the Web, developers began to look for a way to include richer media—including audio and video—in Web pages. Multimedia CD-ROMs were an everyday artifact long before the Web was even a twinkle in Tim Berners-Lee's eyes. Once the Web became the information dissemination tool of the future, it was obvious that it would have to accommodate media of all types to continue to thrive in an eye candy–craving world.

Before the evolution of the Web, there were several different proprietary file formats available for storing digitized multimedia content. Each of these different file formats accomplished the same thing (they made it possible to hear audio and see video on a computer), but each did it in a different way.

To create a multimedia file of any type, you had to buy the software that would convert and store your digitized media using the vendor's proprietary code. To view the file, you'd need a player, almost always from the same vendor and usually for free, that recognized the file type and could display it. The problem was that file types were not compatible across multiple players.

Developers were forced to choose a particular file format and software package, and once they did, they were usually stuck with it because these tools are often expensive. In addition, users had to have a different player to view each audio or video clip saved in a proprietary file format. Although players were usually free, they weren't always available for every platform. Therefore, when choosing a particular file format, developers ran the risk of excluding one group or another from the viewing audience.

The same problem with proprietary file formats and different viewers has persisted as multimedia has become a regular part of the Web. To allow developers to include multimedia files in their Web pages, multimedia software vendors created plug-ins that would play audio and video files embedded directly within Web pages. Even though these plug-ins are technically part of the browser and the HTML used to embed multimedia files is platform and OS independent, you still must have the correct plug-in for the correct media type to view a file within a Web page successfully. Not all plug-ins are available for all platforms, and the multimedia file formats are still proprietary. One plug-in won't play every type of audio and video file. Figure 24.1 shows the browser display a user sees when they don't have the right plug-in needed to view a multimedia file.

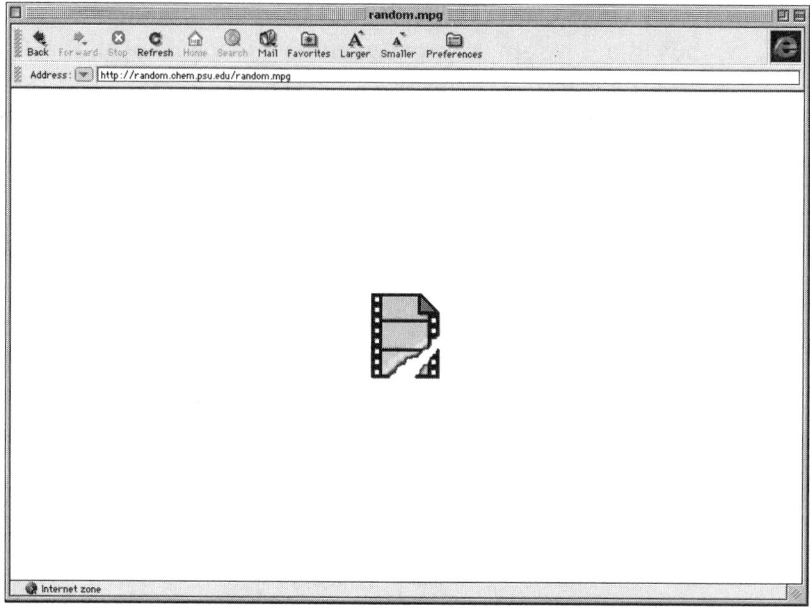

FIGURE 24.1: The browser display seen by a user without the correct plug-in

The major players and their products in the Web multimedia world are

- Apple Computer's Quicktime
  `http://quicktime.apple.com/`
- RealNetworks RealAudio and RealVideo
  `http://www.real.com/`
- MPEG (Moving Pictures Expert Group)
  `http://www.crs4.it/HTML/LUIGI/MPEG/mpegfaq.html` (FAQ)
- Macromedia Director and Flash
  `http://www.macromedia.com/`

Of these four vendors, all have plug-ins available to play files saved in their proprietary format, but none can read the other's files. In Figure 24.1, you saw what happens when a browser tries to play a file it doesn't have a plug-in for. Figure 24.2 shows how the browser reacts when the required plug-in (an MPEG player in this case) is installed.

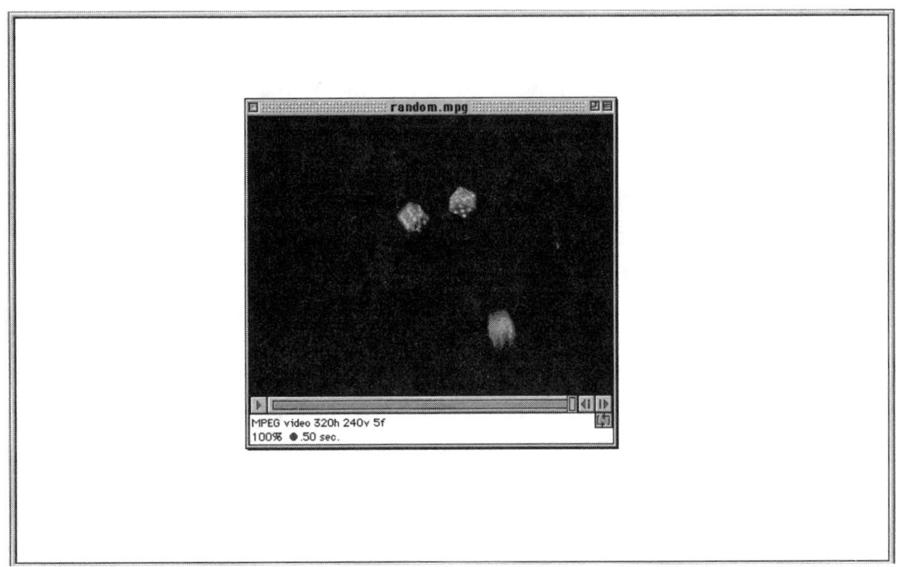

FIGURE 24.2: An embedded MPEG file played on a browser with the required plug-in

The bottom line is that there are several different ways to store and view multimedia files via the Web, but each uses an exclusive format and requires its own specific player to process and display the files. Needless to say, this is a cumbersome way to do business, and it makes the dissemination of multimedia files more difficult than it should be. Hence, the creation of SMIL.

SMIL as the Universal Multimedia File Format

The developers of the SMIL specification represent many of the industry organizations most interested in the dissemination of multimedia over the Internet, including RealNetworks, Lucent/Bell Laboratories, CNET, Apple, and Netscape.

The group that defined the initial SMIL proposal (as well as those who worked to make it an official W3C specification as of June, 1998) had a specific goal: to define a single format for describing multimedia information that could be read and processed by a wide variety of browsers and players. The idea was to remove the stumbling blocks caused by a large number of proprietary formats and make it possible for a single file to be displayed by many players.

If there is a standard multimedia data format, just as HTML is a standard Web page format, then users only have to install one multimedia player instead of five or six, and they can still be assured that they can view multimedia files from a variety of resources. Now users can choose their player based on its compatibility with their computer and operating system, its stability, and the features and interface that it includes rather than the special file format it supports. Developers no longer need to worry that their users won't have access to the appropriate plug-in. By working with a standardized file format, they can be guaranteed that a wide variety of players will support and display their files.

In its most basic form, SMIL can be used to describe a series of media files that should be played in order. The following code shows a valid SMIL file that defines three Quicktime movie files to be played in the order they are listed:

```
<smil>
     <body>
          <audio src="/movies/f1.mov"/>
          <audio src="/movies/f2.mov"/>
          <audio src="/movies/f3.mov"/>
     </body>
</smil>
```

Granted, the player that processes and displays this SMIL file must also be able to process and display Quicktime files (.mov files), which are in a proprietary file format. The eventual goal of the SMIL working group is that standard media formats will eventually be supported by all players in addition to SMIL support—just as GIFs, JPGs, and PNG files are all supported universally by Web browsers. Although the fulfillment of this goal won't happen for a while, it is neither impossible nor unreasonable. The descriptions of the SMIL elements in the "SMIL's Primary Constructs in Detail" section provide a more in-depth explanation of the different SMIL constructs and how you can use them to define a multimedia presentation.

Once again, an XML vocabulary is being used to bring consistency to data so a large selection of client software can view that data. Information only has to be stored in one format, but it can be interpreted and viewed by users via the tool that best fits their individual needs. If SMIL lives up to its potential, every multimedia player available in the next year or so will be SMIL compliant. However, because SMIL is a new technology and many vendors are hesitant to give up their own formats until they are sure SMIL—and XML in general—isn't just a passing fad, SMIL development and browsing tools will be slow to develop. In the next section, you'll find out which vendor is already supporting SMIL and which tools are available for creating SMIL documents.

Implementing SMIL

The idea that drives SMIL—one file format, many players—is a good and solid one. But you must be wondering exactly what are the here and now realities of using SMIL. Because SMIL is already a W3C standard, it shows great promise for a long and useful life. One of the most influential multimedia vendors, RealNetworks, has already begun the development of SMIL authoring tools and has built SMIL support into its newest multimedia display tool, G2.

RealNetworks, the creators of RealAudio and RealVideo, were pioneers in the streaming multimedia industry. When audio and video were first served via the Web, users couldn't hear or view a file until it was downloaded in its entirety. Because audio and video files comprise complex data, they are often large in size, even when well compressed, and it can take up to five minutes to download a 30-second video clip. The technology behind streaming audio and video allows the user to begin hearing or viewing the contents of a sound or video file before the file is completely downloaded. The content streams onto the user's computer, even as they are browsing the file.

RealNetworks maintains a large portion of the Web multimedia market share and has contracts with nationally known organizations, such as CNN and NPR. You can view a live Webcast of CNN's daily news shows at `http://www.cnn.com/` using the RealPlayer as well as listen to NPR broadcasts at `http://www.npr.org/`. Before the development of SMIL, RealNetworks developed its own proprietary format for storing audio and video files. You also have to install a special RealServer on your Web server to serve RealNetworks audio and video files. All of these proprietary technologies still exist, but they're not alone now that SMIL is on the scene.

Because RealNetworks has taken a liking to SMIL and has already included support for it in their new G2 player, it's a safe bet that other multimedia vendors will quickly begin to integrate SMIL support into their development tools and players. The SMIL resources page on the RealNetworks site is at `http://www.real.com/technology/smil/index.html` (shown in Figure 24.3), and it includes a nice collection of resources for authoring SMIL documents.

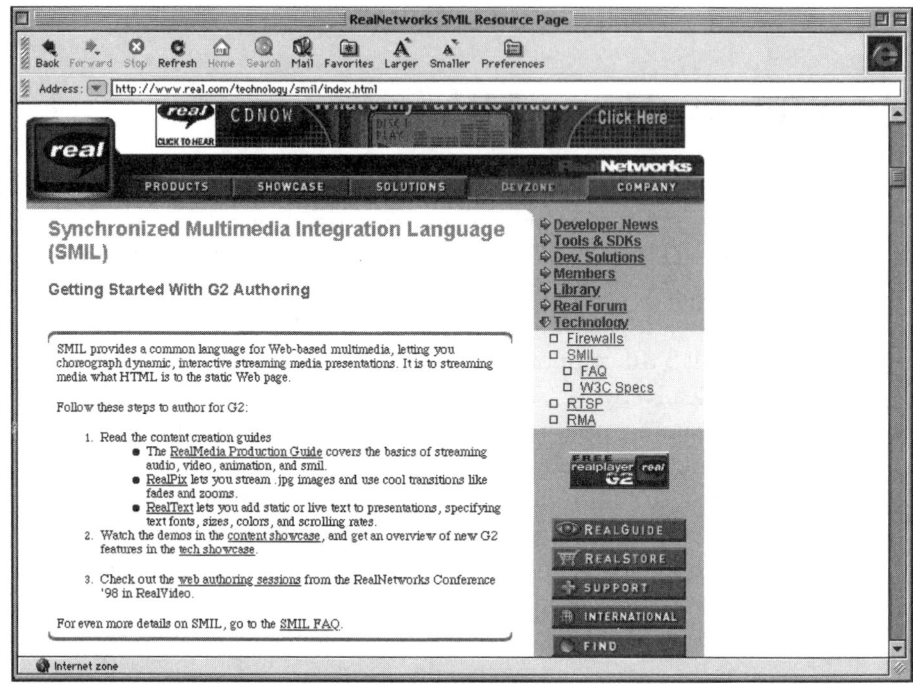

FIGURE 24.3: The RealNetworks SMIL development page

Although this site focuses on using SMIL with RealNetwork's own G2 player, know that the SMIL documents you create for G2 will also be viewable with other SMIL-compatible players as they begin to emerge.

Authoring a multimedia presentation isn't a simple undertaking. Important issues such as digitizing the media, analyzing your users' bandwidth capabilities and your server capabilities, and compressing the data for streaming are just a few of the things you'll have to deal with as you put your presentation together. RealNetworks includes an exceptional guide at `http://www.real.com/technology/smil/production.html` that you will want to take the time to read through if you're serious about multimedia development. To find out more about using SMIL specifically with RealNetworks media files, read the "Assembling a Presentation with SMIL" section of the production guide at `http://service.real.com/help/library/guides/production/htmfiles/smil.htm#1072`.

NOTE

To use SMIL with a RealNetworks G2 player, you must have a copy of the RealNetworks server and be able to save your audio and video files in the RealAudio and RealVideo formats, using RealNetworks authoring tools.

It's obvious that the RealNetworks SMIL solution is still closely intertwined with their proprietary RealAudio and RealVideo solutions, but it won't stay that way forever. If you think SMIL is the right solution for your multimedia needs, you'll want to spend some time at the RealNetworks site reading through their development materials. You should learn what it takes to put together a quality multimedia presentation to be viewed with the RealNetworks G2 player using SMIL. What you learn will be useful later as you develop other multimedia presentations outside of the G2 world using SMIL. The next section of the skill provides an in-depth look at the different SMIL elements and the role they play in describing a multimedia presentation. This will show you how SMIL describes multimedia presentations and give you an idea of the different things you can do with SMIL.

SMIL's Primary Constructs in Detail

The SMIL elements are designed to divide a document into a head and body section and then describe the various multimedia elements that are part of the presentation. The document element for every SMIL document is the `SMIL` element. As with any other document element, all of the other SMIL tags and their content are nested within the `<SMIL>...</SMIL>` tag pair, as shown in this code:

```
<SMIL>
     ...document content
</SMIL>
```

The next several sections describe the major parts of a SMIL document, as well as the elements you'll find inside of them, and show you how they can be used to build a valid SMIL document.

NOTE

The SMIL DTD is too long to include within the skill, but you can find a copy of it on the Sybex Web site, www.sybex.com. Once there, go to the Books page where you'll be able to download Appendix A.

The Document Head

As in HTML, the header portion of a SMIL document is designed to contain those elements that provide information important to the document but that don't affect its final display. The following elements can all be used within the document head.

The HEAD Element

The `<HEAD>...</HEAD>` tag pair defines the portion of a SMIL document that contains header information. The element's content and attribute specifics include

- Content: `LAYOUT`, `META`, `SWITCH`
- Attributes: `ID`

You can only have one head section in any SMIL document, and it must always immediately follow the opening `<SMIL>` tag:

```
<SMIL>
     <HEAD>
     </HEAD>
</SMIL>
```

The LAYOUT Element

The `LAYOUT` element specifies which layout language the presentation uses. If a browser doesn't recognize a particular language or the user has a preference, it may skip one layout specification in favor of another.

- Content: `REGION`, `ROOT-LAYOUT`
- Attributes: `ID`, `TYPE`

The `<LAYOUT>...</LAYOUT>` tag pair uses CSS-2 or the SMIL Basic Layout Language properties and values to specify where the multimedia presentation should sit within a display area (Web browser window, printed page, etc.). The first of the following code samples uses CSS to specify that the presentation should sit one inch from the left and one inch from the top of the display area. The second code sample uses SMIL Basic Layout Language to do the same:

```
<SMIL>
     <HEAD>
          <LAYOUT TYPE="text/css">
```

```
        [region="a1"] {left: 1in; top: 1in}
        </LAYOUT>
    </HEAD>
</SMIL>

<SMIL>
    <HEAD>
        <LAYOUT TYPE="text/smil-basic-layout">
            <REGION ID="a1" TOP="1in" LEFT="1in" />
        </LAYOUT>
    </HEAD>
</SMIL>
```

For more information on the SMIL Basic Layout Language, review section 3.3 of the SMIL specification.

The REGION Element

The EMPTY `<REGION />` tag is used with the SMIL Basic Layout Language to associate the layout with a particular region of the presentation. The same is accomplished with the CSS method using the `[region="a1"]` syntax.

- Content: SKIP-CONTENT
- Attributes: BACKGROUND-COLOR, FIT=(FILL | HIDDEN | MEET | SCROLL | SLICE), HEIGHT, ID, LEFT, TITLE, TOP, WIDTH, ZINDEX

Using multiple `<LAYOUT>...</LAYOUT>` and `<REGION />` tags, you can define multiple layouts for several different regions in the presentation that contain different types of information. This provides for the overlapping of text and movie media as well as other interesting layout effects within the presentation.

The majority of attributes for the REGION element provide tools for describing the region's physical properties. Use the BACKGROUND-COLOR attribute to specify a backdrop color for the region, and use the HEIGHT and WIDTH attributes to set the region's dimensions. The values for LEFT and TOP attributes can specify the exact placement of the region within a display, and the ZINDEX attribute identifies the region's order if several regions are stacked one on top of the other. The HEIGHT, WIDTH, LEFT, and TOP attributes are identical to the CSS2 properties by the same name. The FIT attribute specifies how a region should be sized and how much of its content should show if the content is bigger than the size of the region. The default value for this attribute is hidden. Finally, the ID attribute provides a way to assign a unique identifier to the region. Use as many or as few of the element's attributes as necessary to specify how a certain region within the presentation should be displayed:

```
<SMIL>
     <HEAD>
          <LAYOUT TYPE="text/smil-basic-layout">
               <REGION ID="a1" TOP="1in" LEFT="1in"
                BACKGROUND-COLOR="teal" ZINDEX="2"/>

               <REGION ID="a2" TOP="1.5in" LEFT="1.5in"
                BACKGROUND-COLOR="white" ZINDEX="1"/>

          </LAYOUT>
     </HEAD>
</SMIL>
```

The ROOT-LAYOUT Element

The EMPTY <ROOT-LAYOUT /> element specifies the overall size and background color for the ROOT element (<SMIL>...</SMIL>). This information establishes the size of the window display area the SMIL presentation will need to display correctly.

- Content: none
- Attributes: BACKGROUND-COLOR, HEIGHT, ID, TITLE, WIDTH

The BACKGROUND-COLOR, HEIGHT, ID, TITLE, and WIDTH attributes work the same way with the ROOT-LAYOUT element as they do with the REGION element or in CSS2. Make sure that your display area isn't so big that users with smaller screens won't be able to see it. In this code, the display size for the presentation is set to 600 pixels by 400 pixels:

```
<SMIL>
     <HEAD>
          <LAYOUT>
               <ROOT-LAYOUT TITLE="My First SMIL Document"
                HEIGHT="400px" WIDTH="600px" BGCOLOR="yellow" />
          </LAYOUT>
     </HEAD>
</SMIL>
```

The Document Body

Once you've used the elements in the head of the document to define its display area and set up layouts for other areas within the presentation, use the document's body to describe the actual pieces and parts of your presentation. The following sections describe each of the elements you can use to describe a part of the presentation.

The BODY Element

- Content: A, ANIMATION, AUDIO, IMG, PAR, REF, SEQ, SWITCH, TEXT, TEXTSTREAM, VIDEO
- Attributes: ID

The <BODY>...</BODY> tag pair contains all of the elements within a SMIL presentation that will actually be displayed within a SMIL browser. Any given SMIL document may have only one body, and it immediately follows the document head, as in this code sample:

```
<SMIL>
     <HEAD>
          <LAYOUT>
               <ROOT-LAYOUT TITLE="My First SMIL Document"
                HEIGHT="400px" WIDTH="600px" BGCOLOR="yellow" />
          </LAYOUT>
     </HEAD>

     <BODY>
     </BODY>
</SMIL>
```

The PAR Element

- Content: A, ANIMATION, AUDIO, IMG, PAR, REF, SEQ, SWITCH, TEXT, TEXTSTREAM, VIDEO
- Attributes: see the following note

The <PAR>...</PAR> tag pair describes a collection of elements that must be played at the same time instead of in a sequential order. Using the <PAR>... </PAR> element, you can cause a series of images to slide from one to the next while an audio file is playing in the background.

NOTE

The <PAR>...</PAR> tag pair includes a large number of attributes for controlling how the multimedia components nested within it are played. For a complete description of each of these attributes in detail, read section 4.21 of the SMIL specification.

The SEQ Element

- Content: A, ANIMATION, AUDIO, IMG, PAR, REF, SEQ, SWITCH, TEXT, TEXTSTREAM, VIDEO
- Attributes: see the following note

Just as the <PAR>...</PAR> tag describes elements not meant to be played in a specific sequence, the <SEQ>...</SEQ> pair describes elements that do need to be played in sequence. This allows you to combine several media components together into a single presentation. Using this technique, you can reuse components, such as introductory materials and standard notices, in combination with new materials specific to a presentation.

NOTE

The <SEQ>...</SEQ> tag pair includes a large number of attributes for controlling how the multimedia components nested within it are played. For a complete description of each of these attributes in detail, read section 4.22 of the SMIL specification.

The ANIMATION, AUDIO, IMG, TEXT, TEXTSTREAM, and VIDEO Elements

- Content: ANCHOR
- Attributes: see the following note

This group of tag pairs, known collectively in the SMIL specification as the Media Object Elements, describes all of the different pieces and parts of a multimedia presentation. As you might suspect, the <ANIMATION>...</ANIMATION> tag describes an animation, while the <AUDIO>...</AUDIO> and <VIDEO>...</VIDEO> tag pairs describe audio and video files respectively. The <IMG>...</IMG> tag describes an image, while the <TEXT>...</TEXT> tag pair describes a block of text. Finally, the <TEXTSTREAM>...</TEXTSTREAM> element describes a block of text that should move from one side of the presentation to another.

Each of these tag pairs uses the SRC= attribute to reference an external file that actually contains the presentation component, regardless of its type. These tags are pairs instead of singletons. This is because you can nest an <ANCHOR HREF=> tag within each tag pair to make a section of the component that the element describes a hyperlink (similar to an image map described with HTML), which may point to another SMIL file or Web page. When the user clicks on the hyperlinked component, the SMIL file or Web site is automatically accessed.

NOTE Each of the media-object tag pairs includes a large number of attributes for controlling how the components they describe are handled. For a complete description of each of these attributes in detail, read section 4.23 of the SMIL specification.

To see how all of these different elements come together to create a real, live SMIL document at work, visit the RealNetworks Technical showcase at `http://www.real.com/showcase/realplayer/tech/index.html`. To see the SMIL behind the Razor's Edge file, click on the link to "See the code." For a different look at SMIL, you can also visit http://www.justsmil.com/.

Beyond Vocabularies to Solutions

The goal of this skill was to introduce you to the XML vocabulary known as SMIL and give you a good idea of how it was designed to be used to further the inclusion of multimedia in the collection of Web technologies. As with all of the other skills in Part IV of this book, I've only touched on the basics of the SMIL vocabulary. It is my hope that by now you have a good grasp of what people are doing with XML and how they are doing it. The variety of XML applications you've seen in the previous four skills and in this one should help you understand the many uses XML has in the world of information dissemination.

Now that you know what XML is, understand how it works, can build your own DTDs and documents, and have seen what others are doing with XML, it's time to move onto the last section of the book, "XML in the Real World." In the first skill of this section, "Deciding Whether XML Is the Right Solution," you'll learn how to closely analyze your needs and resources to determine whether XML is the right solution for you. Included in the skill is a look at some real-world implementations of XML as well as a discussion of why XML was the right solution to a problem when other technologies weren't.

Are You up to Speed?

Now you can...

- ☑ Explain how multimedia works on the Web
- ☑ Define SMIL and explain its role in defining multimedia for the Web
- ☑ Describe the different SMIL elements and the content they describe

PART V

XML in the Real World

SKILL 25

Deciding Whether XML Is the Right Solution

- Answering three key XML questions
- Using XML as one part of a larger solution
- Reviewing what others have done with XML

You know how to create DTDs and documents, you've been introduced to some of the XML vocabularies already under development, and you probably have a good understanding of the many uses of XML. The question you have to answer now is whether XML is right for you. In this skill, you'll learn how to answer three important questions realistically and decide whether XML is the right solution for your information dissemination needs. To get your creative juices going, we'll show you what others have already done with XML and inform you of entire XML solutions packages already available on the market.

Three Key Questions

Before you can truly put your XML knowledge to use for something other than an academic exercise, you need to analyze your needs and make sure that XML is truly the right solution for you. Throughout the book, I've said time and again that the potential XML holds is enormous, but the current realities are limited. You're not going to find WYSIWYG XML editors and servers. Web browsers don't support XML documents well or easily, and they may not do so for a couple of versions to come. You'll never hear or read the phrase "You don't need to know XML for this solution to work for you."

However, the promise of XML is that you can describe, store, and disseminate your data over the Internet and Web in ways never before possible. The following three sections present you with three key questions as well as related questions that will help you analyze your needs and determine whether XML is right for you.

Invariably, the answers to these questions will spawn more questions, but it is better to take the time now to answer them than to find out half way through a project that your chosen solution was the wrong one.

What Are Your Needs?

As a first step, ask yourself these questions:

- What am I trying to accomplish?
- What type of information do I need to disseminate?
- What format is the information in, and what format does it need to be in?

- Why isn't my current dissemination solution working, and why do I need a new one?
- How soon do I need this solution up and running?
- How many people need to have access to this solution, and which types of computers, operating systems, and software will they need to access it?

The answers to each of these questions will give you a good handle on the type of information you're trying to disseminate, who your audience is, what your time line is, and what your technology requirements are. While you're thinking about your information, also consider how XML can be used to meet your various needs. Rank the needs by importance, and if XML can't be used to meet a very important need, then it probably isn't the right solution. If you need the solution yesterday, then it's entirely possible that XML isn't the right solution for you. It might be simply because developing a complete XML environment and converting your data to XML takes time. However, if you need to disseminate information currently stored in a database over the Web and current HTML-based technologies just aren't working for you, then XML may be the solution.

What Will It Take to Implement XML?

If you feel that XML is the right solution for your information dissemination needs, you should think carefully about what it will take to develop your complete solution. Ask yourself the following questions:

- Will I need to create a DTD from scratch, or can I use one that has already been developed?
- How difficult is it to create documents for my DTD? Are there specialized tools available?
- What will it take to convert my information from its current state into XML? If the information is in a database, how difficult will it be to program an XML front end for that database?
- Do I need to build a parser, or will one of the ones already in existence work?
- Do I need to develop my own interface or browser for my data, or can I use one that's already been developed?

Creating a CDF channel to be served to Internet Explorer users takes about an hour, and the content for it may take another hour. Setting up a server to send the information to users is a snap. The development time for an active channel using CDF is short because Microsoft has already developed everything you need, such as

- The DTD
- The CDF editor
- The CDF server
- A browser that parses and displays CDF

The more components of the solution that you have to develop from scratch, the longer the development will take, and the more human resources you'll need to complete it. If you create a custom DTD and documents for your solution and your own unique browser (even if you use a freeware parser that's been developed by someone else), you are looking at several months development time. You'll need to employ both a DTD expert and a programmer to create a well-developed DTD and a solid user interface.

Before you decide to reinvent the XML wheel, take some time and examine the tools and vocabularies others have already developed. Review the discussion in Skill 19, "Creating Documents for XML Applications," of how to choose between a vocabulary already in existence and developing your own. Take advantage of what others have done, and don't be afraid to combine their work with yours to create your final solution.

What Are Your Resources?

To determine what your resources are, you must answer some specific questions, such as

- What type of human resources do you have?
- What type of technical resources do you have?
- What type of financial resources do you have?

Remember in Skill 23, "Exchanging Money with OFX," I mentioned that setting up your own OFX server can take up to 90 man-months, or nine months with ten individuals working full-time on the project, in addition to investing in the necessary hardware and software. Other XML solutions may require more or less man-hours. Before you can think of XML as a potential solution, you need to make sure you have enough people on hand, with the right skills or the ability to acquire those skills, to complete the project. You'll need a DTD and document developer and probably a programmer, as well. If your project is small, it may be that one person can serve in both capacities. If your project is large, you may need several of both types of people. After you've evaluated your needs (what it will take to implement your solution), it's easier to figure out what types of human resources you'll need to design and implement your XML solution.

In addition to human resources, you'll need technical resources for developing the various pieces and parts of the solution. Do you have enough of the right types of computers? What XML development tools do you need? (Check out Skill 27, "Choosing the Right XML Tools," for more information on that subject.) You'll need at least one of every type of computer that you expect to be used to access your information for testing purposes alone. In the world of XML, people need a combination of the knowledge, skills, and computing power to develop a solution.

The reality is that human and technical resources cost money. You won't be able to develop an XML solution without some type of budget. Development dollars don't always generate a quick return, especially if the project is going to take a year or more to develop. Factor in the costs of man-hours and technology, as well as other overhead costs, and then add an extra 25 percent for good measure to plan for unexpected delays. After you've examined your needs and looked at what it will take to develop your solution, if you don't think you can afford the costs of development, go back and see whether you can't modularize your solution and develop one or two sections at a time.

The decision to use XML as a solution isn't determined by your answers to one or the other of these three main questions, but instead, the decision is dependent on your answers to all three as well as any others you come up with. One of the best ways to help you make a decision, if you're still uncertain after answering all these questions, is to investigate how others have used XML as a solution and what it has taken to get them there.

A Look at How Others Have Used XML

The majority of XML solutions at work today are tied directly to one vendor product or another. As I've stressed throughout the entire book, XML alone doesn't do much. To be truly useful, it requires processing and display tools that know what to do with an XML document and that can make the document's contents easily available to a human user. For the most part, vendors have begun using XML as their data description and storage language of choice. They create tools that convert database information into XML documents that can be read by specialized browsers. Most of the browsers that read these documents are Web-based and can be used to collect data from the user and transfer that data directly to the back-end database.

Developing a total XML solution from scratch is not a simple activity completed quickly. As you learned from the questions you answered in the previous sections, you'll need lots of resources, both human and financial, to build your own XML DTD, documents, and display devices. However, because so many vendors are rapidly adopting XML as a part of a complete, customizable solution's package, it may be that you won't need to build your own, but rather, for approximately the same cost, work with the tools already developed by a vendor.

If you are truly committed to using XML as a primary part of your information-dissemination solution, you owe it to yourself to investigate the XML solutions already offered by a variety of vendors. Your knowledge and experience with XML won't be wasted, because you still have to understand the most basic inner-workings of XML. In addition, you have to understand XML's strengths and weaknesses so you can use even the most advanced tools to create a complete XML solution. The vendor tools and interfaces will make your development of an XML solution easier, but without your own XML knowledge, they are worthless.

In the following sections, I've summarized solution descriptions from DataChannel, a major information-dissemination solutions vendor that focuses heavily on the use of XML to manage information.

These descriptions are not intended to be endorsements or suggest that they are the only things you can do with XML, but instead, they are held up as good examples of how XML can be used as part of a total information-dissemination solution. You may find that what DataChannel has to offer and how they use XML fit your requirements to a tee. It's also possible that you may not find anything they have to offer useful. Regardless, there is a great deal you can learn from what others have already done.

DataChannel Solutions

DataChannel, one of the first companies to work with XML exclusively, has developed a product called RIO that is designed to better manage data over a corporate intranet. DataChannel coined (and trademarked) the phrase "Save to the Web."

In nonmarketing speak, this means that their solution involves saving all of a company's information, regardless of type or purpose in a database or set of databases on the intranet server with a Web front end. Data is then delivered to users via channels created using the XML vocabulary CDF.

Users can customize the information they have delivered directly to their desktop by selecting which corporate channels they want to subscribe to; remote access to information is as easy as firing up a Web browser and logging in. When new information is added or existing information is updated, all subscribers automatically receive an updated version of the information. This process assures that the information everyone has is current, a key factor in keeping a company's business running smoothly, regardless of its size.

The RIO suite is a collection of tools that provides an organization with all they need to set up RIO-compliant databases or to convert existing databases, set up client computers to receive channel updates, as well as to publish data to the intranet. The CDF vocabulary plays a key role in the RIO system because it governs the way data is distributed among company users. Databases and Web servers also play an important role in the total RIO solution, but in reality, databases with Web front ends are a dime a dozen these days. It is the use of CDF to deliver the most current information to users in a timely manner that makes RIO so powerful.

The RIO suite provides a complete collection to create a framework that manages intranet and extranet content. RIO runs on top of any ODBC-compliant database, which is easily configured upon installation. Client computers with a minimum of 8MB of RAM and 100MHz processing speed can run Windows 3.11, 95, 98, or NT and access their RIO channels or folders through version 3 or higher of a browser. The client can publish data to their intranet or extranet from Office 95 applications, and they can drag-and-drop from their desktop or within Windows Explorer or merely from the browser itself.

The RIO interface hides channel creation and subscription from intranet administrators and users. It also makes publishing to the intranet a matter of clicking a button. (However, setting up templates does require someone with a bit more knowledge.) To give you an idea of how RIO is designed, Figure 25.1 shows a screen shot of the tab in RIO used to publish a channel. Figure 25.2 shows the tab used to subscribe to a channel.

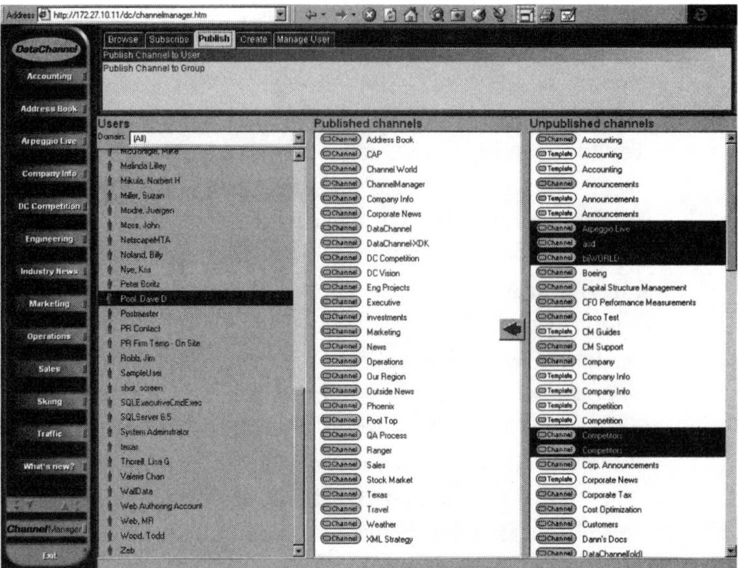

FIGURE 25.1: Publishing a channel using RIO

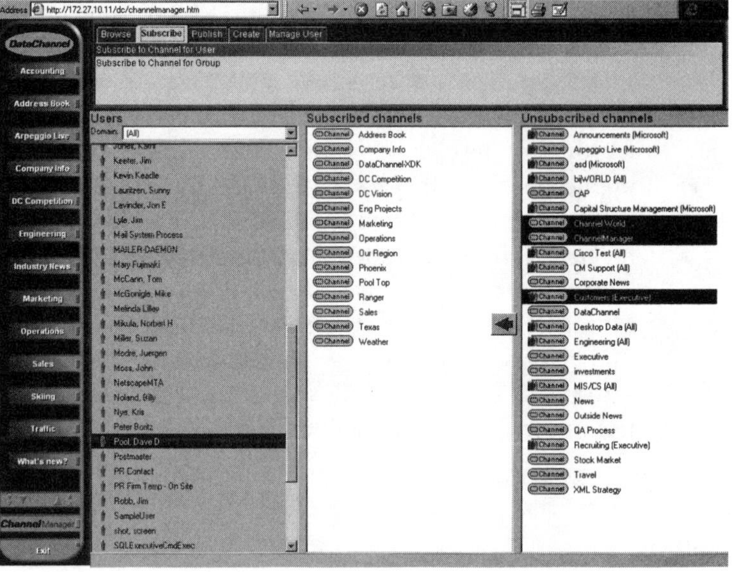

FIGURE 25.2: Subscribing to a channel using RIO

The folks at DataChannel have been wildly successful in their development and installation of RIO as a total information management tool. The following three sections will summarize three examples of RIO solutions. To find out more about RIO visit `http://www.datachannel.com/products/`.

Sales Information Desktop

Everyone involved in sales at a company needs to have access to immediate information about everything from product information and availability to customer service and technical support. At a busy company, this information changes almost constantly, but many of those who need access to it are on the road, where they don't have a direct connection to the company's database. The bottom line is that there is a great deal of key information that needs to get to a variety of individuals, both in and out of the office, as quickly as possible.

The RIO solution to this problem is to save all of the sales information to a database and publish it to the corporate intranet. Everyone with a connection to sales subscribes to the sales channel. When new information is published, the subscriber's channel content is updated automatically. Those who are on the road only have to log into the corporate network using the nearest phone line and click a button to update their channel content remotely. A database is used to centralize the data, but XML makes immediate delivery of important information to key personnel simple and automatic.

Engineering Information Desktop

Engineers, technical support specialists, project managers, and field representatives often need to have access to the same types of information:

- What parts and products are in stock and available?
- When is a project expected to be done and is it on track?
- What technical schematics are relevant to a current product or project?
- How a developing product will work with an existing product?

Depending on the person's role in an organization, chances are they will need to be able to put their hands on some or all of this information at any given time. The problem—in addition to needing an easy way to centralize and distribute the data—is how to provide all of the necessary information to those who need it without overloading those who don't.

The RIO solution, once again, uses CDF to meet this need. All of the related engineering data is stored in a database and is published to the corporate intranet. However, when using CDF, several different engineering-related channels of data can be set up. Who subscribes to each of those channels is dependent on the type of information they need to know. A manager might need to have access to all engineering-related information, but unless the information is broken up into well-organized groups (channels), it's difficult to sort through. By using channels, it is easy to see which new projects or areas have updated information that needs to be attended to and which do not.

Technical support specialists and field specialists may need to know the status of projects, but they don't necessarily need to be kept apprised of each new technical development in the project. Separate channels can be set up for individual facets of a project. This helps keep the information organized and delivered to those who need it without overwhelming those who don't. Once again, it's the XML portion of this solution that helps focus and control the delivery of different groups of related information to different people within a department or group based on who needs to know what.

Private Customer Information Desktop

In today's competitive market, it's important to acquire and then retain customers. One of the best ways to do this is by providing solid customer support and keeping customers apprised of new developments and information. The simplest and easiest way to do this is to post customer support and new information to your Web site. However, for your customers to access this information, they have to first know it exists and then come to your Web site to get it.

Instead of making customers come to you for information, you can use RIO to go to them. Using RIO you can set up individual channels for limited groups of customers. Because RIO has a built-in security and permissions system, you can limit who has access to what information. You can use your private customer system to provide existing customers with special technical-support information as well as targeted marketing information about new products. If a bug report or patch is released, you can quickly and easily spread the word to your customers by publishing the information using RIO.

Again, this solution uses CDF to create highly focused channels of information that are delivered from a centralized location to a select group of people. Such services can be used to entice customers and help make a product more attractive. Any customer with a Web browser or other display tool that supports channels can subscribe to the channel related to their product with the click of a button.

NOTE

Any client running a Javascript-enabled browser (not CDF) can take advantage of RIO's technology. The database and publishing tools are not proprietary—the database can be any ODBC-compliant relational database, and the user can publish to a channel from either Netscape Navigator 3 or Microsoft Internet Explorer 3 browsers.

All three examples of the RIO solutions involve disseminating information to a variety of users, both local and remote, in a timely manner. By using the XML CDF vocabulary already supported by the Microsoft Web browser, RIO takes advantage of a nonproprietary technology to disseminate the information. Any client running a CDF-compatible browser can take advantage of RIO's technology, even though the actual database and publishing tools use a proprietary DataChannel format. This combination of a proprietary solution with XML makes it easy for RIO to serve a large collection of users running clients on a variety of platforms and operating systems. Without XML, it would've been hard to make RIO a success.

Other Solutions Providers

DataChannel is certainly not the only information-dissemination solution provider that uses XML as a key part of their technology. However, many vendors are just now beginning to see the benefits associated with using the various XML vocabularies, or one of their own, as part of a new and better way to share information resources. WebMethods, Microsoft, and ArborText have products already developed.

WebMethods focuses on business-to-business e-commerce solutions that allow businesses to share information with each other across the intranet. WebMethods uses XML to standardize data descriptions to make it possible for businesses with disparate systems to share data. You can find out more at `http://www.webmethods.com/solutions/index.html`.

Microsoft uses XML in conjunction with their database, Web server, and Active Server Pages (ASP) technologies to create Web-based applications. Their XML scenario's page is at `http://www.microsoft.com/xml/scenario/intro.asp`; it discusses how XML was used in several instances as part of a total information-dissemination solution.

ArborText is an established SGML software vendor that has created a series of tools for developing and publishing large quantities of documents. ArborText focuses on providing a way for several people in an organization to collaborate on the development of a single document in a controlled and organized way. Read more about ArborText's use of XML at `http://www.arbortext.com/`.

These companies—DataChannel, WebMethods, Microsoft, and ArborText—are beginning to develop XML-based solutions for everything from Web publishing to inventory management. In the end, the possible uses of XML are limitless. Once you've decided that XML is the right solution for your information-dissemination needs or is part of the right solution, you're well on your way to meeting those needs.

Implementing XML After You've Decided to Use It

Once you've decided the XML is the right solution for your needs, you'll need to tackle some of the major issues involved in the actual implementation. These issues include the volatile nature of XML and its related specifications as they develop into key Web technologies as well as which vendors support XML, and what it will take to get your project off the ground and running. In Skill 26, "Dealing with the Implementation Realities of XML," I'll review the particular implementation issues you'll need to address before you begin your project and let you in on a few trade secrets that will make overcoming implementation problems easier than you might expect.

Are You up to Speed?

Now you can...

- ☑ **Answer three key questions about your need for XML as a solution**
- ☑ **Describe other cases where XML has been used as a solution and explain why**
- ☑ **Decide if XML is the right solution for your information needs**

SKILL 26

Dealing With the Implementation Realities of XML

- Identifying and addressing implementation issues
- Acquiring the right skill sets and tools to build an XML solution
- Selling XML to the boss
- Creating an implementation check list

Once you've decided that XML is indeed the best solution to meet your needs, or will be a component in a larger solution, you'll need to address several important implementation issues before you dive into developing your solution. Because XML is a new and developing technology, you will be a pioneer, and you will be faced with all the problems pioneers encounter. However, if you tackle each issue in a careful and logical way, you'll find that they are easier to deal with than you'd expect. This skill identifies potential implementation problems you may face and shows you how to go about solving them.

Identifying Potential Implementation Problems

In Skill 25, "Deciding Whether XML Is the Right Solution," you answered a variety of questions designed to help you decide whether XML is the right solution to meet your needs. Many of the questions revolved around new skills or technologies you would need to develop an XML solution. Even if you feel confident that you have the resources on hand to create a successful XML solution, you'll still need to consider several implementation issues and decide how you're going to address them. Most importantly, you'll need to accurately identify the different implementation issues you'll be dealing with, be honest with yourself and your team about what it will take to address them, and define a plan that integrates the implementation issues into your overall development strategy.

Each of the following sections identifies several common issues that anyone implementing an XML solution will need to deal with. The importance of these issues, the steps you'll need to take, and the resources you'll need to spend to address each individual issue will be different for each and every XML solution. There is no right or wrong way to address these issues. Instead, you'll want to look at each one in the context of your proposed solution and determine how it might affect the completion and implementation of your XML plan. These sections are designed to get you thinking about what it would really take to implement XML and make you acutely aware of all that goes into developing a well-designed and functioning XML solution.

Acquiring the Right Skills

You've made it through almost the entire text of this book, so you are well on your way to acquiring the most basic skills you'll need to begin working with

XML. However, as you know by now, XML never does anything by itself, so developing a total XML-based solution will require several different skill sets, including

- Project management
- DTD and document development
- Browser and interface programming
- Internet and intranet networking administration
- Interface design

How much access you need to each of these different skill sets depends entirely upon the scope of your project and how much of it you intend to develop from scratch. If you are using an XML-based tool, such as the DataChannel RIO package discussed in Skill 25, then the skill sets you will need are greatly reduced. Yes, you'll have to understand XML and how it works, as well as spend some time getting caught up with the basics of channels, but you'll find most of that information in the RIO documentation. RIO installs on an existing intranet, so if you have an intranet, then you probably already have the network administrator you need to deal with RIO's client-server functionality. RIO comes with a predesigned and preprogrammed interface, with a built-in DTD and with all the tools you need to publish your data to both the intranet and to individual desktops. In short, to implement this solution, the only new skills you'll have to acquire are the ones you need to administer and install the product. The same is true of any other tool designed to implement your XML-based solution quickly and easily and without much work on your end. However, what you don't spend to acquire new skills will easily be spent licensing the RIO product.

If you are not buying a tool like RIO, then you'll be responsible for developing most, if not all, of the components of your solution. If you don't already have the skills in place to do so, you will need to get them. If your project is large scale and will affect a great number of users, you may need to have several people with specialized skill sets, such as programming and interface design, working on it. If the project is on a smaller scale, you may have individuals with multiple skill sets, such as a programmer who designs interfaces or a network administrator who writes DTDs.

A key factor in the development of any XML solution is one that includes both DTD design and document development. If you are going to be developing your own DTD, then you'll need to build extra time into your development schedule to design and test the DTD. You'll want to have an experienced DTD writer on hand as well as someone who can write documents for the DTD that you develop.

Although this process may require more time and resources, you will be working with a DTD customized for your data.

One way of saving time and resources is to use a DTD already developed or under development, especially if you are part of an industry already working on a standard DTD for describing data, such as the financial and multimedia industries. If you use someone else's DTD, there is a strong possibility that you will be able to use tools and processors already designed specifically for that DTD. This means you won't have to program your own browser or may only need minimal programming work to customize an existing browser, which is faster than building it from the ground up.

Of course, the downside to working with an existing DTD is that it may be limited in some way or another or may not include support for all of the different kinds of data you need to describe. One solution to this problem is to modify an existing DTD to meet your needs, but after you do, the tools associated with that DTD may be of limited use to you. For a discussion of how to decide whether you should design your own DTD or use someone else's, revisit Skill 19, "Creating Documents for XML Applications."

The easiest way to figure out which new skill sets you'll need to have access to and which you won't need is to make a list of all the proposed components of your solution and describe what skills will be required to develop and implement them. For those you will be building from the ground up, try to estimate how many man-hours they will take to develop and make sure you have access to enough people with the right skills. For those with components that have already been developed by a third party, make sure you have access to someone who understands the component, can modify it as necessary, and can integrate it smoothly with the other parts of the solution.

Working with New Software

It's likely that your XML solution will require that you work with at least one or two new software packages. To figure out which new software you'll need to acquire, consider which tools are available to make development easier and which tools you will absolutely have to have. XML tools are designed to make the development of an XML solution easier, and many are quick and easy to learn. Once you standardize a specific set of XML tools, you'll need to make sure everyone on your development team has time to learn to use them well. Build that time into your schedule up front.

It's also possible that you will need to learn how to use other software, such as a database or visual-programming environment, to complete the development of your solution. To identify those tools and account for the time it will take to learn them in your project time line, reexamine the component's list you generated and determine the skill sets you'll need to complete the project. Decide what special software, if any, you'll need to learn for the development of each individual component. Keep in mind that the person, or persons, with the skill set needed to complete the component may also already know how to use a particular software package. It's best to inquire about this immediately to avoid duplicating training or not providing adequate training.

New software and development tools will contribute to the financial resources you'll have to spend on your project as well as to the time it will take to complete the project. Identifying software licensing and training costs, as well as how much time it takes learning a new tool, will add to a project's completion time. Assessing all these factors will help you keep your project both on time and on budget.

Platform and Operating System Issues

A major issue when dealing with an XML solution is what it will take to make your solution function equally well across a variety of computer platforms and operating systems. Although XML is designed to be platform independent, as is all markup, the reality is the tools designed to develop and browse XML documents are decidedly proprietary. Regardless of how much of your solution you're developing from scratch and how much you are using from already-developed solutions, you'll need to decide from the beginning which platforms and operating systems the solution will need. The more platforms and systems you'll need to support, the longer it will take to develop your product. You may also need to revise the list of skill sets required for the project.

Of course, the kind and number of different computers you'll need to design for is entirely dependent upon the ultimate goal of your solution. If you're creating a solution for your company intranet, then you only have to make it work on the kinds of computers found in your company. If you're designing a solution for the Internet at large, then you'll have to account for the variety of operating systems and platforms at use around the world.

If you're going to develop for more than one system and platform and plan on using components that have already been developed by third parties, such as parsers and browsers, you'll need to find out which systems and platforms they support. If they don't support all of the systems that you need, then find out whether you can

- Port existing code from one platform to another

- Find another tool that supports the other platforms you need, and use both in your total solution
- Work with the developer of the tool to create a multiplatform tool

Java is turning out to be one of the best cross-platform development environments available today. Many of the developing XML parsers are Java-based, as is the JUMBO browser created for the CML vocabulary. Java is designed as a write-once, run-anywhere programming language, which means that a single Java applet should be able to run on any computer regardless on which platform the applet was developed. Applets can also be embedded directly into Web pages, making it easier to bring XML solutions to the Web. In the real world, things aren't this easy. Java implementations differ from Web browser to Web browser and from platform to platform, but a good Java programmer knows how to deal with these issues. If you'll be developing your solution for multiple platforms, then you'll want to seriously consider Java as your primary programming language for the parsers and browsers that will read and interpret your XML files.

Determining how many platforms you need to support and what it will take to do so is one of the most important issues you need to address. If you plan from the beginning for a solution that supports a variety of platforms, then you can build the extra time and resources you'll need into your schedule.

Planning for Change

One of the most important things you can do as you plan your XML solution is to anticipate changes in the underlying technologies and be prepared to deal with them. XML is officially a standard now, but it is constantly changing and growing. Its accompanying specifications—Xlink, XPointer, and XSL—are all still in the working draft phase and won't begin to become specifications until early 1999.

Although you will have to develop your solution using what you know to be true in the present, don't get so set on working with XML in one way that you are caught off guard when a new version is released and changes have been made. Be comforted by the fact that the W3C does not make decisions or changes to a specification arbitrarily, and it always takes into account backward compatibility and what's best for developers. Vendors get to make their own decisions about what aspects of a technology they support, but if you research the developers of tools and components and select those committed to meeting and adhering to standards, you'll find tools that change and grow as the specification does.

Stay current with the technology. Read online resources and trade magazines regularly. Participate in newsgroups and e-mail discussion lists to find out what others are thinking and doing with XML. Skill 27, "Finding the Best XML Resources," includes all you need to know about finding these XML resources that will help you stay up-to-date on the developments in the XML world.

Selling XML to the Boss

The last and most important implementation issue is convincing management that XML is really your best solution. Managers get to be managers because they are conservative and prudent. They're not going to buy into a major technology change and devote a hefty chunk of resources to a project without a good reason or several good reasons. However, because you're dealing with a new technology, bringing the boss up to speed on what XML is, how it is different from HTML, and why it's better can be a bit difficult.

One of the best ways I've found to help managers understand why I've developed a particular solution or chosen a particular technology is to point them to well-written articles that support my case. One of the best XML-related articles I've seen, written specifically for managers, is called "XML for Managers" and is located on the site at `http://www.arbortext.com/xmlwp.html`. The topics the article covers include

- Who Should Read This?
- XML: For SGML on the Web
- XML's Inventors
- The Growing Momentum behind XML
- The Limitations of Browsing: Why HTML Is Limited to Document Delivery
- HTML: Today's Web Technology
- Why HTML Isn't Enough
- SGML: Father to HTML and Brother to XML
- SGML's Limitations for Web Delivery
- XML = SGML with Minor Changes
- XSL and XLL: Companions to XML
- XSL: Doing XML with Style
- XLL: Superior Linking for XML

- Is XML Easier than SGML?
- XML for Nondocument Applications
- Conclusion: When to Use XML and SGML
- HTML vs. XML: An Application Example

The article is a quick read (no more than 10 or 15 minutes) and provides an easy and accurate way to bring your manager up to speed on what XML is and how it is useful as a solution. If your boss is well informed about XML, you've cleared the first major hurdle.

Make sure you present your manager with a good project proposal that stresses the facts that XML is an open standard supported by the W3C, Microsoft, Sun, Netscape, IBM, and other major players and that XML is extensible. Finally, if you've already isolated and found solutions for your other implementation issues, you'll be prepared to answer hard questions with quick and effective answers. Once you've convinced the boss that your XML project is worthwhile and a good investment, you'll be on your way to creating a quality XML solution.

Creating an Implementation Checklist

The development of an XML implementation begins with a need to be met and ends with a complete XML solution. After you've identified your need and settled on XML as the solution, you'll want to create an implementation checklist that identifies all of the components you'll need to complete the solution and how you'll go about developing those components. For each individual component, you'll want to list the following:

- Is the component to be developed from scratch or licensed from another developer?
- Any special skills required.
- The number of man-hours needed to build or modify and integrate the component.
- The different platforms the component will have to support.
- Any special development tools needed to build the component.
- Any special tools needed to work with the component (databases, Web browsers, etc.).

Once you've created this list, you'll want to check each item off after you've included a plan for addressing it in your overall project documentation. You will also need to reassess your original time and resource costs to make sure that you've included enough human, financial, and time resources into your project schedule. After completing this evaluation, you will be well prepared to show your boss your solution as well as check off your final implementation issue.

Tools Aid in All Aspects of XML Development

The right tool always makes any job easier, whether it's building a house or building an XML solution. In this skill and in the previous one, you met some of the realities associated with developing and implementing an XML solution. In Skill 27, "Choosing the Right XML Tool," you'll meet many of the quality XML tools currently available for the development of XML DTDs, documents, and other solution components. Every developer's tool box will be different, and in the next skill, you'll find all you need to begin filling yours.

Are You up to Speed?

Now you can...

- ☑ **Explain why it is important to identify implementation issues up front**
- ☑ **Identify key skill sets and tools you may need to develop an XML solution**
- ☑ **Use resources to bring your managers up to speed on XML and get their support for an XML solution**
- ☑ **Create an implementation checklist**

SKILL 27

Choosing the Right XML Tool

- How to find the best XML tools for you
- XML parsers and editors
- XSL editors
- CSS editors

The right tool can be a most important asset to your successful development of XML DTDs, documents, and applications. Although XML is a new technology, a variety of tools from DTD editors to document management systems have already been developed, with many more on the horizon. This skill provides a rundown of the currently available XML parsers, document and DTD editors, and style-sheet tools.

XML Toolbox

If you were to sample the best developers in any field, especially those in the Internet and Web industry, you'll find that no two use the same set of tools to ply their trade. Instead, each developer's tool box contains a set of software tools best suited to meet their individual needs. As you begin to fill your own XML tool box, several different factors will affect the tools you choose, including

- Your operating system and platform
- Your role in the development of an XML solution, such as
    - A DTD designer
    - An interface or parser programmer
    - A project manager
    - A document developer
- The bells and whistles, or lack there of, you prefer
- Your budget

To find the set of tools that best fit your needs, you'll have to do a bit of research and shopping around. The remaining sections of this skill provide you with information about all of the currently available XML tools, broken down by category. The beginning of each section includes a table that summarizes the important information about each tool, including its author, platform, and URL.

Following the table in each section, you'll find a brief description of each tool, platform, and operating specifics. I will also give you URLs you can visit on the Web to peruse more detailed information about each tool as well as downloadable demonstration versions to try out before you commit to one.

TIP

It has been my experience as a developer that you'll work with several combinations of tools before you find the set that is right for you. Once you do find the perfect collection of tools, you shouldn't completely ignore new tools that are either under development or in full release version. The items in your toolbox can become like a comfortable pair of shoes or your favorite jacket. They're serviceable and have proven themselves over time, but they aren't always the best solution to your needs. Take the time to read about new products and demo them to see if they include capabilities you might never have known you wanted or needed.

Parsers and Browsers

XML parsers and browsers are at the heart of XML processing. You'll recall from Skill 14, "Processing XML Documents," that parsers are the software programs responsible for reading an XML document and breaking it down into a format that a front-end program—such as a Web browser—can read and display. These front-end applications that display the parsed XML data are called browsers. Table 27.1 lists all of the currently available parsers.

TABLE 27.1: XML Parsers

Name	Author	Platform	URL
Ælfred	Microstar	Java	`http://www.microstar.com/XML/AElfred/`
DXP	Datachannel	Java	`http://www.datachannel.com/xml_resources/dxp.shtml`
expat	James Clark	C	`http://www.jclark.com/xml/expat.html`
HEX	Anders Kristensen	Java	`http://www-uk.hpl.hp.com/people/ak/java/hex.html`
JUMBO	The Virtual School of Molecular Science	Java	`http://ala.vsms.nottingham.ac.uk/vsms/java/jumbo/index.html`
Lark	Tim Bray	Java	`http://www.textuality.com/Lark`
Larval	Tim Bray	Java	`http://www.textuality.com/Lark`
LT XML	Language Technology Group	C	`http://www.ltg.ed.ac.uk/software/xml/index.html`
SP	James Clark	C++	`http://www.jclark.com/sp/index.html`

TABLE 27.1 CONTINUED: XML Parsers

Name	Author	Platform	URL
xmlproc	Lars Marius Garshol	Python	http://www.stud.ifi.uio.no/~larsga/download/python/xml/xmlproc.html
XML Parser in Java	IBM Alphaworks	Java	http://alphaworks.ibm.com/formula/xml
XP	James Clark	Java	http://www.jclark.com/xml/xp/index.html
XParse	Jeremie Miller	JavaScript	http://www.jeremie.com/Dev/XML/

In Skill 14, "Processing XML Documents," you'll find a detailed description of each of these parsers with information about the ability of each to validate XML documents as well as to check whether they are well formed.

XML Editors

You've seen throughout this book that the only tool you need to create XML DTDs and documents is a text editor or other application that creates plain text documents. However, when you use an everyday text editor to create your DTDs and documents, you'll have to type in every less-than and greater-than sign yourself as well as everything that goes in between.

An XML editor is a specialized text editor that is designed to simplify the creation of XML DTDs and documents. A good XML editor warns you when you make a common mistake, such as forgetting to close a tag pair or accidentally omitting a less-than sign. Often, these editors color code the text in your documents to differentiate markup from text, making both easier to read. Finally, some editors are smart enough to read a DTD and make sure the document you are creating is both well formed and valid. Table 27.2 lists all of the XML editors available at the time this book was written.

TABLE 27.2: XML Editors

Name	Author	Platform	URL
CLIP	Techno 200 Project	Win 95/NT, Sun Solaris 2.5	http://xml.t2000.co.kr/product/clip.html
Near and Far Designer	Microstar	Win 95/NT	http://www.microstar.com/Products-And-Technologies/index.html
tdtd	Mulberry Technology	Emacs compatible	ftp://ftp.mulberrytech.com/pub/tdtd/

TABLE 27.2 CONTINUED: XML Editors

Name	Author	Platform	URL
XED	Language Technology Group	Win 95/NT, Sun Solaris 2.5	`http://www.ltg.ed.ac.uk/~ht/xed.html`
XML Notepad	Microsoft	Win 95/NT	`http://www.microsoft.com/xml/notepad/intro.asp`
XML Pro	Vervet Logic	Win 95/NT	`http://www.vervet.com/prod.html`
Visual XML	Pierre Morel	Java	`http://www.pierlou.com/visxml/`
WebWriter	Stilo Technology	Win 95/NT	`http://www.stilo.com/products/xmlbody.htm`

CLIP

Clip, from Techno 2000 Project for the Windows 95/NT and Sun Solaris 2.5 platforms is a visual XML editor whose capabilities include validation, advanced search and replace, and the use of dialog boxes to make applying markup easier. Figure 27.1 shows the CLIP information page at `http://xml.t2000.co.kr/product/clip.html` and includes two screen shots of the CLIP interface.

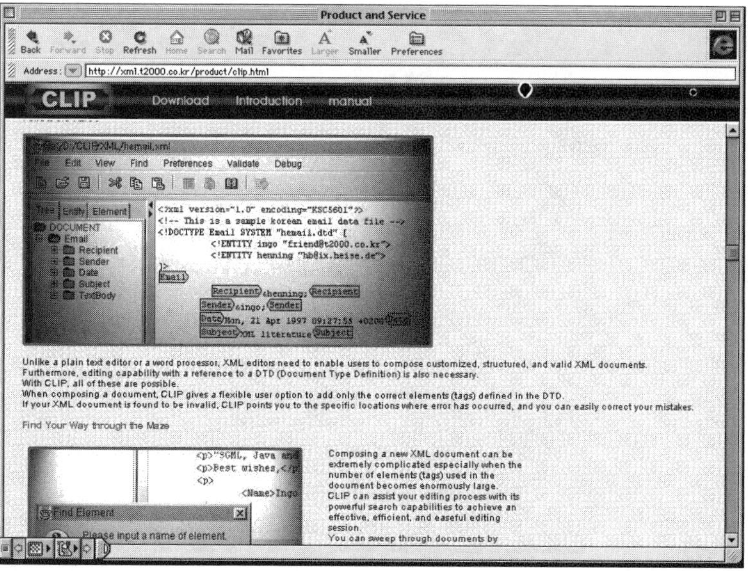

FIGURE 27.1: The CLIP information Web page

As shown in Figure 27.1, markup tags are visually represented as tags by CLIP to distinguish them from the text they describe, and the editor also shows the structure of the elements in a document as a tree. CLIP is still in the development phase, but it looks to have all of the makings of a quality XML editor and will include both XSL and XLL support. To download a demo version of CLIP, visit `http://xml.t2000.co.kr/product/agreement.html`.

Near and Far Designer

Near and Far Designer from Microstar for the Windows 95/NT platform is a DTD and document editor that has parsing capabilities. One of this editor's greatest strengths is that it comes with full support for several industry DTDs including CDF, OSD, and OFX. In addition, Near and Far Designer can import SGML documents and convert them to well-formed or valid XML documents. The editor's interface is based on a tree representation of a document, so it is easy to see how groups of content and their markup relate to one another as well as navigate through them.

To download a demonstration copy of Near and Far Designer, visit its description page at `http://www.microstar.com/Products-And-Technologies/index.html`, shown in Figure 27.2.

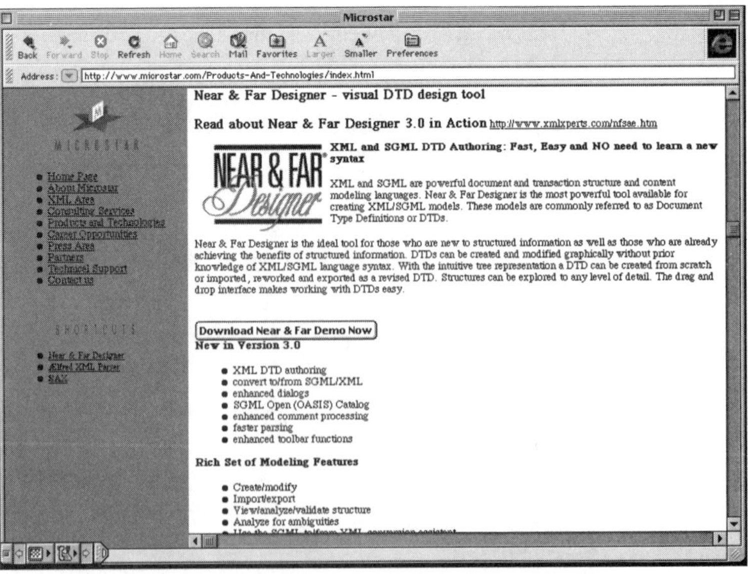

FIGURE 27.2: The Near and Far Designer Web page

tdtd

Not for the inexperienced user, tdtd is a set of macros built specifically for the Emacs text editor. Any system running a version of Emacs can use these macros. Included in the macro package are tools for storing frequently used markup tags in aliases for quick retrieval and use as well as other helpers for creating XML DTDs. If you're a regular Emacs user, then you'll appreciate this macro tool kit. To download the macros, a `readme.txt` file, and a tutorial, visit `ftp://ftp.mulberrytech.com/pub/tdtd/`.

XED

XED is an XML document authoring system created by Henry S. Thompson at the University of Edinburgh for the Windows 95/NT and Sun Solaris 2.5 platforms. This editor is a WYSIWYG editing tool whose primary focus is to ensure that your documents are valid. It accurately parses the DTD you are writing the document for, and it will make sure you don't violate any of its content rules or leave out any required elements and attributes. The editor also keeps track of the changes you've made to a document so you can go back later and review them.

If you are new to the world of XML and document creation, then XED is a good tool for both developing XML documents and learning to avoid common document development mistakes. It provides error messages when you violate a precept of the DTD and helps you work easily with both element and mixed content. To find out more about XED or to download a copy, point your Web browser at `http://www.ltg.ed.ac.uk/~ht/xed.html`.

XML Notepad

The latest addition to the Microsoft XML arsenal is XML Notepad, a souped-up version of the Windows OS Notepad built specifically for editing XML documents. Notepad is a free offering from Microsoft, but it doesn't come with technical support. However, the documents and tutorials found at `http://www.microsoft.com/xml/notepad/intro.asp` provide you with all the information you'll need to get started.

The XML Notepad interface provides a graphical representation of an XML document, as shown in Figure 27.3.

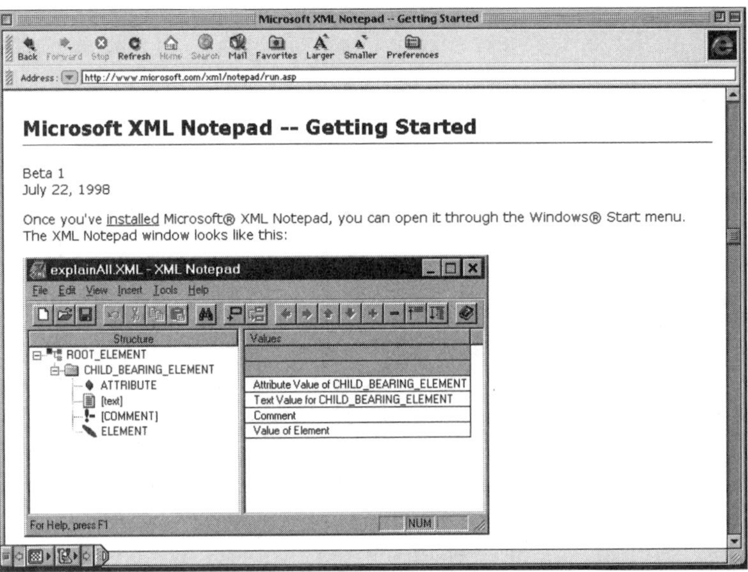

FIGURE 27.3: The XML Notepad information page

Each element in a document is listed in a tree-based representation, as are text and other XML structures, such as entities and comments. One of XML Notepad's strengths is that it helps you visualize the structure of your document and see how different markup elements relate to each other and the text they describe. You can download your own copy of this useful tool at `http://www.microsoft.com/xml/notepad/download.asp`.

XML Pro

A commercial XML editor from Vervet Logic for the Windows 95/NT platform, XML Pro is a fully functional XML and DTD editor with a WYSIWYG interface, as shown in Figure 27.4.

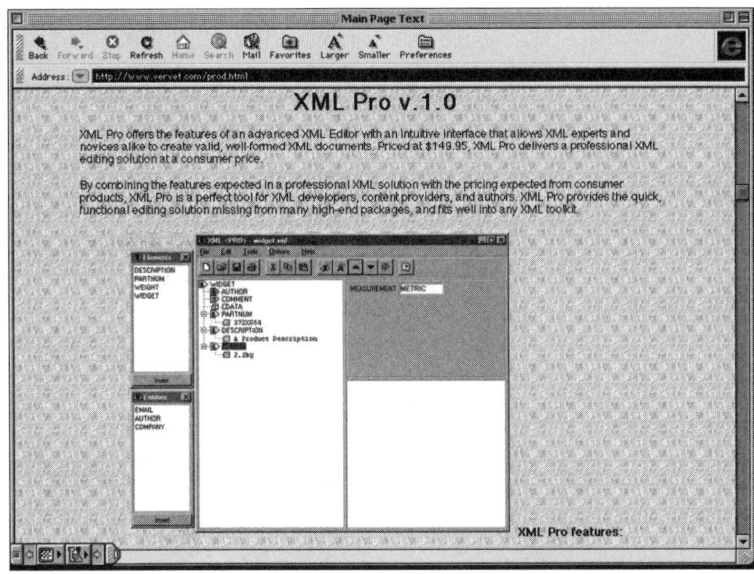

FIGURE 27.4: The XML Pro information Web page

Using the same tree-based representation of XML documents that many other XML editors employ, XML Pro also makes use of floating pallets for quick access to elements and attributes. The editor also includes wizards that make creating elements and attributes in DTDs quick and easy. Finally, XML Pro will validate documents against their DTDs and check to make sure a document is well formed. You can read more about XML Pro and download a demo version at `http://www.vervet.com/prod.html`.

Visual XML

Visual XML is the only Java-based XML editor currently available. This editor, developed by Pierre Morel, can run on any platform that has a Java runtime environment installed on it. Once again, in Visual XML you'll find the tree-based representation of a document's content and markup. The interface is clean and easy to use, and it even provides you with your choice of three look-and-feel options, as shown in Figures 27.5 through 27.7.

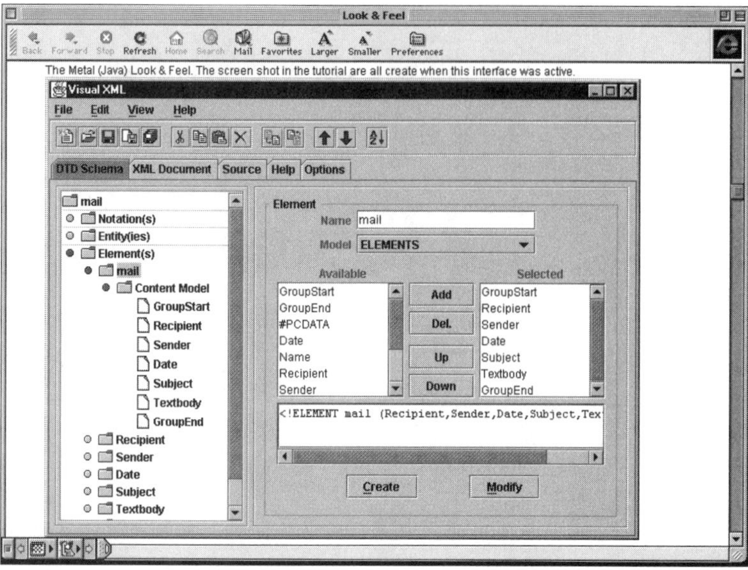

FIGURE 27.5: The Visual XML metal interface

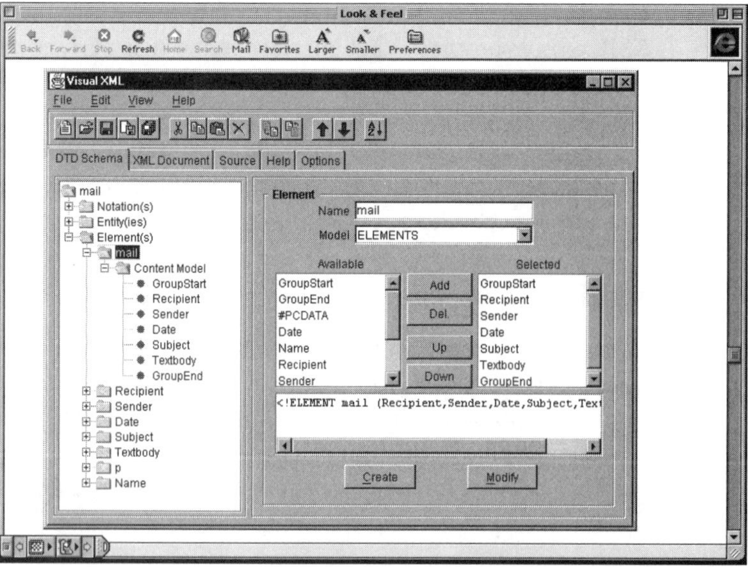

FIGURE 27.6: The Visual XML Windows interface

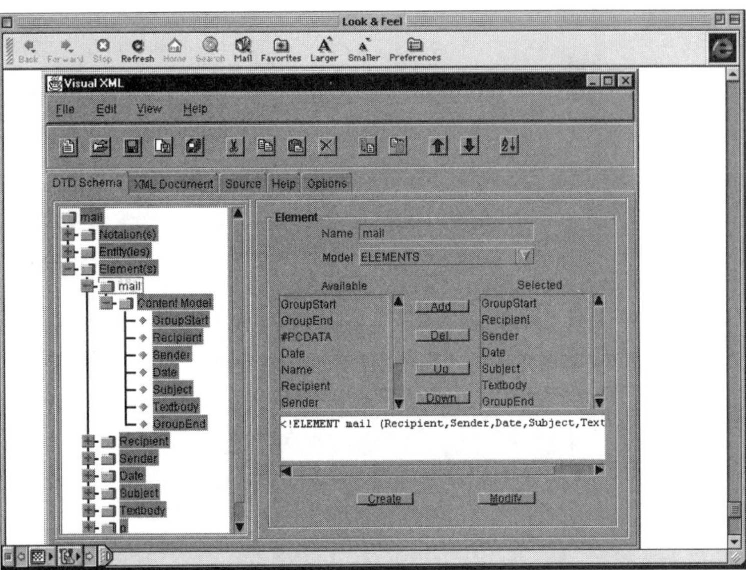

FIGURE 27.7: The Visual XML motif interface

In addition to being easy to use and learn, Visual XML will parse a DTD and ensure that any documents you create for it are both well formed and valid. It includes many other functions you expect to see in a good HTML editor, including the ability to edit both DTDs and documents, search-and-replace functionality, and several options for viewing your XML source.

For those XML developers not using the Windows or Sun Solaris operating system, Visual XML provides a nicely executed XML editing option. Find out more about it and download a copy at `http://www.pierlou.com/visxml/`.

WebWriter

WebWriter is a tool from Stilo Technology for the Windows 95/NT platform. WebWriter is a unique editor that generates XML documents based on data you enter into a database-like interface shown in Figure 27.8.

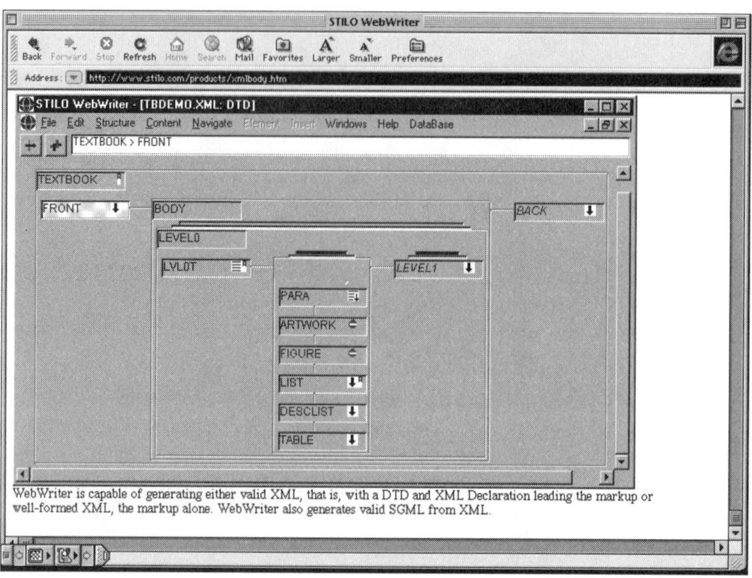

FIGURE 27.8: The WebWriter interface

WebWriter reads and parses the DTD for which you are writing your document and ensures that the document is both well formed and valid. WebWriter uses an easy-to-learn and easy-to-use interface, and because it is based on a tested and popular SGML product, Stilo's SGML Document Generator, it tends to be more reliable and stable than other editors still in the early phases of development. WebWriter allows you to edit an existing XML file, start a file from scratch with or without a DTD, as well as edit an existing DTD. You can also use WebWriter to create SGML documents from XML documents. To read more about WebWriter or download a demo copy, point your Web browser at `http://www.stilo.com/products/xmlbody.htm`.

XSL Editors

The XML style-sheet language, XSL, is a robust and extensible language that you use to write style sheets that drive the final display of XML documents. Because XSL is so powerful, its constructs can often be complex to create and edit. To speed this process along and ensure that you create functioning and usable style sheets, you might want to include an XSL editor in your XML toolkit. There are currently only two stand-alone XSL editors available, as shown in Table 27.3, but several of the XML editors described in the previous sections either include XSL support or will include it in future releases.

TABLE 27.3: XSL Editors

Name	Author	Platform	URL
xslj	Language Technology Group	Win 95/NT, Sun Solaris 2.5	`http://www.ltg.ed.ac.uk/~ht/xslj.html`
XML Styler	ArborText	Java	`http://www.arbortext.com/xmlstyler/index.html`

xsjl

Created by Henry Thompson at Language Technology Group (the creator of the XED XML editor), xsjl is a tool for the Windows 95/NT and Sun Solaris 2.5 platforms. This XSL is designed to work specifically with a tool created by James Clark, called *Jade,* and it converts XSL style sheets into DSSSL style sheets (the original style-sheet mechanism for SGML) that can be parsed and processed by Jade. This is another tool that isn't for the novice user. If you're familiar with SGML and DSSSL, then xsjl is for you; otherwise, you'll find yourself more frustrated and confused than assisted by it. To read more about xsjl, visit `http://www.ltg.ed.ac.uk/~ht/xslj.html`, and to read more about Jade, visit `http://www.jclark.com/jade/`.

XML Styler

A Java-based XSL editor from ArborText, XML Styler is a XSL style-sheet editor that runs in your Web browser and has a nice WYSIWYG interface. All of the style sheets in the XSL demo discussed in Skill 16, "Converting XML to HTML with XSL" were created and modified using the XML Styler.

One word of caution: This editor was written to the original XSL proposal and does not reflect the current XSL working draft. The folks at ArborText are right on top of things and are sure to release an updated version of the XML Styler when the working draft becomes more stable.

If you're new to XSL or are looking for an easier and faster way to create XSL style sheets that are syntactically correct, you'll want to look into XML Styler. It's even free. For more information and to download your copy, visit the XML Styler Web page at `http://www.arbortext.com/xmlstyler/index.html`. You can also see the XML Styler page in Figure 27.9.

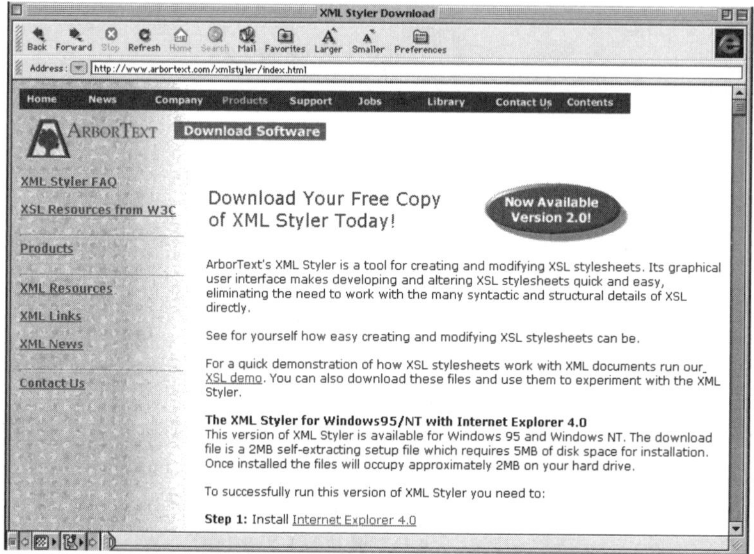

FIGURE 27.9: The XML Styler information Web page

CSS Editors

As you learned in Skill 15, "Adding Style with CSS," Cascading Style Sheets will be the first style mechanism used with XML documents to drive their display in Web pages. CSS is much easier to learn than XSL, and it is already an official W3C standard. CSS editors have been slow to emerge, but Table 27.4 lists three of the best ones available.

TABLE 27.4: CSS Editors

Name	Author	Platform	URL
Cascade	Balthisar Software	Win 95/NT	`http://www.balthisar.com/html/cascade_2.0_section.html`
StyleMaker	Danere Software	Win 95/NT	`http://danere.com/StyleMaker/`
StyleMaster	Western Civilization	Macintosh	`http://www.westciv.com/style_master/`

Cascade

Cascade is a compact and very usable CSS editor for the Windows 95/NT platforms from Balthisar Software. It's just been rewritten entirely from scratch, so the currently available version is the most up-to-date. It includes a WYSIWYG interface that allows you to create style rules for HTML elements as well as your own elements, so it is readily useable for the creation of XML documents. This nice piece of shareware provides you with an easy way to create syntactically correct CSS style sheets as well as to learn about CSS along the way. To read more about Cascade and to download a free copy, point your Web browser at `http://www.balthisar.com/html/cascade_2.0_section.html`.

StyleMaker

StyleMaker is a shareware product from Danere Software for the Windows 95/NT platforms. Its intuitive interface allows you to formulate style rules and then preview the affect they will have on your document, as shown in Figure 27.10.

You may wonder what kind of results you'll get by combining certain style properties and values as well as how style rule inheritance will affect the final display of your document. Using StyleMaker you'll never need to wonder again. Another advantage to using a CSS editor like StyleMaker is that you don't have to worry about accidentally forgetting a colon or semicolon in your style sheet. StyleMaker uses all of the properties and values supported by the leading Web browsers as well as CSS positioning. To read more about StyleMaker and to download a demo version, visit `http://danere.com/StyleMaker/`.

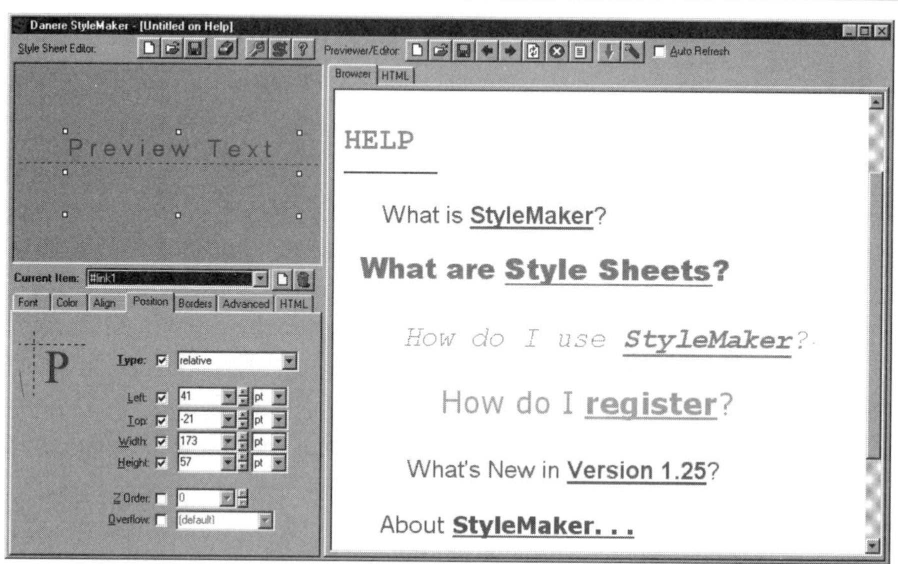

FIGURE 27.10: The StyleMaker interface

StyleMaster

StyleMaster is a Macintosh CSS editor from Western Civilization that helps you design and implement style sheets for both your Web and XML pages. One of StyleMaster's more unique capabilities is that it allows you to create style sheets targeted for specific browsers or for all browsers that support style sheets. If you're working on a style sheet for an intranet, you can take advantage of those styles only supported by your local browser. If you're working on a style sheet that will be viewed by a variety of users across the Internet, however, StyleMaster will help you create style sheets that are safe for all CSS-compatible browsers. This editor also allows you to preview your styled documents in any browser you have installed on your computer directly from within the editor. To find out more about StyleMaster or to download a demo copy, visit the StyleMaster site at `http://www.westciv.com/style_master/`. The StyleMaster Web page is shown in Figure 27.11.

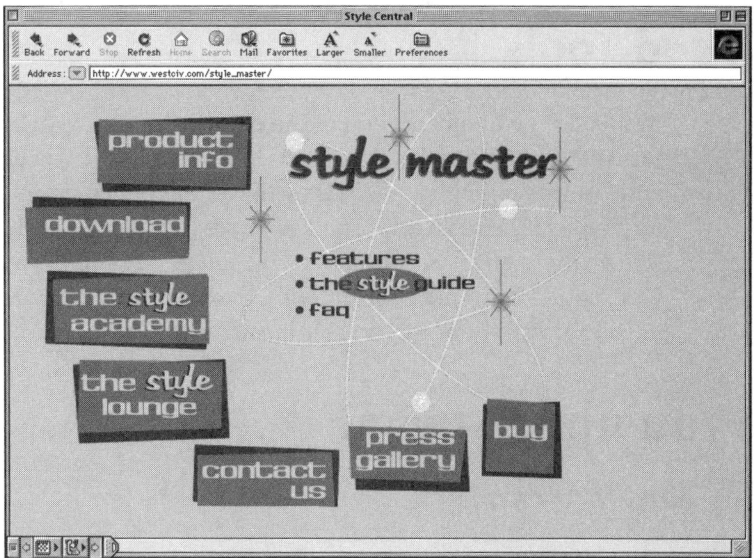

FIGURE 27.11: The StyleMaster information Web page

HTML Editors with Built-In CSS Support

Many HTML editors also have CSS support built right into them, including

- HoTMetaL Pro from Softquad
  `http://www.softquad.com/`
- Dreamweaver from Macromedia
  `http://www.macromedia.com/software/dreamweaver/`
- FrontPage 98 from Microsoft
  `http://www.microsoft.com/frontpage/`
- HotDog from Sausage Software
  `http://www.sausage.com/soft1.htm#hotdog`
- QuickSite 3 from Site Technologies
  `http://www.sitetech.com/QuickSite3.0/qsintroduction.html`

Good Resources Are Just As Important As Good Tools

In this skill, you met several of the best XML development tools available on the market today. With the right set of tools, your XML development will be easier and your documents and DTDs will contain fewer errors. Although your tools are some of the most important XML resources you can have, you'll also need to know where on and off the Web you can go to keep up with the ever-changing world of XML. In Skill 28, "Finding the Best XML Resources," you'll learn all you need to know about locating and using key XML resources.

Are You up to Speed?

Now you can...

- ☑ **Explain how software tools can make XML development easier**
- ☑ **Describe the currently available XML parsers and editors**
- ☑ **Locate the best XSL and CSS editors**

SKILL 28

Finding the Best XML Resources

- **Working with XML as a developing technology**
- **The top five XML Web resources**
- **Participating in XML mailing lists and newsgroups**
- **Collection of XML resources in print**

XML is a newborn technology, and you can bet it will change significantly as it matures. Growing pains are to be expected. As you work with XML and make it part of your information dissemination solution, you'll need to have at your disposal the best online and offline resources available. When you know where to turn for the latest and most accurate information, you'll be more able to anticipate changes in the technology and adjust your XML products accordingly. This skill serves as a guided tour to the key online XML resources and includes some tips and tricks for building your own paper-based collection of resources outside of cyberspace.

Remember: XML Is a Developing Technology

If you've spent any time at all working with Internet and Web technologies, you know that nothing ever stays the same for very long. If you're relatively new to the wonderful world of the Web, then my disclaimers about the volatility of the XSL specification in Skill 16, "Converting XML to HTML with XSL," provided you with a brief insight into the regular goings-on of the Web and the tendency of its technologies to change in a heartbeat. There's no real solution to the problem except to get used to this quickly changing landscape and to arm yourself to deal with it.

Luckily, the Web itself makes it possible for a wide variety of resources to be posted and updated in a relatively short period of time. In addition, your local bookstore most likely carries a large number of computer and Internet-related works (much like this one) that can serve as both learning and reference tools. There definitely isn't a shortage of information, but that's not always a good thing.

One of the most difficult things about using the Web and printed materials as resources and references is sorting through all of the fluff to get to the good stuff. A search on "XML" at `www.infoseek.com` finds over 9,000 Web pages, whereas the same search at `www.altavista.digital.com` comes up with over 23,000 possible Web resources. Just digging through the results from the search engine can take more time than a busy developer has.

As you work with any technology for an extended period of time, you find those resources, both online and offline, that you come to rely on as the best and most accurate repositories of the most up-to-date information. The process of finding these resources can literally take months, if not years, and more often than not, you don't have the luxury of that much time when you're working with a new technology. The remaining sections of this skill are designed to save you those months and years and point you to the best and brightest XML resources around.

At the time of publication, all of the information in this skill, from URLs to newsgroup and mailing-list information, was up-to-date and correct. Because it is the nature of the Web to change from day to day, I can't promise that all of these resources will be available indefinitely. However, I am confident that the majority of these resources will be maintained and serve as quality sources of information for quite a while.

Take Advantage of Online Resources

Possibly the best source of current and accurate XML information is the Web. Publishing on the Web is much less expensive than publishing in print, and it's easier to update information on a Web site than in a book or magazine. In addition, several of the developing XML information Web sites are actually using XML to deliver their content. These sites not only provide useful resources but are good examples of XML at work.

The Web isn't the only Internet-based information resource that is a good source of XML information. Usenet newsgroups (a bulletin board–like system that allows users to read and post messages about different topics) and mailing lists (e-mail distribution programs that send copies of e-mail messages to everyone who has subscribed to the list) are two ways XML developers can ask questions of and share ideas with other developers around the world. The following sections look at the different types of online resources you have to choose from, explain how they work and what you'll need to access them, and highlight the best-of-breed resources of each type.

The Top Five XML Sites to Watch

New XML Web sites are springing up left and right every day. Although this is a good indicator that XML is here to stay and will soon be a moving force within the Internet and Web world, it also means that it's becoming harder to root out resources you can trust. My work on this book and other XML projects has caused me to look for quality resources from one side of the Web to the other. In this section, I'll introduce you to my five favorite XML Web sites. They are all included in my bookmark collection, and I make a point of visiting them on a weekly basis just to see what's new. In general, I find that these sites

- Include useful and accurate information
- Are updated frequently

- Keep up with the pace of XML's rapid development
- Are well organized, well designed, and easy to use
- Are maintained by individuals or groups committed to the development of XML as a nonproprietary standard

Site 1: The World Wide Web Consortium's XML Page

Because the W3C is the governing body for the XML standard it only makes sense that their collection of XML Web pages would be at the top of the list. Shown in Figure 28.1, and found on the Web at `http://www.w3.org/XML/`, the W3C's XML page includes a timeline of the most recent XML-related events as well as links to specifications and press releases.

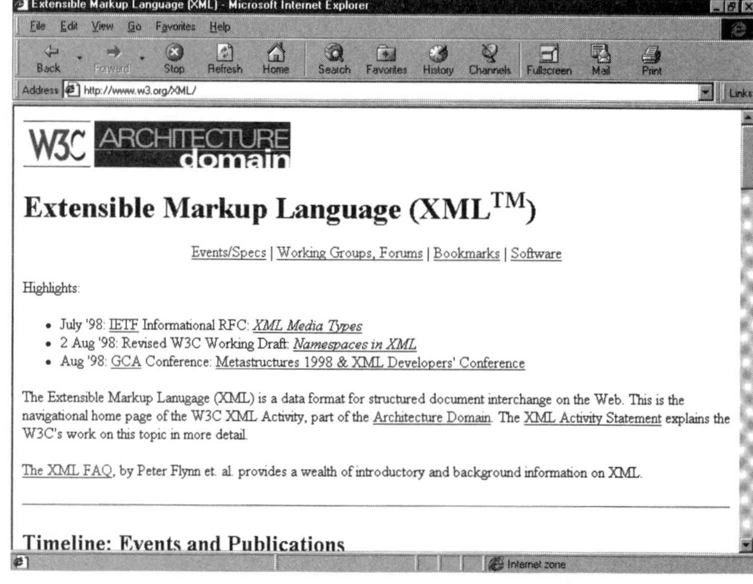

FIGURE 28.1: The World Wide Web Consortium's XML Web page

One of the most important features of the W3C's online XML resources is the timeline. It highlights the important events and changes associated with XML. If you want to know how recently a specification was released or when to expect a new release, then look to this portion of the page. The W3C also keeps tabs on the latest XML Web sites and software, although their listing isn't always as up-to-date as others described in this chapter. Finally, whenever new versions of specifications are released, they are always announced and posted first at this site. It's well worth your while to take a few minutes once a week to visit this site to see what's new in the world of XML.

Site 2: James Tauber's XMLINFO.COM

During my XML research and writing activities, I find myself returning to this well-designed and information-rich Web site at `http://www.xmlinfo.com/`. Maintained by James Tauber, an active member of the XML development community, XMLINFO.COM includes a variety of XML resources, including sections on both XSL and XLL as well as how people are already using XML. Figure 28.2 provides a brief glimpse at the beginning of this incredible site.

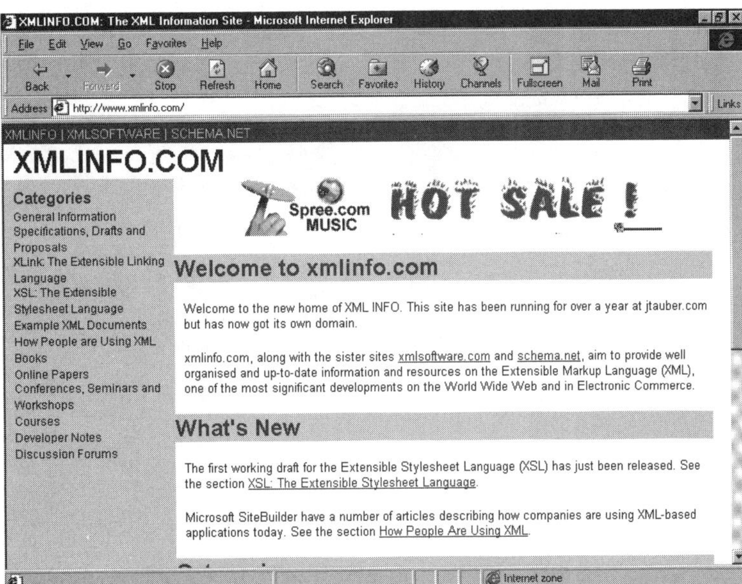

FIGURE 28.2: James Tauber's XMLINFO.COM site

In addition to links to basic XML resources, the site also includes the most comprehensive listing of XML books, conferences, courses, and developer notes that I've found to date anywhere on the Web. Tauber is devout in his maintenance of the site and updates it on a regular basis. The site always includes information on the most recent developments in the XML world along with relevant links to other sites and resources on the Web.

XMLINFO.COM also has two sister sites, XMLSOFTWARE.COM and SCHEMA.NET. The first is dedicated to collecting information about XML-related software and includes links to XML editors, parsers, XSL style-sheet creators, and complete document management systems. The second site, SCHEMA.NET, is a listing of all of the XML vocabularies currently under development. It divides the vocabularies into groups by type, provides a description of each vocabulary, and links to the vocabulary's specification (when available) and other relevant resources.

Site 3: Robin Cover's XML Resources

If you're looking for the most complete listing of available XML resources to be found in cyberspace or the real world, then you'll want to visit `http://www.oasis-open.org/cover/xml.html`, shown in Figure 28.3.

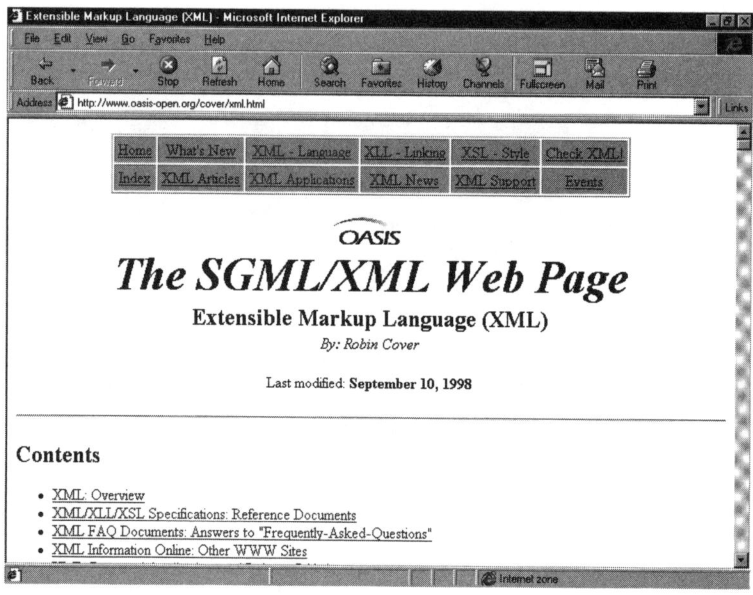

FIGURE 28.3: Robin Cover's XML Resources site

Think of this site as the ultimate XML hotlist. The site (in reality, a very long single document) divides its myriad links to XML resources into several categories, including XML overviews, specification information, FAQs, books, articles, software, and other specific groupings. Although many of the other XML Web sites focus on a few important types of information, Cover's listing includes links to all resources related to XML in any way. This site is particularly useful if you're looking for information on a specific topic, like XML/SGML Namespaces or XML Media/MIME Types. Be forewarned that the site can take a while to load, simply because it is a single document. However, once loaded, it is an invaluable resource.

Site 4: XML.com

Sponsored by two heavy hitters in the publishing industry, O'Reilly and Seybold, XML.com is another excellent source of useful XML resources. Found at `http://www.xml.com` and shown in Figure 28.4, this site includes several one-of-a-kind resources you won't find anywhere else on the Web.

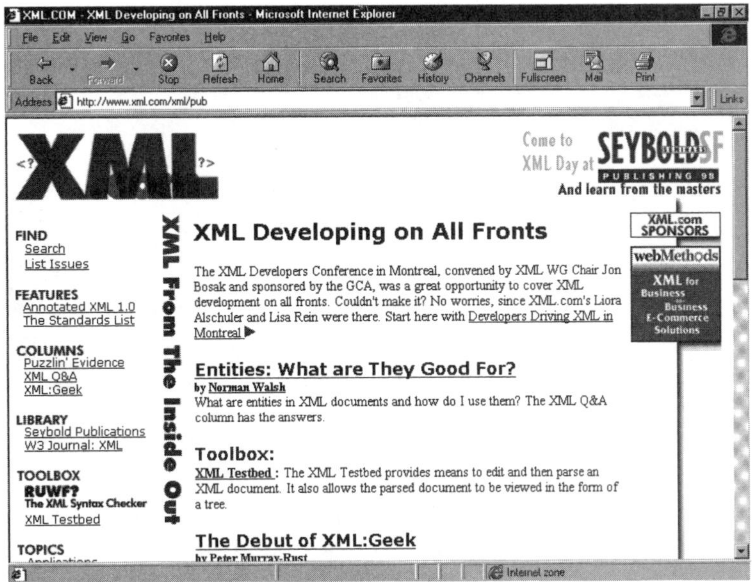

FIGURE 28.4: XML.com

Because publishers maintain the site, it includes a list of magazine articles about XML published in Seybold publications at `http://www.xml.com/SeyboldReport/index.html`. Two of the site's most extraordinary sections are an annotated version of the XML specification and an XML syntax checker.

Tim Bray, one of the editors of the official XML specification, created the annotated XML specification for XML.com. Shown in Figure 28.5, the annotated version of the specification provides a roadmap and lengthy explanations of each element in the specification.

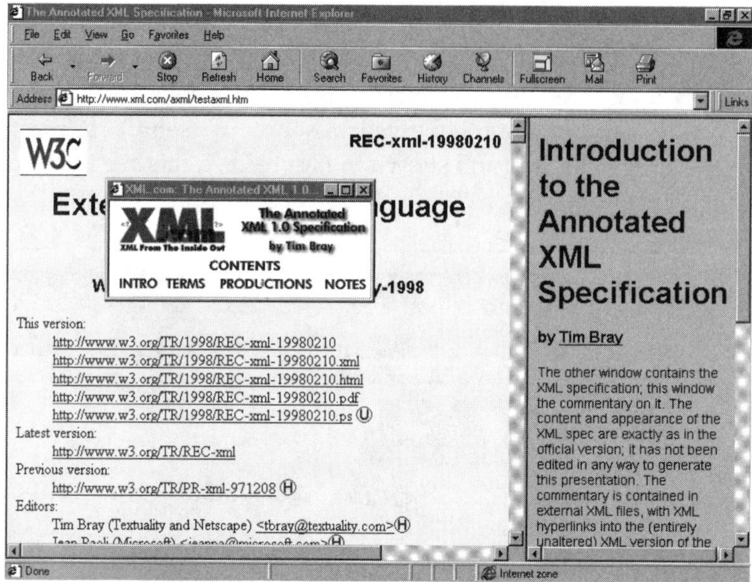

FIGURE 28.5: Tim Bray's annotated XML specification at XML.com

This framed presentation includes a copy of the specification, as you'd see it in at the W3C in the left frame and a running description of the various pieces and parts of the specification in the right frame. A floating navigation window provides a quick and easy way to move around within the specification. All and all a very nice tool, and if you've never read a specification before, you'll want to start here.

In addition to the annotated specification, XML.com also includes RUWF? (are you well formed?), an XML syntax checker. This valuable tool will check to make sure that your XML documents are well formed, and it will spit out a list of errors that you can use to fix the document and ensure that it will be processed correctly by a parser. To use RUWF? simply enter the URL of the document to be checked in the text field on the page, as shown in Figure 28.6, and click the RUWF? button. It's really that simple.

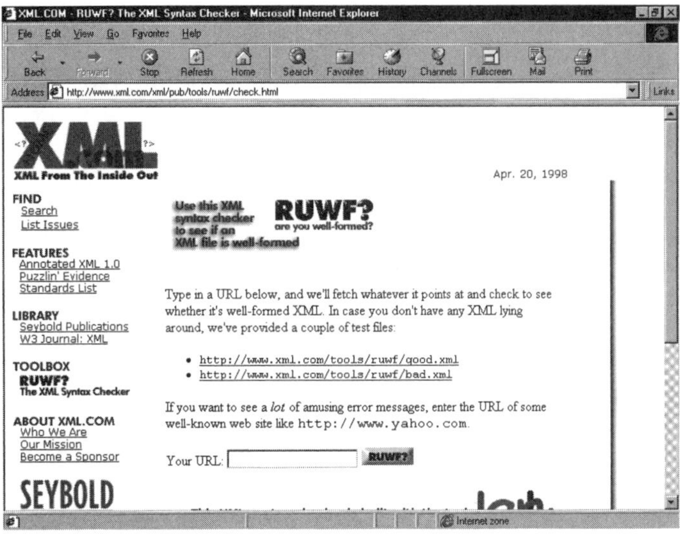

FIGURE 28.6: The RUWF? syntax checker at XML.com

XML.com also includes links to other XML sites as well as book reviews, information about using Java and Perl with XML, information on the various XML applications, and more. New to XML.com is the XML Testbed, shown in Figure 28.7.

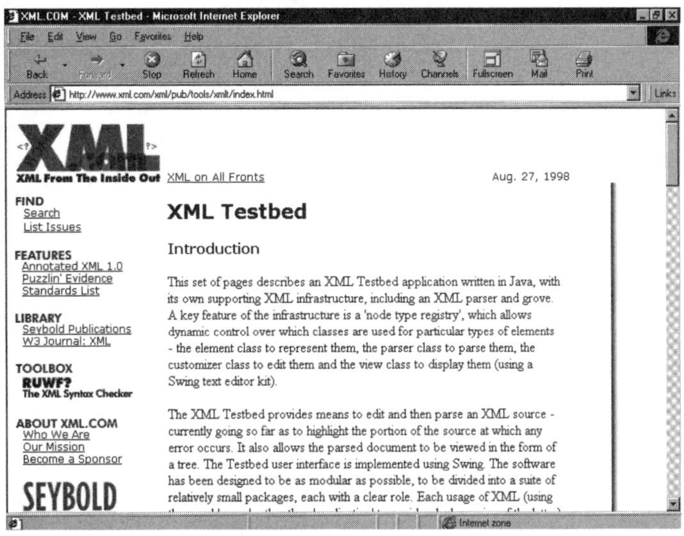

FIGURE 28.7: The XML Testbed at XML.com

Created in Java, the testbed allows you to parse an XML document and see the output in a tree-structured hierarchy. This is useful if you're learning about XML documents or are thinking about writing your own XML processing application. You'll have to have a Java runtime environment (like a Web browser) to run the Java applet in, and it's only just now being developed, so look for later releases to have more functionality than the current one does.

All in all, XML.com is a resource-rich site with a commitment to providing quality XML tools in addition to text-based resources. Because it's backed by Seybold and O'Reilly, it should have an extended shelf life and is updated frequently as things change in the XML world. So, if you haven't done so, visit XML.com right now and take a look around.

Site 5: Microsoft's XML Resources

Although it's not often that I count a vendor's Web site as one of my most useful resources for any topic because they are usually focused on a product and not a technology, I have to make an exception this time. Microsoft is committed to supporting XML as a major industry initiative. To that end, the Microsoft Site Builder site includes a variety of very useful XML resources, including a well-designed FAQ, shown in Figure 28.8.

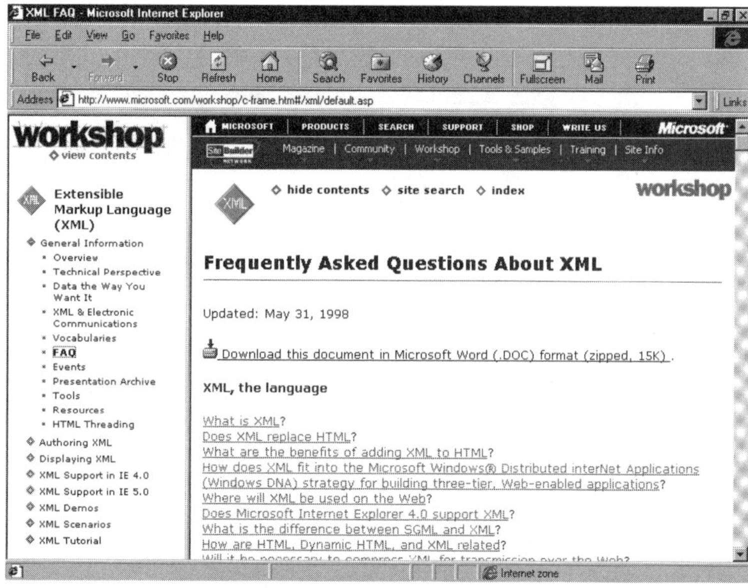

FIGURE 28.8: The FAQ at the Microsoft Site Builder XML site

The Microsoft site also includes an XML tutorial, white papers, demos, and links to other online XML resources. Microsoft's ultimate goal is to use XML as part of its Web-based applications development solution, so the resources at this site also include quite a bit of advanced information about creating applications with XML. Be aware that the solutions described at the site rely 100 percent on Microsoft technologies and are not designed to work on non-PC platforms, operating systems other than Windows, or with browsers other than Internet Explorer. However, if you're looking to learn more about advanced applications of XML and what it takes to create them and put them into place in the real world, the Microsoft site has quite a bit of useful information that you can use as a starting point: `http://www.microsoft.com/xml/default.asp`.

The Best Sources for Specifications

All of the sites just listed are good places to find the current version of many of the XML-related specifications, including XSL and XLink. Of course, the definitive resource is the W3C's XML pages. Throughout the book I've referenced this site time and again as *the* place to find a particular specification or another. To recap (and to list them all together in one convenient and easy to find place), here are the URLs for the key XML specifications that you'll need to reference as you work with XML:

- The XML 1.0 Specification
  `http://www.w3.org/TR/REC-xml`
- The XSL Working Draft
  `http://www.w3.org/TR/WD-xsl`
- The XLink Working Draft
  `http://www.w3.org/TR/WD-xlink`
- The XPointer Working Draft
  `http://www.w3.org/TR/WD-xptr`
- The HTML 4.0 Specification
  `http://www.w3.org/TR/REC-html40`
- The CSS-2 Specification
  `http://www.w3.org/TR/REC-CSS2`

Many of the XML vocabularies, such as CDF and SMIL discussed in Part IV of the book, are notes to the W3C or have made it to the working draft or even recommendation level. For a complete listing of all the notes, working drafts, and recommendations governed by the W3C, point your Web browser at `http://www.w3.org/TR/`. Visit this page about once a month to see whether the status of the particular vocabularies or specifications that you are working with has changed.

Some Final Words on Specifications

Before leaving the discussion of specifications behind, let me once more refer you to Tim Bray's annotated version of the XML specification, discussed a few sections earlier in this skill. Specification-speak can be a bit difficult to read and takes a bit of getting used to. Bray's annotated version lets you get your feet wet in the specification pool before diving in headfirst. From past experience, I can say that your first attempt to read a specification can leave you feeling like you've drowned in geek-speak and DTD lingo.

Also let me point out that specifications, although developed and maintained by a standards body, are not requirements that vendors must follow but, instead, are a set of guidelines that, if followed, will make interoperability among applications and data easier. Always read the documentation for any XML processing application that you are working with to see whether it follows the relevant specifications to the letter or whether it has incorporated its own proprietary elements. I encourage you to choose and use those tools that abide by the guidelines set down in the specifications and do your best to follow them when developing your own XML projects.

Joining Mailing Lists and Newsgroups

Although the Web is the most prevalent source of XML information, it is not the only online alternative for finding useful and timely XML information. The content of Web pages tends to be largely posted text and graphics, unless the page provides the front end to a tool like the RUWF? syntax checker, and then the content is largely form-based. On the other hand, the content you'll find within mailing lists and newsgroups consists primarily of the musings of other human beings much like yourself.

Mailing Lists

A mailing list is comprised of subscribers who send e-mail to each other by way of a mail server running a special mailing-list program (usually called a listserv or majordomo). The program sends each piece of mail it receives to all of the subscribers on the list. This makes it possible for one person to e-mail a thousand other people via one e-mail address. Mailing lists are always organized around a particular subject, such as XML or XSL, and are designed to foster frequent discussions among the mailing-list members about different issues and topics related to the general subject. As a member of the mailing list, you can ask questions, share your thoughts and ideas, and respond to other members' questions and comments. There are certain spoken and unspoken rules you'll need to abide by when you become part of a mailing list. If you're new to the world of mailing lists, see the sidebar "Mailing List and Newsgroup Etiquette" for some important advice that will keep you from accidentally winding up with virtual egg on your face.

There are several XML-related mailing lists that you can join to take part in discussions about the development of XML. Many of the major players in the XML world, including some of the members of the various XML working groups, participate regularly in the mailing-list discussions. The W3C maintains a variety of mailing lists for the discussion of all the technologies they govern.

The one mailing list maintained by the W3C that will be most useful to an XML developer is the `www-style` mailing list. The list focuses on the issues that surround the use of style sheets on the Web, and because both CSS and XSL are key factors in bringing XML to the Web, much of what is discussed on this mailing list is of use and interest to XML developers. To subscribe to the mailing list, send an e-mail message to `www-style-request@w3.org` with a subject of "subscribe" and nothing in the body. You will receive an acknowledgment message that includes important information about the newsgroup and its posting requirements. Read this message carefully, and save it for later reference. If you'd like to see what topics have been discussed recently on this newsgroup, you can visit the archive online at `http://lists.w3.org/Archives/Public/www-style/`.

Watch the W3C's listing of newsgroups at `http://www.w3.org/Mail/Lists.html` for the establishment of future XML-related mailing lists. Other XML related mailing lists include

`XML-L` A general XML discussion list. To subscribe, send an e-mail message to `LISTSERV@listserv.hea.ie` with "subscribe XML-L *firstname lastname*" in the body of the message.

`XSL-LIST` A general XSL discussion list. To subscribe, send an e-mail message to `majordomo@mulberrytech.com` with "subscribe xsl-list" in the body of the message. Visit the list's information page at `http://www.mulberrytech.com/xsl/xsl-list`.

`XML-DEV` A technically oriented mailing list for XML developers. To subscribe, send an e-mail message to `majordomo@ic.ac.uk` with "subscribe xml-dev-digest" in the body of the message. Visit the list's information page at `http://www.vsms.nottingham.ac.uk/vsms/xml/jewels.html`.

Both the XMLINFO.COM site and Robin Cover's site have specific sections on XML-related mailing lists. Keep an eye on them to find out when new mailing lists are set up.

Mailing-List and Newsgroup Etiquette

If you've never participated in a mailing list or newsgroup, there are a few matters of etiquette, often called Netiquette, that you'll want to be aware of.

- It's customary to "lurk" on the list or group for a while before you begin posting or responding to messages. Lurking involves hanging out behind the scenes and reading the messages and posts without actually participating. This will help you to get a feel for the type and tone of messages common to the list or group and help you decide whether the list or group is the right forum for your questions and comments. When you are ready to post, you'll be more apt to post an appropriate and well-worded question or response.
- Read the FAQ for the list or group to review those common questions asked and answered time and again. It may be that many of your questions or comments are addressed in the FAQ, and you won't have to waste valuable time and bandwidth asking what's already been asked many times. The members of lists and groups are willing to help you with almost any topic-related question or problem, but if you ask a question already in the FAQ, you'll most likely get the equivalent of the Internet cold shoulder: e-mail silence.

continued ▸

- Don't respond with rude or insulting messages to those list or group members whose opinions you don't agree with. This type of behavior is called "flaming" and is the fastest way to be kicked off of a list or barred from posting to a group. Always be polite and respectful in your posts and responses and you can expect the same from other members of the list or group.
- Only post questions or comments directly related to the list or group's topic. If you are exchanging posts with another member of the list or group and your discussion becomes personal or off-topic, move it to private e-mail.

One final word about posting to newsgroups and mailing lists: advertisements are a no-no. There's nothing that will raise the hackles of all the list members faster than unsolicited advertisements, regardless of what you're selling or how useful you may think it is to them. In general, if you use good common sense when interacting with other members of newsgroups or mailing lists, you'll find that your experience with them will be both fun and informative.

Newsgroups

Newsgroups are like electronic bulletin boards where you can read and post messages about different topics. The number and focus of newsgroups has grown in the last several years, and you can now post messages about everything from waterskiing to XML development. To view and post to a newsgroup, you'll need two things:

- A news feed
- A news reader

You can usually get a news feed from your ISP. The number and type of newsgroups supported by ISPs varies from place to place, but you can usually count on being able to receive and post to technically oriented newsgroups like the ones related to XML development. To find out more about which newsgroups you have access to and how to access them, check directly with your ISP.

To read and post to newsgroups, you'll need a news reader. This is a piece of software that understands the protocol that governs newsgroups—NNTP—and provides you with an interface to read and post message to any given newsgroup. Most of the major Web browsers from versions 3 and later have newsgroup support built right in. Microsoft Outlook and Outlook Express both have news support, and there are a variety of stand-alone news readers you can download for all platforms and operating systems. If you don't have a news reader built into your Web browser or e-mail package, you can visit `http://www.tucows.com` or `http://www.shareware.com` to download one for free or little cost.

There are currently two newsgroups that focus on topics of interest to XML developers: `comp.text.sgml` and `comp.text.xml`. In addition, Microsoft maintains a publicly available XML newsgroup that focuses on the use of XML with Microsoft technologies: `microsoft.public.xml`. Finally, the newsgroup `comp.infosystems.www.authoring.html` includes discussions about all aspects of Web page development including, but not limited to, XML.

To read the messages for any of these newsgroups, simply subscribe to the newsgroup, and see what nuggets of information you can find. Figure 28.9 shows a sample listing of the messages in `comp.text.sgml` newsgroup as displayed by the Outlook Express newsreader.

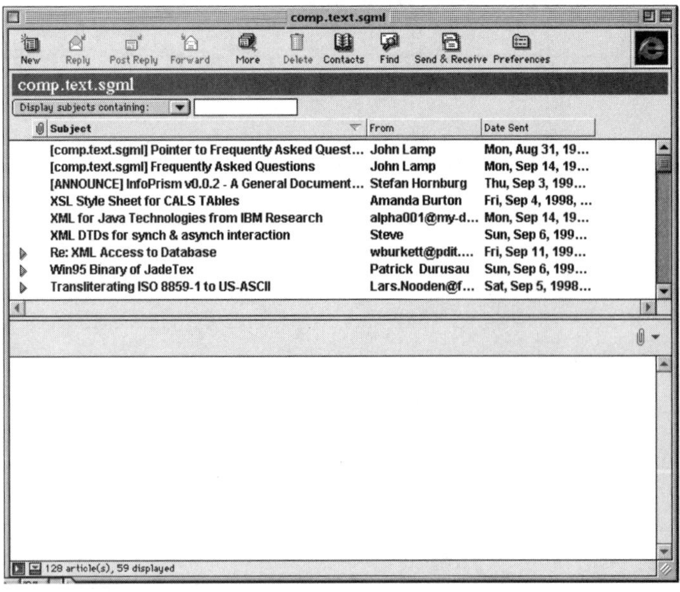

FIGURE 28.9: The `comp.text.sgml` newsgroup listing as displayed by Outlook Express

Note that the first two messages in the list are pointers to FAQs for the mailing list. Make sure to read these before posting any messages to the list.

Collecting Offline XML Resources

The Web isn't the only place you can find solid XML resources and useful XML information. Indeed, there are many books and articles already in print that can provide you with a quality library of reference material you can thumb through on the spot. The next two sections take a look at how you should go about establishing your own XML library and what to look for when you visit the magazine rack at your local newsstand.

Establish Your Own XML Library

There are many different kinds of XML books already out on the market, each with its own particular slant on XML and XML development. It's often difficult to find a set of books that's right for you. If you're just reading about XML to see what all the fuss is about, then this book should meet your needs well. If you're planning on moving into the complex world of XML development, you'll want to arm yourself with a more formidable collection of XML literature.

In general, when you're shopping for books to fill your XML library, you'll want to have at least one introduction to XML (this book is perfect!) and then two or more intermediate and advanced books that focus on a particular area of XML development that you're interested in. In addition, you might want to pick up a good set of Java and scripting books because it's doubtful that your final XML solution will be independent of programming.

The best place to start looking for additional XML offerings is at `http://www.amazon.com/`. If you search for XML titles, you'll find a variety of listings that include a synopsis and purchase information for the book as well as reader reviews and comments from the authors and publisher. Figure 28.10 shows the results from a recent search I performed at amazon.com on the subject XML.

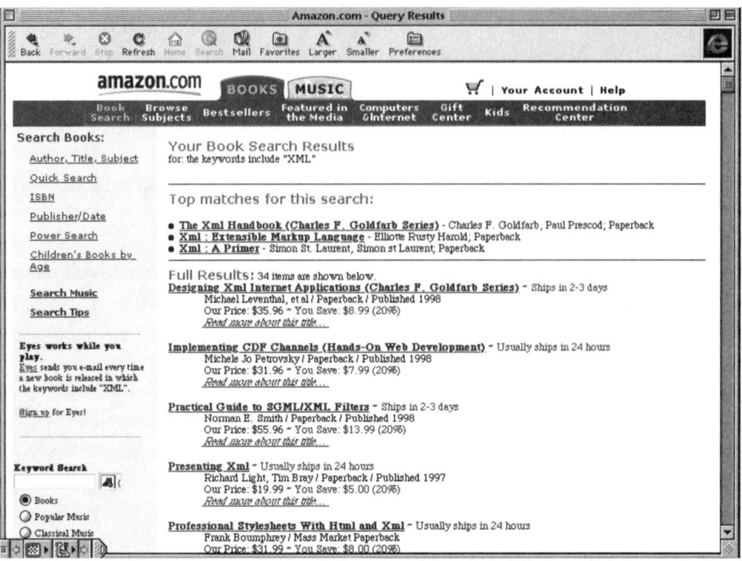

FIGURE 28.10: The results of an XML search at amazon.com

Frequent the Trade Magazine Newsstand

One of the best resources for up-to-date print information are the trade magazines you'll find at your local bookstore or newsstand. There are so many to choose from these days, and it's just not practical to subscribe to them all. Instead, I recommend dedicating a couple of hours one Sunday a month to visit your favorite magazine stand for some constructive browsing. Grab a stack of Internet and Web trade mags, take a seat in one of the inevitable chairs most bookstores include, and start flipping. If you see an article of interest, especially one that includes sample source code, links to useful Web sites, or a step-by-step how-to, purchase it and take it home to read in detail.

A good collection of magazine articles can provide you with a reference as complete as many of the books you can buy, and the articles are usually more up-to-date than any book can be. If you keep your article collection well organized and even cataloged, you'll find that you can lay your hands on useful and important information almost instantaneously. Some of the magazines you'll want to watch for are

- *Inter@ctive Week*
- *Internet Magazine*
- *Internet Professional*
- *Internet World*
- *Web Developers Journal*

The End

And we're finally here. I hope you've enjoyed the ride as much as I have. Thanks for sticking with me through it all, and I am confident that you're well informed about the wonders and realities of XML and have the knowledge you need to consider XML as a potential solution to your information dissemination needs. Always remember that by itself, XML can't do much, but when you team it up with a quality data collection and good interface, its applications are virtually limitless.

Are You up to Speed?

Now you can...

- ☑ **Explain why it's important to keep up with the latest XML developments**
- ☑ **Describe the five best online resources**
- ☑ **Discuss mailing lists and newsgroups as information resources**
- ☑ **Compile an XML book and article collection that meets your individual needs**

GLOSSARY

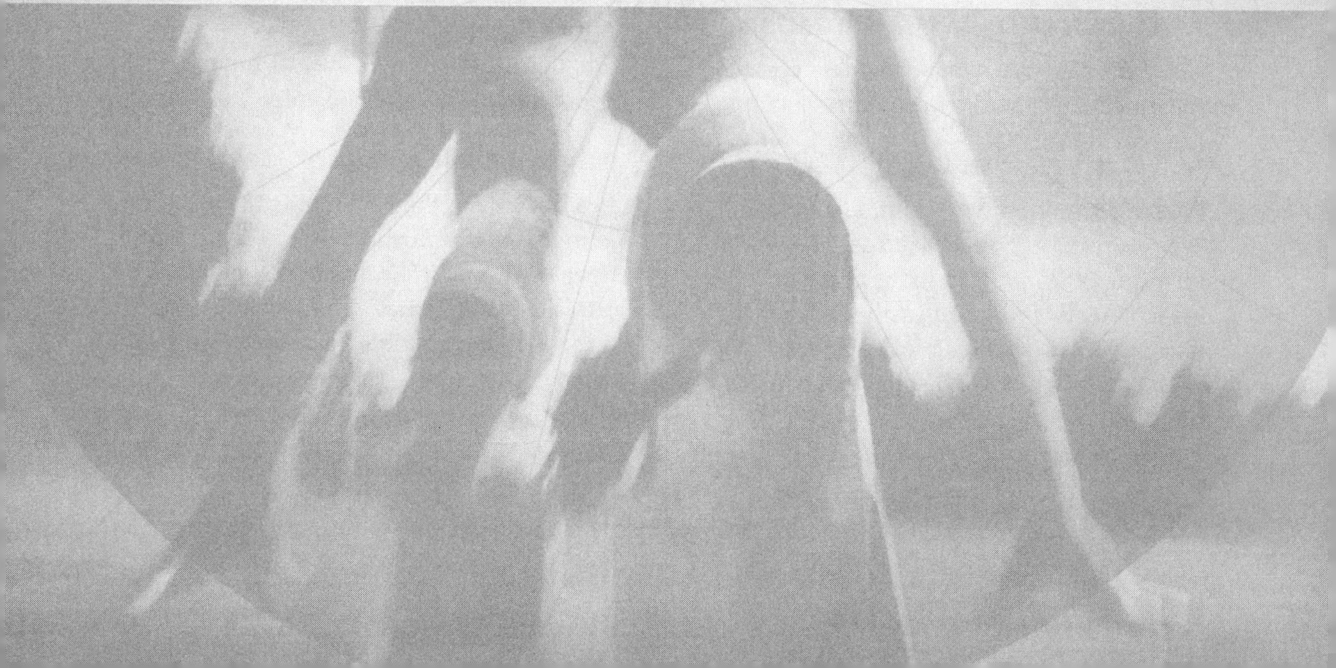

a

action

The part of an XSL or DSSSL style rule that specifies how the rule's pattern (element) should be formatted.

Active channel

A technology adopted by Microsoft and others that uses the XML CDF (Channel Definition Language) vocabulary to define channels of regularly updated Web-based information. Users can subscribe to channels using CDF-compliant browsers, such as Internet Explorer.

ActiveX control

A lite version of an OLE (Object Linking and Embedding) control. The control's size and speed have been optimized for use over the Internet. ActiveX controls provide added functionality to both Web environments and regular desktop environments.

API (Application Program Interface)

A software interface that provides access to the functions of another program.

ASP (Active Server Page)

A Web programming technique that links Web pages to back-end databases using scripting. ASP configurations allow developers to store their content easily and logically in a database and dynamically generate a Web page template to display that content via the Web.

attribute

A component of an XML or HTML element that provides additional information about a specific instance of the element. The attributes you can use with any given element are predefined within a DTD. `SRC=` is an attribute of the `<IMG>` tag.

attribute-list declaration

The notation in a DTD that specifies which attributes can be used with which elements and the type and values of those attributes.

attribute name

The character string used in both DTDs and documents to refer to an attribute. The name of the hypertext reference element used with the `ANCHOR` (`<A>`) tag in HTML is `HREF`.

attribute specification

The individual listing for an attribute in an attribute-list declaration.

attribute type

Within the attribute specification, it's the notation that identifies the attribute as an enumerated, string, or tokenized attribute.

attribute value

In a document, the attribute value is the value assigned to the attribute by the document developer for each individual instance of the attribute. Within the attribute specification, it's a list of all the possible values for an attribute.

b

binary entity

An entity that references any file that's not an XML-encoded resource. Audio, video, and graphics files are all examples of binary entities.

box properties

In CSS, box properties are the collection of properties and values that control the formatting of the margins, padding, height, width, and border aspects of any element.

c

CDF (Channel Definition Format)

An XML DTD that sets up server-push channels for routine delivery of Web-based information to users.

CGI (Common Gateway Interface)

Computer programs or scripts that run on a Web server and connect Web pages with back-end applications, such as databases and image map utilities.

channel

See *Active channel*.

character data

All of the text, other than markup, contained in an element in XML documents. For an element to contain character data, the element's definition with the DTD must include `CDATA` in its content model. All elements do not necessarily have to contain character data.

character entity

A virtual storage location referenced in an XML document that associates a text string with a non-ASCII character and causes the non-ASCII character to be displayed by the processing application. For example, the character entity `©` represents the copyright symbol (©).

CHILD element

An element that is nested (contained) within another element.

classification properties

In CSS, classification properties are the collection of properties and values that control the formatting of white space and lists.

CML (Chemical Markup Language)

An XML DTD that describes chemistry formulas and data.

comments

Content in both XML DTDs and documents (contained within <!– and –> tags) that is ignored by an XML processor.

construction rule

The base element of an XSL style sheet. A construction rule contains the formatting instructions for any given element within an XML document. Also called a *template rule*.

content

Anything, including other elements, character data, and entities, found between the `START` and `END` tags of an element.

content-based markup

Markup that describes content intended to be read and processed by a computer to accomplish a task instead of displayed for a user. The Open Software Description (OSD) vocabulary, which is designed to describe software packages to be installed by a server across a network, is an example of content-based markup.

content model

In a DTD, the definition of the content (element or character) that can be nested within any given element.

CSS (Cascading Style Sheets)

A style-sheet mechanism designed to govern how HTML and XML documents are displayed by display mechanisms, such as browsers. CSS is a W3C standard that is currently in its second version (CSS2).

d

default rule

An XSL convention that describes how all elements not governed by specific construction rules should be formatted.

document element

The main element of an XML document that contains all of the document's other elements and their content. The document element for an HTML document is `<HTML>...</HTML>`.

document-type declaration

A markup convention that associates an XML document with its corresponding document-type definition (DTD). The document-type declaration is often referred to as the `<!DOCTYPE>` declaration.

DOM (Document Object Model)

The way processing applications and programming languages view an XML document. The DOM represents the document's elements and content as a series of objects in a hierarchical tree that the application or programming language can easily access and manipulate.

DSSSL (Document-Style Semantics and Specification Language)

A style-sheet mechanism originally designed for the Standard Generalized Markup Language (SGML). DSSSL is an ISO standard and an established tool for specifying how documents described by advanced markup languages should be formatted when displayed by various devices, such as Web browsers or printers.

DTD (document-type definition)

A specification for an SGML or HTML document that specifies structural elements and markup definitions that can be used to create documents that describe content.

e

element

A markup convention that refers to a markup tag and the text contained within the tag. The elements (tags) that may be used within any given document to describe text are defined in the document's related DTD.

element content

A description of the elements that can be nested within any given element within an XML document. The specific element content for an individual tag is defined for each element within the document's DTD.

element declaration

The notation within a DTD that specifies which element's documents associated with the DTD can be used to describe content. Element declarations also include a content model for each element that specifies which other elements and data can be contained within the element.

EMPTY element

An XML element that cannot contain data. EMPTY elements are singleton tags rather than tag pairs.

entity

A virtual storage unit that associates a unique name with the content of the storage unit. Entities can be used to store XML text and markup (text entities), binary data, such as audio or graphics files (binary entities), or non-ASCII characters (character entities). When an entity is referenced in an XML file, the entity's content replaces the reference.

extended link

An XLink convention that defines a hyperlink stored in an external file and that allows you to express a relationship between two or more resources.

extended link groups

An XLink convention that stores the definitions of a collection of extended links together in one group.

external DTD subset

The portion of a document's DTD that is stored in an external file. The external DTD subset usually contains the bulk of the DTD and is stored in its own file so it can be referenced by a large number of documents.

external entity

An external entity stores information in a file located outside of the document that references the entity. External entities can contain text, binary data, or character data.

fixed attribute

An attribute whose value cannot be changed by the document developer. If an attribute is designated as fixed and its value in a document is other than the value specified by the DTD, the document is invalid.

flow object

An XSL convention that contains the specific information about how the content of an element within a document should be formatted. Construction rules link flow objects to their elements.

font properties

In CSS, font properties are the collection of properties and values that control the fonts used in the display of a document.

g

GedML (Genealogical Data in XML)

An XML DTD that provides a description format for genealogical data.

h

hexadecimal color-notation system

The notation system designed to define color values for attributes in HTML documents. The hexadecimal system is based on the RGB (Red-Green-Blue) method for describing color.

HTML (Hypertext Markup Language)

A markup language for describing the content in documents on the World Wide Web.

HTTP (Hypertext Transfer Protocol)

The protocol that governs the way client computers request and receive HTML documents from a Web server.

inline link

An XLink convention that describes where the content of the linking element acts as a resource. An example of such a link is a link created using the HTML <A> tag.

internal DTD subset

The portion of a document's DTD that is included within the document. The internal DTD subset contains information that is specific to the document, such as text and binary entities, as well as adjustments to the DTD that will affect only the individual document.

internal entity

An entity that contains information stored in the entity declaration itself. Internal entities can contain only text or character data.

intranet

A private network, usually internal to a company or organization, that is built on the same standards and protocols as the Internet.

Java

An objected-oriented application programming language developed by Sun Microsystems. Whereas Java is not used exclusively for Web programming, a large portion of its implementation is Web-related. Many of the XML parsers available or under development are written in Java.

Java applet

A Java executable (application or program) that can be embedded in a Web document or run independently in a Java runtime environment.

Java class files

The file or set of files that comprise a Java applet and contain the actual programming instructions that run the applet.

Java runtime environment

An application, usually a Web browser or operating system extension, that can interpret and run Java applets.

JavaScript

A scripting language developed by Netscape that is used to script Web pages. Netscape 2 and later and Internet Explorer 4 and later support JavaScript-enabled Web pages.

l

link

An XLink convention that provides a description of the relationship (or connection) among data objects or parts of the data objects. (Data object are XML documents.)

linking element

An XLink convention used to describe elements. In addition, a linking element is used to describe the existence of a link and its characteristics.

local resource

An XLink convention that describes the content of an inline linking element and specifies the content-tile and content-role of the link.

location term

An XPointer convention that describes the basic addressing information unit in an XPointer. A location term refers to the exact location in a resource to which a link is linked.

locator

An XLink convention that describes a part of a link that identifies a resource. The locator is used to locate the resource.

m

MathML (Mathematical Markup Language)

An XML DTD that describes mathematical data.

metadata

A resource that provides information about another resource.

metalanguage

A language that describes other markup languages. XML is a metalanguage for describing other XML vocabularies.

mixed content

A content model for an element that combines both element and character data.

multidirectional link

An XLink convention that describes a link that joins several documents together in a single link and can be traversed from any one of its resources.

n

namespaces

An advanced XML convention. Namespaces use PIs (processing instructions) to assign unique names in a document to URIs (Uniform Resource Identifiers).

nesting

A term used to describe how elements are contained within other elements.

nonvalidating parser

A software application that checks to make sure XML documents are well formed but does not check whether they are valid.

notations

An XML declaration that associates a processing application (such as Paint Shop Pro) with a type of binary entity (such as a JPEG file).

o

OSD (Open Software Description)

An XML DTD that describes software packages to set up remote installation of software and components on an intranet or the Internet.

out-of-line link

Links between documents that don't have to be stored in either of the documents that make up the link.

p

parameter entity

A special entity type reserved for use in a document's DTD that is designed to hold lists of attributes and content models.

PARENT element

An element that has one or more elements nested within it. Elements nested within a PARENT element are called *CHILD elements*.

participating resource

Any resource that is part of a link; all resources can potentially be part of a link, and a resource becomes a participating resource only when a locator is used to include it as part of a link.

pattern

An XSL convention that describes the portion of a construction rule that identifies the element in a document that receives the rule's formatting (action).

PCDATA (parsed character data)

Element content that comprises just plain text.

presentation-based markup

Markup that describes content mainly designed to be displayed by a device for a user. HTML can be defined as presentation-based markup because its primary goal is to describe content that a user will view with a Web browser of some kind.

processing instructions (PIs)

An XML convention that allows instructions to be passed from the document directly through the parser to the display software to instruct the software on how to process the entire document or just a part of it. PIs can be placed in any location in an XML document.

r

RDF (Resource Description Framework)

An XML DTD that describes resources of all types for easy cataloging, searching, and referencing.

RMD (Required Markup Declaration)

An attribute in an XML document that specifies whether the processor needs to read and process a DTD along with the document.

root rule

The construction rule that specifies what action should be applied to an XML document's document element.

s

scripting language

An interpreted programming language used to direct the behavior of a Web page based on the action performed by users.

selector

A CSS convention that defines the element that a rule will affect.

SGML (Standard Generalized Markup Language)

A text-based markup language used to describe the content and structure of complex documents without regard for the operating system or device that will eventually process the documents.

simple link

An XML convention that uses the `HREF` attribute to point to a single resource. For example, every HTML link is a simple link.

SMIL (Synchronized Multimedia Integration Language)

An XML DTD that describes collections of multimedia resources, such as audio and video files, that are played together in a single presentation.

style sheet

A formatting document that provides information about the structure of other documents. A style sheet tells the software package used to parse and process the document how the information should be displayed.

text entity

An entity that associates character data with an entity name.

text properties

In CSS, text properties are the collection of properties and values that control the text specifics for elements within the document.

U

Unicode

The ISO 10646 character set that uses 16-bit patterns to represent characters. It was created to describe every known language character and a large collection of special characters using unique bit patterns that computers can recognize and display.

validating parser

A software application that checks XML documents for the presence of the document's document-type definition (DTD) and whether the document conforms to it.

valid XML document

A document that adheres strictly to the DTD specified in its document-type declaration.

well-formed documents

A document that conforms only to the XML standard but not to any particular document-type definition (DTD).

WIDL (Web Interface Definition Language)

An XML DTD that defines Application Programming Interfaces (APIs) for Web services and information.

XLink

The linking language created for XML (used to be called the Extensible Link Language or XML-Link). XLink allows users to create a variety of different kinds of links within and between XML documents.

XML application

A specific DTD (or set of DTDs) developed according to the XML specification and that are designed to serve a specific purpose. XML applications are often called *XML vocabularies*.

XML declaration

A declaration within an XML document that identifies to the processor the specific version of the XML specification the document was developed with.

XML processor

A software application that reads XML documents and provides access to their structure and content to display or process applications.

XML specification

A technical document that describes the conventions and mechanisms of XML. The XML specification is often referred to as the XML standard.

XML vocabulary

See *XML application*.

XPointer

An XML specification that details how links should point to the various places inside a document.

XSL (Extensible Style Language)

An advanced style-sheet mechanism that provides browsers with formatting and display information.

Index

Note to Reader: Page numbers in **bold** indicate the principal discussion of a topic. Page numbers in *italic* indicate illustrations.

A

B

C

D

F

G

H

I

M

N

O

P

Q

R

S

T

U

V

X

Z